# Secular Theology

CW00553966

*Secular Theology* brings together new writings by some of America's most influential theological and religious thinkers, providing new resources for philosophical theology. Secular theology is not a contradiction; rather it acknowledges that philosophy and religious reflection are deeply implicated in theology and contemporary culture, and cannot disavow or overcome them. The theologians whose work is gathered together here argue that secularity does not oppose religious practice and belief, but is in fact much concerned with possibilities for thinking about religion and the sacred, God and humanity. The essays in this volume cover such themes as:

- Postmodern theology
- Ethics
- Aesthetics
- Psychoanalysis
- The Death of God
- Medieval theology
- Literary theory
- Epistemology

These essays set forth an agenda for theological and religious reflection, opening up creative and important possibilities for looking at religion and theology in an encounter with Continental philosophy and Radical Orthodoxy. *Secular Theology* contextualizes American radical theology from Paul Tillich onwards and points towards new directions for thinking about religion and humanity in the twenty-first century.

**Clayton Crockett** is a Visiting Assistant Professor of Religion at the College of William and Mary. He is the author of *A Theology of the Sublime*, also published by Routledge in 2001, and managing editor of the online *Journal for Cultural and Religious Theory* (www.jcrt.org).

# Secular Theology

## American radical theological thought

**Edited by Clayton Crockett**

London and New York

First published 2001
by Routledge
11 New Fetter Lane, London EC4P 4EE

Simultaneously published in the USA and Canada
by Routledge
29 West 35th Street, New York, NY 10001

*Routledge is an imprint of the Taylor & Francis Group*

© 2001 Edited by Clayton Crockett

Typeset in Times by RefineCatch Limited, Bungay, Suffolk
Printed and bound in Great Britain by
MPG Books Ltd, Bodmin

*British Library Cataloguing in Publication Data*
A catalogue record for this book is available from the British Library

*Library of Congress Cataloging in Publication Data*
A catalogue record for this book has been requested

ISBN 0–415–25051–X (hbk)
ISBN 0–415–25052–8 (pbk)

For the memory of my grandfather, Thomas Denny Spivey

# Contents

# Notes on contributors

**Leora Batnitzky** is Assistant Professor of Religion at Princeton University. She is the author of *Idolatry and Representation: The Philosophy of Franz Rosenzweig Reconsidered* (Princeton University Press, 2000), as well as numerous articles that have appeared in, among other places, *Journal of Religion*, *New German Critique*, *Oxford Journal of Legal Studies*, *Journal of Jewish Thought and Philosophy*, and most recently *Jewish Studies Quarterly*. She is currently completing a book on the philosophies of Emmanuel Levinas and Leo Strauss and also beginning a new project on modern Jewish, Christian and secular conceptions of law.

**Peter Canning** has taught comparative literature at Berkeley and Minnesota and published essays on contemporary French philosophy and psychoanalysis as well as on the fabulation of "Jews" in Christianity and modernity. He is completing a book on cosmology.

**Thomas A. Carlson** is Associate Professor in the Department of Religious Studies at the University of California, Santa Barbara, where he teaches courses in modern philosophy, theory and the history of Christian culture. Author and translator of many articles and books treating religion and modern thought, he has published, most recently, a study of mystical theology and post-Heideggerian philosophy, *Indiscretion: Finitude and the Naming of God* (University of Chicago Press, 1999), and a translation of Jean-Luc Marion's *The Idol and Distance* (Fordham University Press, 2000).

**Clayton Crockett** is Visiting Assistant Professor of Religion at the College of William and Mary. He is the author of *A Theology of the Sublime* (Routledge, 2001), and Managing Editor of the online *Journal for Cultural and Religious Theory* (www.jcrt.org).

**James J. DiCenso** is Associate Professor in the Department for the Study of Religion at the University of Toronto. Recent publications include "*Totem and Taboo* and the Constitutive Function of Symbolic Forms," "Religion and the Psycho-Cultural Formation of Ideals" and *The Other Freud: Religion, Culture, and Psychoanalysis*.

**Luca D'Isanto** received his doctorate in religious studies from the University of Virginia. He has taught there, as well as in religious studies and in the Department of Rhetoric at the University of California at Berkeley. He is currently a Visiting Fellow in the Centre for Advanced Religious and Theological Studies at Cambridge University. He has published in Europe and North America on the secularization of philosophy in contemporary hermeneutics. He is currently working on a book provisionally entitled *The Kenosis of Sense*, on parallel themes in baroque mysticism and early romantic philosophy.

**Martin Kavka** is an Assistant Professor of Religion at Florida State University. He received his Ph.D. from Rice University, where he wrote a dissertation on the appropriation by modern Jewish thought of the Greek concept of non-being. His published work focuses on the empirical and phenomenological groundings for the "religious turn" in postmodern thought.

**Gregg Lambert** is Associate Professor of English at Syracuse University. He is the author of *Report to the Academy: The New Conflict of the Faculties* (Davies Group Publishers, 2001), *The Critique of Pure Fiction: Essays on Gilles Deleuze and the Image of Thought* (forthcoming) and *The Culture of Strangers: Psychoanalysis and Ethnography in Modern Literature* (forthcoming). He has published numerous essays dealing with Deleuze, culture and psychoanalysis.

**Carl A. Raschke** is Professor of Religious Studies at the University of Denver. He is the author, or co-author, of various well-known books on contemporary postmodernist theology, including *Fire and Roses*, *Theological Thinking*, *The Alchemy of the Word* and *Deconstruction and Theology*.

**Theresa Sanders** is Associate Professor of Religious Studies at Georgetown University. She is the author of *Body and Belief* (Davies Group Publishers, 2000). She has published articles in the *Journal of Philosophy and Theology*, *Continuum*, *Horizons* and *The Journal of Religion*, among others.

**Victor E. Taylor** is the author of *(Para) Inquiry: Postmodern Literature, Culture, and Theology* (Routledge, 1999) and co-editor of *Postmodernism: Critical Concepts, I–IV* (Routledge, 1998) and *The Routledge Encyclopedia of Postmodernism* (Routledge, 2000). He is an Assistant Professor of English and Humanities at York College of Pennsylvania.

**Gabriel Vahanian** is retired from the University of Strasbourg, France. He has published numerous theological works dealing with themes of secularity, language, utopia and technology. His books include *The Death of God* (1961), *Dieu anonyme ou la peur des mots* (1989) and *L'utopie chrétienne* (1992).

**Noëlle Vahanian**, born in Valence, France, is Visiting Assistant Professor of

Philosophy, LeMoyne College. Her dissertation develops a constructive vision of theological language using insights from Julia Kristeva, Alfred North Whitehead and others. She works at the intersection between philosophy and theology, reason and faith, determinism and creativity, the absurd and the other.

**Charles E. Winquist** is Thomas J. Watson Professor of Religion at Syracuse University. He is the author of many works including *Desiring Theology* (University of Chicago Press, 1995) and *Epiphanies of Darkness: Deconstruction in Theology* (Davies Group Publishers, 1999).

# Acknowledgements

Above all, I want to thank the contributors for their willingness to write for this book, as well as their patience and dedication. The rigor and creativity of their thinking makes this what it is. In particular, I would like to thank Gregg Lambert, for suggesting the original idea to me, and providing valuable advice. I also want to thank Charles E. Winquist, for his enthusiasm and assistance throughout the process.

The editors and editorial staff at Routledge have been consistently friendly and helpful, particularly Roger Thorp, Hywel Evans, Adrian Driscoll and Anna Gerber. I would like to thank Phillip Blond and Keith Putt for their input and suggestions, which contributed to the final shape of the volume. I also have to thank Phillip Blond for his edited volume, *Post-Secular Philosophy*, which provided a model and inspiration for this project, which is intended in part as a counter-instance and counter-argument.

Although indirect, the support of my teaching by the Department of Religion at Wesley College, particularly Jeff Mask, as well as the Department of Philosophy and Religion at Lebanon Valley College, including John Heffner, Eric Bain-Selbo and Noel Hubler, have afforded me the confidence and energy to sustain this project, even as they have competed for my time and concentration.

I could not undertake projects such as this without the love and support of family and friends. My wife, Vicki Bryan Crockett, is my inspiration and joy, and she helps to make my work worthwhile. My parents and brother, my grandmother, my in-laws, and friends, both academic and non-academic, provide constant encouragement. Finally, I would like to acknowledge Ed Connell's Amoco service station, as the place where this work has been predominantly conceived and constructed.

# Introduction

*Clayton Crockett*

## I. A secular theology?

At first glance, the notion of a secular theology appears contradictory, even oxymoronic. Does not theology concern itself with what is not secular, that is, the sacred, holy, God? And secular, that generally means non-religious, independent of theological concerns and interests. As with the "Death of God" theology before it, secular theology produces a superficial confusion, based on the inherent tension of the two terms it brings together.

And yet, perhaps we do not understand either term as well as we might. One of the original Death of God theologians, Gabriel Vahanian, has insisted for decades that secular does not mean the opposite of sacred. Rather, the term secular refers to a *saeculum*, or a shared world of human experience. This *saeculum* is generated out of a fundamentally Jewish and Christian theological worldview, and underlies the secondary opposition between sacred and profane. For Vahanian, a *saeculum* is a theological notion which implies that we live in a world of immanence which functions as the location of human and divine meaning and value.

In this way, Vahanian's notion of a *saeculum* approaches what Gilles Deleuze calls a plane of immanence. According to Deleuze (and Félix Guattari), a plane of immanence is the "image of thought" which provides consistency for the creation of philosophical concepts.[1] Deleuze and Guattari stress the plane of immanence as a condition for the creation of concepts. In a similar way, taking Vahanian's notion of secularity, I want to emphasize the importance of the *saeculum* as a condition for the creation of theological conceptions. But does the emphasis on a *saeculum* as a plane of immanence, or a shared world of human experience, eliminate the possibility of transcendence, which many consider the proper domain of theological thinking?

One of the trajectories of modern theology has been towards an elimination of otherworldliness, in favor of attention to the concrete, immediate reality in which human beings live, think, suffer and die. Nietzsche's philosophical protests helped spur this trend. On the other hand, immanence became identified with an autonomous secularity linked with a naïve belief in human progress, which came to a crashing halt in the twentieth century.

From the debris of the First World War, Karl Barth issued a cry against autonomous humanity in favor of a free and transcendent God. His 1919 commentary on Paul's Epistle to the Romans touched off dialectical or Neo-Orthodox theology, which sought to reaffirm transcendence and orthodoxy over against the arrogance of human immanence and autonomy.[2] Transcendence figured as a protest against the status quo, and a realm for God's freedom to operate unconstrained by human conceptions and manipulations.

The problem became how to discuss that transcendence in human conceptions and language without undermining or undoing it. In his magisterial *Church Dogmatics*, Barth was forced to assume the perspective of transcendence in order to relate the story of God's self-revelation in Jesus Christ, along with what Dietrich Bonhoeffer called a biblical "positivism of revelation" in order to justify his hermeneutical methodology.[3] The more stress one lays upon divine transcendence in opposition to human immanence, the harder it becomes to disentangle oneself from worldly concerns and contexts. Neo-Orthodoxy after Barth has been forced to contextualize its theological positions in terms of self-enclosed narratives, with the result of walling itself off from the world and undermining its theoretical and theological relevance. Nevertheless, various forms of Neo-Orthodoxy are usually seen as the sole legitimate forms of theological expression, because they can be recognized as theological in form.

The question is less one of immanence versus transcendence, than the acknowledgement of a minimal imperative of intelligibility, along with an orientation towards the world rather than otherworldliness. Theology needs to pay attention to the form it takes, even if it attempts to surmount that form, and formulations of transcendence must at least be indexed in terms of immanence, secularity or a shared world of human experience. Another way to frame the question is to translate it into the language of desire. Admittedly, theology desires to speak of transcendence and transcendent reality; however, such attempts have been complicated by critical reflections both external and internal to theological thinking. An honest theologizing must recognize its implication in (at least) a human discourse of desire, which functions as a plane of immanence, which does not initially settle the question of transcendence, or another plane. If I desire God, that may say as much about my desire as it does about God, and at least it raises the epistemological question of how I can know whether what I desire when I desire God (Augustine) is truly God or my desire. A reflection upon a secular component to theological thinking is the insistence on a minimal and formal attention to the reflexivity of human thinking and desire.

## II. Radical Orthodoxy

Recently, a new variety of theological thinking has emerged, which in some ways articulates another protest against immanence for the sake of transcendence. With the publication of collections such as *Post-Secular*

*Philosophy* and *Radical Orthodoxy*, Cambridge Radical Orthodoxy has taken shape as a coherent theological movement, based on the work of John Milbank, Phillip Blond, Catherine Pickstock, Graham Ward and others. Radical Orthodoxy envisions itself as a truly postmodern theology because it critiques all of secular modernity as inherently atheistic and violent. Although the thinkers are sophisticated and complex, in some ways the basic story is extremely simple: modern philosophical and scientific thinking emerges as a rejection of the medieval synthesis of faith and knowledge, so-called postmodern philosophers expose the aporias and contradictions which underlie modern presuppositions and aspirations to universality, but such postmodern philosophers themselves end up in nihilism because they take over the basic assumptions of secular modernity. What is needed is a truly postmodern theology which overcomes all independent, autonomous reason with a revitalized Christian faith which carries along with it the possibility of harmony and transcendence.

On the one hand, Radical Orthodoxy seems to provide an opening, and a breath of fresh air, because it affirms intellectual scholarship and provides an impressive breadth for its field of inquiry, which is the whole of Western history and culture. Radical Orthodoxy also takes "postmodernism," or the most recent forms of Continental philosophical inquiry, very seriously, and it reads such thinkers in sophisticated and intelligent ways. The works of Radical Orthodoxy assist readers and scholars in their attempts to assess and evaluate the importance of so-called postmodern philosophy for religion and theology. On the other hand, however, the conclusions of Radical Orthodoxy can appear very simplistic and one-sided. John Milbank and others provide important and subtle critiques of politics, power and contemporary secular society, which must be taken seriously, but the wholesale rejection of modernity, secularity and philosophy in favor of what sometimes appears to be an idealistic and romantic notion of Catholic Christendom can be frustrating to thinkers and theologians with a much more complicated understanding of modernity and/or postmodernity. These conclusions can appear incredibly simplistic: modernity is bad; postmodernists deconstruct modernity but end up in nihilism because they accept the basic presuppositions of modernity; the only way out is a leap (*salto mortale*, death leap) back to a place anterior to modernity and all of its discontents. These conclusions also appeal to conservative and traditional theologians who want to use deconstruction and postmodernism to purify theology of any metaphysical or philosophical corruption. So Radical Orthodoxy appeals to a desire to use postmodern critique but not get lost in its nihilistic conclusions, and also provides a way to approach and understand such postmodern philosophers and their writings, but some thinkers of a more radical constitution wonder if Radical Orthodoxy ends up in an all-too-familiar orthodoxy, and represents merely one more version of Neo-Orthodoxy and its contemporary American representative, the Yale school of Post-Liberal theology.

If many of the ends to which theological appropriations of philosophy are aimed are conservative, what are the possibilities of a genuinely radical theological thinking, which allows contemporary philosophical expressions to inform, affect and even distort theology itself? Secular theology represents an encounter between postmodern philosophy and theology on a much deeper and ultimately more fruitful level. This encounter allows a much riskier and transformative discourse to take shape, one which is not simply concerned to argue point by point with Radical Orthodoxy, but which constructively imagines alternative appropriations of Continental philosophy and constitutes more complex, nuanced and ambivalent understandings of secularity, modernity and postmodernity.

## III.  Back to Tillich

In many ways, radical theological thinking in the United States traces its roots to the work of Paul Tillich. Tillich opened theology up to secular culture, and seriously engaged discourses of philosophy, anthropology and the sciences in an effort to situate theology as a responsible academic discipline which carries along with it important existential and ecclesiastical implications. At the same time, Tillich's work on symbols stressed the symbolic nature of theological discourse, and allowed reflection on the discursive nature of theological language. Finally, Tillich's engagement with Mircea Eliade at the end of his life opened up theology to the discipline and methodology of the history of religions, as well as the pressure of world religions in all of their vitality. Tillich brought a breadth of vision and an honesty to theology which gave him the ability to transform our understanding about what theological thinking is and can be.

Contextually and historically, we can perceive the emergence of "Death of God" theologies in the 1960s as the expression of a radical Tillicheanism, which experimented with the experience of a cultural irrelevance of God along with the philosophical implications of modernity in order to create a unique theological discourse. This discourse became somewhat of a caricature at the popular level, despite the complexity and profundity of the thinkers themselves, including Richard Rubenstein, Gabriel Vahanian, William Hamilton and Thomas J. J. Altizer.

Tillich's method of correlation led theologians to allow contemporary culture to pressure the dogmas of theology, and his definition of theology as ultimate concern was sufficiently formal and minimalist to allow thinkers to apply it in different ways. The Death of God theology included diverse expressions of the death, irrelevance or decline of God as a central concept in relation to religious experience. Some theologians (Harvey Cox, William Hamilton) took a very optimistic view of secular culture, whereas others were more pessimistic or ambivalent (Richard Rubenstein, Gabriel Vahanian). Thomas J. J. Altizer's kenotic notion of the Death of God was at the same time the most idiosyncratic and the most recognized manifestation. Even if other theologians did not share his Hegelian presuppositions, many other radical thinkers were influenced by his work, including his insistence on the continuity between biblical Christianity and modern secular culture. Altizer proclaimed that philosophers like Hegel and Nietzsche, as well as poets like Blake and Joyce, were the true sources of contemporary theological insight, as opposed to traditional representatives of institutional churches.

In the 1980s, an initial postmodern theology developed around the work of Mark C. Taylor, Charles E. Winquist, Carl A. Raschke and others, which combined insights into the situation of the death of God with contemporary Continental philosophy. An important collection appeared in 1982, called *Deconstruction and Theology*, which included essays by Altizer, Taylor, Winquist, Raschke and Robert P. Scharlemann. In his influential 1984 book, *Erring*, Taylor set forth four themes of postmodern a/theological thinking, including the death of God, the disappearance of the self, the end of history, and the closure of the book. Such works set an agenda for radical theological inquiry.

At present, this locus of theological thinking has been obscured somewhat as more conservative forms of postmodern theology have emerged. Now, radical younger American theologians interested in exploring and advancing topics opened up by Taylor and others find that the locus of debate has shifted, so that what passes for postmodern theology is represented by Milbank and Jean-Luc Marion. Both of these thinkers are important, exciting and creative theologians, but their conclusions reinforce a conservative or even reactionary orientation to contemporary culture and its most sophisticated theoretical expressions. This book provides a space for theologians who take Continental philosophy as well as their various traditions seriously, to pursue constructive and creative insights in what can be seen as both a recovery and a continuation of an American radical theology. In addition, such an understanding of theology is not restricted to Christian theology, but includes at least Christian, Jewish, post-Christian and secular approaches and perspectives.

An understanding of contemporary radical American theology in the context of Tillich allows a recognition of continuity and an appreciation of a tradition that possesses vital and possibly under-utilized resources. DiCenso's essay in this collection is particularly significant in this context in that it reexamines Tillich in relation to Lacan as well as contemporary religious reflection in order to reveal how Tillich may be relevant to theological thinking in the twenty-first century.

## IV. Plurality of themes

This collection of essays, centered around the notion of secular theology, does not intend to express a school or a movement. One of the characteristics of intellectual thinking in America, as opposed to the United Kingdom, is the decentralization of schools and ideas, which is reflected in a methodological pluralism. Rather than evidence of confusion, this pluralism can be the source of a creative vitality of connections, suggestions and conceptions. The authors confront and express a variety of overlapping themes and traditions, which contextualizes their location as radical American thinkers about religion.

Despite this plurality, some common approaches can be ascertained. First of all, each of these essays represents not merely a description of theology and/or Continental philosophy, but an intervention into those discourses. These interventions may be more or less experimental or scholastic, but they do not fail to transform our understanding of theology and Continental philosophy. Second, the essays all express a certain secularity; whether explicitly argued or not, a secular perspective is a minimal tool to provide a reflection upon theological thinking as a meaningful discourse. Of course, for Gabriel Vahanian, the secular functions as both a minimal and a maximal discourse, because secularity is the *telos* of theology. Vahanian's essay demonstrates the inextricable relationship between religion and the secular in the human and divine work of the worlding of the world. The dialectical interpenetration of religious and secular originates in a biblical thought which is manifested in every important Christian theologian that follows, including (surprisingly) Tertullian, Augustine, Luther, Calvin and Tillich.

For most if not all of the authors, a minimal secularity functions to allow a rich and multi-layered discourse, where theology, philosophy, ethics and aesthetics are all interwoven and imbricated upon each other, whether one or another is emphasized more clearly. The collection follows an organic trajectory which begins with a focus on theology itself in relation to Continental postmodern discourse. Winquist mines the contemporary resources for a postmodern secular theology by way of an encounter with Derrida, in terms both of Derrida's own religious writing as well as of John D. Caputo's important interpretation of these religious concerns. Raschke then problematizes Derrida's thought in relation to Levinas, and asks whether it is necessary to attend to the prayers and tears of Derrida or rather to bid him *à-dieu*. Such intensive philosophical and theological investigations evince no simple consensus, but provide creative and conceptual resources to assemble and assess a postmodern secular theology. This explicit concern with postmodern theology then gives way to a consideration of psychoanalysis and religion in which DiCenso enacts a compelling relation between Lacan and Tillich around the concepts of risk and anxiety, which allows a reconceptualization of theoretical religious discourse. DiCenso shows how Tillich's theology is not merely relevant, but crucial for thinking about religion in the twenty-first century, even though its form and formulations must be recast in the context of Lacan, Kristeva and other French thinkers.

These opening essays clear the way for a profound grappling with ethical discourse, although ethical issues are never entirely absent from any of the essays. Batnitzky subjects John Milbank to a correlation with Hermann Cohen, an encounter which unsettles Milbank but provides resources to think about the complex relationships between law and love in the context of any secular society. Lambert conducts an intensive and performative reading of a brief passage of Whitehead's *Process and Reality*, which grapples with the notion that life is robbery, that is, fundamentally immoral, and relates that discussion to a consideration of God as love, both for Whitehead and for us. Kavka uses a consideration of the work of Gillian Rose to develop an interpretation of Husserl and Levinas as well as to ask enormously significant questions about the relationship between Judaism and Christianity. Here are no simple moralistic admonishments or edifying consolations; these thinkers complicate and problematize ethical and theological discourse precisely because of their passion for justice and morality.

From ethics emerges an engagement with medieval theology. Sanders interrogates the postmodern discourse surrounding the gift using the anonymous mystical work *The Cloud of Unknowing*. She criticizes Milbank and Marion by associating the gift with prayer, which dislocates a simple affirmation of a gift of being. Carlson then opens his essay, which deals with self-creation, with a discussion of the early medieval theologian John Scotus Eriugena. Carlson juxtaposes the universe of Eriugena with the modern chaosmos of James Joyce, which indicates a concern with an aesthetics of self-creation amid a welter of complicated languages, technologies and cultural conditions. As opposed to many of the current discourses about apophatic theology, Sanders and Carlson are less interested in testing negative theologians against deconstructive theories than in using insights and tools of medieval theologies to illuminate and advance theoretical religious and cultural discourse.

Following the aesthetic turn taken by Carlson, D'Isanto applies Deleuze to Romantic thought in order to develop an aesthetics of kenotic grace. This aesthetics differs from that of von Balthasar and Radical Orthodoxy in that it takes the problem of negativity seriously without merely wishing it away by washing it away with an unworldly beauty. Taylor then uses the work of Ovid to reconsider literary language and the resources for developing a theography, or a writing of divinity, rather than a logos. Theography attends to the figurations, fissures and signs of a broken divinity rather than attempting to put Humpty Dumpty back together again. The end of Taylor's essay considers the discourse of postmodern theology, which points a return to theology, along with a consideration of epistemology and the sciences.

Crockett develops a contact epistemology based on the work of Charles H. Long and then elaborates four sites or currents of contact between Continental and/or postmodern philosophies and American radical empiricism, pragmatism, Anglo-American process thought and American Death of God theology. Noëlle Vahanian wields a dense theoretical language which probes Plato and Aristotle in order to define a contemporary social and religious space with epistemological, ethical and political connotations. Finally Canning's inquiry into the possibility of God which closes the volume issues a powerful demand which functions as a call to engage in cosmological thinking at the risk of failing to understand ourselves and our world. Again, there exists no strict separation or segregation of themes and approaches, but this trajectory merely indicates a superficial progression within the book. The topics explored range from medieval mystics to modern German and Jewish thinkers, to French postmodernists, to American pragmatists, but the purpose is less to historically survey than to construct an image of thought for theological thinking, or a meaningful theoretical discourse about religion which is not hostile to either academic study or religious experience.

Finally, if secular is a minimal tool, the authors use narrow and honed epistemological tools to work on a canvas as broad as life, experience and existence. These broad histories, cultures and traditions serve as a framework which pressures and focuses the tools used to interrogate and interpret them. The tension between a narrow and minimal theoretical tool and a vast canvas on which to work must be held open in order to ask important questions, including whether theological thinking itself matters. There are no easy answers, and the questions are open-ended, provisional. This openness constitutes an invitation to the reader to participate in the process of thinking about religion and theology by engaging the essays that follow.

## Notes

1  Gilles Deleuze and Félix Guattari, *What Is Philosophy?*, trans. Hugh Tomlinson and Graham Burchell (New York: Columbia University Press, 1994), p. 37.
2  See Karl Barth, *The Epistle to the Romans*, trans. Edwyn C. Hoskins (Oxford: Oxford University Press, 1968).
3  See Dietrich Bonhoeffer, *Letters and Papers From Prison*, ed. Eberhard Bethge (New York: Macmillan, 1967), p. 171.

## Select bibliography

Altizer, Thomas J. J. *The Gospel of Christian Atheism*. Philadelphia: Westminster Press, 1966.
Altizer, Thomas J. J., and Hamilton, William. *Radical Theology and the Death of God*. Indianapolis: Bobbs-Merrill, 1966.
Marion, Jean-Luc. *God Without Being*, trans. Thomas A. Carlson. Chicago: University of Chicago Press, 1991.
Milbank, John. *The Word Made Strange: Theology, Language, Culture*. Oxford: Blackwell, 1997.
*Post-Secular Theology: Between Philosophy and Theology*, ed. Phillip Blond. London: Routledge, 1998.
Raschke, Carl A. *et al.*, eds. *Deconstruction and Theology*. New York: Crossroad, 1982.
Raschke, Carl A. *The Alchemy of the Word: Language and the End of Theology* (1979). Republished as *The End of Theology*. Aurora, CO: Davies Group, 1999.
Rubenstein, Richard L. *After Auschwitz: Radical Theology and Contemporary Judaism*. Indianapolis: Bobbs-Merrill, 1966.
Taylor, Mark C. *Erring: A Postmodern A/Theology*. Chicago: University of Chicago Press, 1984.

*Theology at the End of the Century: A Dialogue on the Postmodern with Thomas J. J. Altizer, Mark C. Taylor, Charles E. Winquist and Robert P. Scharlemann*, ed. Robert P. Scharlemann. Charlottesville: University of Virginia Press, 1990.

Tillich, Paul. *Theology of Culture*. Oxford: Oxford University Press, 1959.

Tillich, Paul. *What Is Religion?* New York: Harper & Row, 1969.

Vahanian, Gabriel. *The Death of God: The Culture of Our Post-Christian Era*. New York: George Braziller, 1966.

Winquist, Charles E. *Desiring Theology*. Chicago: University of Chicago Press, 1995.

Wyschogrod, Edith. *Saints and Postmodernism*. Chicago: University of Chicago Press, 1990.

# 1    Theology and the secular

## Gabriel Vahanian

For it was not through law that Abraham, or his posterity, was given the promise that the world should be his inheritance, but through the righteousness that came from faith.

Romans 4:13

If a man merely stares at the world, while another not only sees but questions it, the world does not appear differently to them; but appearing the same to both, it is dumb to one and answers the other. Or rather it speaks to all, but only those understand it who compare its answer with the truth that is within them.

Saint Augustine

## I

"Secular" – no other word has been so pried loose of its semantic context as has this word. Made to bear all by itself the brunt of the Death of God, a cultural phenomenon the size of an epochal "continental divide" for which it has been both acclaimed and vilified, it has become the unwilling syndrome of a metastatic evolution, so irrevocable that we forget it was brought about less by the rise of the secular itself than by the self-inflicted demise of Christianity.

And yet "secular" was only the antonym of "religious," not its antithesis: they formed a pair, never to be cleaved one from the other. Together, they belonged to one and the same worldview, and belonged with one another. And no sooner are they split from one another than each seems to come apart at the seams. And "secular" either has become a shibboleth for a newfangled ideology of liberation from the past or is looked upon as an orphan or as a kind of prodigal son that is in the process of squandering his father's religious inheritance. But this is a positivistic approach which feeds on the assumption that religion is a thing of the past – an allegation which is not entirely undeserved. One must admit that in keeping with just about any traditional definition of it, religion boils down to memorizing the past, even keeping it alive medically through artificial means, if necessary. Either way, however, overlooked is the fact that religion and the secular belong together as do two sides of one and the same coin. Or that just as blood runs through both arteries and veins so does life – and even faith – run through the religious and the secular. Remove the heart, or kill God, and the same finger is pointing at us: we have also killed the secular or turned it into the parody of an obsolescent religion.

No other word has been more maligned than the word "secular." Its connotations encompass so diverse a debauchery of meaning as to throw anyone endowed with the least love of words into a dizzying puzzle of bewilderment. They range the whole gamut from antonym of religious to synonym of atheist. True, words are like Russian dolls: they achieve a meaning by shedding another; or they grow on words, as often acquiring new meanings regardless of their etymological roots as because of them. But "secular" is a word whose fate has been worse even than that of the word "God," though the latter is a noun which, naming that which has no name, is neither proper nor common, putting us in the strange situation of being caught between conflicting demands: that of the secular, on the one hand, which eschews God by extruding him from the realm of daily concerns; and on the other, that of a religion which can only posit God by intruding him into the kernel of memory and thus by identifying religion with memory before turning it into a survival kit. It's as though religion had and need have only one fear – that of having no future. Indeed, from time immemorial, religion, not unlike the albatross burdened by its wings, has been weighed down by this fear instead of discarding or shedding itself of it in keeping with the biblical tradition which holds, precisely, that true religion has no future and none certainly beyond this world – the *saeculum*.[1] There is no religion in the new Jerusalem or in Jesus' parable of the Last Judgement or again in Thomas More's *Utopia* or even in the world come of age as celebrated by Bonhoeffer, though Bonhoeffer himself continued to be caught in the throes of a residual Lutheran dualism, and, despite Luther, the condescending look it casts upon the world, upon the secular.

The secular is what outgrows religion; it looms on the incompressible horizon of memory as what's left when religion is loosened from the fossilizing effects of memory and fades into hope. To wit Israel: instead of merely remembering the past, listens to that God that would be no God should God not make room for the world and should there be no world here and now, should there not be once and for all a world as ephemeral and contingent as it is secular, i.e. a pro-vision of the new heaven and the new earth, of the newness of the world – its worldhood. The secular is not merely secular. Nothing is secular that is not at the same time symmetrical with something religious. And just that is the paramount reason why traditional "theology must address its own irrelevance"[2] ("secularized" as others are wont to say, giving that term a negative inflection meant to drown all positivity to which its pristine meaning is intrinsically entitled).

## II

We talk of the secular much as we do of religion. Used to presuming there is an essence of religion, more immutable than not, we likewise tend to think of the secular as though it too must have an essence. And, of course, that essence should both set it at the opposite end of the spectrum from religion and keep it from shying away from the least pretense of an incontrovertibly self-adjudicated status at the apex of an equally self-programming ideology.

Unfortunately, no sooner has under the guise of "secularism" such an essence been identified than its true nature becomes manifest. It festers the secular, just as its counterpart, fundamentalism, festers religion. Worse still, however antagonistic their respective claims may be, fundamentalism and secularism similarly result from an equally positivistic coercion of one prong of the dialectic of the religious and the secular into subservience to the other. Faking each other, they are interchangeable. Not being real twins, they are not self-limiting, either, and they counterfeit or blur and pervert the respective realms of the absolute and the relative, of the transcendent and the imma-nent. Either by absolutizing the relative (fundamentalism) or by relativizing the absolute (secularism) they disfigure the intrinsic autonomy whether of the religious or of the secular. Either way, there is inaugurated a process which consists in reducing language to some kind of Newspeak, so terrorized that it will carry any ideology. And, in fact, from East to West, this is the age neither of secularism nor of fundamentalism, but of each joyfully blending with the other. Not that, here and there, people live in some dark age whereas others do not. Ironically, this is an age when no religion can claim to be the best or the only religion; when, in other words, every religion is the whole religion and yet every single one of them shies away from embracing the only thing they have in common: not religion (which is why they are divided), but the secular – a language all the religions have in common, just as *mutatis mutandis* language is also what the religious and the secular have in common. Or else language would not be iconoclastic, which it must be if the religious is iconoclastic of the secular and the secular is of the religious.

## III

In this light, neither secularism nor fundamentalism can claim to be viable projects. They do, however, provide sociology, or a sociologically attuned mindset such as ours has become, with enough fuel to keep it sliding down the slippery path at the end of which not only the religious but also the secular lose their respective identity, melted as they are in a process that is neither fish nor fowl and is no less abusively called secularization, though it has less to do with any drive towards the secular – which in keeping with bib-lical faith is vested in and vindicated by true religion – than it does with the dis-habilitation of religion or the obsolescence of Christianity. Dis-heveled, bruised, maimed, kidnapped or raped by would-be specialists more concerned with their own press than with pressing the real issue in the after-math of the death of God, secularization needs to be salvaged and retrieved. It must recover the meaning of its pristine thrust as one prong of a dialectic in which, in the biblical tradition, the other is perceived as hallowing (or sanctification).

Saying that these are theological terms nowadays deprived of their down-to-earth significations is hardly questionable. What is questionable, oddly if ironically enough, are the reasons – in the very sense in which Archibald MacLeish's Job declares in *J.B.* that "God is reasons" – for which the effects of the interface between hallowing and secularization have deserted the mindscape of the imagination even among the American people, whose cultural heritage would no doubt sink into oblivion if Thanksgiving should perchance cease from being emblematic of its spirit. And yet whether Thanksgiving is a religious or a secular holiday makes no difference. And it doesn't, precisely because of the phenomenological principle at work in the inescapably mutual compatibility between church and world, which held that *ecclesia in mundo latet* while *mundus in ecclesia patet*, or, as Tillich will say, that religion is the substance of culture and culture the form of religion.[3] Precisely because religion means the overcoming of religion (Buber) and its secularization, it can be overcome only by religion. So that correspondingly secularization can refer to the gradual dismissal of religion only by adepts of a sociology of religion already sentenced to extinguish itself. The situation is like that of Pinocchio's nose: should it keep growing, there would soon be no Pinocchio left to tell a lie. But of course sociologists who have to make a living will doubtless find then another half-truth and switch from one funda-mentalism to another, from one secularism to another, prone as some of them are to mistake the sign for what it points to.

Hallowing and secularization are, on the contrary, the cutting edge of a process through which by "world" is designated not so much a datum as a mandate, not a fate but a destiny, not only the realm of *anankē* (necessity) but also that of *nomos*, i.e. of the possible though it may seem impossible.[4] And so, by "world," is ultimately designated the realm of *logos*, the empowering of the will unable by itself even to do the good that possibly is within its reach, inasmuch as the will precedes everything except itself. No world comes of age except through the word, as illustrated according to the biblical tradition of creation and incarnation and the fullness of time. Nor do any of these notions entail the least contempt for the world, though they require its defatalization; or entail disparagement of nature, though they require its desacralization.

## IV

In other words, biblical religion is not geared with a dualism of the sacred and the profane. It is tackled by a dialectic of a different order, that of the holy and the secular, or, for a better consonance with the biblical outlook on the world, of the holy and the not yet holy.[5] And then, one might as well go the further step of identifying it as a dialectic of the secular and the not yet secular, if only in order to bear in mind that, on account of this same perspective, nothing is more religious than the secular, and more secular than the religious. It bears repeating: they belong together.[6]

They belong together, although not as do the sacred and the profane. Take Eliade's well-known definition. Its laconic succinctness is more telling than any disquisition that would only burden the evidence. The sacred, says Eliade, is that which is not profane and the profane is that which is not sacred. Standing between them is something like an altar rail. Each is confined within itself rather than to the other, but neither is really self-limiting. Things are the way they are by reason of *ananke* or *physis*. Greek is set above barbarian, Jew above goy. They evince a statically structured order, quite in contrast to the dynamic configuration achieved by the religious and the secular, where the "altar rail" of the sacred and profane lingers on until it is erased from the symbolic imagination by the iconoclastic move towards the priesthood of all believers. Ordered to one another, the religious and the secular limit them-selves, they are self-limiting insofar as each consists, not in secluding itself from or being secluded by the other, but in making room for the other.[7] The Israelites are expected to make room for the stranger that is within their gates, all the more "naturally" since, unlike Athenians of old, the Israelites form a people, by virtue, not of their origin, but of their calling. Whatever their identity or morality, they only can catch a glimpse of it, not in the mirror of nature, nor in that of history, but in the iconoclastic mirror of the word. Identity does not result from natural sedimentation or from historical seden-tarization, but in spite of them: it lies in the future, in that which is yet in need of coming to pass. And morality is not a matter of conformity either with natural necessity or with historical convention, but of eschatological pro-vision. Receiving a stranger may be a show of human morality, but it is above all an eschatological act – the identification of oneself, not with, but through the other and likewise of the chosen people through the nations, of the religious through the secular: ultimately or, put in biblical terms, eschatologi-cally speaking, what counts is what Israel and the nations have in common, and, in view of the parable of the Last Judgement and Paul's understanding of the Body of Christ, what they have in common only comes about where there is neither Jew nor Greek, neither master nor slave, neither man nor woman, but one world as worlding of the Word become flesh.[8] It comes about wherever faith is not the monopoly of religion; and this world is the only world in which one may live by faith – that is, *eschatically*.

## V

Remember, the Greek word from which *eschatic* is derived refers to that *last* thing or event, by whatever name it is identified, in the light of which all that is at stake in this life stands revealed and "justified," that is at all events in need of that grace without which it would have no grounds upon which it could stand to begin with. In this light, the ultimate is nothing that lasts or is everlasting unless it is so contingent as to happen – once for all. Nor does it consist in opposing this life and the next, this world and the other world, the temporal and the eternal, much less in the classic opposition between the spiritual and the material, the good life and the goods of life.[9] It does not consist in changing worlds, but in changing the world. It has a utopian rather than a sacral edge, as is actually illustrated by Paul's way of putting forward his Roman citizenship even though "here we have no lasting city" and though "our commonwealth is in heaven."[10] Heaven is that which is no place but takes place when the religious is superseded by the secular and, conversely, the secular by the religious. It even occurs on earth[11] whenever or wherever you did not do what you did in view of some "pie in the sky."[12]

As *eschatic* existence, faith is moreover to be lured neither by apocalypticism nor by historicism, neither by the catastrophism, millennial or otherwise, of the end of the world, nor by the progressivism of salvation through some historical evolution from this world to the next. Insofar as faith lies at the juncture of commitment to God and involvement in the world, *eschatic* existence entails a worlding of the Word, a process whose threefold iteration is indicated by creation as spacing of time, by incarnation as timing of the eternal, and by the fullness of time as overcoming of any gap between transcendence and immanence, between the holy and the secular. But then secular is only the name of that for which time, rather than becoming timeless, happens once for all.

*Eschatic* existence, being then as autonomous as it is theonomous, is all the more vulnerable: it is alienated from itself as well as from God and driven into heteronomy by the joint antagonism of fundamentalism and secularism. If theonomy is the name for the religious method of putting man into question, autonomy rightfully is its secular counterpart. And should we proceed further in this line of thought, I should gladly entertain the contention that if theocracy is the religious name for anarchy, anarchy is the secular name for theocracy – supposing that such vocables can still be trusted, and then, provided that, instead of some kind of arbitrary rule, human or divine, they mean, each in its mode, that none of us is *per se* good enough to lord it over anyone else. No one. Not even God, so to speak. God entrusts the creation to Adam – a move whose ultimate significance is woefully misconstrued if it is not viewed as entailing and combining both the desacralization of nature and the defatalization of history; in a word: the secularization of religion. The human is no phenomenon exclusively emanating either from nature or from history. It makes sense only because it is, at least, as self-transcending as it is self-affirming. In the biblical tradition, it relates to God, to that which is emblematic of otherness in its radicality, yet without grinding that radicality into alienation whether from God or simply from other people, whatever their language. No God can be mine unless God can also be God for others. Which explains why in the biblical tradition God is language, rather than this or that. God need not be deified: the Word becomes flesh.

## VI

Neither polytheism nor atheism, much less secularism, has ever achieved such an iconoclastic conception of God. What language can attest, it can also test and contest. It deconstructs as well as it re-structures, and tempers *physis* with *nomos* as well as law with grace. Only language can spell the law, but then only so long as it does not fall short of grace. Giving to God what is God's and to Caesar what is Caesar's,[13] it surrenders neither to the supernatural nor to the natural.[14] All the more symbolic for being literal, it brings about the only world apt for being lived in by humans, amending and emending it, trimming and pruning it. Just as there would be no brains were it not for the mind, there would be no heart were it not for prayer, and no lips, either, were it not for language. But to the extent that language is what makes us human, we are its instrument, just as through it also we are that of God and of the world: we speak to the extent that we are spoken for, are responsible for God as well as for the world. And speak we must: silence would tell either more than we would, or less than we should. And just as an instrument needs to be kept clean, so do lips and the heart need cleansing. To this end, the believer implores God, saying: *munda cor meum ac labia mea* (purify my heart and my lips), as pointed out by Catherine Pickstock, who, commenting on this excerpt from the Roman liturgy of the Middle Ages, writes: "The heart and lips of the Deacon are worlded."[15] She even takes the trouble of reminding the reader that here "worlded" is to be heard in the sense of *munditia*, one of the noun forms of the verb *mundo* (to purify)! Astonishing the reader, she willfully neglects a gem – the fact that evidently from the same root are also derived the adjective *mundus* (pure, clean) and the noun *mundus* (world). In other words, no cleansing, no hallowing, and no worlding either, except through that temporal synonym of "world," the *saeculum*.

Possibly, worldliness and otherworldliness, laden with negative connotations, still affect the religious imagination in general and piety in particular. One thing rings loud and clear, however. Perhaps they muted the biblical emphasis upon the covenant between God and all that is, upon a world so loved by God that he sends his only son. But they never eclipsed either the covenant or God's love for the world. From Tertullian to Hegel and the Death of God, "world" is a constant that furthermore invariably discriminates one theological discourse from another, provided that the cultural pregnancy of the Christian faith remains a *sine qua non* of its religious habilitation. In keeping with the biblical stress on the original goodness of creation, the otherworldly contempt for the world will in the course of history give way to the affirmation of the world, paving the way for an ecological awareness of nature, not to mention the emergence of a world where everyone who comes or will come into the world has a right to a place in the sun and where in other words radical innocence can be as fraudulent as the notion of original sin it has replaced.[16]

And yet even Tertullian, who died in 240, need not be decried more than he deserves. His way of equating *saeculum* and paganism or his contention that Athens and Jerusalem have nothing in common are certainly consonant with the rather arrogant otherworldliness abruptly displayed in his writings. These are the same writings, however, through which, with equal composure, he further demonstrates his talent by goading the Christian faith into developing its own rhetoric and stocking with its first conceptual tools. Nor does he, given the naturalism that pervades the paganism to which he reduces a bedeviled *saeculum*, shrink from contending that the soul is by nature Christian (*anima naturaliter christiana*). Bewildering! Yet coherent. He has sensed the religious dimension inherent to the secular. And if Athens and Jerusalem stand at opposite ends of the pole, this may only mean that what is at stake in their divergence actually deals but with the question on hand at that juncture, namely what kind of religion will rightfully constitute the substance of culture. Even from the ultraconservative Tertullian's standpoint, it deals with the cultural embodiment of the Christian faith – with its acculturation and not its inculturation, a strategy developed of late by the Vatican and ascribing it to the role of a mole. What Tertullian is saying is not that culture is not a necessary form of religion much less of true religion, but that no *given* culture is necessary *per se* and none exhausts religion as when, claiming it did, Roman secularism leveled the charge of atheism at the Christians, or when, realizing it did not, Christianity was overtaken by the Greek legacy through the gradual Hellenization of its metaphysical development. Tertullian himself was pointing his finger at a soft spot: though suspicious of it, he nevertheless allows in turn for a suspicion to be levied on him, to wit: the *saeculum* is what precisely paganism and Christianity have in common.

Muted by Tertullian, this is an insight whose credibility becomes more and more persuasive even before Augustine. In *The City of God*, the latter's other *magnum opus*, it would seem even that not only was Tertullian being understood better than he understood himself, but that moreover Augustine's vision of the relation between Athens and Jerusalem amounts to a deconstruction of their alleged opposition. For the epistemological bent of Tertullian's ill-secured fideism, Augustine substitutes a phenomenologically oriented dialectic of the Word become flesh,[17] of that which, for being eternal, is no less standing in the Now, in that which has no past.[18] For Tertullian's provocative notion of the absurd, he substitutes the no less challenging if equally paradoxical notion of grace, which, as Thomas Aquinas will later assert, does not abrogate nature but perfects it. Paganism, Augustine contends, may well have been shot through with vices, but they were "splendid." In this way, "natural man" is both asserted and challenged: no man is natural except through grace. In contrast to the prevailing assumption of natural man as sinful man, there is emerging with Augustine more than a hint to the effect that to sin is to go against nature.[19] And should he, on the contrary, appear at times to identify paganism with secularism, this only goes to show that secularism is merely the effect of an otherworldly puritanism, of which Augustine steers clear on the whole. "It is," he writes, "the peculiarity of secularism that it worships a god or gods, by whose aid it may reign victorious in temporal peace, animated not with the love of wise counsel but with the lust for possession. For the good use this world in order that they may enjoy God; but the evil use God in order that they may enjoy this world."[20] Clearly, whatever the merits of Augustine's case, the point he wants to make is not that for the good God comes first and, for the evil, only secondarily if at all. The point is not that God comes first, as the evil think who therefore use him in order to enjoy the world, but that God comes *down* all the while the world is being and it must be used in order for God to be enjoyed. The world is what the city of God and the city of man have in common, even to the extent that, Augustine keeps saying, they are "interwoven as it were in this present transitory world, and mingle with one another."[21] And between them what will make the difference is the church, as principle not of segregation but of hallowing God throughout the world. If with Tertullian Christians tend to form a society within society, this is no longer the case with Augustine. The church must instead mesh with society.

## VII

The church should mesh with society, though not to the extent that, as under Charlemagne, *ecclesia* becomes so identified with the *imperium* that she will in fact designate the empire itself: theocracy? secularism? How could one tell the difference? That there ought to be one – though not so much between those two as between church and world or between *corpus Christi* and *corpus christianum* – will soon be brought into evidence.

At the apex of the Middle Ages, pope and emperor, challenging one another, compete for supremacy. The church manifests her supremacy by defining herself as the Body of Christ and thus the better subordinating the world to her rule, yet without going so far as to absorb it. On the contrary, drawing a line between reason and revelation, philosophical and theological truth, Thomas Aquinas will draw a line between the religious and the secular. Not a Berlin wall, to be sure. But rigid enough in its consequences for dissenting voices to sound forth and be raised, especially – and no less ironically – from among the more "religious" pool of the church and, strangely enough, within the spiritual wing of the ecclesial structure. In an age when "nothing would seem to be more otherworldly and apolitical – indeed, downright idealistic – than the doctrine that because Christ, Mary, and the apostles had practiced total poverty," one would expect that "it was incumbent on the church to obey their example and to abstain from owning anything." And they did expect no less than that. But "by one of those curious ironies with which history and perhaps especially the history of the church, is fraught, this otherworldly position formed an alliance with various secularists of the fourteenth century, who were asserting the authority of the state over against that of the church."[22] With arguments culled from as devoted a churchman as William of Ockham, "the emperor and his supporters cast themselves in the role of liberators of the true church from the burdens of property and power." Doubtless, the emperor was stretching Ockham's views. Two things must be noted, however. One is that these are views that reverberate an image of Jesus the latter shares with his fellow Franciscans. The other is that, already with Ockham himself, civil power emanates neither from God nor from nature, but from the people. And the upshot leaps to the eye: with this image of Jesus, what is achieved is "a contribution to the formulation of the founding principles and 'secular values' of modern political philosophy."[23]

## VIII

But the ideology of salvation and its changing-worlds motif still holds, though not, perhaps, in as dualistic a mood as with Tertullian. It continues to control the texture of the good life and its ramifications into the various goals of human existence, whether ultimate or penultimate, individual or social, spiritual or temporal. But it has not, if only because of its roots, abated the biblical concern for the worldhood of the world, though it was somewhat held in ontological abeyance by the metaphysical turn of Christian thought. This is a concern which evinces two aspects, both of which stem from Augustine's dialectic of the two cities and, by way of Saint Thomas on the one hand and of William of Ockham on the other, are woven, though perhaps unequally, into the fabric of the Reformation, or at least some segments of it. Indeed, one of these aspects bears the stamp of the sacramentarian, while the other stands for the charismatic approach to the secular or worldhood of the world. The former subordinates the world to the church. The latter, considering this world as the sole arena of faith, views accordingly the church as a principle of social novation.

Most instrumental in this respect is the concept of vocation. Even in its medieval version as calling to the priesthood and before its enlargement through the Reformers' doctrine of the priesthood of all believers, vocation illustrates the public relevance of social mobility, even of social criticism if one should, in view of their attitude *vis-à-vis* the church established, so credit the emergence of monastic orders, each of them emblematic of a small-scale utopia, bent on changing the world by first changing the church. This is precisely what the Reformers will seek to do. But, in the various walks of life, forerunners had not been missing. For example, until the fourteenth century, Saint James the Less is represented with the fuller's tool with which he was tortured. By the end of the Middle Ages, however, crafts and trades had all so evolved that society had to reflect their effects, and for this ancient tool of Saint James's martyrdom was substituted a recent carder's instrument.[24] In similar fashion, we move from the church as mystical body to the church as principle of social novation when the Last Judgement scene of a cathedral's classical tympanum is replaced on a tympanum like that of the basilica of Avioth by the figures and emblems representing the various crafts and trades making up society.

Luther and especially Calvin will elaborate on this charismatic approach to the secular. Though Luther, for his part, continues to adhere to the dichotomous theory of two realms (religious and secular, private and public), he nevertheless holds the view that one can and need only serve God *in* any calling or whatever function one happens to fill. A prince must accordingly govern as should a prince rather than a Christian, although in 1520, barely two or three years after posting his *Ninety-Five Theses*, he still was of the opinion that the civil authorities should – and therefore could – summon a church council.

It is Calvin who will explore in a more dynamic fashion this overlapping of religious community and civil society. It is not only *in vocatione*, but through one's vocation (*per vocationem*), that one is to serve God, should it for that purpose have to be changed. Meanwhile, mayor and minister, so to speak, are equally vicars of Christ and according to their own respective functions. As Karl Holl stated it in his famous dictum, the Reformation consists in secularizing religion and in spiritualizing culture. More specifically, in Cassirer's assessment of it,

> The Reformation seems to agree with the Renaissance in giving new value and new sanction to life on earth. It too calls for a spiritualization of the content of faith; and this spiritualization is not confined to the ego, the religious subject, but encompasses also the being of the world, placing a new relation to the basis of religious activity. The world is now to be justified on grounds of the certainty of faith. Thus again the ascetic demand for negation of this world is met by a demand for world affirmation, that is, in activity within the secular order.[25]

Here is an activity which, Max Weber notwithstanding, deserves a better appraisal than it receives when, supposedly in contrast to the otherworldly asceticism of the Middle Ages, it is identified in terms of an innerworldly asceticism. One appreciates the intention, and it is well taken. But if medieval otherworldly asceticism had to cope with a world marred by scarcity, it must be noted that in the aftermath of the Reformation and the Renaissance and in view of the industrial and scientific revolutions that will ensue, abundance rather than scarcity is what looms on the horizon as being in need of stewardship. Not to mention the fact that, somehow, asceticism sounds more religious than secular, self-limiting frugality would better describe the fundamental principle of the Protestant ethic, should for that purpose a label be needed at all. Asceticism remains the hallmark of a life hemmed in by scarcity; frugality harks back to the biblical injunction according to which social justice and solidarity cannot be achieved unless the rich "have nothing over," and the poor have "no lack,"[26] unless life abundant is available to all who, regardless of where they come from, should be reduced to "hoping against hope."[27]

# IX

Even the notion of salvation cannot quite survive the impact of the Reformation on the secularization of religion. Although no ablation of it is advocated frontally, it will, at least substantially, recover its biblical orientation. Already with Luther's faith and its thoroughgoing self-examination, the heretofore basic question "What must I do in order to be saved?" gives way to "Who or what kind of God is this God who saves me?" Luther's insight amounts to a virtual shaking of the foundations of traditional religion. In his treatise on Christian liberty, he writes: "Quite voluntarily and without recompense the Christian does all that he does without thereby seeking his own advantage or salvation. What is done is done just to please God thereby."[28] Faith lies in being released from the very obsession of salvation – an idea which, strange as it may sound, is embedded in Calvin's doctrine of predestination. Losing at all events its ontological moorings, salvation is recast in relational terms, and faith turns into a mode of being: the believer himself or herself is according to Luther a Christ unto his or her neighbor. Using a Tillichean image, one is compelled to observe that the vertical already lies in the horizontal. Or that transcendence consists in making room for that which is immanent.

As grandiose an idea as this may have been in its conception, it will however give way or subsequently fall a prey to a drive towards a would-be radical immanentism more aptly described as an immanentism with a vengeance. Always lurking in the horizon of Western culture, it never was as ominous as it will henceforth be, when theology itself is in fact either driven out of the church or so domesticated by the church that Schleiermacher himself will barely succeed in reanimating it in his attempt to disarm the cultural despisers of religion. But by then theology has for all practical purposes already bifurcated into law and civil polity, on the one hand, and into law and political philosophy on the other. The gap that had already been yawning between the church and the world, faith and culture, will not only widen; it will result in artificially pitting the religious and the secular one against the other and meretriciously plaguing them both, accordingly.

Consider, in this respect, the "idealism" of Hegel. Not to mention Kant on one side and Heidegger on the other, with its roots going back to Luther, what is this idealism actually concerned with if not the worldhood of the world, its secularity? Denouncing the otherworldliness of the established church and what he calls its "sacramental materialism," Hegel displays nonetheless an amazing fondness for such classical, if not worn out, expressions as "the invisible church" or, for that matter, "the kingdom of God." And what do they mean? They simply mean that the reality of God is at stake in the reality of the world: if no God is God, no world is without God. The world is like a manger, in which lies but one for whom there is no room in the inn, in the church. Coping with the world, as though it were its trust, the invisible church has indeed little to do with the visible church. But we must here go back to Calvin.

## X

Calvin similarly castigates all those for whom the kingdom of God lies tucked away in some heavenly realm instead of paving the way towards the "true country." Retrieved from the substantialized metaphysical order of an other-worldly salvation, the church is now geared to the task of changing the world, to the extent that Calvin's ecclesiology reads more like a declaration of political theology than like a mystical treatise about a community sheltered and segregated from the world. At the risk of an oversimplification, we move from the *imperium* as essence of the church to the church as matter of civil government. Not that the religious and the secular are confused with one another. Rather, they will court such a confusion if, left to their own devices, they drift into either fundamentalism or secularism as the case may be. The separation of church and state is a matter of pragmatic reflective equilibrium, traumatically lost sight of as soon as one ideology is pitted against the other in battles so dubious as to vouch for nothing short of mutual extermination. Power, whether religious or secular, becomes tyrannical and arbitrary, unless it limits itself. Calvin was a lawyer. Taking the measure of the new situation to whose insemination Calvin contributed, Michael Walzer writes, most judiciously: "Religion produced a counterpolity to the state; as a prelude to admitting the state to the world of religion, Calvin admitted politics to religion. He often described the church as a commonwealth and the metaphor is a significant key to his thought."[29] And certainly the metaphor was not missed by John Cotton, the Puritan divine who writes:

> It is necessary that all power on earth be limited, church power or other. . . . It is counted [by some] a matter of danger to the state to limit prerogatives; but it is a further danger not to have them limited. . . . And it is meet that magistrates in the Commonwealth and officers in the church should [each] desire to know the utmost bounds of their own [respective] spheres of power.[30]

And what follows from a view like this is no less significant. Having to cope with a commonwealth, no particular church is the church. Denominations do not exhaust the reality of the church, and no less significant is the fact that, on the American scene, the notion of a Holy Commonwealth upstages that of holy church. Nor do, for that matter, denominations altogether exhaust the scope of religion, much less that of faith, especially since denominations are but debris of a church held on a leash by some territory, of territorial churches now still confined within an area but stretching archipelago-fashion across an ocean swept by tradewinds of diverse persuasions. What they have in common is nothing but the secular – which explains why they can merge when the configurations of the secular undergo a drastic change and theological differences lose their ground. It also explains why new religions can today blossom and thrive on the religious veneer *already* spread on the secularized mindset to which they appeal.

Nearly half a century ago, while President Eisenhower, expressing his confidence in whatever future, was declaring that "our Government is based on a deeply felt religious faith," Will Herberg was describing the American people as being at once most religious and most secular. Nearly two millennia earlier, the apostle Paul described a similar situation by saying that the world is full of gods.[31] Unlike Paul, who, I tend to think, cared what kind of gods these were, Eisenhower, in a mood no doubt less apostolic than political, proudly went over the board and enthusiastically teeming with this deeply felt religious faith scuttled it, and, he said, "I don't care what it is." Brutal, surely. And sobering too. Like life the secular can be brutal. And, one would surmise, it is brutal only because or to the extent that, correspondingly, religion has become vulgar – as Nietzsche would say.

It is Nietzsche who points out that, after the collapse of Christian culture, what remains is the Bible. Not a book, but a trace – the emblematic trace of a language, if not of language *tout court*. What remains is a theology of language, the cutting edge of discourse reduced neither to the religious nor to the secular. Indeed, faith is what religion and the secular have in common, regardless of the respective metamorphoses they undergo, even while through a series or process of renewed mutual articulations they come to terms with one another and hinge one upon the other world without end, throughout the ages, *in saecula saeculorum*.

## Notes

1 The cross-fertilization between *mundus* (world, *welt*, *monde*) and *saeculum* (this present age, this world) from which is derived "secular" is of such a staggering magnitude that, from cacophony into symphony, it seems to stretch language beyond some kind of sound barrier: "world without end" simply renders *in saecula saeculorum* and *saeculum* designates the eternal as it breaks into time, a *kairos*, a worlding of the Word become flesh. I cannot accordingly resist considering worldhood and secularity as isomorphous terms. We get a hint of this with Paul Tillich, as I have tried to show elsewhere, especially when he switches from German to English and has to cope with the questionable and philologically hybrid American conundrum of "the sacred and the secular," a coupling against nature yet so widespread in the middle of the twentieth century. No wonder religion was caught in a vice: it could not tell which end was up, supposing it has since then somewhat come to its senses, if at all, considering the general obsession with the sacred, at once the acme and most subtle form of self-crowning achievement in the distortion of the worldhood of the world now downgraded as the realm of the profane. To that extent, I cannot fault Tertullian for identifying the *saeculum* with *paganism* (*De Pudicitia* 1; *De Anima* 46) in contrast to his third-century contemporary Cyprian or to successors like Saint Jerome (331–420) or Saint Augustine (354–430) with whom *saeculum* or its derivatives designate the present order in contradistinction from *religio*, the ecclesiastical order. Though a fragrance of worldliness may surround such use of the term (as it still does with Barth), a step was nevertheless being taken that will become a giant one when with modernity we move from the world as objective to the world as subjective reality.

See Alexander Souter, *A Glossary of Late Latin to 600 A.D.* (Oxford: Clarendon Press, 1949); R. E. Latham, *Revised Medieval Latin Word-List from British and Irish Sources* (Oxford and London; Oxford University Press and the British Academy, 1965); Karl Barth, *Church Dogmatics* I/1 (Edinburgh: T. & T. Clark, 1936), §36; Paul Tillich, *Systematic Theology* (Chicago: University of Chicago Press, 1951) I, p. 46; III, p. 42; Friedrich Gogarten, *The Reality of Faith*, (Philadelphia: Westminster Press, 1968), pp. 113, 170; Martin Buber, *Eclipse of God: Studies in the Relation Between Religion and Philosophy* (New York: Harper & Row, 1952); Philip Hammond, "Religion and the 'Informing' of Culture," *Journal for the Scientific Study of Religion* 3/1 (1963); Gabriel Vahanian, *The Death of God: The Culture of Our Post-Christian Era* (New York: George Braziller, (1957) 1961), pp. 65 and *passim*; *L' utopie chrétienne* (Paris: Desclée de Brouwer, 1992); "Une dogmatique sans dogme: l' impertinente pertinence de Tillich," *Foi & Vie* 97/3 (1998); "The Holy and the Secular versus the Sacred and the Profane," in Gert Hummel and Doris Lax (eds), *Being versus Word in Paul Tillich's Theology?/Sein versus Wort in Paul Tillichs Theologie?* (Berlin and New York: Walter de Gruyter, 1999); and "The Otherness of Time," www.jcrt.org, December 1999.

2 Clayton Crockett, "Foreword" to Charles E. Winquist, *Epiphanies of Darkness* (Aurora, CO: Davies Group, 1998).

3 See Gabriel Vahanian, *No Other God* (New York: George Braziller, 1966), *passim* (where, incidentally, *mundum* should read *mundus*).

4 Deuteronomy 30:11–20.

5 Buber, *Eclipse of God*, p. 28; *The Writings of Martin Buber*, ed. Will Herberg (New York: Meridian Books, 1956); *To Hallow This Life: An Anthology*, ed. Jacob Trapp (New York: Harper & Row, 1958); Vahanian, *Death of God*, pp. 65 ff., *passim*.

6 Ernst Troeltsch, *The Social Teachings of the Christian Churches* (London: George Allen & Unwin, 1951), vol. 2, p. 522.

7 Stanislas Breton, *L'avenir du christianisme* (Paris: Desclée de Brouwer, 1999), pp. 133–4, 142.

8 Matthew 25; Galatians 3:28; Colossians 3:11. On the eschatological dimension of secularization see Walter Jaescke, "Saekularisierung," *Handbuch der Religionswissenschaft* (Stuttgart: 2000).

9 Troeltsch, *Social Teachings of the Christian Churches*, p. 49.

10 Hebrews 13:14; Philippians 3:20.

11 In his commentary on the Gospel of John (3:3), Calvin writes: "ceux-là s'abusent qui prennent le Royaume de Dieu pour le ciel."

12 Matthew 25:40; 25:45.

13 Matthew 22:21; Mark 12:17; Luke 20:25; Psalm 137:4.

14 *Greek Acts of Andrew* 38:4–5.

15 Catherine Pickstock, *After Writing: On the Liturgical Consummation of Philosophy* (Oxford and Malden, MA: Blackwell, 1998), p. 217; see also p. 189.

16 See Albert Camus, *The Fall* (New York: Alfred A. Knopf, 1957).

17 Commenting on the Gospel of John, Saint Augustine writes: "Understanding is the reward of faith." "We believe that we might know; for if we wished first to know and then believe, we should not be able either to know or to believe" (In *Joannis evangelium tractatus* XXIX, 6 and XXVII, 9, quoted from Erich Przywara, *An Augustine Synthesis*, p. 58).

18 Saint Augustine, *Confessions* XI, 26–7.

19 Saint Augustine, *The City of God* XII, 3.

20 Saint Augustine, *The City of God* XV, 7, quoted in C. N. Cochrane's rendering of it in *Christianity and Classical Culture* (New York: Oxford University Press, 1944), p. 500.

21 Saint Augustine, *The City of God* XI, 1.

22 Jaroslav Pelikan, *Jesus through the Centuries: His Place in the History of Culture* (New Haven and London: Yale University Press, 1985), p. 141.

23 Ibid.

24 Jacques Le Goff, *La civilisation de l'occident médiéval* (Paris: Arthaud, 1964), pp. 253–4.

25 Ernst Cassirer, *The Philosophy of the Enlightenment*, trans. Fritz C. A. Koelin and James P. Pettegrove (Boston: Beacon Press, 1951), pp. 138–9.

26 2 Corinthians 8:15; Exodus 16:18.

27 Romans 4:8.

28 "The Freedom of a Christian" as well as "Secular Authority" are included in John Dillenberger, *Martin Luther: Selections from His Writings* (New York: Anchor Books, 1961). On this question of salvation or the history of salvation, see in particular Rudolf Bultmann, *Theology of the New Testament* II (New York: Charles Scribner's Sons, 1955), pp. 8–9; "The Idea of God and Modern Man," in *Translating Theology into the Modern Age*, ed. Robert W. Funk and Gerhard Ebeling (New York: Harper & Row, 1965); Paul Tillich, *Theology of Culture* (Oxford: Oxford University Press, 1959), p. 44; "Salvation," *The Princeton Seminary Bulletin* 57/1 (1963); *Gesammelte Werke* V (Frankfurt am Main: Evangelisches Verlagswerk, 1980), pp. 22–3; J. Christiaan Beker, "Biblical Theology Today," *The Princeton Seminary Bulletin* (Winter 1968); Gabriel Vahanian (ed.), *Le salut: du salut dans l'au-delà au salut sans au-delà* (Strasbourg: Association des publications de la faculté de theologie protestante, 1994).

29 Michael Walzer, *The Revolution of the Saints: A Study in the Origins of Radical Politics* (Cambridge, MA: Harvard University Press, 1965), p. 51.

30 Quoted from William G. McLaughlin, "The Diverse Origins of the American Tradition of Separation of Church and State," *Cimarron Review* 2 (1967) p. 50.

31 1 Corinthians 8:4–6.

# 2 Postmodern secular theology

Charles E. Winquist

I want to assess the possibilities and to reflect on the meaning of the development of a postmodern secular theology. I especially want to think about theology as a way of thinking. Theology sometimes has had to think under conditions not of its own choosing. In its Western cultural expression and in its close alliance, since Aristotle, with first philosophy or wisdom it has generally followed a trajectory of epochal transformations from philosophies of Being to philosophies of consciousness to philosophies of language. This last transformation has been further complicated by the explosive expansion of information technologies and parallel developments in the neuro-sciences. The notion of postmodern theology does not entail a specific agenda but is more importantly a thinking theologically that accounts for the conditions under which we think that are themselves indexical marks of the postmodern condition. Postmodernity cannot be simply dated and the postmodern is not synonymous with the contemporary. There are instead distinctive traits of a postmodern sensibility that call for theological understanding and thereby characterize the meaning and possibilities for postmodern theological thinking. It is the image rather than the object of thought that has been radically reconfigured.

The publication of *The Alchemy of the Word* (Raschke 1979), *Deconstruction and Theology* (Altizer *et. al.* 1982) and especially *Erring: A Postmodern A/theology* (Taylor 1984) brought the deconstructive philosophy of Jacques Derrida into the arena of theological discourse. The shaping influence of Derrida was soon augmented by attention to other, mostly French, theoreticians such as Jacques Lacan, Jean François Lyotard, Julia Kristeva, Gilles Deleuze and Michel Foucault. Theology also had to rethink its achievements in relationship to their precursor figures Nietzsche, Marx and Freud to better understand the meaning of the postmodern condition. Together, these precursor figures loosely constituted a movement that Paul Ricoeur labeled the hermeneutics of suspicion. They plumbed hidden forces that have disrupted an easy alliance with Enlightenment consciousness which was marked by clear and distinct ideas authenticated by expressions of force and vivacity. The ideality of consciousness was subverted or at least displaced by the materiality of history (Marx), the materiality of the body (Freud), and the materiality of language (Nietzsche). The nineteenth century extended the Kantian problematic separating the phenomenality of experience from the noumenality of reality by focusing on quasi-transcendental structures as conditions for thinking that complemented Kant's more limited transcendental interrogation of the conditions that make possible objective knowledge. The ideological structures of class consciousness, the psychoanalytic formulation of the unconscious, and the general metaphoricity of all language usage as substitutive structures make self-consciousness problematic in a way that is implicated in a new and radical thinking.

Theology itself took a radical turn in the 1960s that in some ways was a catching-up with the hermeneutics of suspicion but was not yet what can be called postmodern theology. This radical theology was almost synonymous with the "Death of God" theologies of Thomas J. J. Altizer, William Hamilton, Gabriel Vahanian, Paul Van Buren and Richard Rubenstein. There was a linguistic turn in theological thinking, and the radical question was whether theology was possible as a mode of meaningful discourse. The declaration of the Death of God had different meanings among these radical theologians but there were common implications of their diverse discourses. A challenge to the hegemony of neo-orthodoxy was clearly announced. History and society were understood as thoroughly secular. The human subject was privileged as the agent within theological discourse. Theology was a textual reality. And, most importantly, God is dead.

It wasn't long before it was recognized that there were important resonances between this radical theology and the appearance on the North American scene of Derrida's deconstructive postmodernism. Taylor's publication of *Erring* was a manifesto for a deconstructionist postmodern a/theology deeply influenced by radical theology and Derrida. He claims early in his argument that "*deconstruction is the 'hermeneutic' of the death of God*" (p. 6). This parallels Raschke's claim that "[d]econstruction . . . is in the final analysis *the death of God put into writing*" (Altizer 1982, p. 3). In what appears to be an oxymoronic formulation, the death of God is celebrated as a possibility for a new theological thinking. Quoting from Gilles Deleuze: "Theology is now the science of nonexisting entities, the manner in which these entities . . . animate language and make for it this glorious body which is divided into disjunctions" (Deleuze 1990, p. 281). The deconstructionist critique of the onto-theological notion of presence allows theology to think itself otherwise.

This "otherwise" is a valuation of "otherness" or the "other" that implicates the proclamation of the Death of God in other senses of irrevocable loss and incurable fault as outlined by Taylor. Implicated in the loss of supreme authorship and total presence are the displacement of the self, the end of history as a paradigm of explanation and the closure of the book of encyclopaedic proportions.

The God who died is the God of classical theism: a primal origin, an ultimate end, transcendent and eternal. This God is thoroughly implicated in an onto-theological understanding of total presence. The humanistic atheism of radical theology was a writing large of the privileging of the conscious subject over the supreme authorship of God that began with the turn from philosophies of Being to the philosophies of consciousness emblematically associated with Descartes and the beginnings of the Enlightenment. As the Enlightenment matured it soon became clear that, with the loss of total presence of a supreme authorship, the self experienced its own profound displacement, first with the Kantian fissure of the phenomenality of experience from the noumenality of things-in-themselves, and secondly with the articulation of hidden material forces through the hermeneutics of suspicion further distorting representations of the phenomenal world. Absolute self-identity and self-sameness expressed in "I am that I am" gave way to identity in difference marked by otherness. Without a supreme *Logos* present to consciousness the *telos* of history and the authoritative completeness of the book were subverted.

A postmodern theology has had to rethink its warrant without authority from outside its own productive formulations. That is, theology is a textual production that is always in the middle of existing discourses and there is always an outside of its achievements, but postmodern anti-foundationalism leaves it without special privilege. It makes a place of its own through strategies and tactics within a cacophony of diverse textual voices.

There are secular and what have recently been identified as postsecular postmodern theologies. In each case there are diverse strategies and tactics. There are more differences than similarities among neo-evangelical post-modern theologies, radical orthodoxy, and secular deconstructive theologies. What is similar is the acknowledgment or recognition of an epistemological problematic that is not resolvable by using straightforward Enlightenment categories. Reason is challenged. In neo-evangelical theologies revelation and scripture are privileged, which is in contrast to radical orthodoxy that rejects a reason/revelation duality. Radical orthodoxy appears more Catholic than Protestant as its seeks to recover and deepen the epistemic framework of the analogy of being with a knowing participation in reality. Generally, neo-evangelical theologies and radical orthodoxy understand secular deconstructive theologies as nihilistic.

This accusation of nihilism coincides or conflates with the apprehension of epistemological undecidability that is characteristic of a postmodern sensibility. The postmodern denial of a master narrative refuses the privileging of any particular revelations or metaphysical formulations that reside outside of the textuality of experience. A secular theology begins with an assertion that there is no special exemption from the conditions that make possible any discursive practices.

The traits of postmodern theories of discourse are preliminary markers for defining a postmodern theological agenda. Aside from the proclamation that "God is dead," traditional theology has been undermined by the dismantling of the centered and unified subject. Theological subjectivity is constituted as it is written and dispersed throughout the theological text. Theology is text production and the deconstruction of constituted subjectivities denaturalizes the onto-theological frame of theological discourse. The frame is instead a materialistic fold in a specific nexus of forces relative to its social and intellectual location. Because of this folding the inside is implicated in an outside so that the achievement of thinking is nonidentical with itself. There is an undecidable excess in theological thinking. Theology thinks not the "other" but traces of the "other."

These traces manifest themselves in fissures, gaps, paradoxes and incongruities on the surfaces of theological expressions. They transgress or violate any law of closure within a symbolic order. Postmodern theologies work against the totalization of thinking also by attending to extreme formulations, even in traditional theologies, that convolute the discourse of any symbolic order instantiating a radical negativity that marks an "other" within and of language. That is, postmodern theological analyses seek incommensurabilities within discursive practices that are internal traces of the "other" in the subjective fold of discourse. The "other" includes those forces that are not included in the expressivity of representational economies of ordinary discourses. In this sense, postmodern theology is a commitment to an extraordinary discourse.

There is sometimes a longing for primordial realities or primary processes that can only be marked on textual surfaces by aporetic formulations that refuse assimilation within a continuum of existing discursive practices. What is important is what the discourse is not even if this is marked inside of the discourse. These aporetic formulations facilitate a negative theology that could possibly be a clearing for apophatic disclosure or could simply be a negation of meaning within a discursive practice. It is not always clear what is valued by deconstructive theologies about an *aporia*, an impassable passage. Is it that it is a passage, or that it is impassable? Negative theologies emphasize impassability but there are other strategies that emphasize passage even when they articulate themselves in figurations of rupture, fissure or gap.

Deconstructive postmodernism is parasitic in that it works with already existing texts. It can choose to work within the textuality of traditional theology. It is a common strategy in postmodern thinking to critically intervene in already existing textual practices. There is the awareness that the text could always have been otherwise. This thread of criticism is particularly evident when feminists read patriarchal texts, and in Marxist ideological critiques. The text is read to be problematized, fissured and opened to the excluded other. Derrida in his readings of the Western philosophical tradition is a clear and even paradigmatic witness to this strategy. Derrida taught how to read *in extremis*, to read against the grain of a text locating lines of fissure, undecidables of meaning and forces of disruption. Deconstructive critique is a reading technology that implicates its own thinking in the "other" of language. This first strategy makes existing texts unsafe.

There are also writing technologies that generate texts that highlight their fissured surfaces, disfigured language, disorder and incompleteness. For example, Derrida in his experimental and playful texts generated a loose weave through graphic displacements, mixed genres and complex intertextual referencing. This second strategy is the work of the *bricoleur*. It is a work of assemblage amenable to an erring consciousness. The dominant trope is metonymy rather than metaphor. Ideas, images, words and phrases are ungrounded so that their placement is fully contingent. There are no established meanings because new contiguities or metonymical displacements contest fixed meanings and defer closure of any text. Experimental assemblage can be the dispersal, dissemination and dissimulation of what might have been settled meanings. A variation of this second strategy is less playful but is the engagement in the creation of new concepts that resist textual closure. These second strategies generate texts that are unsafe.

A third strategy is recognition of what is already paradoxical or parabolic in existing theological or religious texts and practices. The theologian attends to points of reversal in narratives, notes aporetic formulations of extremity in traditional theologies or sacred texts and attends to discrepancies or incongruities between ritual practices and the lives of their practitioners. Recognition is not intervention or creation but it is a tool of scholarship that helps postmodern theology understand a continuity between its own agenda and the historical traditions from which it draws textual materials to be rethought.

A recent theme in postmodern philosophical and theological thinking has been the return of religion, but it is a religion without religion. This is not so much a strategy as a sophisticated recognition of deconstructive traits as well as incorrigibilities in *fin-de-siècle* cultural and political experience. In Derrida's development we see a series of metonymical displacements of aporetic tropes from *différance* to *khôra*. John Caputo reads this situation as a passion for God, saving the name of God, a capacity to think religion without a forgetfulness of the conditions of a postmodern sensibility. With Derrida deconstruction carries negative theology, even atheism, into the fold of faith. In its latest turn postmodern theology implicates itself in a logic of the impossible. Beyond all philosophemes it is argued that the *khôra* has left its trace in language. A passion is articulated to save the name or names of the wholly other even if this is a theology of God who is not being God.

This recent shift in deconstructive philosophical and theological thinking could be emblematically entitled *Jacques, Jackie, Jack* because it has to do with names and saving a name, some names or the name. Jacques Derrida was, according to his confession, named Jackie and the distinguished religious philosopher John D. Caputo is known to many of his friends and colleagues as Jack. *The Prayers and Tears of Jacques Derrida: Religion Without Religion* is a remarkable book that can guide our reflections in a rethinking of the secular postmodern theological agenda.[1] In a first serious reading it is a book that needs to be marked because it makes startling claims about Derrida's faith and it needs in reflection to be re-marked to help assess who is speaking, Jacques, Jackie or Jack, or a combination of the three. There is in this mix another name that is wholly other, unspeakable but nevertheless spoken of as God in some determinable religions. But, since this is a book about religion without religion there may also be understandings without speaking, without knowing and without seeing.

Derrida's claim that he has been read less and less well over twenty years can be understood in the failure to understand his religion without religion (p. xxviii). It is not simply that his readers are fallible but there is a perverse resistance to understanding Jackie Derrida alongside of Jacques Derrida. Derrida speaks of his mother's knowledge that the constancy of God in his life was called by other names and that he has an "absolved, absolutely private language" in which he speaks of God all the time (pp. xvii, xviii) Derrida does not think of this God as an object of theological analysis. The God of Jackie "is given only in praying and weeping" (p. 288). He distrusts the word *theology* because of its embeddedness in the Western onto-theological tradition and its associations with totalizations, dogmatisms, and institutionalization (p. 289). The privilege that Western consciousness has given to seeing is transformed by the abocular counter-tradition of blindness. This is not a blindness that abhors the light but is instead an understanding of eyes that are "organs not of sight but of passion. Derrida is interested in eyes that are clouded by tears of mourning, tears of impassioned imploring" (p. 327). These are eyes that some readers of Derrida would prefer to be blind rather than be filled with tears. Jackie problematizes deconstructive scholasticism with a passion for meanings that are not determinable by close readings of texts. Maybe saving the name of Jackie, a task accepted by Jack Caputo, is also a saving of the text that is more than a scholarly exercise sanctioned by professional philosophers. Prayers and tears can smudge the ink on a *curriculum vitae* and Caputo is arguing that if this is our concern then we are one of those that have been misreading Derrida for twenty years.

Part of what has been misread is the meaning of epistemic undecidability that is inscribed in Derrida's earliest writings. Of particular importance is Derrida's concept of *différance*, which has sometimes been understood as a master trope constantly challenged by Derrida's metonymical substitutions while always returning as a fundamental expression of an epistemological *aporia*. One of the questions we will have to ask as we move from *différance* to hymen to spur . . . to *khôra* is whether anything important has changed. Has this slippage meant that the early enthusiasm for Derrida as a negative theologian, a charge denied by Derrida, has taken on a new theological or a/theological significance?

Caputo entitles his first chapter and strongly asserts that *"God* is not *différance."* It is, perhaps, more strongly asserted if we say that *différance* is not *God*, not even a hidden God. Caputo writes that "it would be a serious misunderstanding to think that *différance* is a master name, the secret hidden name of Being beyond Being, the hidden name of a presence so pure that it cannot itself appear and be present except by means of the imperfect traces of itself that it leaves behind as it withdraws from the world seated on a cloud of unknowing." (9) Derrida's *différance* is not a simple passageway into an apophatic negative theology. It is instead an aporetic formulation, an impassable passage, that delimits knowing. *Différance* is not a Heideggerian clearing but is a rift or fissure that has a close kinship with the Kantian schematism of the pure concepts of the understanding or transcendental imagination. "*Différance* does not love you or even know you are there ... *différance* could care less." (169)

Like the Kantian schematism, *différance* is a procedure, a transitive process, anterior to the representational economy we know as the world. *Différance* is a condition of possibility for the appearing and differential naming of the world. It is an epistemic reality that lets us name the animals, name ourselves, name the Gods and Goddesses. *Différance* is a condition of possibility for difference. Caputo, like Rodolphe Gasché, thinks of Derrida's *différance* as a quasi-transcendental formulation to contrast it with a constrained Kantian transcendental interrogation of the conditions that make objective knowledge possible. In Derrida, the Kantian problematic is written large so that it can include the meaning of prayers and tears. We see in *The Truth in Painting* that Derrida knew that the problematic of the Kantian first *Critique* was reinscribed in the third *Critique* and that we cannot circumvent *différance* by turning to faculties of desire or feeling.

Caputo argues that Derrida's deconstructive thinking is not a negative theology but it shares the passion of negative theology for the impossible. (3) It also needs to be noted that if his thinking is not a negative theology this does not mean it is not theological even if he steps back from the word *theology*. Theology is not simply an onto-theological doctrine of presence. Perhaps Derrida's religion without religion is accompanied by a theology without theology.

Throughout his text, Caputo rightly keeps bringing us back to *différance* as the key to resituating faith and negative theology so that it is not the apophaticism that is traditionally the engine and hope of negative theology. Deconstruction unsettles all assurances of the same and in this sense delimits simplistic metaphysical claims of theology. That is, deconstruction resituates metaphysical theories so that they are no longer theories of presence and thereby resituates theologies that are metaphysical. Deconstruction denies hyperessentialism in what has appeared and in what will come to appear. "The deconstruction of theology (positive or negative) consists in allowing *différance* its say or sway, allowing *différance* to inscribe and exceed negative theology without return. The deconstruction of theology re-commits theology to the grammatological flux from whence negative theology would take its leave." (11) The notion of the impossible can shatter or fissure conventional discourse, mark its incommensurability, but it cannot be understood as nonlinguistic. Wordlessness is inscribed in language. Discourse can be unsettled and made unsafe but it is still discourse.

This does not mean that there is not an "other" in and of language. Derridean deconstruction does not deny reference. It complicates it. There is no naked contact or immediate presence of Being or beings. As Aquinas and Avicenna so clearly understood well before Derridean deconstruction, women and men do not have angelic knowledge. Our knowledge of the impossible is a knowledge of traces. These traces of the other, possibly a wholly other or even an infinitely other, are the aura of representations and substitutions that let us think. We know that the image *dog* is not a dog and that the word *dog* is not a dog. Reference is complicated and unsettled but not denied. There is an *always already, not yet*, quality to the impossible in discourse. Discourse trembles when it speaks through indirection of what cannot be spoken. Its thinking can apprehend but not comprehend its own extreme formulations such as Anselm's "that than which nothing greater can be conceived," Tillich's "ultimate concern," Barth's "wholly other," the Brahman, Allah as lord of the worlds, the Tao or even the prosaic expression of Lonergan's God as "the complete set of answers to the complete set of questions." These can all be likened to Derrida's name of the *impossible*, the incoming of the *tout autre*. (22)

Derrida's formulation, like those of his predecessors, is an open-ended, indeterminable, disseminative undecidability within discourse. The word and the world are made strange. There are no reductive closures or closures that disguise themselves as totalizations. The notion of a clean, well-lighted place is a transitory fiction that gives way to a sense of the uncanny in our thought or experience.

In traditional language, Derrida's theological thinking, even when it comes forward in disguise, is messianic and eschatological, marked by an apocalyptic tone, rather than apophatic. What is to come will not come in a clearing because what always precedes the thought of Being is *différance*. What comes will come in the clutter and cacophony of marketplace discourse even if the element of undecidability makes us think of the market as a desert. We are always already in the middle of discourse, an economy of representations. What this possibility of the impossible, when spoken, makes strange is the marketplace itself. In a hyperbolic formulation, the kingdom of God is at hand but this doesn't make sense because we have erased the name of God, cannot speak the name of God and do not know how to save the name of God. Derrida sets for himself the task of saving the name of God and Caputo brings this forward as a profound exigency in Derrida's thinking. Jack hears the voice of Jackie that is feared by some of the followers of Jacques. Even the marketplace of ideas that define various postmodernisms is made strange by the pressure of theological formulations.

This is all premature unless we are first about saving the name of God that cannot be spoken or written. This is a God who can be likened to Jean Luc Marion's "God without Being" or Robert Scharlemann's "the being of God when God is not being God." Saving the name of God is an instantiation of a radical *negativity*. The name of God is spoken and crossed out so that it can be spoken otherwise. *Différance* is not God but if the name of God is spoken it is because of *différance*. Is there a way or a place where we can unsay what has been said so that there can be maintained a notion, without knowledge, of a God without Being whose name can be saved? This appears to be non-sense unless there can be a nonconceptual formulation that names such a way or place. This would have to be a nonconcept likened to *différance* but not *différance*. Following Plato and perhaps Julia Kristeva, Derrida names this place *khôra*. This name is a trope of negativity that is neither being nor non-being. (35) "*Khôra* has no meaning or essence, no identity to fall back upon. . . . In short, the *khôra* is *tout autre*, very." (36) He posits what we have not experienced except as the notion of an unheard trace that calls us into language. The name is an aporia. Caputo asserts that the desert *khôra* is for Derrida a nameless name for the desert of *différance*. (40) What comes forth from this desert is the name of God as the wholly other which cannot be the private property of any determinable faith. It is a not knowing and the *not knowing* is itself the trace of what is coming forth that never comes. Caputo writes that "[f]or Derrida, the trace is the element of undecidability, the formlessness in which determinate forms are inscribed, a desert place within which determinate decisions – theological or atheological – are made, each checked and confused by the other, each movement disturbed by a counter-movement, so that we do not know what is taking place; in the desert one never knows whether what is coming is an oasis or a mirage." (57) Undec-idability makes every text, every thinking, unsafe. The trace is an experience of unknowing that leaves us all a little lost. We are not secure in our scholar-ship or in any determinable faiths. While referring to Derrida's *Specters of Marx*, Caputo asserts that deconstruction believes in the ghosts of chance events. (124) Thinking is a throw of the dice. There is nothing philosopically, theologically or politically correct in the place of the *khôra* and yet all think-ing is philosophical, theological and political. The trace always suffers becoming philosophical, theological and political as it is marked and refer-enced in representational economies. Because of profound undecidability, the trace also can suffer becoming tree, becoming cow, becoming dog, becoming river, becoming woman, becoming man as it is marked and referenced in representational economies. And so, God created the world.

These becomings on a plane of immanence suggest a coming that Caputo links to the secret of the *khôra* and *différance*. He writes that "[v]*iens* is rather a certain *Ur*-affirmation, older and lighter than any determinate word or deed, that silently and invisibly tears open lived time and ordinary language, that renders them always already structurally open to what is coming, that prohibits (*pas!*) closure while soliciting transcendence (*le pas*). The *viens* is the order, or disorder, of messianic time, of *venir* and *avenir*, that disturbs the order of presence, that hollows it out, so that what is coming does not, never did, never can, correspond to presence and presence cannot close over." (86) Clearly, Derrida shares a passion with negative theology for the impossible but what this passion engenders in Derrida's thinking is messianism rather than mysticism. What is coming is factually unknown and structurally unknowable. This is the "absolute secret." (101) This coming, incoming, is an invention, inter-vention of the wholly other. The "absolute secret" is an originary experience that sets writing, thinking, in motion accompanied by passion and sparks.

This is a given that is a gift. "The gift, one might say, is *how* things 'come,' how *the* impossible happens." (160) This gift does not reside within a representational economy. There is no knowledge of a giver, no credit, and no debt. The impossible is incompossible within an economic structure. This should be obvious if the place of giving is *khôra* and the giving is *différance*. The gift is known only in the trace of unknowing. The trace is the mark of epistemic undecidability that denies credit, debt and obligation. This deconstructive anti-foundationalism is freedom for an ethical and political decidability. Obligation is a *de facto* obligation to our freedom and not part of a foundational contract.

Caputo writes that "[i]f deconstruction were a theory, it would be a theory that nothing is safe, pure, clean, uncontaminated, monochromatic, unambiguous . . . [d]econstruction is an exploration of as many 'instants' of undecidability as it has time (as it is given time) to study . . . it always tends to say that the undecidability is permanent, that undecidability precedes, follows, and permeates the decision, that the undecidability is first, last, and always, but that decisions must be made and indecision broken." (225) There is a faith that is a known unknowing, a trace. "Our life is a tissue of faith, of little beliefs and credulities, *minima credibilia*, of taking one another's word, of assumptions and presuppositions which, if they form a rich enough and elaborate enough network, may just see us through the day and then, if they are still more complex and subtle enough, might well see us through the week." (312) Life is making arrangements or assemblages, the satisfaction of which involves a measure of their complexity. This appears to be an aesthetic justification of existence but it is not quite that simple because of Derridean messianism. That which comes, but never arrives, disrupts, fissures and enflames all of our arrangements. "We never get out from under the textuality and structural undecidability of our lives." (313)

What is coming never comes because what we understand with Kantian sensibilities, the meaning of *différance*, is that whatever comes is other than the wholly other or it cannot come. There is in Derrida's project a deferral of the parousia. "The whole idea of deconstruction is to deprive *ousia* of its prestige, to expose the present to what is not present, to keep it open to what is to come." (245) Theological formulations of extremity, names of the wholly other, pressure ordinariness, disrupt its flow, distort its meanings, function as a lure to what is not yet, without ever coming to presence. Derridean brokenness is a hopefulness. It is possible to say a Nietzschean yes, a Derridean *oui oui*, to life, to language, and to that from which language arises and accompanies language. We can say yes to what we can name and to that which we cannot name but which is the possibility for naming what we can name. Derrida articulates a theological empiricism rather than a theological mysticism. His "*oui* is not so much a word as a silent companion to words, a quasi-word which provides words with their element and force." (256) His empiricism is an empiricism with a secret.

This brings us face to face with the question why do we want to save the name of what will always remain a secret. Clearly most of us want fire and sparks in our lives. We don't want the everydayness of life to be trivialized. Maybe we didn't know that this intensity will include prayers and tears. This acknowledgement is one of the special contributions of Caputo. He has the capacity to hear, when he reads Derrida, that there is always something more or other than the text. We can liken the *khôra* to a place but it is not a place to live. Neither *khôra* nor *différance* come to full presence. They are conditions of possibility, quasi-transcendentals, and make their mark on the ordinariness of life. They are the extra-ordinary of the ordinary, the general structure of the possibility for religious meaning. The other in the phenomenality of our world is implicated in the wholly other to be what it is. Derrida's and Caputo's worlds are saturated in a divine ordinariness. The paradox of religion without religion is lodged in its ordinariness.

"[T]he knight of faith extraordinaire is an exemplar of the ordinary." (208) What is exceptional is recognition that every other is implicated in the wholly other, every possible world is implicated in the impossible. The knight of faith lives the passion for the impossible. "Faith is a passion of unknowing." (311) It is a passion for unknowing in the midst of what we know. The kingdom of God, a formulation available to us if we have saved the name of God, *tout autre*, is a place of singularities, empiricities and heterologies. We can say yes to the ordinary because the ordinary is now extraordinary.

## Note

1 John D. Caputo, *The Prayers and Tears of Jacques Derrida: Religion Without Religion* (Bloomington: Indiana University Press, 1997). All future textual references will be a citation of page numbers from Caputo's book in the body of this article.

## References

Altizer, Thomas J. J. *et. al.* (1982) *Deconstruction and Theology.* New York: Crossroad.

Caputo, John D. (1997) *The Prayers and Tears of Jacques Derrida: Religion Without Religion.* Bloomington: Indiana University Press.

Deleuze, Gilles (1990) *The Logic of Sense*, trans. Mark Lester with Charles Stivale. New York: Columbia University Press.

Derrida, Jacques (1995) *On the Name*, trans. David Wood. Stanford: Stanford University Press.

—— (1994) *Specters of Marx*, trans. Peggy Kamuf. New York and London: Routledge.

Carl Raschke (1979) *The Alchemy of the Word: Language and the End of Theology.* Missoula, MT: Scholars Press.

Taylor, Mark C. (1984) *Erring: A Postmodern A/theology.* Chicago: University of Chicago Press.

# 3    *À-Dieu* to Jacques Derrida

## Descartes' ghost, or the Holy Spirit in secular theology

### Carl A. Raschke

> That which was from the beginning, which we have heard, which we have seen with our eyes, which we have looked upon and touched with our hands.
>
> 1 John 1:1

## I

As we head into the new millennium, a ghost can be heard shuffling through the passageways of the postmodern.

As is the case with all hauntings, the specter is difficult to spot, let alone to name. Naming a ghost would dispossess it, strip it of its aptitude to distress, and for that reason it cannot be spoken – yet. There are still many slumbering in their chambers who still have no inkling of it, who have not, and cannot even constitutionally, awaken from what the painter Goya called the "dream of reason" in which philosophical and theological thought since Descartes has been steeped. The specter has not yet materialized, rendering its theological signature even more exquisite and dreadful.

The fearfulness of the ghost has already been apprehended, curiously and epochally, by the prince of the postmodern himself, Jacques Derrida. It is the ghost of Emmanuel Levinas, to whom Derrida professes to leave the "last word," the "word that says *à-Dieu*." It is a ghost that can only be named "Sinai." It is the "proper name 'Sinai'," which Derrida says is "as enigmatic as the name 'face'," which is "untranslatable."[1] Levinas has called forth this peculiar "spirit" for Derrida. But it is a spirit that does not allow him to simply say "farewell" to the celebrated postmodern Moses who brought down from the mount of modernism the tablets of a new ethic, the (post-Kantian) "law" of responsibility to *l'autre*.

It is a spirit that compels Derrida to say something once more about the "*à*," the intrusive vowel that has long cast the shadow of differ*à*nce, but now in an even more fateful way. It is the *à* of *à-Dieu*, the *à* of accountability, the *à* that circumscribes the discourse "to (*à*)", the other. The *à* cannot be said to the "passage" – that which is now "past" – of the text. It must be said to what continually "passes" over us, the unspeakable presence of the Most High, that which can only be regarded in terms of the traces such a Presence leaves in our presence. It is this superlocutionary Presence that absents itself not in the "past," but in that which "passes for" time, as beings. The Levinasian trace, as with Derrida, cannot be named, but for an entirely different reason. The trace can be located in the *à* of *à-Dieu*, in the "good"-bye, in the act of "letting go." But this letting-go or "letting be past" is also a letting-be-present in the most radical sense. This "saying to (*à*)" the other that is "wholly other" is truly frightful, because it forces philosophy on its knees in the "fear of God." But how can philosophy fear God, especially if God is dead? One does not fear living. Only the most self-composed mentality, however, will not fear a ghost.

Descartes' ghost! No, even Descartes has encountered the ghost – *Geist*, *Gast*, guest – from Sinai. In his *Wille zur Macht* Nietzsche spoke of nihilism as "the strangest of guests." But this "presence" – the Levinasian trace that is a presence that cannot be known or named as present – is strangest of all "strangers." If in Nietzsche's words nihilism "stands at the door" of the twentieth century, and by Heidegger's reckoning skulks at the borders of Western philosophy with its "white mythology," its metaphysics of presence, then the strangest thing is the way in which the trace can be recollected as a double inscription, as the gratuitous and gloomy ghost of a dead Deity, or as the *parousia* of the unrepresentable present that history has named "Sinai."

The *aporia* of postmodern religious thinking is itself a kind of *aporia*, a displacement of the fundamental zone of undecidability for the "Western," not simply Greek, philosophical tradition. The option is not Athens or Jerusalem; it is Derrida or Levinas! It is the *duplex Hebraicum*, the two "faces" of the text of Western thought that is not Greek, or Roman, or even European, but Levantine. It is Torah, Law, Word, Scripture – the signature behind the "philosophical" play of signs. It is the Code of codes, the tablets of transcendence that came down from the mountain. Metaphysics as the history of the text of "pure reason" (Kant) was never the text in this sense. Kant's problem of metaphysics, which is also Heidegger's, is not the peculiar problem of postmodern religious thinking. The text that we have problematized without recognizing the immensity of the problem is the text of pure practical reason, the canon of the Other, the inscription that requires "society" in Levinas' sense, which is beyond the self-presence of consciousness. Nietzsche's *aporia* was simply this – "God or *Übermensch*." But what if *Übermensch* itself was a tracing, an unrepresentable ghost/guest of the unity of self-presencing which the phenomenologists call "consciousness" and Kant dubbed the "transcendental unity of apperception"?

Nietzsche's guest is Descartes' ghost, the infinity that both logically and existentially overwhelms the positing of the finite. But it is even more the specter that cannot be exorcized by any "deconstructive" reading of the entire discursivity of Western history. Kant understood there were at least two texts to be "critiqued." But it required his somewhat fumbling critique of "judgement" (*Urteilskraft*) to discover that something else was still demanded. The "second" critique was not a critique at all, but an articulation of where the writing of the text might go after its limits had been set. The Kantian effort to create a kind of "moral ontology" from the universality of the Law and the "God postulate" simply extended the notion of a "critical metaphysics" to the point where it had first been inscribed, in the temple itself. Both Athens and Jerusalem had their temples. Without knowing it, in his attempt to subdue Athens, Derrida has thrown his incense finally on to the altar of the temple in which is enshrined the Law, the Law of writing, the endless "metaphorization" of the text that counts as the history of philosophy. The movement of deconstruction begins and ends inside the temple, the temple of "Holy Scripture." It is still within the confines of Old Jerusalem.

But what of Sinai? The trope is a mountain, rather than a city. If the primordial mountain is Sinai, Zion is the eschatological one. And what would that mean for the postmodern philosophy that has overcome theology? Zion as the "Mount of Olives" where the messiah returns, where the "heavenly city" comes down. The stylization of the mountain from the standpoint of philosophical writing, as Derrida understands, is the pyramid. The pyramid is the location of the altar, the site of sacrifice, the sublation of the letter in the construction of difference, which like the Aztec ritual of dismemberment at the top of the stairs marks the totalitarianism of a wholly textual civilization. But the pyramid is not a mountain, any more than a house is not a home. The mountain is where the face appears. The mountain is where the trace is deposited as law, but remains the infinite "altarity" of the letter itself, even the "a," the alpha and omega of thought as writing. Sinai is where the "tradition" – even the deconstructed passages of the tradition that our new postmodernist and a/theological writers – cannot go, but it is also the name for what Derrida has endeavored to name, without nevertheless naming it. It is Spirit.

What of Spirit? Good Hegelian that he is, Derrida construes Spirit as sublation, as *Aufhebung*. The sublation, of course, is the jarring of the literal, the code of differentiation that contains within itself the entirety of writing. It is the text that is messianic for Derrida, and therefore the text remains the grand pyramid of sacrifice, so far as "meaning" is concerned.

## II

"We are still in the presence of the Aristotelian *representation* of time," writes Derrida.[2]

Derrida's critique of Aristotle, of course, can be found in *The Margins of Philosophy*. Derrida's "marginalization" of the Aristotelian theory of (temporal) representation in turn functions as the fulcrum for his strategy of surpassing the metaphysics of presence by the valorization of the sign as the force of writing. The deconstruction of the "present" of representation requires, for Derrida, a "dynamic" alterity. But this alterity, this "other than" the present, cannot be "originary." It cannot be phonetic, which derives from the written, the "grammatological." It is eminently the presence of the pre-monition of presence, which we experience in the raptness of interior mono-logue. It, therefore, must constitute "a closing of the circle of language," Derrida's "autofellatio," which underwrites the hidden truth of deconstruc-tion. It is the autochthony of the lexical/logical, the very "modernist" principle of totalization.

To call Derrida a "nihilist" at this level is no misreading. The nihilism of the early Derrida peers straightaway from the rhetoric of the *Grammatology* itself. Such a nihilism manifests itself in the infinitely expanded presence of all presences, which is the same as the *grammé*, the line, the trace, the "writing down," the self-scripting or *vorhanden* that is in actuality an *unhanden*, the phantasmal hand that "has no hands" when it writes, the inscription whose "truth" is a further inscription, the temporalization of the temporal that dis-closes nothing because the "no-thing" (*nihil*) is an interminable differencing. The Derridean *a* of difference, henceforth, becomes a self-bounded moment of totality. The *à* of *à-Dieu* is a negation, an absence or "being away" (*Abwesen*) instead of a "being toward." Derrida's *à-Dieu* confirms the "a" of *a-theology*. It is the "a" of the law of the text that leads to death.

When Derrida speaks of "spirit," he speaks of what is dead, absent, what has "passed on" into the trace that is beyond the present, the *geistliche* guest in the house of philosophy that forever haunts us. Derrida declares at the opening of *De l'esprit*: "I shall speak of ghost (*revenant*), of flame, and of ashes."[3] The flame is Hegel. The ashes are the event of deconstruction of the text of speculative philosophy. Not a spirit in ashes, but *a* spirit of ashes. Does not the strangest of totalitarianisms stand at the door of postmodern-ism? All totalitarianisms mis-represent spirit as totality, *ousia* as *parousia*, presence as the revelation of presence, time as eternity, slavery as liberation; it is the new "scholarly" totalitarianism of writing that holds sway.

Derrida imagines that he has thought through Heidegger as follows:

> ... Do you find that what we have in our memory, the abyss of our memory, is not enough?), the thinking of this *Frühe* to come, while advancing towards the possibility of what you think you recognize, in going towards what is quite other than what you think you recognize. It is indeed not a new content. But access to thought, the thinking access to the *possibility* of metaphysics or pneumato-spiritualist religions opens up something quite other than what the possibility makes possible. It opens up onto what remains origin-heterogeneous. What you represent as simply ontological and transcendental replica is quite other.[4]

The "repetition" that is "most vertiginous" and "most abysmal." Do we not have here echoes of Nietzsche's well-known polemics? It is repetition that keeps alive, if only as catachresis, the allusion of presence in the Derridean trace. The "trace of the trace" that is at the same time the "spirit which keeps watch in returning [*en revenant*, as a ghost] will always do the rest. Through flame or ash, but as the entirely other, inevitably." The "entirely other"? *Totaliter aliter. En revenant.* Returning to what? The return that is endless repetition, the endless differencing of difference. Nietzsche's "eternal recurrence of the same" now deconstructed as the "origin-heterogeneous," the trace. The entire Derridean project succumbs to a kind of Nietzschean exhaustion at the rim of the abyss. Derrida has not overcome Nietzsche, but impaled himself on Nietzsche's own "most abysmal" thought, the thought of eternal recurrence. Eternal recurrence of the same. The mark of/*as* the same. The same as the presence of the present that presents itself as pure presence, that keeps erasing itself as *écriture*, but remains "eternally" *la même.* Eternal recurrence. Eternal recurrence as the will to power. The will to writing. That end that is a-theological and thereby forecloses the eschatological. The trace. The rude inscription on the tablet. The law. The presence that makes possible the amnesia, the erasure of the trace, of Sinai. The ghost that stalks, the "literacy" of the letter that kills on the sight.

## III

That is Derrida's *Geist*. But what of a different ghost? Descartes' ghost?

In his 1962 essay *"Transcendence et Hauteur"* Levinas writes about "the rhythm of Cartesian thinking" which "only rejoins the world by passing through the idea of the Infinite." If, Levinas says, "Descartes begins with the *Cogito*, he says a little later that in fact it is the idea of God that is primary, that is the idea of the infinite. The idea of God was prior to the *Cogito*, and the *Cogito* would never have been possible if there had not already been the idea of God . . . it is the direct act and not in the reflective act that philosophical critique begins."[5]

It is curious that the *Meditations*, which have been read throughout the history of late modernist thought, particularly by Hegel and Heidegger, as grounding the subjectivity of the subject, or the metaphysics of self-presence, should not be construed as disclosing the sense of difference that has always confounded onto-theological reflection. Kierkegaard spoke of this difference as the "infinite qualitative difference," as the chasm between the temporality of self-reflective (Hegelian) spirit and the eternal God presence. But Levinas' "direct act" is something much more than the postmodernist, postmetaphysical inscription of the "differend," as Lyotard designates it. The inscription of difference rests on a puzzle within the logic of identity and difference itself. Whether we embark from Leibniz' "identity of indiscernibles," Hegel's "concept" (*Begriff*) of self that is compelled to externalize itself in order to return to itself, or Derrida's discovery that the structuralist theory of the sign as differentiation implies the revelation of the self-presence of consciousness to itself as writing, we remain caught within a conundrum of onto-theology itself.

Is it Descartes who ironically leads us out of the labyrinth of onto-theological self-reflection, and self-reference? Derrida scoffs at Levinas' suggestion. But Levinas makes a critical observation that Derrida (and Heidegger for that matter) has not yet intuited. The observation is that the "question of Being" is "over and above" ontology. Levinas talks not about differencing, but of the "trace" in the sense that Plotinus long ago meant it, as a "signature" upon Being of that which is beyond Being, as an Opening within being that reveals that Being itself is "beyond itself." "This *hither side* of identity is not reducible to the *for itself*, where a being recognizes itself in its difference beyond its immediate identity."[6] The "hither side of identity" is Levinas' "otherwise than being." It is the radical troping of even the most allusive ontological determinations toward what Levinas terms a "height." The troping of the language of predication on which even Heidegger's "fundamental ontology" depends drives the "science" of Being in the direction of what Levinas calls "prophetic signification."

"The intelligibility of transcendence," says Levinas, "is not something ontological."[7] In Descartes such a transcendence is not yet interpretable, but it registers a kind of unthematizable liberty, a "theological" brand of *laissez passer* in anchoring modern subjectivity. We may call this liberty truly "postmodern." It is the liberty of "prophecy," the recognition that philosophy does not have its provenance in rationality *per se*, that it can be admitted into the sphere of "signification of order given to subjectivity before any statement."[8] When we reference the postmodern do we, in effect, mean the prophetic?

The fashionable identification in Anglo-American theological circles of postmodernism with nihilism rudely mislabels the nature of this underlying signification. The postmodern is not, and never was, the Derridean. The prophetic signifier, the infinite pressure of the Cartesian "phantom," reaches into the transcendental recesses of a pseudo-Cartesian modernist ontology of immanence. The delicate rose of a postmodern *parousia* can be sighted within the Cartesian inferno. By the same token, the Cartesian fire is a "holy fire," the fire "from heaven," the fire of the Holy Spirit. Postmodernism is ineluctably eschatological – and hence "prophetic" in the way Levinas understands it – inasmuch as it reverses the inclement nihilism of onto-theology with the covert and timed "fulfillment" of what appears to be the empty mirror of the signifier. Such a reversal is precisely the moment Paul Tillich enunciates in the phrase "God beyond God." But this enunciation is neither "ontological" in Tillich's turn of phrase nor strictly "ethical" along the lines characteristically laid out by today's "Levinasians." The prophetic signification of the reversal of nihilism in Descartes' "direct act" constitutes a lightning-like event that is yet to be encountered – perhaps it is beyond even the thinking of an unthought presence – in the disentanglement of the "onto-theological."

The lightning, like that which accompanies the advent of the Son of Man, has only been barely descried in even the most timely attempts to overleap postmodernity by some kind of "discourse of participatory perfection," as John Milbank has called it. Milbank's work consists in a bold, but highly unsatisfactory, endeavor to think out the contradictions in the Derridean wing of postmodernism, when the "differentialist" view holds that deconstruction by dint of its disfiguring of the sign is impervious to the semantics of contradiction. Milbank's critique of postmodernist "ontology," on the other hand, is not as interesting as his declaration that "theology" alone can overcome metaphysics. What does Milbank have in mind?

Ironically, Milbank makes almost precisely the same point as Levinas. Milbank argues that "modernism" as a whole, of which postmodernism is but a truncated postlude, signifies the immanentization of the infinite. Where Levinas finds in Descartes a point of leverage for the deconstruction of deconstruction itself, Milbank locates it in Saint Thomas' *analogia entis*. This peculiar move, which earmarks the whole of so-called "radical orthodoxy," is not as reactionary or as idiosyncratic as it looks on first inspection. Milbank discerns that concealed within the *analogia* is a full-armored hermeneutical strategy that disrupts the Derridean parousia of the text. The *analogia* generates a system of signs that can never be determinations of being and, henceforth, can never survive as a moment of any ontology, or de-ontology for that matter. These signs bespeak an order of signification that is genuinely "mysterious," as the Latin meaning of *mysterium* suggests. They show the way toward an understanding of God not as Being, but as the One who is revealed in the compendium of signs. Milbank talks about revelation as an Augustinian form of "illumination" that is instantiated in the Christian sacrament, and derivatively in the domain of "ecclesiology." Milbank's "orthodoxy" is not in any sense a theological trope; it is an argument for the restoration within the West of clerical, and therefore "theological," authority.

Milbank embroiders this position from his own admittedly "strange" reading of Christian soteriology. If the *analogia* entails a radical terrain of differentiation between Being and the divine, there is a "second difference" as well. Where Milbank speaks of a "second difference," he is dealing with the distinction within the Trinitarian conception of God. The act of differentiation names the "person" of the Holy Spirit that fills out the "doctrine" of the Holy Trinity. The idea of the Trinity is what Milbank cryptically characterizes as "the true validity of postmodernity."[9] The postmodernist "myth" is a hermetic one, according to Milbank. It is the myth of the demigod as scribe, who usurps "the verbal power of the god." In separating the principle of *pneuma* from *logos*, Christian Trinitarianism "takes absence as the occasion for rhetorical community, and not dialectical unity, nor infinite concealment and betrayal."[10]

The soteriology of radical orthodoxy, on the other hand, does not overcome the hermetic myth. The hermetic myth is, of course, a gnostic one. Milbank dubs his new gnostic soteriology the "Gothic vision." The phrase "Gothic" in Milbank's usage is as slippery and equivocal as it has been for hundreds of years within Western arts and literature. Milbank draws his own version of neo-Romantic, post-postmodernist "Gothicism" from the thought of John Ruskin in the nineteenth century. Following Ruskin's aesthetics of architecture, Milbank claims that Gothicism allows for a "complex space" that confirms the person in relation to the transcendent through both eucharistic mediation and sacerdotal power. Just as the Gothic cathedral interweaves the vertical grandeur of prelatical hierarchy with the horizontal overgrowth of communal life space, so a "Gothic" vision implies the intricate integration of priestly signs of hierophany with a practical social ethic. It is as though the Reformation never happened. Like all historic forms of gnosticism, the new Gothicism constitutes a seductive pastiche of religious symbols and affiliations that supply the "initiate" with an insight unavailable within the discourse of popular culture. Milbank's gnosticism is no different.

Milbank contrasts Gothic "complexity," which he sees as a kind of "conservative" heterology, with the totalizing singularity of the Enlightenment. Milbank's Gothic vision is admittedly a Romantic type, as his appeal to Ruskin shows. Milbank's attempt to supplant a hermetic/scribal gnosticism with a Gothic/communitarian (read "Anglo-Catholic" or neo-Victorian) one comprises one more negative moment of reading in what Habermas has called the "dialectic of Enlightenment." Milbank's "second difference" on that score is not a significant difference at all. The "differentiation" of *pneuma* still belongs to the "gnostic" complex. A pneumatology that remains a force of cultural paleontology must be essentially gnostic. From an onto-logical vantage point such a second difference is tantamount to an identity-within-difference, not as an interval within the history of the metaphysics of Being but as a kind of gnostic apriorism that Milbank himself takes as a sort of mystic insight. It is a mysticism that encircles, and therefore serves to totalize, the space of heterology that Levinas allows for the presence exhibited in the face of the other.[11] It is an illuminism that counts as a kind of ahistorical "simulacrum" in Baudrillard's sense, not as rich representation of historic orthodoxy, but an illuminism that can entrance a theological public wearied by the discursive libertinism of the Derrideans and suffering from the same vague sentiment of "twentieth century disaster" from which Milbank's "Gothic vision" offers redemption.[12]

There is, however, a gaping chasm between Milbank's "second difference" and the difference engendered within the infinite "spirit" of Levinas. Whereas Milbank's difference is decidedly gnoseo-metaphysical, the differentiation between Being and Levinas' "otherwise than Being" carries us back to the original vanishing-point of the Word that eucharistic mysticism is unable to assimilate. Radical orthodoxy may offer an "origination" of sorts in the theological simulacrum of the Johannine "Word made flesh." But it knows not the (Levinasian) Word from "the heights" that tabernacles in the Johannine liturgy. It knows not Sinai. Because it knows not Sinai, radical orthodoxy is incapable of framing theologically what is actually implied in the simulation of Christian" presence" it names as *ortho-doxa*. The refusal of such an "orthodoxy" is not nihilism, as we can be easily led to believe. For orthodoxy historically has cast its nets of discursivity within the sea of onto-theology.

The creedalism of the patristic tradition is an obvious case in point. The shattering of every orthodoxy is not nihilism, but eschatology. In its very conception eschatology betokens the overcoming of the metaphysics of presence by the Presence alone. The presencing of Presence means the smashing of the onto-theological pattern of writing as presence, of inscription as the double sentence, of the regime of being itself. Eschatology is both "the end of theology" and the end of all "orthodoxies" that purport to stand in for the Father, that usurp the throne of signification and raise their own spectral authority within the temple as the name of sacred names. Only there dwells Sinai. The name of the Son and the "second difference" of the Spirit retain this same moment of infinite decidability. On the theological scale the "second difference" that is the power of the Holy Spirit, therefore, has its origins at the moment that follows the rending of the veil of the temple. It begins with the "new harvest" of Pentecost. The event at Pentecost entails the parousia of all signification that is the "outpouring" of the Spirit, the "miracle" of glossolalia that signifies a fullness of the phonological in a way that cannot be captured within the articulation of the grammatical. It is an event that explodes both the hermetical/grammatological authority of the priestly order and the horizontal indeterminacy of the "tradition" of temple scribes. The "arrival" of the Holy Spirit has little to do with any second "metaphysical" differentiation within the domain of theology that has somehow re-established the mediating role of the ecclesiastical. Speaking both historically and semiotically, we grasp that the "second difference" is not a difference at all. It is the negation of the very negativity that inheres in writing, and hence in theology itself.

The site of Sinai, for Levinas, both grounds and confounds the history of Western philosophy. Any "post-secular" philosophy, as Phillip Blond has termed it, must take into account this peculiar "sit-ing." While in no manner does Western philosophy, according to Levinas, "lose its right to the last word . . . it is not the place of the first meaning of beings, the place where meaning begins."[13] Sinai is not the "high sign" (*Sign-high*) of the theologico-metaphysical stance of truth as "revealed." Sinai recurs in philosophy, particularly in the dead zone of ultra-Cartesian subjectivity.[14] This siting is the difference in both philosophy and theology that takes the "end" of both philosophy and theology, of which Heidegger spoke, to the top of the mountain, to the height. Sinai speaks for the site from which it is possible to speak ontologically at all.

Can Derrida climb to the height? Alas, no, even when he speaks of the possibility of transcendence that cowers as "the absolute invisibility of the origin of the visible."[15] Such an invisibility cannot be named for Derrida. It can only be named as a kind of *Döppelganger* to metaphysics, as "religion," as the presence of the invisible that cannot be made present. The "phenomenon" of religion, writes Derrida, is "phallic," projective from the absent origin. It is defined by "the law of iterability" that inheres in textuality, "or of duplication that can *detach* it from its pure and proper presence." Is such a presence, Derrida asks, "also its phantasma, in Greek, its ghost, its spectre, its double or its fetish."[16] The ghost Derrida embraces is the "spirit" of the text, the undelimitable text, the deconstructed text, the end of the book that becomes writing. That is not the ghost of the *saeculum*, as radical orthodoxy would have it, but the ghost of religiosity that is a most familiar, comfortable, and friendly haunting. There are Christian texts, Buddhist texts, Hindu texts, Parsi texts, Mayan texts, and so forth. There is the religion that has come out of the cloud as writing, though the cloud is now long forgotten. Because we have writing, we have religion, a scholastic "fantasy."

The writing of the history of being, for Derrida, is the being of writing. This being of writing is what we mean by "presence," even among those who would seek to "consummate" writing in its "post-secular," liturgical setting.[17] The "ghost" of writing remains the theological body of Christ, the writing of the religious academy, that has dissimulated the presence and power of the Holy Spirit that comes to the disciples as the "comforter" in lieu of the Son's absence.[18] Radical orthodoxy is far more Derridean than it can confess. For example, Graham Ward in his essay on Jesus' "displaced bodies" moves in a kind of deconstructive sweep of the early Christian tradition. The empty tomb, Jesus' spectral appearance on the road to Emmaus, and his vanishing upon ascension into heaven are all marks of the *parousia* of absence that is the entirety of eschatology. In this sense Ward's presentation differs little from that of the "a-theistic theology" of the last forty years. "Jesus' presence," Ward says, "is mediated through the discourses of those who would comprise the early church."[19] The narrative of the risen Savior which in conventional "orthodoxy" might be rendered as the complete, historical outworking of the Tridentine *ousia* now becomes the fullness of discursivity, which amounts to little more than the Christianization of Derrida's grammatology *sub specie theologiae*. Ward cannot say *à-Dieu* any more than Derrida himself.[20]

How does one, then, say it? Levinas himself writes:

> Yet to the Other – a relationship. A relationship and a non-relationship. Is that not the meaning of the question? As the relationship to the absolutely other – to the nonlimited by the same – to the Infinite – would transcendence not be equivalent to an originary question? A relationship without simultaneity of terms: unless we are to say that time itself lasts in the guise of this relationship/nonrelationship, this question. Time being understood in its dia-chrony and not as a "pure form of sensibility." The soul in its dia-chronous temporality in which retention does not annul lapse, nor protention the absolutely new – the soul in the passive synthesis of aging and of the to-come (*à-venir*), in its life, would be the originary question, the to-God (*à-Dieu*) itself. Time as question: an unbalanced relationship with the Infinite, with what cannot be comprehended. Nor encompassed, nor *touched. But also the way in which the Incomparable concerns the finite and that is, perhaps, what Descartes called the Idea of the Infinite in us.*[21]

The *à-Dieu* is indeed the "originary question." For it is the question of "where we go from here," insofar as the "here" is understood as the fate of the postmodern that has come to the "end" of all onto-theological possibilities, even the disguised soterio-ontology of a Christian "rhetorical community." The *à-Dieu* is a saying "bye" to the "deconstructive imagination," the imagination of the word made text. It is a "bye" to the now excessively cheapened construct of "postmodernity," as it has been popularly delineated, though it is also a farewell to so-called "post-secular" theologies of identity which have not succeeded in bursting out of the "metaphysical" maze of religious signifiers. But the *à-Dieu* is also a saying "to" the infinite that can only be engaged in the differencing of the *proposa*, the "persons" or transcendental expressions of the one and awesome Presence that establishes every sense of alterity, the "absolute other" that *is*, Levinas tells us, *the* other, the presence of infinity. Like a gray ghost, this infinity haunts all subjective philosophies. It is "outside" the Cartesian circle. It is "outside" the scriptorium of deconstructive labors. It is "latent" in Freud's sense. It is spooky, evanescent, and uncanny. It cannot be si(gh)ted. It is not some metaphysical wraith of unresolved secular contradiction. It is not a creature of the *Jenseits*, or the "hereafter." Unlike a ghost, it is forcing itself into embodied presence. But what do we mean by such a "meta-notion"?

It is the notion, as Levinas reminds us, of "being's other," *autrement qu'être*. The sense of *autrement* is crucial in understanding Levinas' "alternative" to what typically is both an ontological and a theological strategy of entertaining the "transcendent" in language. "If transcendence has meaning," Levinas says, "it can only signify the fact that the *event of being*, the *esse*, the *essence*, passes over to what is other than being."[22] Such a passing over corresponds to the "way back" to which Heidegger alludes. But the "way back" is not into the autochthony of representation, as it is for Heidegger, the Being that glimmers in the showing of beings. It is the "way toward," an "amphibology" that retraces once and for all the "spirit" which constitutes writing which enables Derrida's "double sentence." It is a "going forward" into the temporalization of time that discloses what is "essence." It is a walk up the mountain to "the hither side."

Levinas' "hither side," of course, is equivalent to Heidegger's "unsaid" but with an epochal difference. "If being and manifestation go together in the said, it is in fact natural that if the saying on the hither side of the said can show itself, it be said already in terms of being."[24] To speak "on the hither side of the said" is to speak at the originary situation, the moment of Sinai; it is to speak to that which has already spoken, but not yet in the history of onto-theology been "spoken for." It is to speak within the cloud, within the translucency that is making its way into the realm of the visible. It is to say *à-Dieu*. The alterity of ontology is not so much "the way of faith," though faith is crucial. It is the way toward *parousia*. By *parousia* we understand "the fullness of time," the temporalization of all essentiality which philosophy cannot acquire in thought, but only meet on the dusty road of history, the

Grand Emmaus, Pentecost, the eschatological event that is the "coming" of *Spiritus Sanctus.*[25]

On the road to Emmaus the disciples met what they first believed to be a ghost. That is a spirit from the temporal standpoint. Let us, therefore, say *à-Dieu.* It is at that point that we say, and make, the *final différance.* The final differànce is the one Levinas has enunciated in such a way that renders the distinction between theology and philosophy less consequential than we are wont to acknowledge and underscores how the "end of theology" is at the same time an eschatology of each and every sign, consolidating and abrogating at once the metaphysical regulation of equality between *signum* and *res,* running back to Augustine. We find a slightly less cryptic construal of this eschatological differencing stated by Levinas toward the end of *Otherwise than Being.* The challenge by the infinite, the calling of Presence, Levinas' "one-for-the-other," is "the very signifyingness of signification," Levinas asserts. It is a challenge to philosophy to discover the Sinaic site of "saying." "Philosophy has at its highest, exceptional hours stated the beyond of being and the one distinct from being, but mainly remained at home in saying being, that is, inwardness to being, the being at home with oneself, of which European history itself has been the conquest and jealous defense."[26] Western thought, therefore, bears "the trace of events carrying another signification." And this signification is one of utter alterity, the "final difference" of thought that is the ending of the thought of alterity itself.

The ending of the thought of alterity is the breakthrough to intimacy through "others" with others and *with* the *autrement* that is at once the Spirit's indwelling, not its "Golgotha" in Hegel's sense, but its ascension. It is the intimacy Levinas calls "proximity," which can only be understood in any age when the thought of the postmodern has thought through alterity to its one-and-the-same, the sameness of total presence or immanence, the incarnation of the "secular." It is the proximity of Pentecost, the revolution from "on high" that rattles and shatters the temple of the tradition, Levinas' "breakdown of essence" that "baptizes" the other as nearness, that installs him or her as a citizen of the "kingdom of midstness." The proximity of the "otherwise," the speaking of that which sets down being as being through being from the "hither side." Sinai, Emmaus, Pentecost!

If we must say *à-Dieu* to Derrida and the interregnum of deconstruction, it is only because we are forced into the radical space of the *à* which is known by its diacritical mark that points to the heights. This space is far more radical than the theological space of any "radical orthodoxy." It is the space of the "saying to" and the "hearing from" the Presence that presences in time and in history from the peak of Sinai to the mount of Zion. It is the saying that can only be heard through the rumbling in earth and heavens. It is the saying of the guest whose advent arrives as the sign of the "Son of Man" in the heavens. It is what we truly mean by "the end of theology."

# Notes

1  "The proper name 'Sinai' is thus just as enigmatic as the name 'face.' In the singular and the plural, retaining the memory of its Hebraic synonym, what is here called 'face' also starts to resemble some untranslatable proper name." Jacques Derrida, *Adieu to Emmanuel Levinas*, trans. Pascale-Anne Brault and Michael Naas (Stanford, CA: Stanford University Press, 1999), p. 119.
2  Jacques Derrida, *Of Spirit: Heidegger*, trans. Geoffrey Bennington and Rachel Bowlby (Chicago: University of Chicago Press, 1989), p. 91.
3  Ibid., p. 1.
4  Ibid., pp. 112–13.
5  Adriann T. Peperzak, Simon Critchley and Robert Bernasconi (eds), *Emmanuel Levinas: Basic Philosophical Writings* (Bloomington, IN: Indiana University Press, 1996), p. 25.
6  Ibid., p. 86.
7  Ibid., p. 147.
8  Ibid., p. 148.
9  John Milbank, *The Word Made Strange: Theology, Language and Culture* (London: Blackwell, 1997), p. 189.
10  Ibid., p. 189.
11  See Levinas' comment: "Between a philosophy of transcendence that situates elsewhere the true life in which man, escaping from here, would gain access in the privileged moments of liturgical, mystical elevation . . . we propose to describe, within the unfolding of terrestrial existence . . . that is not a totalization of history but the idea of infinity. Such a relationship is metaphysics itself. History would not be the privileged plane where Being disengaged from the particularism of points of view . . . is manifested." Emmanuel Levinas, *Totality and Infinity: An Essay on Exteriority*, trans. Alphonso Lingis (Dordrecht: Kluwer Academic Publishers, 1991), p. 52. Radical orthodoxy has not escaped this strategy of mere "elevation."
12  Milbank, *The Word Made Strange*, p. 288.
13  Emmanuel Levinas, *Ethics and Infinity: Conversations with Phillipe Nemo*, trans. Richard A. Cohen (Pittsburgh, PA: Duquesne University Press, 1985), pp. 24–5.
14  It is significant that the movement of radical orthodoxy does not accede to the Levinasian reading of Descartes, though it is certainly aware of it. Such an accession would, in effect, undermine its systematic critique of postmodernism as the culmination of modernist metaphysic. In a recent article Jean-Luc Marion seeks to refute the notion that there is a Cartesian "argument to the other" by insisting that the position Descartes develops in the third meditation belongs within the sphere of metaphysics and is not an implicit critique of onto-theology. The Cartesian argument is actually, according to Marion, "the thought of the cause completing the principle. Cartesian thought thus belongs strictly to metaphysics since it twice fulfills its onto-theo-logical constitution." That dyadic fulfillment, for Marion, derives from the Scholastic ideal of "sufficient reason," which is an ontological principle, not an opening to the "otherwise," as it is for Levinas. See Jean-Luc Marion, "Descartes and Onto-Theology," in Phillip Blond (ed.), *Post-Secular Philosophy* (London: Routledge, 1998), p. 96.
15  Jacques Derrida, *Dissemination*, trans. Barbara Johnson (Chicago: University of Chicago Press, 1981), p. 167.
16  Jacques Derrida, "Faith and Knowledge," in Jacques Derrida and Gianni Vattimo (eds), *Religion* (Stanford, CA: Stanford University Press, 1996), p. 48.
17  I have in mind, of course, here the argument of Catherine Pickstock, in *After Writing: The Liturgical Consummation of Philosophy* (Oxford: Blackwell, 1997).
18  See John 14.
19  Graham Ward, "Bodies: The Displaced Body of Jesus Christ," in John Milbank,

Catherine Pickstock and Graham Ward (eds), *Radical Orthodoxy* (London: Routledge, 1999), p. 174.

20  In one important sense radical orthodoxy simply follows the "Christian" line of Israelite salvation, replacing the Derridean messianism of the *ganz Andere*, with the liturgical community of faith. Both radical orthodoxy and deconstruction are involved in spectral conversations. As John Caputo says of Derrida, "deconstruction talks with (*s'entretenir avec*) ghosts, with a spectral messianic figure, a figure of the impossible, of a *tout autre* whose comings we can only invoke but cannot foresee." See John Caputo, *The Prayers and Tears of Jacques Derrida: Religion without Religion* (Bloomington, IN: Indiana University Press, 1997), p. 149.

21  Emmanuel Levinas, *On Thinking-of-the-Other Entre Nous*, trans. Michael B. Smith and Barbara Harshav (New York: Columbia University Press, 1998), p. 73.

22  Emmanuel Levinas, *Otherwise than Being, or Beyond Essence* (The Hague: Martinus Nijhoff, 1981), p. 1.

23  See Levinas' discussion of being as "apophansis," the verbalization of the nominative that points us in the direction of the *autrement*. "In a predicative proposition, an apophansis, an entity can make itself be understood verbally, as a 'way' of essence, as the *fruitio essendi* itself, as a *how*, a modality of this essence or this temporalization." Levinas, *Otherwise than Being*, p. 38. Tracing back the temporalization into the "otherwise" is a "reading before" to the moment we call Sinai.

24  Ibid., p. 43.

25  "I will not leave you desolate; I will come to you. Yet a little while, and the world will see me no more, but you will see me; because I live, you will live also. In that day you will know that I am in my Father, and you in me, and I in you" (John 14:18–20). The "in that day" (*ekeinē tē ēmera*) is the eschatological *signum*, the mutual indwelling of Father and Son within the sanctified Christian "body." It is the Body *qua* Spirit, the indwelling of the "Holy Spirit," the full presencing of the "secret presence" that even those who know "the Son" prior to Pentecost do not know.

26  *Otherwise than Being*, p. 178.

# 4 Anxiety, risk and transformation

## Re-visiting Tillich with Lacan

James J. DiCenso

## I

In the world of philosophical theology, the work of Paul Tillich remains one of the most significant attempts to bridge the polarities of tradition and innovation, past and present, universality and particularity. Tillich made it an explicit theme of his thinking to resist tendencies to reify tradition so that it becomes isolated from the experiences, concerns and reflective thinking of contemporary individuals. In this vein, it is important that Tillich begins his *Systematic Theology* with a critique of religious fundamentalism, arguing that "Fundamentalism fails to make contact with the present situation, not because it speaks from beyond every situation, but because it speaks from the past. It elevates something finite and transitory to infinite and eternal valid-ity."[1] The closed and totalizing tendencies represented by, but no means exclusive to, fundamentalism sustain a worldview that excludes and represses anything or anyone inimical to that world. Such orientations are hence incapable of transformation and response in relation to personal and cultural innovation, and at their worst they give rise to destructive intolerance. Half a century later, the problematic tendencies here indicated by Tillich remain very much in evidence, and therefore issues related to them continually need to be addressed.

In contrast to closed religious orientations, which, in debasing innovation and freedom, actually disconnect worldly activity from guiding religious and ethical principles, Tillich continually sought to bring theology into a fruitful, living relationship with the existential situations of contemporary human beings. The implications of this strategy are profound and, for some, they can be rather disturbing. This is the case because, in genuinely opening theological reflection to the shifting temporal world of "the present," to the ideas and insights that emerge in the course of secular historical experience and inquiry, Tillich relinquished the security of immutable *a priori* truths. The *risk* involved in this endeavour is quite consistent with the formulations at the heart of Tillich's reflections, which push theology away from fixation on a determined past and toward the challenge and openness of the future.

The following analysis attempts to continue in the spirit of Tillich's efforts to speak to the present situation by bringing his work into engagement with some recent conceptual developments. Primarily, I will trace the connections between anxiety and potential self-transformation as discussed mainly by Tillich and Jacques Lacan. By bringing these two thinkers into engagement, I am also concerned to clarify Tillich's status in relation to issues and orientations associated with contemporary emphases on themes such as *decentering, resistance to totalization* and the *linguistic constitution of subjectivity*, all of which are prominent in Lacanian thinking. Reciprocally, Tillich's theological and existential orientations maintain an emphasis on the crucial problems of mortality, ethics and meaning; they thus provide a counterbalance to the waning of these concerns in much recent thought. The general implication here is that Tillich's work is best served not by being embalmed as an immutable "classic," but by being revisited from a conceptual distance and thus reread so as to foster an active relation with contemporary ideas.

## II

My point of departure is Tillich's repeated comments concerning the experience of *finite freedom* and its relation to processes of *self-transcendence*. Under these categories, Tillich analyses moments of rupture in human existence, wherein the finite, as the closed, opens out into the infinite, as the possible. In this way, Tillich translates metaphysical postulates, concerning infinitude and God, into dynamic categories related to self-transcendence on existential and psychological levels. For example, Tillich states that "infinitude is finitude transcending itself without any a priori limit," and further describes this as "the power of infinite self-transcendence."[2] In other words, infinitude comes to be understood as a quality inherent in human being-in-the-world; it expresses a potentiality opening ahead of or beyond immediacy into new configurations on conceptual, cultural and psychological levels. More specifically, Tillich links this potentiality to dimensions of subjective experience that allow a transcending of givenness, fixity and particularity, that is, of relations on a closed and deterministic level. There is a free and creative quality to self–object relations that exceeds the scope of reactive responses, and it is this freedom that introduces features of meaning and value into human existence. Most importantly, for Tillich the freedom manifest in human existence is always "finite freedom,"[3] that is, it occurs within particular limiting relations within the world and is, as we shall see, at least partially dependent on those relations and the linguistic media within which they occur.

It is in terms of this project that Tillich discusses the concept of God, traditionally associated with transcendence and infinity, as "the quality of the world which expresses itself in finite freedom, the quality we experience within ourselves."[4] This view is not unlike that expressed by Emmanuel Levinas, who establishes a correlation between "the idea-of-the-Infinite-in-me" and "my relation to God." As with Tillich, this Levinasian sense of the divine becomes manifest in existential situations and relations. For Levinas, this means that the relation to God "comes to me in the concreteness of my relation to the other man, in the sociality which is my responsibility for the neighbor."[5] For both thinkers, the term "God" designates a quality inherent in reality itself, especially the sphere of human relations. This quality has to do with the possibility of going beyond the given in a creative relationship to existence (or, in the case of Levinas, in an ethical response to the other encountered in the world) wherein the possibility of both meaning and ethics arises.

Within this set of issues, concerning existential moments occurring within finitude but opening beyond the closure of finite determinations, I am specifically concerned with negative, disruptive instances related to processes of self-transcendence and transformation. In the course of my analysis, it should become clear that this negative focus not only reflects the concerns of religious thinking from a variety of sources but, most importantly, it links that thinking to the conflicts, uncertainties and suffering so characteristic of human experience.[6] Tillich discusses these negative dimensions of developmental dynamics ontologically under the category of *nonbeing*. Within the related, but more circumscribed psychological realm, nonbeing is primarily manifested in experiences of *anxiety*, defined by Tillich as "the state in which a being is aware of its possible nonbeing."[7] For Tillich, this subjective experience is grounded in reality, in the nature of finitude itself: "As an ontological quality, anxiety is as omnipresent as is finitude. Anxiety is independent of any special object which might produce it; it is dependent only on the threat of 'nonbeing' which is identical with finitude."[8] It is in thus being linked with the perpetual threat of nonbeing that is intrinsic to finite existence that anxiety comes to represent the essential tension between finitude and reflection on finitude that in some ways transcends it.

Before developing these points further, I want briefly to indicate some background to this issue in order to clarify what is at stake here. The problem of anxiety has been a recurring theme at the intersections of religious, philosophical and psychological thought at least since Kierkegaard's pioneering analyses. Kierkegaard sets the stage for much that follows in distinguishing anxiety from "fear and similar concepts that refer to something definite," that is, to the "special objects" of which Tillich speaks. By contrast, Kierkegaard emphasizes that "anxiety is freedom's actuality as the possibility of possibility."[9] Kierkegaard explicates the matter further by linking anxiety with what he terms "spirit's relating to itself," and, particularly, to the human potentiality or "being able" inherent in freedom's possibility.[10] As with Tillich, these comments by Kierkegaard indicate the inevitability of negative and unsettling experiences inherent in the spiritual qualities of human existence *as inherently free*. Anxiety arises in that space where the vertiginous possibilities of choosing confront us, and this allows for freedom in the sense of committed, responsible and meaningful existence. This is not simply freedom from constraint, but the freedom to be, to choose and to act. However, what remains crucial, and perpetually unresolved, is the challenge contained in Kierke-gaard's statement that "whoever has learned to be anxious *in the right way* has learned the ultimate."[11] In the present context, I will decline to take up issues related to ultimacy, at least in strict terms. I will focus instead on the problem of *modes of response*, that is, on the possible inner transformations in relation to anxiety, contained in Kierkegaard's declaration. Anxiety may be an experiential indicator of the subjective potentiality for freely made decision, but the *way* in which the individual is able to engage and respond to these unsettling experiences remains pivotal.

In *The Courage to Be*, Tillich furthers Kierkegaard's analysis of anxiety as a moment of possible freedom by differentiating between neurotic and exist-ential anxiety.[12] There may be an intrinsic difference between the two types of anxiety, with the neurotic form having a narrow, obsessional focus, and the existential related to the nature of existence itself in its qualities of nonbeing as finitude, contingency and open-endedness. One might argue, however, that it is also the individual's *mode of response* that differentiates the neurotic from the existential. As we have seen, anxiety is understood by both Kierkegaard and Tillich as a general inner unrest and dis-ease, without a specific causal source or object. Qualifying anxiety as "existential" highlights this lack of specific referent; it is rooted in the nature of human being-in-the-world, with its continuous threats of "nonbeing" arising on levels of finitude, morality and meaning. Thus, Tillich discusses ontic anxiety related to finitude as *mor-tality*, to the inevitability of death, and then postulates two further distinc-tions within existential anxiety. Anxiety is also related to "nonbeing" on the *moral* level, that is, to the uncertainty of ethical decisions and the resulting threats of guilt and condemnation. Finally, anxiety appears in relation to *spiritual* issues, i.e. as related to the question of meaning, in the accompany-ing threats of emptiness and meaninglessness.[13]

Existential anxiety reflects human existence within a finite world which not only does not offer certainties when it comes to matters of life and death, ethics and meaning, but continually confronts us with new questions and situations unassimilable to pre-established views. It is here that anxiety indi-cates the possibility of unique individual *choice* and *response* in relation to these issues and dilemmas. It is precisely the lack of an isolated referent that relates anxiety to ontological issues, that is, to questions of modes of exist-ence, to the overall *quality* of our being-in-the-world. Existential anxiety provides a conceptual framework for grasping disturbing aspects of human experience outside of pathologizing explanatory systems. If the experience of anxiety is understood as "a call to ourselves"[14] (and here Tillich appropriates Heideggerian language), it might generate an opening towards the type of response that manifests human possibility. The interplay between existential anxiety and our responses to it is indicated in Tillich's discussion of existen-tial courage. As Tillich states, "courage does not remove anxiety. Since anxi-ety is existential, it cannot be removed. But courage takes the anxiety of nonbeing into itself. Courage is self-affirmation 'in spite of,' namely in spite of nonbeing."[15] Here courage correlates with existential anxiety in that it addresses one's life or being as such, rather than some specific challenge within life. The affirmation that ensues can be seen as evoking the capacity for creativity, responsibility and decision, and hence as stimulating the "self-transcendence" in which an individual moves beyond previously entrenched attitudes and modes of being. These points, of course, bring us into the realm of psychological processes, and will require further discussion.

By contrast, what Tillich calls a *neurotic response* to anxiety results from a failure to engage anxiety courageously.[16] Such responses seek to repress the threat to one's mode of being heralded by anxiety and would, as a defence against this threat, translate anxiety (albeit unconsciously) into the kind of symptomatology characteristic of neurosis. It is significant that it is the quality of "indefiniteness" which maintains the distinction between anxiety and fear. In light of this, the category of pathological anxiety falls between existential anxiety and fear. It blurs the distinction between a nameless existential dis-ease, and the fear of some definite threat, and thus creates intermediary, or transitional, anxiety objects of an imaginary nature, such as the phobic ones discussed by Freud. (I will return to this point in my discussion of Freud in section IV.) In some ways, the neurotic response is "safer"; although painful and unpleasant it familiarizes and domesticates the threat of anxiety. In Tillich's words, "neurosis is the way of avoiding nonbeing by avoiding being."[17] That is, insofar as being itself is characterized by openness (and hence includes nonbeing), with the concomitant possibilities of freedom and uncertainty, the closing down of the self into a focus on a specific (neurotic) issue or problem evades both the nonbeing of contingency and the affirmative being of freedom.

## III

Tillich is quite consistent in maintaining awareness of polarities and tensions in both life and thought, and of the need to mediate extreme or one-sided stances on every level. The more encompassing, dynamic perspective that emerges from such an overview is evident throughout Tillich's engagement with the issue of anxiety. It seems to me that this Tillichean sensibility is lost by psychological solutions emphasizing "wholeness" and "centering." To be sure, as one commentator on the relations between Tillich and psychological theory has stated, contemporary existence seems generally to be characterized by qualities of anomie, dissolution and meaninglessness.[18] However, I disagree with the view that this psycho-social context requires the counteracting influence of stabilizing, centering psychological models, which cover over the risk inherent in Tillich's relational and forward-looking formulations. Of course, Tillich himself frequently appropriates the discourse concerning the "centered self" current in his time. However, we must inquire into the precise meaning of this language within the overall context of Tillich's existential and ontological analyses. Thus, in *The Courage to Be*, after stating that "the subject of self-affirmation is the centered self," Tillich proceeds to refine his analysis by emphasizing that the personality is always correlated with "world," including individual others, social structures and language.[19] The key statement here is that "self and world are correlated, and so are individualization and participation."[20] In this respect, we might say that the self or subject is not merely a self-enclosed center, but that it is permeated in various ways and on various levels by that which it is not, the not-I, the other, and otherness. Tillich states this quite explicitly in *Systematic Theology*, indicating that the interpenetration of self and world, via society, occurs both consciously and unconsciously: "The centered self is dependent not only on the influences of its social surroundings which are consciously given and received but also on those which are effective in a society without being apprehended and formulated."[21] Tillich seems to indicate that the self, even as "centered," is not always aware of the extent to which it is enmeshed in socially constructed networks of meaning. From this there emerges the issue of *opening* the self, beyond the circumscribed sense of identity habitually operative, to greater degrees of awareness of the forces constituting and shaping it. In this way, a *constructive de-centering of the self* seems intrinsic to the processes of reflective self-transcendence and transformation characteristic of free beings. To neglect this de-centering abrogates the dynamic quality of Tillich's thinking and makes it impossible to understand his inquiries into anxiety. Binding and structuring also entail the danger of totalization, closure, stagnation, and hence the inhibition of processes of self-transcendence. Therefore, taken within the context of the overall quality of his thinking, Tillich's allusions to a centered self are best understood in contradistinction with *one-sided* and/or *fragmented* forms of subjectivity. These would be manifested in "neurotic" tendencies to fixate on particular features of existence to the exclusion of others, that is, to sustain a condition of repression that inhibits self-awareness and self-transcendence. The centered self can be understood to be integrated, not in the sense of being closed or totalized, but rather in being able to be in relation, to see things in broader perspective, to question and to address issues from more than one side. It is therefore permeated by otherness and by negativity (in the sense of nonbeing as the not-yet and the other-than-what-is), and hence remains open to possibility and transformation. It is here, once again, that the question of anxiety indicates a necessary feature of meaningful existence rather than simply a difficulty to be overcome.

This argument can be substantiated and augmented by reference to an ongoing suspicion of closed systems that characterizes Tillich's work. This suspicion appears in relation to obvious targets such as the comprehensive conceptual systematization of Hegelian philosophy,[22] but it is also directed toward totalizing trends in religious belief and practice. For example, Tillich argues that

much courage to be created by religion, is nothing else than the desire to limit one's own being and to strengthen this limitation through the power of religion. And even if religion does not lead to or does not directly support pathological self-reduction, it can reduce the openness of man to reality, above all to the reality which is himself. In this way religion can protect and feed a potentially neurotic state.[23]

This argument shows that Tillich's relation to religion – he may be speaking of Christianity but the argument can just as well apply to any religion – is a differentiated one. Religion can be a resource for courage – indeed, it can be a name for the dimension of transcendence manifest in courage. Yet religion can also harden into closed heteronomous frameworks that provide ready-made responses to the existential dilemmas of death, moral uncertainty and loss of meaning, thereby suppressing the possibility of inner engagement and of autonomous responses that address the uniqueness of life situations. Here, Tillich's comments parallel his critique of fundamentalist attempts to elevate historically conditioned doctrines to the status of closed eternal truths. These strategies ward off the threat of uncertainty by enclosing an individual and a community, their ways of thinking and relating, within fixed, circumscribed worlds of meaning. Tillich associates these tendencies with pathological responses to anxiety, which also involve *fixation* (and here his reflections converge with psychoanalysis). For example, Tillich discusses pathological responses to moral anxiety as seeking to reduce the realm of ethical decision and action to a narrow focus that can be perfected and controlled.[24] He then argues that "the pathological forms of anxiety of emptiness and meaning-lessness show similar characteristics" to these "moralistic" responses to existential guilt. In each case, "existential anxiety of doubt drives the person toward the creation of certitude in systems of meaning, which are supported by tradition and authority."[25] This is why *doubt*, *risk* and *courage* are such pivotal terms in Tillichean thought; these qualities enable meaningful resistance to the powerful human needs for consolation and protection from the contingent dimensions of existence that appear on the levels of mortality, morality and meaning.

It is with regard to these arguments that one can understand Tillich's emphasis that Christian theology should always "decide for truth against safety, even if the safety is consecrated and supported by the churches."[26] Here, "truth" has to do with engaging qualities of existence that cannot be absorbed into fixed doctrines and systems of meaning. These qualities, such as temporality, innovation and interdependency, necessarily make of truth an ongoing relational process that eludes totalization. One is reminded of William James, who argued with regard to the temporality of existence and of knowledge that "when larger ranges of truth open, it is surely best to open ourselves to their reception, unfettered by our previous pretensions."[27] Interestingly, James shares with Tillich the awareness that being open to new experience can be a painful, traumatic process, as is so well described in his analyses of the "sick soul" and "the divided self."[28]

Without lapsing into teleological thinking, Tillich exhibits a confidence that the disrupting inner processes manifested in anxiety can engender meaningful responses. The features of non-necessity, open-endedness, and individual response-ability are, of course, clearly delineated by the Tillichean concept of *courage* as the key figuration for meaningful engagements with anxiety and nonbeing. "Courage always includes a risk," states Tillich, "it is always threatened by nonbeing."[29] More is contained in this statement than simply an awareness of the forces – psychological, social and existential – that work against our capacity for meaningful response. Nonbeing, as variously manifest in threats to our ontic, moral and spiritual certainty and security, is *intrinsic* to the very processes of human self-becoming. There is a dialectical interdependence of being and nonbeing, manifested psychologically as the interdependence of courage and anxiety. Indeed, the modality of self that responds to the threat and risk engendered by nonbeing carries these unsettling realities within it. Tillich states the matter quite forcefully: "the self-affirmation of being without nonbeing would not even be a self-affirmation but an immovable self-identity."[30] The model of the courageous religious personality evident here is one that is very much in play or in process, one that is capable of freedom, creativity and transformation. It is characterized by openness to otherness, and by a responsiveness to the unexpected de-centering experiences of which anxiety is a manifestation.

Having established some general characteristics of courage as responsiveness to anxiety, what is now required are more detailed analyses on the psychological level. Although Tillich's formulations cannot be encapsulated within the framework of psychology, they indicate certain psychodynamic processes related to a capacity for self-transcendence and hence self-transformation. In many places in his work, Tillich speaks to this issue by emphasizing the importance of psychoanalysis for theological thinking insofar as it intersects with the question of subjectivity. Generally, he sought not merely to establish dialogue between theology and psychoanalysis, but to do so in such a way that the established doctrinal and disciplinary boundaries of each were opened to the other in a process of mutual augmentation. Thus, in speaking of psychoanalysis and theology, Tillich argues that "the relationship is not one of existing alongside each other; it is a relationship of mutual interpenetration."[31] Elsewhere, Tillich offers a clue to the fruitful engagement of religious thought with psychoanalysis in noting that in the Freudian view "anxiety is the awareness of unresolved conflicts between structural elements of the personality."[32] This comment opens issues related to the inner differentiation of the personality, and indicates the specific tasks of clarifying the nature of those internal structural elements and of analyzing the type of transformation toward which their conflicts might point.

**IV**

Perhaps the most significant difference between Tillich's religious–
existentialist analyses and mainstream psychoanalytic ones concerns the
issue of possible connections between anxiety and subjective transformation.
Tillich's arguments would seem to be generally incompatible with
psychoanalytic interpretations of anxiety that posit definite underlying
causal factors. These approaches attempt to state the "hidden object" of
anxiety as something that can be therapeutically resolved and hence
removed. Speaking of such approaches, Tillich forcefully argues that "they
call all anxiety, all guilt, all emptiness, illnesses which can be overcome as any
illness can be, and they try to remove them. But this is impossible. The
existential structures cannot be healed by the most refined techniques."[33]
Here again, Tillich connects anxiety with qualities inherent to human existence as interlaced with nonbeing, arguing, in essence, that it can be *faced* but
not *eliminated*.

It is precisely this tendency to pathologize anxiety by interpreting it as a
manifestation of a localized problem that seems to restrict the religious and
existential significance of psychoanalysis. This problem is especially evident
in Freud's earlier treatment of the issue (1894), in which anxiety is seen as the
psychical manifestation of the quantitative build-up of repressed libido.[34] In
this model, the excess of excitation producing anxiety is clearly disconnected
from qualitative changes in personality. Tillich is aware of this limitation, this
lack of a vision of what he terms the "new man" in Freud's work. Most
presciently, however, he points out that "fortunately, Freud, like most great
men, was not consistent."[35] That is, despite his many deterministic and
reductionistic proclamations, there are moments of opening in Freud's work
that speak to issues of what Tillich would refer to as transformation on a
more spiritual level, that is, to self-transcendence.

Elements of a less biologistic approach to anxiety appear sporadically in
Freud's later work, particularly in *Inhibitions, Symptoms and Anxiety* (1926),
where he defines anxiety in a way that is closer to the existentialist tradition.
That is, in his understanding, *angst* or anxiety "has a quality of *indefiniteness
and lack of object*," which differentiates it from fear concerning specific
objects.[36] Metapsychologically, in terms of the structural model of inner
psychodynamics, Freud indicates that "the ego is the actual seat of anxiety,"
which he specifically differentiates from his earlier view that "the repressed
impulse [is] automatically turned into anxiety."[37] Here, anxiety is understood
as manifesting some *nameless threat to the ego*, arising from within the
personality and related to "perceptions and ideas which it [the ego] has up
till now made a rule of avoiding."[38] This implies, as Jacques Lacan states,
that "Freud came to evaluate anxiety itself as a signal."[39] The quantitative
explanation shifts toward a qualitative one that touches upon issues of
*communication* and *meaning*.

Nevertheless, Freud resists seeing such threatening signals as emerging from inadequacies in the entrenched orientations of the ego. Likewise, he tends to neglect issues of self-transcendence (what Lacan would call ego-transcendence) and the ensuing qualitative transformations of the personality. Thus, in confronting the problem of anxiety, Freud still seeks to reduce the *unnameable* to the *nameable*. In doing so, emphasis remains fixed on the cause of anxiety as an extrinsic irritating factor, somewhat modeled after an illness that intrudes into an otherwise healthy organism. This reductive tendency is apparent in Freud's example of anxiety manifest in animal phobias. The most famous instance of animal phobia is the case of "Little Hans," in which a five-year-old boy developed such a fear of horses that for some time he was hardly able to set foot outside the house.[40] Freud offers a general account of such phobias: "It was the same in every case: where the children concerned were boys, their fear related at bottom to their father and had merely been displaced onto the animal."[41] In this view, animal phobias represent a displaced and symbolized expression of anxiety, related to the father. Indeed, Freud takes this analysis a step further and concludes rather unequivocally that "the anxiety felt in animal phobias is the ego's fear of castration."[42] Anxiety related to "castration" seems to be traceable to some definite, determinable source (and this tendency is reinforced by Freud's tracing anxiety back to fear, so as to blur the previously made distinction). Once the source is discovered, the problem can presumably be rectified and the healthy ego can return to "normal" existence unimpeded by disturbing sensations and unchallenged in its self-image and attitudes. This may be an appropriate therapeutic method in relation to manifestations of "pathological anxiety" as Tillich defines it; however, it closes down the path of possible self-reflection and transformation in relation to "existential anxiety." In fact, the objectification of the posited source of anxiety serves to collapse the existential dimensions into the pathological, thereby avoiding the issue of dealing with the more encompassing life issues surrounding anxiety. With this approach, the analyst becomes the accomplice of the entrenched and defended ego structures that refuse the call to self-transformation. Lacan's approach differs significantly from these tendencies toward closed explanation, evident in much of Freud's work and predominant in the practice of most of his "orthodox" followers.[43]

However, it is noteworthy that Freud himself indicates a possible *symbolic* significance of the threat of castration, and it is precisely here that we find one of those seminal inconsistencies to which Tillich refers. In what appears as an aside to the main argument, Freud argues that "just as the father has become depersonalized in the shape of the super-ego, so has the fear of castration at his hands become transformed into an undefined social or moral anxiety."[44] This single statement unravels Freud's attempts to reduce anxiety to a response to a definite object or threat, that is, to fear. It opens the posited cause, the threat of castration, into a relation with the more encompassing existential issues of *moral anxiety* and guilt. In this way, Freud surreptitiously reintroduces the problem of a challenge to the habitual attitudes and worldview of the ego, appearing in anxiety, without a simple determinable source, and with possible moral significance.

It will be useful to extrapolate upon the symbolic opening evident in Freud's comment, in order to illustrate its possible connections with Tillich's existential concerns as well as with a Lacanian model of self-transformation. I will draw upon Julia Kristeva's alternative analysis of the case of Little Hans, which deliteralizes and dereifies a Freudian analysis that seeks to replace one definite object (the horse) with another (the castrating father). By contrast, Kristeva's interpretation indicates a psychical process of designating and giving form to a nameless anxiety with a symbolic, or, more precisely, imaginary object. "By means of the signifier of the phobic object, the 'horse,' it calls attention to a *drive economy in want of an object* – that conglomerate of fear, deprivation, and nameless frustration, which, properly speaking, belongs to the unnameable." She thus sees phobia as a "metaphor of want as such."[45] This interpretation opens another dimension to Freud's analysis that pushes it away from positing determining facts or events. Rather, the symbol emerges from the inherent *lack*, nonbeing, or, in Lacanian terms, *manque-à-être*[46] (want-of-being or want-to-be) characterizing the level of the drive. Its source is not a literal event, object, or person, but the unformed, open-ended and hence potentially terrifying nature of the "drive economy," that is, the dynamics of internal and external relations. The psychical dynamics at work here are well summarized in Lacan's statement that "*angoisse* is not the fear of an object, but the confrontation of the subject with an absence of object, with a *lack of being* in which he is stuck or caught, in which he loses himself and to which anything is preferable, even the forging of that most strange and alien of objects: a phobia."[47] Unlike Freud, Lacan explicitly maintains the distinction between existential and pathological anxiety, and both he and Kristeva view phobia as representative of the latter.

Kristeva introduces the term *abjection* to characterize the experienced threat of a breaking down of identity, system and order. As she puts it, "the phobic has no other object than the abject."[48] This definition is remarkably close to Tillich's understanding of anxiety, which, as he states, "has no object, or rather, in a paradoxical phrase*, its object is the negation of every object.*"[49] The non-referent of both abjection and anxiety is not directly nameable, and hence requires indirect, displaced, symbolic expression. Symbolization can be pathologized, however, falling under the category of what Lacan and Kristeva refer to as *imaginary* orientations that seek to disguise anxiety with a definite referential image. Hence Kristeva describes "the phobic person as a subject in want of metaphoricalness," and relates this to "fetishist denial."[50] Fetishism can be understood as a mode of "pathological anxiety": it allows for a *familiarization* of nameless anxiety by transferring it to a determinable referent. In thus fixating on a specific substitute object such as a horse, fetishism represses the irreducibility of lack. It inhibits a working-through of abjection or anxiety via the symbolic resources of language, and welds the phobic individual to a fearful association with the substitute fetish-object.

## V

The analyses of Kristeva and Lacan develop a line of inquiry (latently present in Freud's work) that traces a process in which anxiety emerges as a threat to the closed representational (imaginary) structures of the ego. This threat arises from something "nameless," the inherently open-ended nature of subjectivity which can only be tentatively masked by closed identity formations. In light of these insights, Lacanian psychoanalysis formulates a metapsychological model that, in emphasizing the ego's status as a circumscribed identity within a potentially more differentiated subject, finds a point of convergence with a great deal of religious reflection.[51] Lacan analyzes the ego as a limiting and, to variable degrees, distorting personality formation through his model of the mirror phase. Because the infant is characterized by an unformed quality, a lack or *want-of-being* related to what Lacan calls the inherent "prematuration" of human beings, an initial sense of identity is gained from identification with bodily images reflecting "wholes."[52] Lacan thus refers to the ego as being founded upon "imaginary, narcissistic, specular identification."[53] The ego represents the result of the "want-to-be," the identification with an illusory "completeness" responding to our inherent want-of-being. The imaginary ego serves as a defence against, and organization of, the inchoate condition of the infant by filling the lack – or nonbeing – within the self by a fixation upon a closed self-image. The ego is a necessary "binding" of the personality that establishes a fixed sense of identity, but by that very fact it entrenches tendencies toward limitation, closure, fixity and exclusion.

Unity of the ego is gained through what Lacan calls a "fascination" with a clearly defined self-image.[54] This fascination leads to a process of *alienation* by creating a split between the more fluid, open-ended, multifarious qualities of subjectivity, and the more defined, but constricting, rectilinear structure of the imaginary ego. The irony is that the ego builds its self-image on an identification with an external image, and yet in doing so closes itself off from genuinely transforming relations of reciprocity.[55] In Lacan's definition, narcissism is ultimately alienating because its self-containment inhibits a reflexive engagement with otherness, that is, an open type of relation that "acts back" upon the subject, potentially putting one's own presuppositions and viewpoints into question. The relation to alterity occurs both existentially in the form of external others, and intra-psychically in the form of undeveloped or repressed dimensions of the self. Indeed, the two dimensions are correlated, so that "internal" modalities condition ways of being and relating in the world.

In light of these formulations, we may approach Lacan's dictum that *"anxiety is that which does not deceive."*[56] Anxiety does not deceive precisely because it recalls us to the nonbeing that is habitually repressed by the ego. It thus signals the inadequacy, that is, the rigidity, one-sidedness and exclusiveness of the dominant ego structure. Anxiety is a call to the ego from the other-than-ego. Lacan distinguishes the ego from the subject, insisting that "the ego is an imaginary function, it is not to be confused with the subject."[57] Indeed, the subject is defined in mainly "negative" terms as that which is blocked and masked by the ego: "we call the ego that nucleus given to consciousness, but opaque to reflection, marked by all the ambiguities which, from self-satisfaction to 'bad faith' (*mauvaise foi*), structure the experience of the passions in the human subject; this 'I' (*moi*) who ... opposes its irreducible inertia of pretenses and *méconnaissances* to the concrete problematic of the realization of the subject."[58] The subject is that dimension of ourselves which appears when the fixity and blockage of habitual identity structures is opened up. In contrast to the "closed" ego, it is defined as a process, as relational, and as temporal; i.e. *as taking nonbeing into itself*.

Lacan describes a process whereby the ego begins to be engaged by repressed dimensions of subjectivity; with the repressed also characterized as the desire of the subject. Lacan explicates this process as (1) characterized by *anxiety* when the ego faces its own incompleteness or nonbeing, and (2) occurring within the medium of *language* (or, more precisely, speech):

> That is the moment when desire is sensed by the subject – which cannot happen without the conjunction of speech. And it is a moment of pure anxiety, and nothing but. Desire emerges in a confrontation with the image. Once this image which had been rendered incomplete is completed, once the imaginary facet which was non-integrated, suppressed, repressed, looms up, anxiety then makes its appearance. That is the fertile moment.[59]

Lacan sees de-centering the ego (in which there occurs recognition of "oneself" in manifestations of discourse that seem to come from "elsewhere," from outside the habitual ego-stance) as necessary to an ongoing process of self-transcendence. The ego is threatened by the not-I excluded by its closed structure, and this is experienced as anxiety. This is the "fertile moment," poised between courage and pathology. A pathological response to this anxiety would take the defensive form of further repression, leading to both a more closed, rigid personality structure, and greater likelihood of unintegrated, problematic eruptions (or "returns") of the repressed. The subject, by contrast, can be seen as Lacan's term for a courageous response to anxiety, resulting in a widening of the personality that takes on nonbeing in the form of alterity, open-endedness and possibility.

It is crucial that Lacan's argument that the unconscious is structured like a language is connected with an awareness that inner-generated "ego-threatening" experiences are irreducible to blind drive activity (i.e. to a quantitative problem). The interior otherness of the personality becomes manifest within symbolic resources, as Lacan emphasizes in stating that "desire always becomes manifest at the joint of speech, where it makes its appearance, its sudden emergence, its surge forwards. Desire emerges just as it becomes embodied in speech, it emerges with symbolism."[60] Here it may be seen that, just as otherness arises within a linguistic form, so too is the response, the transformation of the I, necessarily one that occurs linguistically, that is, in terms of the production of new meaning. Key to this production are slippages of meaning, polysemy, over-determinations, and the production of new semantic avenues through re-combination and re-contextualization. These pluralizing linguistic processes enable a capacity to *see otherwise* that characterizes the subject-in-process. In this respect, Lacan emphasizes that it is not the ego alone, but also the unconscious aspects of personality, that are transformed by language acquisition. As he states: "the unconscious is constituted by the effects of speech on the subject, it is the dimension in which the subject is determined in the development of the effects of speech, consequently the unconscious is structured like a language."[61] This approach opens an inquiry into the modes of discourse associated with the unconscious, such as representation in images, displacement (related to metonymy) and condensation (related to metaphor).[62]

The dimensions of unconscious potential meaning that exceed ego awareness are not based on a self-contained innate order, but on the intermeshing between the drives and symbolic (cultural) worlds. Hence Lacan also emphasizes that "the unconscious is the discourse of the Other."[63] Acculturation is not confined to the ego but involves the wider personality, or subject. Therefore, language is not merely a tool controlled by the ego. Language is a constitutive factor in the formation of subjectivity and of the cultural worlds we inhabit. In exceeding, in its origin and function, the utilitarian procedures of fixed communication, language discloses meaning that exceeds or offsets ego intentionality. This appears in Lacan's statement that the

> passion of the signifier now becomes a new dimension of the human condition in that it is not only man who speaks, but in man and through man *it* speaks (*ça parle*), that his nature is woven by effects in which is to be found the structure of language, of which he becomes the material, and that therefore there resounds in him, beyond what could be conceived by a psychology of ideas, the relation of speech.[64]

The "it speaks," playing upon and modifying Freud's concept of *das Es*, is indicative of a creative tension between ego and non-ego, that opens the subject to repressed dimensions of signification. Lacan further argues that "the tension between the subject . . . and the *ego* . . . is the starting point for the dialectic of consciousness."[65] This dialectic operates by a process of displacement and decentering, and offsets ego tendencies toward control, closure and repression.

Lacan offers the example of metaphor as paralleling the effect of anxiety upon the ego, but brought to the level of meaning. "It is in the action of the metaphor, insofar as certain original circuits impact upon the everyday, banal, commonly recognized circuits of metonymy, that the emergence of new meaning is produced."[66] Metaphor, symbolism and other non-literal forms of discourse sustain an is/is-not juxtaposition, as has been illustrated at length by Paul Ricoeur.[67] This adds a semantic dimension to the being/ nonbeing dynamic manifest in anxiety. We may recall Kristeva's point concerning the phobic person as being "in want of metaphoricalness." Existential anxiety is reduced to pathological anxiety by a closure within literalized, objectified, and hence fetishized representations. Kristeva formulates the problem in stating that "anxiety appears as a failure of emotional life, incapable of mobilizing the mental work of cognitive, logical, and rhetorical assimilation."[68] From this standpoint, meaningful courageous responses to anxiety involve a communicative process: not simply "seeing as," but rather seeing both "as" and "not as," enabling a widening of perspective. Lacan makes this point most explicitly in stating that "anxiety is only overcome where the Other names itself."[69]

In this regard, Lacan refers to the dialogical orientation of "full speech" related to metaphorical displacements of the ego's control of meaning. This disclosive process breaks the cycle of repetition and familiarity characteristic of the ego's "empty speech." This also indicates that for Lacan the subject is not a pre-given entity, and not a "whole."[70] Again, the gap or lack inherent in human beings is not to be filled, but becomes a key to the transformations of subjectivity. The subject comes into being by means of a series of displacements and questionings of the closed (imaginary) ego within interpersonal communicative relations. This emerges when Lacan refers to the Other (*Autre*) as being for the subject "the locus from which the question of his existence may be presented to him."[71] Within this questioning, wherein the problems of meaning and the transformation of meaning arise, one might find, in Lacan's words, "a corridor of communication between psychoanalysis and the religious register."[72] Therefore, the plurivocal resources of language, enabling an expansion and renewal of meaning in confrontations with the alterity and nonbeing that threaten closed identity, are intrinsic to the capacity for a courageous response to anxiety in Tillich's sense. Courage, as related to the process of finite transcendence, seems predicated upon an ability to see, to state things, otherwise than as they are (without positing a final answer to the perpetual existential questions of death, morality and meaning). The key issue here is the capacity to respond to and mediate decentering and destabilizing experiences of anxiety. Existential courage becomes something of an empty concept without attention to the linguistic media that allow for sustaining tension while enabling meaningful affirmation.

## VI

It is not surprising to find that emphasis on language as the medium for self-transformation also appears throughout Tillich's writings (although the link with existential courage is not explicitly formulated). Nevertheless, there are evident connections between courage and representational transcending of closed, routinized frameworks of understanding. There are indications that courage and self-transcendence are impossible without language as non-literal, without symbols in Tillich's sense of the term (i.e. language pointing beyond itself to levels of significance that remain closed to literal description).[73] This point can be framed within a distinction made in *Systematic Theology* between *denotative* and *expressive* language. While denotative language is descriptive, literal language pointing at a world of things, expressive language has the power "to disclose and to communicate personal states."[74] It is within this latter category that Tillich articulates some of the relations between language and self-transformation. This appears in his statement that language provides "the power to abstract from the concretely given and, having abstracted from it, to return to it, to interpret and transform it. The most vital being is the being which has the word and is by the word liberated from bondage to the given."[75] However, the transformative quality of linguistically constituted worlds of meaning frees us, but also alienates us in our relations to immediacy, precisely because it is correlated with choice and possibility. In this regard, Tillich discusses the production of meaning intrinsic to living within humanly constituted worlds, noting that "the ambiguity of this process results from the fact that the word, while creating a universe of meaning, also separates the meaning from the reality to which it refers."[76] Tillich further clarifies the point in stating that "the inherent ambiguity of language is that in transforming reality into meaning it separates mind and reality."[77] Thus, the freedom inherent in being "speaking beings" also engenders alienation, rootlessness and anxiety.

Tillich locates the response to this problem within language itself. He connects meaningful distancing from a one-dimensional relation to particulars with the capacity of language to generate *universals* that structure experience. As he states, "without language there are no universals; without universals no transcending of nature and no relation to it as nature."[78] Human beings exist and develop within shared worlds of meaning exhibiting a semi-autonomous, distanciated relation to the environmental world of objects. This spacing, similar to what Lacan refers to as the *negativity* of language, is what allows creative participation in reality.[79] Liberation from a one-to-one correspondence with particulars allows language to generate universals; in Tillich's words, "language, as the power of universals, is the basic expression of man's transcending his environment, of having a world."[80]

Universals speak to recurring dilemmas of human existence, and provide a sense of meaning and orientation "in spite of" the perpetual threat of non-being. However, a question arises here as to the status of the term "universal" within this argument. Charles E. Winquist, in *Desiring Theology*, raises issues that can help us probe more deeply into the meaning of Tillich's statements. Winquist argues that "neither epistemological nor ontological concepts are determinate in themselves. Their fundamental concepts have an internal undecidability or incompleteness that resists their universalization or naturalization in a general system."[81] There is what he terms a "heterogeneity" to such concepts, in that they necessarily derive from and refer to something outside themselves, subverting semantic closure. Recognizing this, he further argues, "works against Tillich's confidence that with language we have universals which liberate us from bondage to concrete situations."[82] Because of the necessarily situated and relational nature of all discourse, argues Winquist, "transcendental philosophy does not have a domain that is proper to itself. It does not resolve itself in epistemological or ontological categories. It is always implicated in alterities that it cannot determine from its own determinate standpoint."[83] These important caveats push us away from facile assimilations of Tillich's thinking into hypostatized metaphysical or onto-theological categories. They lead us to inquire if universals must be contained within totalized systems of meaning that are not themselves conditioned in relation to something outside themselves, to new contexts and experiences arising within finite existence.

I would argue that Tillich departs from notions of *static* universals, just as he resists the positing of fixed *eternal* truths, and just as he sees the *symbolic* (and hence open-ended) dimensions of language as intrinsic to self-transcendence. His work seems to indicate a capacity for *universalizing* associated with processes of moving beyond particulars, i.e. particular perspectives and modes of relation. In outlining such ongoing processes of *finite transcendence*, there is no need to assume absolute reference points or systemic closure in which linguistic universals refer to something like "Platonic ideas." Indeed, the *incompleteness* of which Winquist speaks can be seen as a feature of language that frees it from one-to-one correspondences with a world of objects. There is always a gap, a dimension of nonbeing inherent in linguistic experience and this keeps experience open, enabling freedom for questioning and reflection. In light of Tillich's existentialist view, universals can be seen to arise from within experience itself, as engaged by beings capable of posing questions of life and death, ethics and meaning in the face of nonbeing. Universals are neither *a priori* nor closed and final; they are subject to modification in light of new experience and argumentation. Tillich, as we have seen, understands universals as constructed within linguistic worlds of meaning, a point also shared by Levinas.[84] These linguistic resources are therefore, for Tillich, a constitutive feature of human freedom, responsibility and hence of courage on an existential level – the courage to affirm existence and choose meaning. In affirming existence we mediate the particular situation, within which we find ourselves, in relation to a larger perspective and understanding involving concepts such as freedom, justice, equality, truth or goodness. However, these ideals are never *given* in some final way, but must be individually grasped and applied within finite, contingent, concrete existential situations – hence the involvement of risk and courage.

A compatible definition of universals providing further clarification has been formulated by Luc Ferry and Alain Renaut. In their view, "the universal does not mean some norm . . . in the name of which violence is done to the particular." They argue that, if the distinguishing feature of human beings "is nothing but freedom, if it is the ability to wrench free of multiple codes that constantly threaten to imprison individuals, the idea of universality is the horizon within which this wrenching occurs."[85] Universalizing, then, is the capacity of the subject-in-language to question and transcend the closure of pre-established rules and codes. Relatedly, we may see Tillich as discussing language not as a descriptive tool for definitive "naming," nor as reflecting fixed *a priori* ideals, but as the vehicle of freedom as an ongoing, open-ended task. This appears in Tillich's argument that "language is endlessly variable," and that it is this variability (within time), rather than reference to a static truth, that links it with universals and with finite transcendence. In this vein, Tillich concludes that "semantics could and should become a door to life in the dimension of the spirit."[86] We find a parallel point made by Kierkegaard, also within the context of his discussion of anxiety, in stating that "freedom is always communicating" and that "language, the word, is precisely what saves, what saves the individual from the empty abstraction of inclosing reserve."[87] Here again, "spirit" is characterized by a *divergence* from absolutizing and enclosing tendencies.

Both Tillich and Lacan share a vision of human subjectivity as intrinsically in-relation and in-process, that is, as characterized by futurity. Neither would subscribe to a view of religiosity that involves relinquishing human freedom and individuality; yet, for each the essence of being-human always involves a continuing being-in-relation with an other on multiple levels.[88] It is this relatedness that sustains self-reflection and self-transcendence, allowing us to respond courageously to the dilemmas of nonbeing on levels of mortality, morality and meaning. Relatedness occurs as self/other, self/language, self/being, self/nonbeing, and in a variety of other forms. In all of these relational interdependencies, the connecting hinge, generating the possibility of openness and change, can appear in the form of anxiety. The discourses of Lacan and Tillich, so different in so many respects, converge at this point. Anxiety signals nonbeing for Tillich, lack (or *manque-à-être*) for Lacan; the response, described respectively as courage or the realization of the subject, has in each case to do with our capacity for ongoing creative renewal, with engaging the other, and with affirming life, morality and meaning *in spite of* . . .

## Notes

1 Paul Tillich, *Systematic Theology*, vol. 1 (Chicago: University of Chicago Press, 1951), p. 3.
2 Ibid., p. 191.
3 Paul Tillich, *Systematic Theology*, vol. 2 (Chicago: University of Chicago Press, 1957), p. 32.
4 Ibid., p. 8.
5 Emmanuel Levinas, *Of God Who Comes to Mind*, trans. Bettina Bergo (Stanford: Stanford University Press, 1998), p. xiv.
6 This focus on "the negative," or nonbeing, overlaps with much current postmodernist religious thought in its fascination with *negative theology*. A key source

for this line of reflection is Jacques Derrida, *On the Name*, trans. D. Wood, J. P. Leavey, Jr., and I. McLeod (Stanford: Stanford University Press, 1995). However, the *existential* approach of Tillich and the *psychoanalytic* approach of Lacan both maintain stricter focus on the human experiential significance of negativity.

7  Paul Tillich, *The Courage to Be* (New Haven: Yale University Press, 1952), p. 35.

8  Tillich, *Systematic Theology*, vol. 1, p. 191.

9  Søren Kierkegaard, *The Concept of Anxiety*, trans. Reidar Thomte in collaboration with Albert B. Anderson (Princeton: Princeton University Press, 1980), p. 42.

10  Ibid., p. 44.

11  Ibid., p. 155 (emphasis added).

12  Tillich, *The Courage to Be*, pp. 65ff.

13  Ibid., p. 41.

14  Ibid., p. 148.

15  Ibid., p. 66.

16  Ibid., pp. 66 and 77.

17  Ibid., p. 66.

18  William R. Rogers, "Tillich and Depth Psychology," in *The Thought of Paul Tillich*, ed. J. L. Adams, W. Pauch and R. L. Shinn (New York: Harper & Row, 1985), p. 113.

19  *The Courage to Be*, pp. 87–8; also see ibid., p. 91 for the necessary interdependency of self and other: "only in the continuous encounter with other persons does the person become and remain a person." I will further discuss the crucial role of language in Tillich's thought below (section VI).

20  Ibid., p. 88.

21  Tillich, *Systematic Theology*, vol. 2, p. 42.

22  See, for example, *The Courage to Be*, pp. 125 and 133.

23  Ibid., p. 73.

24  Ibid., pp. 75–6.

25  Ibid., p. 76.

26  Ibid., p. 141.

27  William James, *The Varieties of Religious Experience* (New York: Macmillan, 1961), p. 266.

28  See Ibid., Lectures 6, 7 and 8. A similar point could also be made with regard to Levinas' thinking. See, for example, his comments concerning the "traumatism of awakening" in "God and Philosophy," in *Of God Who Comes to Mind*, pp. 63–6, 66, 70, 75, and 78.

29  Tillich, *The Courage to Be*, p. 155.

30  Ibid., p. 179.

31  Paul Tillich, "The Theological Significance of Existentialism and Psychoanalysis," in *Theology of Culture* (New York: Oxford University Press, 1959), p. 114. In *Systematic Theology*, Tillich also emphasizes that theology requires the ideas and insights of depth psychology (vol. 2, p. 28). In both passages, Tillich is at pains to formulate an additional "interpenetration" between psychoanalysis and existentialism. This move is associated with Tillich's understanding of psychoanalysis as located between the worlds of scientific, potentially closed, reductionistic and pathologizing modes of analysis, and the more open, humanly engaged type of thinking he associates with existentialism. Here Tillich is reading psychoanalysis in a way that correlates with the work of Lacan, Kristeva and many others, both within and without France.

32  Tillich, *The Courage to Be*, p. 64.

33  Tillich, *Theology of Culture*, pp. 122–3.

34  See Sigmund Freud, "On the Grounds for Detaching a Particular Syndrome From Neurasthenia Under the Designation 'Anxiety Neurosis'," in *The Standard*

*Edition of the Complete Psychological Works of Sigmund Freud*, translated under the editorship of James Strachey (London: Hogarth Press, 1953–74 (hereafter *SE*), vol. 3, esp. pp. 99ff. In the "sequel" to this paper ("A Reply to Criticisms of My Paper on Anxiety Neurosis"), Freud re-emphasizes that "I maintain that there exists a specific aetiological factor for anxiety neurosis which can be replaced in its operation by stock noxae in a *quantitative* sense, but not in a *qualitative* one." *SE* 3, p. 131.

35  Tillich, *Theology of Culture*, p. 120. I develop issues related to conflicting tendencies and multiple levels of meaning in Freud's work, with specific reference to psychoanalytic interpretations of religion, in *The Other Freud: Religion, Culture and Psychoanalysis* (London: Routledge, 1999).

36  Sigmund Freud, *Inhibitions, Symptoms and Anxiety*, *SE* 20, p. 165.

37  Ibid., p. 93.

38  Ibid., p. 159.

39  Jacques Lacan, *Seminar VII: The Ethics of Psychoanalysis*, trans. Dennis Porter (New York: Norton, 1992), p. 103.

40  Sigmund Freud, "Analysis of a Phobia in a Five-Year-Old Boy," *SE* 10, pp. 5–149.

41  Sigmund Freud, *Totem and Taboo*, *SE* 20, p. 127–8.

42  Sigmund Freud, *Inhibitions, Symptoms, and Anxiety*, *SE* 20, p. 109.

43  As Lacan emphasizes, "the art of the analyst must be to suspend the subject's certainties until their last mirages have been consumed." Jacques Lacan, *Écrits: A Selection*, trans. Alan Sheridan (London: Routledge, 1977), p. 43.

44  Freud, *SE* 20, p. 128. Symbolic rereadings of "castration anxiety" are a common feature of Lacanian thinking. For examples, see *Écrits: A Selection*, p. 324. See also Kaja Silverman, *The Subject of Semiotics* (New York: Oxford University Press, 1983), pp. 172 and 183.

45  Julia Kristeva, *Powers of Horror: An Essay on Abjection*, trans. Leon Roudiez (New York: Columbia University Press, 1982), p. 35.

46  See, for example, Lacan, *Écrits: A Selection*, p. 323.

47  Jacques Lacan, *Speech and Language in Psychoanalysis*, translated, with notes and commentary, by Anthony Wilden (Baltimore: Johns Hopkins University Press, 1981), pp. 150–1 (emphasis added).

48  Kristeva, *Powers of Horror*, pp. 4–6.

49  Tillich, *The Courage to Be*, p. 36 (emphasis added).

50  Kristeva, *Powers of Horror*, p. 37.

51  Here I will offer only the example of Emmanuel Levinas, who consistently associates the ego with closure, control and "the Same." See his *Otherwise Than Being or Beyond Essence*, trans. Alphonso Lingis (Pittsburgh: Duquesne University Press, 1998), pp. 112, 116–17, 124, 141, 164, for some representative passages.

52  Lacan, *Écrits: A Selection*, p. 19. Elsewhere, reflecting on this inherent want or lack, Lacan is close to Tillich in emphasizing that "it isn't the lack of this or that, but lack of being whereby the being exists." *The Seminar of Jacques Lacan, Book II: The Ego in Freud's Theory and in the Technique of Psychoanalysis*, trans. Sylvana Tomaselli (Cambridge: Cambridge University Press, 1988) p. 223 (hereafter *Seminar II*).

53  Jacques Lacan, *The Seminar of Jacques Lacan, Book I: Freud's Papers on Technique*, trans. John Forrester (Cambridge: Cambridge University Press, 1988), p. 188 (hereafter *Seminar I*).

54  Lacan, *Seminar II*, p. 50.

55  See Samuel Weber, *Return to Freud: Jacques Lacan's Dislocation of Psychoanalysis*, trans. Michael Levine (Cambridge: Cambridge University Press, 1991), p. 107.

56  Jacques Lacan, *The Four Fundamental Concepts of Psychoanalysis*, trans. Alan Sheridan (London: Penguin Books, 1977), p. 41 (emphasis added).

57 Lacan, *Seminar I*, p. 193.
58 Lacan, *Écrits: A Selection*, p. 15.
59 Lacan, *Seminar I*, p. 188.
60 Lacan, *Seminar II*, p. 234.
61 Lacan, *The Four Fundamental Concepts of Psychoanalysis*, p. 149, and cf. *Écrits: A Selection*, p. 234. The use of the term "like" must be emphasized. This is obscured by attempts to conceive of the unconscious as operating according to the laws of structural linguistics, which is too rigid and formalized a model (as has been noted by Jean-François Lyotard and others).
62 See DiCenso, *The Other Freud: Religion, Culture and Psychoanalysis*, pp. 54–5, 126–9, 146.
63 *Écrits: A Selection*, p. 172.
64 Ibid., p. 284.
65 *Seminar II*, p. 177.
66 Quoted in Richard Boothby, *Death and Desire: Psychoanalytic Theory in Lacan's Return to Freud* (New York: Routledge, 1991), p. 161. Boothby develops the point in stating that "metaphor announces a complexity and ambiguity incapable of expression in the register of the imaginary." Ibid., p. 163.
67 Paul Ricoeur, *The Rule of Metaphor*, trans. Robert Czerny (Toronto: University of Toronto Press, 1977), p. 306.
68 Julia Kristeva, *New Maladies of the Soul*, trans. Ross Guberman (New York: Columbia University Press, 1995), p. 69.
69 Quoted in Weber, *Return to Freud*, p. 164.
70 As Lacan states: "If we were whole, we would each be in our corners, whole, we wouldn't be here, together, trying to get ourselves into shape, as they say. It is the subject, not in its totality, but in its opening up." *Seminar II*, p. 243.
71 Lacan, *Écrits: A Selection*, p. 194.
72 Lacan, *The Four Fundamental Concepts of Psychoanalysis*, p. 8.
73 For a general discussion of symbolism, see Paul Tillich, *Dynamics of Faith* (London: George Allen & Unwin, 1957), ch. 3. Elsewhere, with specific reference to symbols and transcendence, Tillich states that "every religious symbol negates itself in its literal meaning, but it affirms itself in its self-transcending meaning." *Systematic Theology*, vol. 2, p. 9, quoted in Charles E. Winquist, *Desiring Theology* (Chicago: University of Chicago Press, 1995), p. 74.
74 Tillich, *Systematic Theology*, vol. 1, p. 123.
75 Tillich, *The Courage to Be*, p. 82.
76 Paul Tillich, *Systematic Theology*, vol. 3 (Chicago: University of Chicago Press, 1963), p. 69.
77 Ibid.
78 Tillich, *The Courage to Be*, p. 91. Also, in *Systematic Theology*, vol. 2, p. 31, Tillich links finite freedom, transcendence and language. As he states: "Man is free in so far as he has language. With his language, he has universals which liberate him from bondage to the concrete situation."
79 For Lacan on the "negativity" of language, see *Écrits: A Selection*, p. 95.
80 Tillich, *Systematic Theology*, vol. 1, p. 170.
81 Winquist, *Desiring Theology*, p. 70.
82 Ibid.
83 Ibid.
84 As Levinas states: "Language, far from presupposing universality and generality, first makes them possible." Emmanuel Levinas, *Totality and Infinity: An Essay on Exteriority*, trans. Alphonso Lingis (Pittsburgh: Duquesne University Press, 1969), p. 73.
85 Luc Ferry and Alain Renaut, *Heidegger and Modernity*, trans. Franklin Philip (Chicago: University of Chicago Press, 1990), pp. 4–5.

86  Tillich, *Systematic Theology*, vol. 2, pp. 58–9.
87  Kierkegaard, *The Concept of Anxiety*, p. 124.
88  Tillich discusses these issues in terms of the tensions between autonomy and heteronomy. He resolves the tension by introducing a revised notion of "theonomy," indicating not the supreme manifestation of heteronomy under the law of an objectified God, but rather "autonomous reason united with its own depth." See *Systematic Theology*, vol. 1, pp. 84–5.

# 5 Love and law

## John Milbank and Hermann Cohen on the ethical possibilities of secular society

*Leora Batnitzky*

John Milbank defines his theological project as an attempt to divorce Christian theology from what he calls "secular reason." By this Milbank means that he intends to free theology from "two characteristic forms of confinement." Milbank argues in the introduction to his monumental *Theology and Social Theory* that

> Either it [theology "positioned" by secular reason] idolatrously connects knowledge of God with some particular immanent field of knowledge–"ultimate" cosmological causes, or "ultimate" psychological and subjective needs. Or else it is confined to intimations of a sublimity beyond representation, so functioning to confirm negatively the questionable idea of an autonomous secular realm, completely transparent to rational understanding.[1]

Methodologically, Milbank's distinctly postmodern theology is an attempt to reinsert linguistic mediation at the core of Christian theology, mediation that he argues secular reason, and more specifically Christian theology indebted to secular reason, implicitly denies. In his more recent *The Word Made Strange*, Milbank begins by identifying Kantian transcendentalism as one, if not the, modern methodological source of a non-linguistic approach to theology.[2] As such, Milbank locates Kant and modern Kantianism at the heart of the "secular reason" that must be overcome if this theological linguistic reinsertion is to be made possible.

While this methodological reorientation of theology and hence social theory is the philosophical goal of *Theology and Social Theory*, Milbank, both in this seminal work and beyond, also makes a substantive argument not just about the form that Christian theology must take but about Christianity's eternal content. While arguing that Christian theology cannot be expressed non-linguistically, Milbank maintains that the meaning of Christianity is that "Christianity . . . recognizes no original violence." Milbank's critique of secular reason thus corresponds to what he argues is the essential message of Christianity:

The real perspective of the book [*Theology and Social Theory*] turns out to be that of virtue . . . from the perspective of Christian virtue, there emerges to view a hidden thread of continuity between antique reason and modern, secular reason. This thread of continuity is the theme of "original violence." Antique thought and politics assumes some naturally given element of chaotic conflict which must be tamed by the stability and self-identity of reason. Modern thought and politics . . . assumes that there is only this chaos, which cannot be tamed by an opposing transcendent principle, but can be immanently controlled by subjecting it to rules and giving irresistible power to those rules in the form of market economies and sovereign politics.[3]

In contrast to both antique and modern secular reason, Milbank contends that Christianity recognizes no originary violence but only "a harmonic peace which is yet beyond the circumscribing power of any totalizing reason." Significantly, Milbank describes what he argues is Christian non-violence as a "peace beyond the law."

I focus in this chapter on the connection between Milbank's argument about Christian non-violence, a "peace beyond the law," and his desire to "sketch out a theology aware of itself as culturally constructed, yet able to elaborate its own self-understanding in terms of a substantive and critical theory of society in general." I argue that despite Milbank's protestations to the contrary, his arguments share an important feature with certain "Kantianisms" as well as with Kant himself. I have in mind here the Jewish ethical monotheism of the founder of the Marburg neo-Kantian school, Hermann Cohen. Cohen's late nineteenth-century and Milbank's late twentieth-century projects share an important formal similarity: both attempt to develop, in Milbank's terms, a "critical theory of society in general" by way of arguments about the interrelation of the nature of law and Judaism's or Christianity's respective contribution to culture. The difference between Milbank's and Cohen's projects is that while Milbank's theology and social theory are ultimately attempts to reject secular society and "secular reason," Cohen's theology and social theory are attempts precisely to embrace secular society and "secular reason." As such, exploring the relation between Cohen's and Milbank's thought is valuable for it calls into question the very nature of Milbank's critique of "secular reason."

## I. Differences between Milbank and Cohen

Before beginning to explore the formal similarities between Cohen's and Milbank's projects, it is necessary to acknowledge the differences between the two. At first glance, the comparison between Milbank and Cohen seems an unlikely one. Cohen, a late nineteenth-century German-Jewish neo-Kantian, and Milbank, a late twentieth-century British Christian theologian seem worlds apart on issues of both method and content.

Let us explore briefly their methodological differences. Cohen's quest for a critical idealism is a quest for a philosophy linked to science. Cohen in fact defines idealism with reference to its scientific aspirations: "idealism as critique of knowledge has scientific facts as its objects, not things and events, not even those of simple consciousness."[4] Cohen's approach to religion does not break with this methodological approach.[5] As Cohen maintains in both his *Der Begriff der Religion im System der Philosophie* (*The Concept of Religion in the System of Philosophy*) of 1915 and in his posthumously published *Religion der Vernunft aus den Quellen des Judentums* (*Religion of Reason out of the Sources of Judaism*) of 1919, religion, and religion of reason in particular, must be understood and evaluated from within the critical idealist perspective. In *Der Begriff*, Cohen writes:

> It must be pointed out, ever more clearly and precisely that philosophy is a homogeneous factor with religion, if true cultural maturity is ever to be the dominant factor in philosophy. The question cannot have a different development than that of the other fundamental cultural phenomena. . . . Physics and mathematics, as well as law and the state and, lastly, the cultural fact of art have had to subject themselves to this transcendental investigation. How could religion be dealt with as a fact that can escape the question on the ground of the right to its existence and stability?[6]

Cohen maintains that religion too must be subjected to the transcendental investigation of his critical idealism. In *Religion of Reason*, Cohen is even more explicit:

> What holds true for every science holds no less true for religion. Insofar as religion, too, consists of concepts and is based on concepts, its ultimate source can only be reason. This connection with reason determines and conditions its connection with philosophy, understood as the universal reason of human knowledge.[7]

At its most basic level, Cohen's approach would seem to be at the heart of what Milbank regards as the bankruptcy of the intersection between Kantian transcendentalism and the implications of post-Kantian theology. Recognizing, in Cohen's terms, religion's share in reason requires, among other things, distinguishing between being and existence: God's provenance is the former while the world's and the human being's is the latter.[8] The unique God, for Cohen, remains not only wholly separate from the human world but can be known only negatively, if at all.[9] In this sense, Cohen's approach to religion, to use Milbank's terms, functions "to confirm negatively the questionable idea of an autonomous secular realm, completely transparent to rational understanding." So, too, religion of reason is a wholly human and rational affair for Cohen. In his succinct formulation, "*The religion of reason turns religion into a general function of human consciousness.*"[10] In these most fundamental ways, Cohen's methodological approach to religion conforms to Milbank's critical summary of Kant: "knowledge of God for Kant is confirmation of this world as it is, or else a 'sublime' aspiration which is a contentless bad infinitude, unrelated to actual social behaviour."[11]

## II. Cohen on law

The differences between Cohen and Milbank would seem to go even deeper as we come to what is the centerpiece of each of their philosophies: their respective philosophies of law. At the end of the nineteenth century, Cohen argues that Kant's Christian and particularly Pauline prejudices led him to misjudge seriously the nature of law by contrasting it to freedom. In contrast, Milbank's late twentieth-century theology is an attempt to reassert the Pauline dichotomy that Cohen rejects, and with it the "secular" legal and social theories of modernity. Let us turn first to Cohen's conception of law and then to Milbank's.

In his *Ethik des reinen Willens*, published first in 1904, Cohen attempts to reassess completely Kant's conception of law and to make the science of law the focus of both his critical idealism and his ethical socialist vision. Cohen writes:

> Kant . . . did not deduce ethics with reference to the science of law, as he had done for logic with reference to the science of nature. There can be no doubt that the consequence of this would inevitably be an irreparable error in the concept of the transcendental method. If it is true for logic, why should it not be true for ethics? . . . it is still a question of knowledge . . . here lie the profound difficulties with Kant's system.[12]

On a technical level, Cohen criticizes Kant for distinguishing morality from right, a distinction to which we will turn briefly below. Cohen argues that Kant's distinction denies law the status of science. Cohen maintains that Kant is inconsistent in this regard on the basis of his own philosophical premises. Significantly for the purposes of this essay, Cohen blames Kant's inconsistency on what he argues are Kant's Pauline prejudices. Cohen writes:

> Kant had made law the center of gravity of his ethics. And thereby he distinguished legality from morality. Morality is rooted in law; but it is not legality . . . [these points] have in fact no legal and no philosophical source, but an unambiguous religious one. They originate in the polemic, in which Paul criticized the Mosaic teaching, which he called and characterized law.[13]

Cohen is certainly correct that Kant has in mind a reading of Paul when he evokes his distinction between law and right. We need but recall Kant's definition, in *Religion Within the Limits of Reason Alone*, of freedom: "To become free, 'to be freed from bondage under the law of sin, to live for righteousness' – this is the highest prize he [the morally well-disposed man] can win." Here Kant repeats Paul's words in Romans 6:18: "and, having been set free from sin, have become slaves of righteousness."[14] Cohen maintains that Kant's Pauline prejudice is responsible for the Kantian split between public law as the mark of coercion and private, or individual, law as the mark of freedom. Kant makes this distinction perhaps most succinctly in division one of book three of his *Religion*. He writes:

> A *juridico-civil* (political) *condition* [*Zustand*] is the relation of men to each other in which they all alike stand socially under *public juridical laws* (which are, as a class, laws of coercion). An *ethico-civil* condition is that in which they are united under non-coercive laws, *i.e., laws of virtue* alone.[15]

Kant goes on in book four to describe religion within the limits of reason alone as that which subscribes to the latter view of law and virtue, while pseudo-service, or clericalism, subscribes to the former. Famously, Kant maintains that Jewish law epitomizes both clericalism and the coercion intrinsic to public juridical laws.

Before turning to Cohen's response to Kant let us turn briefly to Kant's reading of Paul. We saw above that Kant quotes Romans 6:18: "and, having been set free from sin, have become slaves of righteousness." He seems also to have in mind the preceding verses, and especially verses 14–15: "For sin will have no dominion over you, since you are not under law but under grace. What then? Are we to sin because we are not under law but under grace? By no means!" Kant associates bondage and coercion with the law and argues that freedom exists only outside of the law. Kant, following most Protestant readings since Luther, reads Paul as implicitly criticizing Jewish law and arguing for grace over law as the only means for salvation. Reading Paul as if he is offering an implicit criticism of legality, Kant associates legality with coercion and argues that freedom exists only outside of the law. Kant's distinctly modern concept of moral freedom is thus premised precisely on a reading of Paul, and Christianity by implication, as a repudiation of legality.[16] Cohen is certainly right in attributing Kant's seemingly paradoxical position of arguing for a moral law that is non-legal, a law that is not a law, to this reading of Paul.

Recent New Testament scholarship has questioned this reading of Paul that Kant perpetuates. The assumption of Kant's reading of Paul is that Paul is repudiating law for the sake of grace. Kant assumes, as most Protestant readers especially after Luther do, that the question Paul is asking is an either/or one: does law *or* grace provide freedom?[17] As we have seen, Kant assumes that the answer to this question is that only grace provides freedom. And to put it simply, Kant translates this connection between grace and freedom into his arguments about moral autonomy being the basis of an *ethico-civil* association that is non-coercive by nature. But, as a growing number of scholars have argued, this reading works only if one assumes that Paul is addressing Jews and Gentiles alike. In contrast to this view, a number of scholars have argued that Paul is only addressing a Gentile audience. Once this is recognized, the argument goes, Paul's arguments about the law, in Romans and Galatians particularly, begin to look quite different.

As John Gager argues, recent New Testament scholarship paints a different picture of Paul.[18] The question that Paul is asking concerns not whether grace is superior to law but what means of salvation is available to the Gentiles. According to this revised view of Paul, Paul's arguments need to be understood within the context of an internal Jewish debate about the possibility of salvation for Gentiles; in particular, this debate concerned whether or not Gentiles needed to be circumcised. Once seen in this context, Paul's arguments are not against law or legality. Rather, his arguments concern the path to salvation for Gentiles. The law remains valid for Jews. Among other things, this reading of Paul has the advantage of making sense of Paul's arguments precisely for the continued validity of the law for the Jewish people – such as Romans 3:31 "Do we overthrow the law through faith? By no means, we uphold the law" – arguments of which the "traditional" view of Paul have not been able to make sense.[19]

Cohen seeks to vindicate from Kant's harsh critique not only a concept of law, but also, as he would argue in greater detail in his final work on religion, a Jewish view of law. But while Cohen rightly recognizes that Kant's concepts of law and freedom are based on a "Pauline prejudice" (or, better put, a prejudiced reading of Paul) against legality, I suggest that Cohen nonetheless maintains this very prejudice in his redescription of law. While Cohen argues against Kant and "Paul" that law is intrinsic to morality, he goes further and argues that law has no relation to coercion. In this sense, Cohen accepts what had become the traditional Protestant reading of Paul's equation between law and coercion by merely inverting it. Kant and "Paul" equate law and coercion. Cohen accepts the terms of this argument about law by merely denying this equation. I will return to this issue below.

Let us turn now to Cohen's argument. To return to a point from above, in his *Ethik des reinen Willen*, Cohen maintains that recognition of Kant's inconsistency in regard to his transcendental approach to law leads not only to the recognition of the scientific status of law but also to a solution of the problem of coercion and law. In other words, recognizing, as Cohen argues we should, that law is the scientific foundation of ethics also dissolves the problem of coercion. Cohen writes:

> Ethics can confidently allow the concept of coercion to fall away for right, as ... the concept of law steps forward: in the norms of right [*Recthsnormen*]. ... [These] are the mathematically original shape [*Urform*] of a law, in so far as they form the measure of an angle of the

regulations and the guiding principles. In the norms [of right], right is legitimated for the concept of law.[20]

Cohen argues that because the norms of right speak to every person, and hence produce what we might call modern individuality, the problem of coercion disappears. The norms of right create the possibility of ethics because they create the possibility of the free individual. Simply put, every person is the same under the law. Hence the law – public, juridical law – produces (to use Cohen's neo-Kantian vocabulary) free individuality. Cohen augments his philosophy of law in his posthumous *Religion of Reason*, but his argument that law produces free individuality without coercion remains unchanged. Let us turn now to Milbank's conception of law and then back to Cohen's arguments in his *Religion of Reason*.

## III. Milbank on law

As we have seen, Milbank maintains that he rejects the premises of Kantian philosophy. And while he is critical of Hegel also, he does, in the context of the question of Kantian morality, favor Hegel's notion of ethics as *sittlich*, as tied to society and social roles as opposed to Kant's (and Cohen's) view of the morality of private individuality.[21] Nonetheless, as I will argue, Milbank retains the Kantian attempt to extract all coercion from law. From a formal perspective at least, Milbank's construction of Christian peace is remarkably similar to Kant's construction of moral freedom in that both are attempts to define a realm wholly free of coercion.

Of course, Milbank would reject this characterization from the start. He maintains after all that what differentiates the Christian notion of peace is that it is precisely not predicated on violence. In his terms, Christian peace enjoys an "ontological priority." As he argues:

> In the "heavenly city", beyond the possibility of alternation, the angels and saints abide in such a fellowship; their virtue is not the virtue of resistance and domination, but simply of remaining in a state of self-forgetting conviviality. Here there is nothing but "the vision of peace", a condition that originally pertained also for the temporal creation, before the sinful assertion of pride and domination introduced a pervasive presence of conflict leading to death in both society and nature.[22]

Moreover, the meaning of "the name of Jesus," Milbank argues, is found precisely in the transformation of "the world of violence and suffering . . . [of] human conventions" and most profoundly a transformation of and overcoming of "the law."[23] "Whereas 'Moses' is just the name of the mediator of the law, 'Jesus' is the name of the new law itself, because now the word of God is found to be located, not in the dead letter of the law over against the power of bodies, but in true, strong, peaceful, relationships, beginning with the practice of Jesus."[24] Drawing on what he claims is Paul's criticism of the law, Milbank maintains that morality itself cannot be Christian because morality is ultimately tied to the violent law, while Christianity is precisely the ontological rejection of this violence. Milbank contends that the law itself is the realm of sin and violence:

> Whereas Augustine had discovered original sin to be pride and desire, Luther and then Kierkegaard claimed that the desire to command, desire to possess and prideful delight in domination of others all originate in a still more original fear that the unknown is not to be trusted, so requiring legal security in ourselves.[25]

Much of Milbank's argument about a Christian peace beyond the law is drawn from Augustine. Milbank is well aware that Augustine, as John R. Bowlin succinctly puts it, "encouraged Christian bishops and magistrates to coerce and constrain religious dissenters . . . participated in these activities almost from the start of his career as presbyter under Valerius, and . . . offered justifications for what he did."[26] Milbank's response to this tension between his interpretation of Augustine and the reality of Augustine's practice is to conclude that the latter is sadly inconsistent with the former. Nonetheless, Milbank maintains, the vision of an ontological peace beyond coercion remains Augustine's legacy.[27]

But as Bowlin has recently and convincingly argued, Augustine believed that "just coercion is in fact possible . . . we find Augustine insisting that justice sets a standard that cannot be transgressed . . . the justice we know of in this world is a wretched business, an awful necessity."[28] On Augustine's own terms, coercion is not only often a necessity but it is part of the Church's moral practices. In Bowlin's formulation, because Augustine "believes that negative liberty is a genuine good he refuses to conclude that every negative liberty lost can be justified by this or that positive liberty gained. Instead he assumes a rough collection of criteria that must be met for coercion to proceed justly and for negative liberty to be sacrificed for the sake of positive."[29]

I would like to suggest, rather boldly, that from a formal perspective Milbank's arguments about a peace beyond the law have more in common with Kant's than they do with Augustine's. Both Kant and Milbank attempt to carve out an earthly space in which coercion has no place. Moreover, despite the fact that Milbank maintains that Christian peace is "originary" and not predicated on violence, his concept of Christian peace, like Kant's notion of an *ethico-civil* condition, is predicated on a violent substructure: what Milbank calls "secular violence" and what Kant calls a *juridico-civil* (political) *condition*. For these reasons, although Milbank himself acknowledges that his theology is particularly contemporary, what he calls postmodern, and not, in this sense, an attempt to recapture some idealized past, I'd like to suggest that his theology is more "modern" than it might seem.

Like Kant's argument about morality, Milbank's argument (unlike

Augustine's) about Christian peace is particularly modern in that it is possible to separate out a non-violent sphere (if only in theory) precisely because church and state are themselves separate. Milbank argues of course that Christian peace beyond the law is made possible only by way of Christian virtue. Despite his arguments against Kant, Milbank's utopian conception of Christian peace is predicated on the same dichotomy between a non-coercive morality (what Milbank calls Christian peace) and the violent substructure that supports that morality (what Kant calls public-juridical law and Milbank calls "secular reason"), upon which Kant's vision is predicated. As such, Milbank's notion of law is predicated upon what he has denounced as "secular reason."

It might appear particularly ironic that Milbank's conception of law seems closer to Kant's "secular reason" than Cohen's concept might seem to be. Both Kant and Milbank find public-juridical law violent and coercive, while Cohen does not. Yet, as I suggested above, Cohen, despite his criticism of Kant, retains, as he himself thought, the spirit of Kant's interpretation. Like Kant and Milbank, Cohen attempts to define a sphere free from violence. Cohen's argument that the norms of right dispel the problem of coercion has as its premise the "Pauline" equation of law and coercion. Cohen does not consider the complex relation between law and coercion, and indeed between modern individuality and coercion, precisely because he is so bent on dispelling Kant's "Pauline" prejudice. But just as Cohen argues that Kant is affected by his "Pauline" prejudices, so too Cohen is affected by a prejudice of his own, one which, I suggest, is intrinsic to modern Jewish conceptions of law.[30]

As Kant argued to derogatory effect, Judaism is a religion of law. In his *Religion Within the Limits of Reason Alone*, Kant bases his negative reading of Judaism on Moses Mendelssohn's arguments in *Jerusalem*.[31] Mendelssohn, the father of German–Jewish thought and arguably of modern Jewish thought, had maintained that Judaism does not contradict the eternal laws of reason because Judaism consists of divine legislation, which are historical truths received by a particular people at a particular place and time. As Cohen himself argues in his *Religion of Reason*, the context of Mendelssohn's contentions was an attempt to defend Jewish particularity in the face of an ever-growing Enlightenment demand for a universal culture.[32] Cohen maintains that Kant's parochialism led to his misinterpretation of Mendelssohn: "[Kant's] view is only possible if one considers it self-evident and beyond doubt that the Jewish laws can be experienced as a heavy yoke."[33] Arguing that Mendelssohn's argument about Judaism was a corrective to changes brought about by the Reformation, Cohen seeks to offer his own corrective to the law based on his own historical context.

Cohen's corrective to Mendelssohn, however, is not a rejection of Mendelssohn's argument but a deepening of Mendelssohn's premises. Cohen takes Mendelssohn's attempt to argue for the validity of a separate though integrated Jewish community further by arguing, in 1919, against the Jewish turn to Zionism. Like Mendelssohn, Cohen contends that Judaism is not a nation within a nation but a community that is bound together by laws that only they are obliged to follow. The Jewish community, as the embodiment of pure monotheism, both maintain, has much to offer German culture at large. But perhaps most important for the purposes of this essay, Cohen's thought is premised on what we might call a particularly modern Jewish prejudice, begun with Mendelssohn: the notion that coercion plays no role in the Jewish community and in Jewish law.

Just as Milbank reads a utopian peace into Augustine, so too Mendelssohn reads a utopian peace into Jewish religion and law: "Religious doctrines and propositions . . . are not forced upon the faith of the [Jewish] nation under the threat of eternal or temporal punishments."[34] Or, more generally, "Divine religion . . . is a moral person, but its rights imply no coercion."[35] While there is no doubt primarily a socio-political motivation to Mendelssohn's arguments that Jewish law is not coercive (i.e. he wants to argue that Judaism is not a nation within a nation) it seems that he too, as Cohen would after him, has internalized the "traditional" reading of Paul. This reading suggests that Paul associates law with coercion. Mendelssohn, as would Cohen after him, accepts this equation and inverts the valuation in arguing that Jewish law has nothing to do with coercion. In the context of *Jerusalem*, Mendelssohn in fact goes further in this attempt at inversion and argues that it is Christianity that is truly coercive for Christianity demands and coerces faith.

We saw above that Cohen maintains that Kant's "Pauline" prejudice is responsible for the Kantian split between public law as the mark of coercion and private, or individual, law as the mark of freedom. Cohen nonetheless follows this premise of Mendelssohn's thought – that Jewish religion and law are non-coercive – and develops it into a view of law in general. Cohen and Milbank after him are certainly correct that in the modern world, defined here simply (though I realize not unproblematically) by the development of the nation state, Christian churches and Jewish communities cannot coerce their members. Christian churches and Jewish communities are, after all, in the modern world, voluntary associations (as Mendelssohn in *Jerusalem* hoped they would be). But this does not mean, however, that these communities have not used coercion historically or, more importantly for our discussion of modern Christian and Jewish conceptions of law, that this use of coercion wasn't consistent with or justified by the theological viewpoints of these communities.[36]

What Cohen and Milbank have in common with Kant is the attempt to define a sphere that is immune to the violence of law. Cohen merely denies that law is violent at all. He is more consistent than Kant in arguing that law and legality are intrinsic to what Milbank calls, in contrast to Christian virtue, "ordinary morality." And Cohen is also more consistent than Milbank in acknowledging the connection between "secular reason" and his attempt to justify Judaism in the modern world. This isn't to say, however, that Cohen's arguments are any more convincing than Milbank's, but they do have the virtue of being squarely and self-consciously placed within modern and spe-cifically post-Kantian discourses on law. It is Cohen's placement within modern attempts to justify religion via "secular reason" that makes the com-parison between him and Milbank productive. Having explored the seeming differences between Cohen and Milbank, let us turn now to what I will argue is their perhaps surprising affinity with one another.

## IV. Guilt, sin, and religion's role in culture

Although, as I have argued, Cohen's and Milbank's respective thoughts have a profound affinity with Kantian conceptions of individuality and morality, each is a critic of precisely these Kantian views. I suggest in fact that what Cohen and Milbank have particularly in common is the attempt to provide a criticism of Kantian individualism in order to chisel out a place for Judaism and Christianity respectively within secular culture. We will see that Milbank's conception of Christian love parallels in important ways Cohen's conception of the contribution that Jewish *monotheism and indeed Jewish law* make to secular society.

Let us begin by considering what is an obvious criticism of Milbank's and Cohen's arguments about the non-coercive nature of the Church and law respectively. Milbank's notion of the peaceful Christian beyond the law and Cohen's notion of the free and moral individual created by the law each, precisely because of their Kantian resonances, call to mind Hegel's critique of the "beautiful soul":

> The "beautiful soul," lacking an actual existence, entangled in the con-tradiction between its pure self and the necessity of that self to external-ize itself and change itself into an *actual* existence, and dwelling in the immediacy of this firmly held antithesis . . . this "beautiful soul," then, being conscious of this contradiction in its unreconciled *immediacy*, is disordered to the point of madness, wastes itself in yearning and pines away in consumption. Thereby it does in fact surrender *the being-for-self* to which it so stubbornly clings . . .[37]

Drawing on the story of the "beautiful soul" in Goethe's *Wilhelm Meister's Apprenticeship*, Hegel argues in his *Phenomenology of Spirit* that the Kantian notion of morality (*Moralität*) leaves the individual bereft of ethical and political ties to larger social structures. The result is impotence; hence the beautiful soul "wastes itself in yearning and pines away in consumption."

Significantly, Milbank and Cohen have a similar response to Hegel's cri-tique. Each tries to describe a way in which the private, isolated individual is transformed individually and also, perhaps most importantly, by way of communal life (what Milbank calls "Christian virtue" and what is for Cohen "the congregation"). Indeed, Milbank tries to outdo Hegel by claiming that "There is . . . no true *Sittlichkeit* in Hegel's ethical and political theory."[38]

Contra Hegel's social theory, Milbank claims that Christian theology uniquely can transform the individual human being into a person organically connected to a community who nonetheless remains a unique individual. So, too, Cohen makes this very claim with regard to Judaism's relation to German culture. Moreover, Milbank and Cohen both claim that the transformation achieved by Christianity and Judaism respectively is for the betterment of humanity at large. In Milbank's terms, once again, he hopes to "sketch out a theology aware of itself as culturally constructed, yet able to elaborate its own self-understanding in terms of a substantive and critical theory of society in general." Cohen argues that the pure monotheism of Judaism fuels the peoples of the world toward a truly just society. And Milbank maintains that by way of his Christian theology "temporality is restored as gift and thereby rendered eternal. Only the vision and hope of heaven makes us socially and politically just on earth – and how is it, one wonders, that we have ever come to think otherwise?"[39] Let us turn then to Milbank's and Cohen's arguments about the respective abilities of Christianity and Judaism to transform the modern individual.

One of Milbank's major criticisms of law is that it sustains only a totality of generic individuals and cannot recognize the uniqueness of the individual. Milbank maintains that Christian virtue stands in contrast to morality in regard to, among other things, ordinary morality's grounding in generality. By this Milbank means the "eternal demand for uniformity" that sustains "a unity of a thoroughly abstract kind."[40] In contrast to ordinary morality's emphasis on generality, Milbank poses Christianity's emphasis on specificity:

> To the abstract generality of law, Paul opposes the specificity of divine gift which always takes the form of particular gifts in the sense of specific talents or chrismata: these are "different gifts according to the gift given to us" (Rom. 12:6). . . . [Paul] says that if we realize that we each have an absolutely specific work to do, we will stop supposing we can compare ourselves in virtue to our brethren. . . . Each gift, each talent ("virtue") is absolutely unique, yet each repeats non-identically and so exactly the grace of God which is transcendentally, inaccessibly One.[41]

Milbank argues that God's grace provides a unity to humanity that does not deny the particularity, indeed the uniqueness, of the individual.

Significantly, Cohen's approach to "religion of reason out of the sources of Judaism" mirrors, at least from a formal perspective, Milbank's attempt to describe the particularity of Christian love. Cohen's task is, in his terms, to describe religion's share in reason, a task, seemingly at least, at odds with Milbank's postmodern theological project. Yet Cohen describes his task as precisely the attempt to recognize the unique individual. He writes:

> Ethics can recognize and give recognition to man only as a member of humanity. As an individual man he can only be a representative carrier of

humanity. . . . Does ethics have the methodological means for establishing it, if its goal is the totality (*Allheit*) which is realized in humanity? Would not such a division and gradation lie in the general direction of plurality (*Mehrheit*) and thus be an aberration from ethics' unifying goal of totality?[42]

As Cohen argues at length in *Religion of Reason*, only religion, represented by the pure monotheism of Judaism, is capable of producing plurality. And as Milbank argues with regard to Christian grace, Cohen argues that for the true particularity produced by Jewish monotheism "each repeats non-identically and so exactly the grace of God which is transcendentally, inaccessibly One."

Cohen and Milbank make their respective arguments about Judaism's or Christianity's ability to produce particular, unique, human beings, who nonetheless are united by a God who is transcendentally one, by means of an argument about sin and atonement. Both maintain that atonement creates a new kind of individual who, through acknowledgment of his or her sin, is made particular and freed from the arithmetic of pure justice. Cohen states the problem this way in the context of his philosophical system:

> In our *Ethics of Pure Will* we have given the following account of the foundation of the criminal law: the judge is authorized to inquire into the crime only according to the definition of the law and to punish the criminal accordingly. However, the judge, in proclaiming someone guilty, must be prevented from also pronouncing judgment on the man's guilt. . . . If man is not permitted to lay aside the consciousness of his guilt then it is ethics which refers man to religion, to the correlation with God.[43]

Cohen stresses that the fact that ethics requires religion, to use his terminology, does not negate ethics. Rather, religion supplements ethics. We will return to this issue below. For now, however, we need to focus on the formal affinity between Cohen's and Milbank's arguments about atonement.

Let us turn first to Milbank's argument about Jesus. Milbank describes the Christian understanding of atonement as follows:

> To answer the question of why only God incarnate can end violence, one must allude to the view of atonement doctrine that Jesus's death is not merely one isolated act of refusal of domination, but is supposed somehow to enable, in a more than exemplary fashion, similar refusals in the future. This can only mean two things: first of all, on the cross . . . Jesus is "substituted" for us, because here . . . he becomes totally a sign, here he is transformed into a perfect metaphor of forgiveness . . . the idea that only God incarnate can make atonement means that an atoning practice can arise only once the new community based upon the absolute priority of human relationship, so perfectly imaging God, is in place.[44]

Milbank maintains that Jesus, as sign, makes possible a new reality for humanity. "Jesus is 'substituted' for us," which means that we ourselves are transformed.

Similarly, Cohen maintains that the prophet/priest Ezekiel creates the possibility of self-transformation. Cohen writes:

> "*Cast away from you* all your transgressions, wherein ye have transgressed, *and make you a new heart and spirit*" (Ezek. 18:31). With this passage Ezekiel excelled all his predecessors. For they have only prophesized of the new heart and the new spirit, which, according to Jeremiah, God will give when he will make a new covenant with Israel; but Ezekiel says: make yourselves a new heart and a new spirit. *Now the individual comes to full fruition in the I.* In the recognition of his own sin, man became an individual. Through the power to create for himself a new heart and a new spirit, however, he becomes the I.[45]

Like Milbank, Cohen maintains that this new symbolic order is only made possible by way of a new kind of community:

> Thus sacrifice as a social institution, as an institution of the congregation, becomes an important means for the origin of the I and its religious meaning, and the latter finds its fulfillment in the correlation of man and God. The priest represents symbolically the purification, which the individual has to accomplish in himself by a penance which has its peak in confession.[46]

There are obviously major differences with regard to the content of Cohen's and Milbank's arguments. Indeed, implicit in each of their respective arguments for Judaism or Christianity is an argument against Christianity or against Judaism respectively. Each in fact argues that his own Jewish or Christian view is "true monotheism" while either Christianity or Judaism is not. In the context of his arguments about Ezekiel's notion of sacrifice, Cohen maintains that Ezekiel liberated sacrifice from what he argues are the idolatry and immorality intrinsic to Christianity.[47] So too, Milbank, though calling "the Old Testament" "the least legal of all legal codes," maintains that "Legality . . . even Jewish, is polytheist and not monotheist, because not diverse enough – not absolutely divine and so absolutely many-in-one."[48]

The issue of true monotheism and idolatry is for Cohen and Milbank each connected to their views of law. For Cohen, law remains the mark of true monotheism. Indeed, Ezekiel is both a prophet and a priest. Cohen contends, both explicitly and implicitly, that the making of the true individual can only occur within the broader context of law. Cohen reiterates in a number of contexts that the problems of sin and sacrifice are intimately connected to the law. It is in fact law that provides the analogy for confession, argues Cohen:

The way legal procedure shows us in the self-confession of guilt by the criminal is the right way. If the individual must have the knowledge of himself as the originator of his guilt, he also must acknowledge and confess himself to be such. . . . [But l]egal procedure cannot be extended to the embarrassing conflicts of the human heart. Where is there an analogy to legal procedure? The return would remain merely a word of admonition, and the confession of guilt, too, would not become an actuality were it not joined to a public institution.[49]

Milbank denies precisely the connection between the law and atonement:

as Paul puts it in Galatians (Gal. 3:10–12), to be under the law is to be under a curse; to remain in the place of cursed impurity, and to have the threat of further slander hanging always over our heads. Whereas if we fail to receive divine grace and to be simultaneously gracious to others, still no judgment, no punishment from God follows: simply we do not receive anything more, we are self-judged, alone, in hell.[50]

## V. Conclusion: on the ethical and theological possibilities of "secular culture"

The differences between Milbank and Cohen are no doubt profound. However, when we began this essay we may have said their differences reflect different assumptions about "secular reason" and modernity. We see now, however, upon further exploration of the premises of each of their thoughts, that their differences are more appropriately described as differences between modern Christian and Jewish polemics about the modern meanings of Christianity and Judaism as well as about the relation between them. Despite his arguments to the contrary, Milbank's project is embedded in the "secular reason" he criticizes so scathingly. The notion that there is a peace, freedom or morality beyond the coercion of law is a distinctly modern idea that is made possible by way of modern notions of autonomous individuals whose freedom and morality exist outside of coercive social structures. Significantly, these notions are also predicated upon an at least historically problematic reading of Paul that posits an absolute dichotomy between grace and law. Kant and Milbank perpetuate this false dichotomy while Cohen attempts to reject it but nonetheless internalizes its fundamental premises within his conception of law.

While this modern utopian notion of the free individual is implicit in both Cohen's and Milbank's thought, they each attempt to reorient modern notions of individuality by way of their respective arguments about the Jewish and Christian communities. Milbank and Cohen argue that Christianity and Judaism respectively transform the modern autonomous individual, and hence by implication offer a critique of modern individuality. But, as I have argued, each of their thoughts is predicated on a particularly modern attempt to argue for a non-coercive sphere in regard to law. Milbank's postmodern attempt to argue for a Christian difference beyond secular reason has much in common with Cohen's modern attempt to argue for Jewish difference as religion of reason. Both are attempts to argue for the relevance of Christianity or Judaism respectively for the ethical and political transformation of modern secular culture.

And it is on the social and political implications of Cohen's and Milbank's thought that we come to a particular irony. If, as I have argued throughout this chapter, Milbank's theology remains, despite Milbank's arguments to the contrary, implicated in what he calls "secular reason," it may be that Milbank's theological project has an important affinity with late nineteenth-century arguments for ethical monotheism. Milbank would certainly reject the suggestion that his thought bears an affinity to ethical monotheism, certainly to the Jewish neo-Kantianism of Hermann Cohen, but also, as he himself details in particular, to the ethical monotheism of Cohen's Christian contemporary, Ernst Troeltsch. Let us consider the following description of ethical monotheism, used to describe Cohen and Troeltsch together. Ethical monotheism is "a religious concentration and intensity that focuses singular attention on God in contrast to other creaturely reality." Moreover, the ethical monotheist maintains "an inclusive interest in culture and society and insist[s] that ethical monotheistic faith energizes the construction of culture."[51] Once we see that Milbank's theology is implicated in the "secular reason" that he describes, we see that Milbank too fits this description.

Should we subject Milbank's theology to the same scathing description of Troeltsch that Milbank himself provides? Milbank writes:

> both Troeltsch and Weber create a "sociology" which is nothing but a spurious promotion of what they study – namely the secular culture of modernity. What is ultimately crucial in their accounts is their integrity of private will respecting the freedom of others (whether in a Kantian "monotheist" or Nietzschean "polytheist" fashion) and on the other hand, the Machiavellian sphere of political "rationality". What is squeezed out in between is, not accidentally, Christianity, and by this I mean a sphere for the operation of charity.[52]

Is Milbank's also "a spurious promotion of . . . the secular culture of modernity"? Answering this question in the affirmative would only further the false dichotomy that Milbank presents between "secular" and "theological" reason. We might ask instead whether the "Christian difference" that Milbank strives for requires a renunciation of "secular reason." Indeed, Milbank maintains that Christian difference can emerge *only through* such a renunciation. And as Milbank argues in great detail in *Theology and Social Theory*, Christian sociology marks precisely this renunciation.

The task of such a theology [Christian sociology] is . . . to tell again the

Christian *mythos*, pronounce again the Christian logos, and call again for Christian *praxis* in a manner that restores their freshness and originality. It must articulate Christian difference in such a fashion as to make it strange.[53]

Ironically, Cohen's Jewish ethical monotheism (in contrast to Troetsch's Christian ethical monotheism) may offer Milbank a model of an argument for difference within "secular reason." Once again, Cohen makes this argument for Jewish difference, what Cohen calls "Jewish isolation," in the context of his argument about the significance of Jewish law. Cohen writes:

> The continuation of the religion of the Jewish monotheism is therefore bound to the continuation of the law in accordance with its general concept – not to the particular laws – because the law makes possible that isolation which seems indispensable to the care for, and continuation of, what is, at once, one's own and eternal.
> Isolation in the world of culture! . . . Monotheism is at stake. . . . With monotheism, the world of culture is at stake. . . . Therefore, isolation is indispensable to Judaism, for its concept as well as for its cultural work.[54]

To put Cohen's argument into Milbank's terms, Cohen contends that it is only possible to tell again the Jewish mythos, to pronounce again the Jewish logos, by way of Jewish law. The law itself is the form of the mythos; it is its very grammar. Ironically, Cohen's position on the law as the grammar of Jewish life may be more in keeping with the historical Paul's view of the law, though not of course with the historical Protestant Church's view. I conclude merely with the suggestion that an engagement with Cohen's distinctly Jewish and modern thought might provide Milbank with an unlikely resource for rethinking Christian difference.

## Notes

1  John Milbank, *Theology and Social Theory: Beyond Secular Reason* (Oxford: Blackwell, 1990), p. 1.
2  John Milbank, *The Word Made Strange* (Oxford: Blackwell, 1997).
3  *Theology and Social Theory*, p. 5.
4  Hermann Cohen, *Das Prinzip der Infinitesimal-Methode und seine Geschichte*, Einleitung von Peter Schulthess in *Werke*, hg. vom Hermann-Cohen-Archiv am Philosophischen Seminar Zürich unter der Leitung von Helmut Holzhey (Hildesheim: G. Olms, 1984), bd. 5, p. 6.
5  There is a long debate about whether Cohen's arguments in *Religion of Reason* break with his system, although Cohen argued that they did not and there are good philosophical grounds for this position. Franz Rosenzweig argued that Cohen's late philosophy constituted an existential break with his idealist system (see *Einleitung*, in Hermann Cohen, *Jüdische Schriften*, vol. 1 (Berlin, 1924). For an extended discussion of this debate see Andrea Poma's *The Critical Philosophy*

*of Hermann Cohen*, trans. by John Denton (Albany: State University of New York Press, 1997).

6    *Der Begriff der Religion im System der Philosophie* (Giessen: Töpelmann, 1915), pp. 5–6.

7    *Religion of Reason out of the Sources of Judaism*, trans. by Simon Kaplan (New York: Frederick Ungar, 1972), pp. 5–6.

8    *Religion of Reason*, p. 44.

9    Ibid., pp. 44–8.

10    Ibid., p. 7, emphasis in the original.

11    *The Word Made Strange*, p. 16

12    *Ethik des reinen Willen*, *Werke*, bd. 7, pp. 227–8.

13    Ibid., pp. 267–8.

14    All translations from the New Testament are taken from *The New Oxford Annotated Bible* (New York: Oxford University Press, 1973).

15    *Religion Within the Limits of Reason Alone*, trans. by Theodore M. Greene and Hoyt H. Hudson (New York: Harper & Brothers, 1960), p. 87; translation altered.

16    See J. B. Schneewind's *The Invention of Autonomy* (Cambridge: Cambridge University Press, 1998) for a broad view of the relation between Christian debates about law and the invention of the modern notion of autonomy as articulated most fully by Kant.

17    Of particular relevance for this essay is Schneewind's discussion of Luther, see *The Invention of Autonomy*, pp. 26–36.

18    John Gager, *Reinventing Paul* (Oxford: Oxford University Press, 2000). See in particular chapter 2, "New Views of Paul." See also Stanley Stowers, *A Rereading of Romans: Justice, Jews, and Gentiles* (New Haven: Yale University Press, 1994); Lloyd Gaston, *Paul and the Torah* (Vancouver: University of British Columbia Press, 1987); and Krister Stendahl, *Paul Among the Jews and Gentiles* (Philadelphia: Fortress Press, 1976).

19    See also Romans 3:1; 7:7; 7:12; 9:4; 11:1; 11:26; Galatians 3:21.

20    *Ethik des reinen Willen*, p. 270.

21    See *Theology and Social Theory*, ch. 4, "For and Against Hegel."

22    *Theology and Social Theory*, p. 391.

23    "The Name of Jesus," in *The Word Made Strange*, p. 153.

24    "The Name of Jesus," p. 156.

25    "Can Morality Be Christian," in *The Word Made Strange*, p. 231.

26    John R. Bowlin, "Augustine on Justifying Coercion," *The Annual of the Society of Christian Ethics* 17 (1997): 49–70. See also Peter Brown, "St. Augustine's Attitude to Religious Coercion," in *Religion and Society in the Age of Saint Augustine* (New York: Harper & Row, 1972).

27    See in particular *Theology and Social Theory*, pp. 417–22.

28    "Augustine on Justifying Coercion," p. 65.

29    Ibid., p. 66.

30    Though beyond the scope of this essay, I would argue that this "prejudice" affects most, if not all, modern Jewish philosophical conceptions of law, regardless of denominational affiliation. For example, the arguments of Joseph Soloveitchik, the foremost twentieth-century spokesperson for American modern orthodoxy, and Yeshayahu Leibowitz, the orthodox Israeli iconoclast, could easily be described according to this schema.

31    Moses Mendelssohn, *Jerusalem*, trans. by Allan Arkush (Hanover and London: University of New England Press, 1983).

32    See Cohen's discussion of Mendelssohn, in *Religion of Reason*, pp. 357–60.

33    Ibid., p. 357.

34    *Jerusalem*, p. 126.

35 Ibid., p. 73.
36 For a broad overview of traditional Jewish society, the use of coercion within that society, and ways in which the emergence of modern Jewish communities made the use of coercion no longer possible or necessary, see Jacob Katz, *Tradition and Crisis: Jewish Society at the End of the Middle Ages* (New York: Schocken Books, 1958).
37 *Phenomenology of Spirit*, trans. by A. V. Miller (New York and Oxford: Oxford University Press, 1977), pp. 406–7.
38 *Theology and Social Theory*, p. 170.
39 "Can Morality Be Christian?," p. 230.
40 Ibid., p. 226.
41 Ibid., p. 227.
42 *Religion of Reason*, pp. 13–15.
43 Ibid., pp. 167–8.
44 "The Name of Jesus," pp. 160–2.
45 *Religion of Reason*, p. 194.
46 Ibid., p. 200. See also Cohen's discussion of public worship, p. 218.
47 See for example *Religion of Reason*, p. 171.
48 "Can Morality Be Christian?," p. 222.
49 *Religion of Reason*, p. 195.
50 "Can Morality Be Christian?," p. 222.
51 Wendell Dietrich, *Cohen and Troeltsch* (Atlanta: Scholars Press, 1986), p. 1.
52 *Theology and Social Theory*, pp. 97–8.
53 Ibid., p. 381.
54 *Religion of Reason*, pp. 366–7. Cohen continues: "the value of the law is in no way exhausted by the negative movement of its isolation. Rather – and this cannot be grasped in its entire profundity by any outsider – inherent in the law, in its many forms and usages, is a positive force that stimulates, inspires, fortifies, and deepens religious ideas and beliefs" (p. 367).

# 6   On Whitehead's proposition "Life is robbery"

## Prolegomena to any future ethics

*Gregg Lambert*

## I

The proposition in question, "Life is robbery", appears in the third chapter of *Process and Reality*.[1] Because the sense of this statement appears truncated next to the complexity of the surrounding propositions, its simplicity is profound, as if the entire text was written to allow the force of this statement "Life is robbery" to deliver a shock. It is presented as the second principle characteristic of the psychological physiology of life in Whitehead's cosmological argument. The first characteristic of life is the reaction adapted to the capture of intensity in a variety of circumstances; the second characteristic is the definition of the capture of *intensity* as "robbery." We should recall here the chapter head is the "Order of Nature," which could also be understood as the description of the natural law that regulates the arrangement between different societies. A living society is situated in the "environment" of other societies, both organic and inorganic. According to Whitehead, the fundamental law of nature is robbery which is then *reactively adapted* by living societies into the form of a hierarchy; thus, the principle of robbery is distributed as the governing relation between different living societies through which the totality of nature is *ordered* (or to use more contemporary terminology, by which it achieves the form of a "structure"). "Thus," Whitehead states, "all [societies] require interplay with their environment; and in the case of living societies this interplay takes the form of robbery" (*PR* 105). In unpacking the sense of this proposition, we must attempt to think through the concept of "life" (defined elsewhere as the *novelty* of a conceptual reaction, or simply as *originality*) which is implied here in the metaphor of robbery.

The first characteristic of life is that of an *empty space*, metaphorically figured by the occasion of night. A robber "breaks in" usually under the cover of night. Night is not neutral to this occasion, but rather constitutes the medium that facilitates the act of robbery and even promotes its actualization by creating the possibilities of stealth, anonymity and concealment. The medium of night is neither inside nor outside, but rather lurks in the "interstices" that permeate the border from both directions, providing the opening through which the robber traverses into and out of another society. In other words, the robber occupies night as an empty space that he makes use of like a diamond stiletto in his "bid for freedom." (I will return to expand on this phrase later on.)

The second characteristic of life is *singularity*. However, this term must not be understood to refer to any unique trait or personality, but rather the sense of being an "outsider." It is first of all because the robber is not a member of a particular living society that he is endowed with the *freedom* to rob it as if to reaffirm the fact that he belongs to another nature and draws all his possibility and his power directly from the outside. Also, the fact that he is an outsider, or stranger, is what provides him with a cloak of anonymity (like the magical cloak of Gynges in the Platonic fable, or Dracula's cape, which in both cases make the wearer invisible).

The first two characteristics – "night" (or the characteristic of an *empty space*), "singularity" (or the characteristic of being an *outsider*) – combine in such a way that each refers to the other in the sense of being its condition or formal cause. The colloquial phrase "like a thief in the night" comes to mind to represent this intimacy. Whitehead states that life does not occur in the spaces already occupied by living societies but lurks in the interstices between societies; it approaches from an "empty space." Yet, it is only through this empty space and by this occasion of robbery that all living societies are first related to one another, or that a living society is put in touch with its environment through the act of robbing it and destroying the inorganic and organic societies that comprise its "food." Therefore, "the conclusion drawn from this argument is that life is a characteristic of 'empty space' and not of a space 'occupied' by any corpuscular society" (*PR* 105). If we were to illustrate this last statement further, we might refer to a game of chess and say that "life" would be the empty square and not the square occupied by any player. Yet, this might give us an insight into where to seek "life" should we ever desire to find it.

The third characteristic belongs to the event itself defined as robbery. In a certain sense, all robbery is destruction. Through the act of theft the robber destroys a relation of satisfaction that belonged to another society by "capturing" an *intensity* that can only exist within the immediacy of enjoyment. For example, the consumption of a morsel or the possession of an object both express a relationship to the present which itself is a vivid immediacy of satisfaction (intensity). Whitehead calls such an intensity "food" which can only be consumed or enjoyed in the present. As an aside, perhaps this explains the selection of certain ideal objects of theft (jewels, gold, objects of art), since they express an almost infinite quantity of satisfaction and promise a duration of enjoyment that lasts longer or achieves a present of the highest order of intensity. Here, we should also note how the principal distinction that determines the nature of the loss that occurs in the act of theft is temporal and conditions the intensity in terms of the presence or absence of a satisfaction (that is, its "vivid immediacy"). What is stolen is what the object only signifies: the satisfaction of a vivid immediacy that is torn into by the teeth or tightly clutched in the hand (or by the claws) and passes from one living society to another only by violence or force of coercion.

The fourth and final characteristic of "life" is *time*, which can be defined very simply in terms of the presence or absence of a vivid immediacy. What is remarkable about this simple distinction is that the future disappears as a temporal designation, or, more precisely, can only be understood as a modification of a past occasion, as the reaction to the loss of a vivid immediacy which Whitehead calls a "negative prehension." An intensity of satisfaction can only exist in relation to the vivid immediacy of the present; to situate it in the past is already to determine this intensity as "lost" or "destroyed," and this reaction itself expresses the relationship of the offended society to the present that now takes the form of a "negative prehension." Death can be understood, on the level of the organism, as a loss of interaction with the environment; in the human, this is represented as the loss of intensity and satisfaction of the present grasped as a "vivid immediacy." When we view a corpse, we understand very well that the "intensity" of a living relationship with the present is now in the past, just as the past covers the corpse with a blanket of anonymity and closes its eyes.

On the other hand, the robber who "clutches at a vivid immediacy" through the act of theft actually enjoys an original and "new" intensity as a super-added degree of his creative power; he appears as having *more life* in proportion to the offended society, which suddenly appears as having less (corollary states of intensity that Spinoza once defined as expressions of either "joy" or "sadness"). Thus, the intensity of satisfaction that formerly belonged to another society now belongs to the society of the robber. Whether or not this intensity is *proper* engages us in a question of morality that either justifies or fails to justify the theft. However, this does not change the temporal accent on the location of the present satisfaction, but rather makes it appear all the more acute. As Whitehead states, "It is at this point that with life morals become acute. The robber requires justification" (*PR* 105). For example, the offended society can always, in turn, rob from the robber by capturing and incarcerating him. The robber is thereby deprived of the "present" (its immediacy is now in the past, "when he was free") and here the robber is *justified* by the force of law. The act of incarceration corresponds exactly to the logic of Whitehead's statement and reveals the fact that the real issue for each living society is a "bid for freedom," and that it is really over the enjoyment of the present (i.e. the degree of power expressed by its vivid immediacy) that a violent struggle between living societies is constantly being waged.

We have thus defined the four principal characteristics of life in Whitehead's proposition "Life is robbery": first, the characteristic of an *empty space* between societies, that is to say, between a particular living society and all the other societies (both organic and inorganic) that constitute its "environment"; second, the characteristic of *singularity*, of being an "outsider," which simply entails not belonging to any society in particular; third, the characteristic pertaining to the event of life itself, the grasping of a vivid immediacy, or *intensity*, accompanied by the destruction of the same from the perspective of another living society; fourth, the characteristic of *time* defined by the presence or absence of a vivid immediacy, which occasions the past in the form of "negative prehension."

## II

In applying the above characteristics to the distinction between ethical and moral discourse in their respective treatment of "life," we might choose to focus on the fourth characteristic, the temporal difference that emerges in the act of *prehension* itself (specifically, its tendency to fall out of phase with itself, engendering the difference between the present prehension defined as a "vivid immediacy" and the past prehension defined as a "negative prehension"). Here, we might conclude that the current division between ethical and moral discourse, which can be traced back to Nietzsche's *Genealogy of Morals*, in actuality refers to this temporal distinction in the two phases of prehension. Whereas ethical discourse often concerns *potentia*, defined as *the power of acting*, strictly from the standpoint of the present (the prehension of a "vivid immediacy" whose goal is an increase of power), morality often concerns those occasions of theft and destruction that take the form of "negative prehensions" and assume the perspective of the past (or future) occasions which become part of a *tradition* (what Whitehead refers to as the historical order of the organism)? The distinguishing characteristic is the "reiteration of a past occasion" in which "action and reaction are bound together" (*PR* 104). In other words, morality views the agency of life from a reactive standpoint, the past, and it is only from this standpoint that "Life becomes questionable." As we will see, this is a problem, since the characteristics that define the agency of life (the capture of intensity) and the affective characteristics of originality and creativity that express the living society's degree of power (*potestas*) – that is, its capacity to act, to play in its environment, but also the capacity to be affected by other living societies – become "questionable" as well.

If life is fundamentally "a-social," as Whitehead argues, then it might appear to us that a morality that attempts to "socialize life" may fundamentally mischaracterize it. Gilles Deleuze gives an illustration of this in his reading of a similar point in Spinoza. In the act of raising my hands and striking an object there is nothing questionable and even represents a positive expression of enjoyment or satisfaction of the body and its capacity to act and to play with its environment. This act becomes questionable only when it is associated with the effect of striking certain specially defined objects – or perhaps more accurately, the association of a past occasion of being struck myself – which brings with it a prehension of violence or destruction that is "reactively adapted," so to speak, as the condition of raising my arms. This can be termed a "negative prehension" in Whitehead's sense. Thus, according to Deleuze's argument, in certain cases morality prevents the relationship to "life" by the creation of reactive consciousness and by the maintenance of "negative prehensions" in the tradition of the organism (in memory) both of which effectively "separate us from life by separating us from our power of acting, and keeping us separate from that power."[2]

Another, equally pressing, problem concerns us which is the following. If the relationship between living societies, or between a living society and its environment which is equally composed of organic and inorganic societies, is only mediated by this violence or interplay of theft and counter-theft, then does the restriction or repression of this violence actually result in a loss of relation between a living society and its environment. Employing White-head's own language again, all living societies need "food" (in the form of new and original intensities) and this food means nothing less than the destruction of other societies. Would the restraint or curtailment of eating result in a weakened and anorexic organism? If robbery is the only means of my relation to the environment, basically to the other societies that comprise my milieu, would this not constitute a loss of relationship with the environment? This might help to further clarify the phrase "life is robbery," meaning that life is robbery and nothing else besides. There is no neutral being called life, which then is defined as having the predicate of robbery. *There can be no life without robbery, and where there is no robbery, neither is there life.* Again, we must stress that Whitehead seems to be implying that life itself never belongs to any particular living society – another sense of its a-social nature – but only appears in the interstices between societies. It is always outside. This would mean that I am living only to the degree that I am related to this outside, open to it, and that it is through this "empty space" that life appears and reappears, establishing my connection with the environment.

According to Whitehead, therefore, life functions as a catalyst of the relationship between a living society and its environment even though this catalyst is a kind of robbery. It is only by robbing other societies that I live; it is only by the act of robbery that one living society is actually related to another. In a certain sense, if I wasn't robbing another living society or being robbed by another, I wouldn't have any basis for a knowledge (*conatus*) of that particular society. This truism will have important implications for science (the knowledge of the World), on the one hand, and theology (or the knowledge of God) on the other. One could go so far to say that science would not have any predisposition to explore the environment composed of organic and non-organic societies, if this relationship was not already established by the act of robbing them for its food, or, in turn, being robbed. Recalling our earlier example of an offended society that seeks to rob the robber of his "intensity," the same principle can be found to operate in the drive to cure cancer or any number of human diseases – as if to capture the intensity or "vivid immediacy" belonging to the living society composed of cancerous cells, or of a virus. In doing so, in finding a cure or an inoculation, does science reduce the virus to the status of "food"? Yes, but only to the degree that knowledge is also a kind of food, that is, knowing how to destroy or separate a particular living society from its power (*potentia*); in turn, this becomes the power of a particular living society over others that comprise its environment in the order of a hierarchy.

If this attribute does not appear, first of all, as a positive characteristic, but rather as something essentially negative and "improper" (as an intruder or a dangerous predator), perhaps this expresses its position in relation to the consciousness of our living society. Does this not imply that the human society perceives life as not part of its own society, but a shadowy figure "lurking in the interstices," as if viewing life from a perspective that is not-life, as death for example? Strictly speaking, however, there is no such thing as death, only robbery. What is death but the event where life robs a particular living society of its own satisfaction which reduces it again to the status of "food"? Rather, what this "improper" character reveals is the perception of a supreme apathy; life is inhuman, not for us, but for itself. It is essentially indifferent – even supremely indifferent! – with regard to this or that society. It is this indifference, wrongly depicted as cruelty or as malign evil, that reveals our reaction of terror in the face of life (fundamentally a "stranger") and which makes us fear it absolutely. Death, the absolute master? Not at all. However, it does no good to correct this misnomer by substituting the name of "Life" either. Here, we might recall the fragment by Heraclitus that Lacan once used to demonstrate the dialectical relationship between these two terms which often leads to a common confusion: "To the bow is given the name of Life (*Bios*) and its work is Death (*Thanatos*)."[3]

Most plots of science fiction and monster films can be seen as narrative representations of this terror, where we see a form of life that is absolutely indifferent to our own society and attempts to use our members as food. It is "science fiction" that most often touches upon the limit of our knowledge of life, that point where life itself becomes personified as a fictionalized subject who returns an indifferent gaze to our own living society, which it sees basically as its own food. We can refer to the film by Ridley Scott, *Alien* (1979), as a representative example of this fictionalized portrait of life, which one of the film's characters describes as "the pure instinct, unhampered by delusions of morality, whose purity of instinct is only matched by its hostility." Throughout the course of the film, each of the characters save one (Lt Ripley) is destroyed by the alien, who regards the human being as an external reproductive organ or uterus, in other words, as an "empty space" it can use in "its bid for freedom." This destruction seems innately justified by the explanation given above that the alien itself is merely the representation of a pure instinct devoid of consciousness (or "negative prehension"), the instinct (or drive) of sexual reproduction. Thus, it is important to note that the terrifying portrait first presented by this film constituted on the level of the narrative, in a certain sense, a problem that had to be resolved in the subsequent productions: the "negative prehension" that is implied in the representation of a pure sexual instinct (life), which always finds its satisfaction (or aim) in the death of a particular living society (the individual members of the species). In the second installment, directed by James Cameron, *Aliens* (1986), Lt Ripley returns as the personification of the maternal instinct of the human society, who engages in a genocidal conflict with the living society of aliens. In both these dramas, we can see vividly illustrated the accuracy of Whitehead's earlier statement that "the robber requires justification"; however, this requirement only seems to appear from the perspective of an offended society. For example, at a point in the second film, one of the characters poses a moral problem concerning Lt Ripley's genocidal desire, stating that neither she nor anyone else has the right to exterminate the entire species. In good heroic form, Lt Ripley's response is very simply, "Wrong! Just watch me."

At the same time, monsters in films are never fair representations of life. Rather, they are an attempt to grasp the purity of the intensity of life, but already take the form of negative prehension. Thus, benign indifference becomes cruelty; unconsciousness with regard to this or that living society becomes the willful destruction of all living societies that comprise a monster's immediate environment, which it perceives very much as an "empty space." Here, we often see this fictional portrait of life go out of its way to destroy certain living societies, as if willfully and knowingly robbing this or that particular society with a character of impunity. Likewise, modern scientific representations of nature attempt to portray this pure indifference, but often confuse the unconsciousness of life with a malevolent face of terror, as if there is a confused desire within the subject of science itself to represent a nature that seeks to annihilate a particular living society, to wipe it out, or eradicate it from the order of nature. Both of these representations of nature can only be an error caused by the "rationalization" on the part of the offended society that life must be willfully seeking its destruction; therefore, it is justified in arming itself to the teeth and, by opposing life, taking steps to end the robber's reign of tyranny.

If historical religions have often split life into two distinct personalities, one represented by pure tyranny and malevolence, and the other, a benevolent King who seeks to conserve certain living societies (often by destroying others in the name of love or favor), this is because the power of nature or life (*potentia*) is confused with a particular "negative prehension" caused by our "reaction" to this power which imbues it with the attributes of a conscious will (whether this will is expressed in terms of destruction and malign hatred, or in terms of favor and benevolent love). It was Spinoza, whose philosophy of nature Whitehead follows in many respects, who first argued that the power of nature (of pure life) must never be attached to an aspect of will, which is anthropomorphic. God does not conceive of possibilities in his intellect, which he would then realize through his will. Thus, he denied that God (or nature) had any power (*potestas*) that could be analogous to that of a tyrant, or for the same reason to that of a good or enlightened despot.[4]

What theological cosmology depicted as God is nothing less than a pre-scientific portrait of the principle of life. This depiction was an attempt to paint a more tolerable portrait, one that worked to the benefit of a particular living society, which resolves in a certain sense the charge of anthropocentrism by giving it a species justification. Can the replacement of theological by a scientific cosmology reveal the essence of the conflict between these two determinations of "Life," that point where science desires to attain a knowledge of life outside the closed circle of our own species, in short, to achieve the perspective or point of view of God or nature itself? Perhaps, even so, the barrier to this knowledge is the presence of a subject who must "react" to this view with either terror or acceptance, which Whitehead calls the "subjective form of prehension," or consciousness. This is the final and perhaps immovable barrier which poses the greatest obstacle for the subject of science today, in which consciousness itself often appears as fundamental impurity that ruins all equations and prevents it from attaining true satisfaction in its knowledge of nature. It is for this reason, as Lacan has suggested, that the desire of modern science to rid itself of consciousness has inversely taken the form of a desire it sometimes "discovers" in nature to rid itself of a particular living society which represents the final, albeit extreme, solution to the mind–body problem first introduced by Descartes. Therefore, despite its goal to capture the prehension of "Life itself" – where knowledge (*conatus*) is identical to power (*potentia*) – the subject of science still represents the conservative impulses of an organism or particular living society. Thus, any knowledge it obtains of the malevolent design of nature (basically, any other living societies that might pose a threat of robbery) is immediately deployed in a search-and-destroy mission as if against a potential enemy. This sets the stage for the hostile and paranoid relationship between a particular living society and its environment which is the characteristic trait of our species today under the dominance of a scientific cosmology which has replaced earlier religious cosmologies. This is not to say that historical religions don't still exert a considerable influence today, only that it is modern science that mediates our relationship to the environment and to the other living societies that comprise it.

## III

The above discussion might help to clarify what seemed to be an odd moment in Whitehead's own discussion. If robbery is the *order* of nature, why is it then in what Whitehead calls the higher phases of living societies that this order first appears questionable (although, even then, only in relation to certain societies and in certain occasions)? Whitehead's use of the phrase "in its bid for freedom" is interesting in this regard. Life is always described as seeking out a state of greater freedom, of new intensities and original occasions. Freedom is defined as the enjoyment of a "vivid immediacy," and life always seeks this intensity most of all. That is, it seeks more – always more – and clutches those occasions of intensity as always already belonging to it by right. However, it is also here that this bid seems to require justification. Where, or from the perspective of which living society, does this requirement enter in? This might explain its temporal character: rather than occupying a pure present and consuming itself in instinct, it reflects on the present from the standpoint of the past. This underlines the ethical characteristic which reflects on an action from the perspective of the living societies it destroys in its "bid for freedom," allowing a moment of reflective judgement to intervene between the living society and its environment to evaluate, weigh and judge its living occasions with its environment that is composed of other societies. It is in this second sense where "Life becomes questionable," meaning that it becomes sensible, reflective, thoughtful. But why, in the higher phases of societies, would this become a factor in inhibiting the full expression of life?

In responding to the question, perhaps this again expresses the fundamental relationship between ethics and the character of human time, since it is only by this dual relationship that a present becomes reflected in the past and becomes a moment of consciousness, where life is split between action and reaction, where life is separated from itself and what it *can* do. Does this imply that in human societies life attains a level of consciousness that is reactive, as if becoming subject to its own violence, or becoming reflective and sensible concerning its own power to rob other living societies that comprise its environment? If so, then this would reintroduce the possibility of a teleological design into the *order* of nature, as if in the higher phases of living societies life is destined to become conscious of itself *qua* subject. A certain Hegelianism must be subtracted from the last statement, since in Hegel the concept of "subject" retains the conservative spirit of an internalized past, of a spirit that is *for itself* but only in the sense that it conserves its own identity throughout all its occasions. Whitehead notes at several points that life is in no way conservative (meaning also that it does not seek to retain or conserve a past), but is essentially destructive. It is only from the perspective of a closed or living society that the need for conservation appears. This returns us again to the subjective feeling of terror that is revealed differently by the knowledges of science and theology.

After addressing the relationship between the law of nature (robbery) and the problem this poses for ethics where this law becomes "questionable," Whitehead immediately discusses the theological personality of God as an expression of this terror and this schism.

> The primordial appetitions which jointly constitute God's purpose are seeking intensity [again, according to the first characteristic of life], *and not preservation* [my emphasis]. Because they are primordial, there is

nothing to preserve. He, in his primordial nature, is unmoved by love for this particular, or that particular; for in his foundational process of creativity, *there are no pre-constituted particulars* [my emphasis]. In the foundation of his being, God is indifferent alike to preservation and to novelty. He cares not whether an immediate occasion be old or new, so far as concerns the derivation of its ancestry. His aim for it is depth of satisfaction as an intermediate step toward the fulfillment of his own being. His tenderness is directed toward each actual occasion, as it arises.

(*PR* 105)

We might see in the above portrait of a God who "gives no thought for this or that particular" (whether we are speaking here of this particular individual, or that particular living society) that there is good reason for terror, that is, to view this God with "fear and trembling." Moreover, in the temporality that defines the moment of creation, which is infinite, our living society does not even exist, since Whitehead states that for God there are "no pre-constituted particulars." God is unconscious; in other words, his gaze looks right through our particular society for the elements that will further the perfection of his own nature. (This is a gaze, as I have discussed above, that science has attempted to depict by describing the universe in which the human is only a relative society amid others societies, both organic and inorganic, within a total process.) Therefore, in the process of creation where there are "no pre-constituted particulars," the moment of creative spontaneity must occur without what Whitehead calls the "shackle of the reiteration of the past." Although this might appear from the perspective of the living society of the human as indifference, uncaring ignorance, even unconsciousness, Whitehead does not paint a picture of a God who is absolutely devoid of "feeling." On the contrary, God expresses tenderness (even love) only toward his own being through the intermediary of each actual occasion as it arises. One might understand this as primordial narcissism, something that Schelling had also remarked as the underlying trait of God's primary nature, which would again underline the "a-social" characteristic that lies at the basis of God's creative process.

The Christian doctrine "God is love," therefore, offers a strange justification for the robber. Rather than being a moral love, perhaps this would be a love that contemporary psychoanalysis is in a better place to teach us something about. Whitehead describes this love in the following manner:

It does not emphasize the ruling Caesar, or the ruthless moralist, or the unmoved mover. It dwells upon the tender elements in the world, which slowly and in quietness operate by love; and it finds its purpose in the present immediacy of a kingdom not of this world. Love neither rules,

nor is it unmoved; also it is a little oblivious as to morals. It does not look
to the future; for it finds its own reward in the immediate present.

(*PR* 343)

Immediately preceding this passage, Whitehead refers to this concept of
"Love" as the law of nature under what he calls the "Galilean origin of
Christianity" which does not fit very well with the other major doctrinal
conceptions of God: as despot (Caesar), as law-giver or sovereign ("ruthless
moralist") and as transcendent creator and eminently real ("the unmoved
mover"). However, in Whitehead's hands, the somewhat chaste portrait of
love (as *agape*) that one finds in the gospels has been tempered by *The Song of
Solomon* and by Spinoza's *Ethics*, both of which address the first principle of
the universe under the command of erotic love. It is only in this manner that
we might begin to comprehend the aim of Life as "clutching after a vivid
immediacy," as "a bid for freedom," as a kind of "robbery." It is only a lover
who knows these feelings of power and intensity. And according to Whitehead, it is only a lover who knows the nature of God, for "He is the lure for
feeling, the eternal urge of desire. His particular relevance to each creative
act, as it arises from its own conditioned standpoint in the world, constitutes
him the initial 'object of desire' establishing the initial phase of each subject
aim" (*PR* 344). But this last statement would imply that God is the initial aim
of every particular desire, and it is because of the inherent polymorphous
nature of desire – and by this I mean the desire of every living society – that
we might understand that this first principle is "somewhat oblivious as to
morals," and consequently, a question for ethics.

In conclusion, Gilles Deleuze once remarked that Spinoza was the "Christ
of philosophers."[5] If this is so, then from the above passage we might have
good reason to call Whitehead our "Paul." For, like Paul, he sought to present the law of nature although, unlike Paul, according to the gospel of
Spinoza. Accordingly, the law of nature is not the law of Caesar, the law of
Calvin or Luther, nor even the law of Aquinas (or Aristotle). One thing is
certain. God does not love us, any more than he loves the cells in our bodies
(even the cancerous ones), or the electrons and protons that make up these
cells. It might be more accurate to say that *God loves the universe . . . himself.*
It is only in this sense that he can be described as the principle of universal
love. But, then, what kind of love is this? According to Whitehead's portrait,
it would be selfish, sometimes unkind, although never intentionally cruel, or
simply oblivious to the moral prehensions of a particular living society.
Nevertheless, this Love suffers long and is tender; it bears all things, believes
in all things, and endures all things. It does not rejoice in inequity, nor think
any evil, but does not rejoice in the truth either – if we mean by this *our* truth.
Are we in a better place today to justify his love? This, in my view, would be
the first question of any future ethics.

## Notes

1 Alfred North Whitehead, *Process and Reality* (New York: The Free Press, 1978), pp. 83–109. Hereafter abbreviated in the text as *PR* with page number(s) in parentheses.
2 Gilles Deleuze, *Spinoza: Practical Philosophy*, trans. Robert Hurley (San Francisco: City Lights, 1988), p. 27.
3 Jacques Lacan, *The Four Fundamental Concepts of Psychoanalysis*, trans. Alan Sheridan (New York: W. W. Norton, 1977), p. 177.
4 Baruch Spinoza, *Ethics*, trans. Samuel Shirley (London: Hackett, 1982), I: 34.
5 Gilles Deleuze and Félix Guattari, *What Is Philosophy?*, trans. Hugh Tomlinson and Graham Burchell (New York: Columbia University Press, 1994), p. 60.

# 7   Saying Kaddish for Gillian Rose, or on Levinas and *Geltungsphilosophie*

*Martin Kavka*

> For [the noble] desires his enemy for himself, as his mark of distinction; he can endure no other enemy than one in whom there is nothing to despise and *very much* to honor!
>
> Nietzsche, *On The Genealogy of Morals* I: 10

One might have foreseen that it would be almost impossible to remember Gillian Rose (1947–95) in such a way as to render her the honor due her. It is difficult for memory to lock on to a writer who oscillates between polemic and tenderness, between the most infuriating of generalizations and the most attentive of close readings. It is even more difficult when this constant change in tone appears to be, intentionally, at the core of her thinking. Throughout her polemical rejections of postmodernism and modern Jewish thought, she hearkens back to a Hegel who argues that the life of spirit is "a ceaseless comedy, according to which our aims and outcomes constantly mismatch each other, and provoke yet another revised aim, action, and discordant outcome . . . comprehension is always provisional and preliminary."[1]

In one sense, her death, and the religious narrative in which it is embedded, is the most comic expression of the constant renegotiation of life's projects in the face of the discord of violence and loss which, for her, characterizes the world and its necessary institutions. The story of her religious life is now somewhat well known. Rose was ethnically Jewish, and she published essays on Jewish philosophers, on the Holocaust and on the nature of halakha (Jewish law) from the mid-1980s onward. These essays, collected in *Judaism and Modernity*, and partially reproduced in the last chapter of *The Broken Middle*, are not easy to read. This is not necessarily because her work is difficult, although this is certainly the case. Rather, it is *emotionally* difficult to read: with laser-beam intensity, she deploys an all-encompassing critique of Jewish philosophy. There is little hope for Judaism in her work. She insists that modern Jewish thought must sunder its formalist attachment to Jerusalem as the sheer other of Athens and embrace the messiness of political jurisprudence, and organizing itself around concrete halakhic rulings. On the flip side, Rose doubts whether such a move is really possible, since halakha has no means of concretely addressing the institutional struggles (e.g. over gender inequality) within the political history of Judaism.[2] What Judaism needs, in her eyes, is a view of its own tradition as the development of a trans-historical (Hegelian) spirit within history. However, the tradition of Jewish thought currently dominant in the academy (responding to the Neo-Kantian liberalism of Hermann Cohen), resists appropriations of Hegel, in part due to anti-Judaic elements in his writings. The tension between Rose's desire to identify as a Jew and her philosophical impossibility to do so resolved itself as she was dying of ovarian cancer in late 1995. On her deathbed, she decided to convert to Christianity, and was baptized and confirmed by the Bishop of Coventry a few hours before her death.[3] She wanted to celebrate her conversion in the midst of her community of friends. Yet she died too soon for this; her baptism was sudden and private. The celebration, as the Archbishop of Canterbury reports, was one of tears and rejoicing.

To honor Gillian Rose after her death, it is necessary to remember this death as the culmination of her Hegelian comedy. Yet none of the published remembrances of her which I have been able to find reflect this. Arnold Wolf openly refers to her life and her death as a tragedy. Perhaps Wolf only means this in the ordinary sense of the term. Yet the Hegelian overtones of tragedy only serve to imply that Wolf perceives Rose to have died alienated from her work, unreconciled, ruined by the hostile expression of her own self-certainty which prohibited her from recognizing herself, in Judaism.[4] Rose would have to accept this as an insult. If her death is the culmination of her comedy, it is the culmination of divine comedy. She must have seen her death in accordance with Hegel's *Aesthetics*, as a manifestation of "the Divine here in its community, as the substance and aim of human individuality."

Nevertheless, one wonders if the Archbishop of Canterbury has done any better than Wolf. He writes that, during her near-death baptism, "she could only make responses with a squeeze of the hand and then she went to meet her Maker, her Saviour, and her true Lover." If this *is* part of the story, it is *only* part of the story. In equating death with the freedom from the pain of spatiotemporal existence, the Archbishop risks recasting Rose's death as a "flight from the finite" – the very Fichtean position that Hegel critiqued in his own philosophy of religion, as Rose demonstrated in her best book, *Hegel Contra Sociology*.[5] To die in Christ, for Hegel, is not simply to fall into the infinite. While incarnation is the *Aufhebung* of the tragic separation between the finite and the infinite, this incarnation means *nothing* without community and its institutions. Christ's death is taken up into the third person of the Trinity; Hegelian Spirit is present as "the universal self-consciousness of the community."[6] This is not simply the community of the Church, but the community of the State and all its citizens in which individuals are able to repeat the actions of Christ and sanctify the world only through the political and legal conditions which enable this repetition to occur.[7] To be blunt, Rose's Hegelianism forbids us to see her death within a discourse of consolation.

Both Wolf and the Archbishop of Canterbury are at fault when they make

Rose's death the result of an individual tragedy (as Wolf does) or of an individual interior quest which can then be imitated by the audience of the Archbishop's sermons in their own interior spaces. Rose's death is relational in a much more intimate fashion. As Christians believe Christ to have died for us, so did Rose in as dense an act of *imitatio Christi* as any of which I know. The death of a messianic figure was wholly unanticipated in the context of the messianic ideologies of the Second Temple period,[8] yet willingly embraced by Jesus in the garden of Gethesemane. Rose's death as a Christian was wholly unanticipated except to her confessor, and willingly embraced in her belief that death is something representable and immanent, concretely meaningful.[9] In this repetition of the death of Jesus of Nazareth, Rose's audience, as Jesus', is those whom she spurned. If the death of Jesus of Nazareth is for Hegel part of the "*Bildung*, formation or education, which is intrinsic to the phenomenological process,"[10] then the death of Rose, when seen in the context of Hegelian comedy, must be our formation and education. Who learns here? Certainly not only Christians, but also the non-believers who were at her post-death celebration . . . and her Jewish audience. To answer in any other way is to betray the friends she had during her life, the very friends who were surprised by the conversion, came to realize that they had misrecognized Rose, and thereby entered into the comic drama.

A resistance to this answer on the part of Jews is inevitable, and Christians who forswear the mission to the Jews can empathize with it. As Martin Jay writes,

> Although a nonobservant Jew unperturbed by any disaffection from the tenets of Judaism, I cannot avoid an involuntary shudder at the news of a positive decision to convert to another religion. I am unable to throw off the troubling memory of nearly two thousand years of eager attempts to convert Jews to Christianity, either through persuasion or coercion, attempts that are intimately related to the sorry history of antisemitism.[11]

I share in Jay's shudder. Indeed, I think that the recent contretemps over the conversion of Edith Stein, at the time of her canonization by Pope John Paul II, is of little magnitude compared to the difficulty with which Judaism is faced in Gillian Rose. For Stein's decision to convert was based on a mystical experience which occurred during her reading of the autobiography of St Teresa of Avila. Completely interior, this experience cannot call forth any response from Jews (or from adherents of any other religious tradition). There is no satisfactory explanation for her conversion. On the other hand, from the evidence of Rose's published writings, her conversion is completely dissimilar to Stein's. It is philosophically justified: Rose's conversion is the result of her passionate attachment to a Hegelian view of the world, her dismissal of modern and postmodern Jewish philosophy, and her struggles with the halakhic life. For Jews not to respond in this instance – to run away into the safe space of pietism or to conclude that "it is not for us to judge matters of identity"[12] – is to cede the territory of philosophy to Christianity, and to inaugurate a path which can only end in the loss of the relevance of university chairs in Judaica and in the return of the asymmetrical power dynamics of medieval disputations. The threat and urgency of this conflict are only heightened for those Jews (and here I include myself) who see themselves as converts from Christianity to Judaism and who made this decision on the basis of a philosophical argument – perhaps the very neo-Kantian arguments about the nature of secular reasoning which Rose excoriates in all of her writings from *Hegel Contra Sociology* onwards.

So the deep problem of Rose's conversion must be answered. However, a sheerly negative response by Jews would be naïve. For a Jewish apostate is "always a Jew nonetheless."[13] There is no reason why Rose, with her knowledge of halakhah, should have been obligated to see her decision to convert as a decision to leave behind her Jewish identity. Additionally, there is nothing in the entirety of her published work (which is the only resource Jews have for their response) that implies that her conversion would have had anything to do with the putative messianic force of Jesus of Nazareth. Rose's Christianity must always transcend the picture-thinking (*Vorstellung*) of the New Testament. Throughout her career, she critiqued models of Christianity and Judaism which failed to express the belonging-together of transcendence and immanence, of God and man, that she found in Hegel. In *Hegel Contra Sociology*, she correctly states that Hegel's account of religion fails to be a complete recognition of the unity of absolute infinite truth and the finite medium which represents that truth, since Hegelian Christianity (and, of course, other religions) misrepresents this recognition "as occurring in a world distinct from the world of real social and political relations, as occurring in heaven."[14] The path to achieving absolute religion and full mutual recognition in "the knowledge that the isolated individual is God, and that God is finite man," however, is stymied by Hegel's inability to adequately represent this recognition, to utter the absolute in anything except abstract language which falls prey to the very problem of *Vorstellung* from which the attempt to think the absolute is trying to extricate itself.[15]

Rose thus argues that recognition is always inextricably intertwined with misrecognition. This agon between the infinite and the finite, insofar as it enacts itself in the conflicts between various finite agents, is the truth of the Hegelian system. The phenomenological path for Hegel thus never has the static predictable quality of classical and postmodern teleologies, because the cognitive intent never directly fulfills itself. The place *toward* which it aims has no different hierarchical value than the place *from* which it aims, as opposed to the teleological models of Aristotle, Hermann Cohen or (for most) Levinas, which narrate the path by which the individual achieves intellectual and moral perfection. Instead, self-consciousness "comes up against, again and again, its own positing of the world, discovering outcomes the inverse of what it intended."[16] As a result, "to fix our relation in domination or dependence is unstable and reversible, to fix it as 'the world' is to attempt to avoid these reverses."[17] This anti-foundationalist reading of Hegel is, by now, common. Another Hegel scholar who seeks to save Hegel from the charges of foundationalism and violence, Robert R. Williams, writes that

> For Hegel any divine comedy is found in and therefore is *inseparable* from the infinite anguish of Good Friday. The metaphysical tradition, under the domination of abstract impassible identity, separated the divine from the human, the comic from the tragic.[18]

Rose sees this agonistic structure everywhere in existence. In the public sphere, the desire to act ethically toward the neighbor is always ensconced in violence, and freedom always operates within prior constraints and in complicity with the coercive constraints which the order of law places on others in the world.[19] In the private sphere, the impulse for erotic love can never be separated from the fear of the loss of the relationship in which that impulse enacts itself. Eros, like philosophy, is risk: "that mix of exposure and reserve, of revelation and reticence . . . we are at the mercy of others and we have others at our mercy."[20] The development of the self occurs not through an extirpation of its vulnerability, but in a tarrying with vulnerability that serves to negotiate the self through the labor of life and love. The ultimate value of living is the knowledge that the self is "decrepit nature yet supernature in one." In spite of the passivity which we are insofar as we are conditioned by the world, it is just as much the case that we are the activity (or "activity beyond activity," as Rose writes in her inversion of the Levinasian "passivity beyond passivity") of Nietzschean nobles that risks partaking in the order of law and its violence in order to love truly and fully. It is this insight that allows one to accept and endure the fact of death and the pain of dying, to "move beyond eternal loss to eternal confirmation."[21]

Rose sees this structure nowhere in Judaism. Orthodox Judaism hastily resolves the agon between the natural and supernatural elements of being human, between freedom and constraint, by opting for the natural: Rose's first teacher, Julius Carlebach, told her that "an Orthodox Jew doesn't need to worry about whether he believes in God or not, as long as he observes the law."[22] (It is precisely this naturalized epistemology of halakhah which makes it absolute, unrevisable and forever the enemy of those Jews who are not heterosexual males.) Liberal Judaism, on the other hand, prematurely resolves the agon of existence by constructing theologies around an absolutely transcendent God who is absolutely unknowable and wholly other. This idea has no content for consciousness, being purely "in-itself," completely abstract and hence, for Hegel, lacking real existence.[23] This is nihilistic, and while it is not the only species of nihilism which Rose treats in her work – in the 1984 *Dialectic of Nihilism*, Rose has not made the Jewish turn but focuses her critique on the postmodern thinkers who come from a broadly construed neo-Kantian and phenomenological heritage (Heidegger, Deleuze, Derrida, Foucault) – it is the case that after she begins writing on the other-centered ethics of the Jewish phenomenologist Emmanuel Levinas in the early 1990s, nihilism is primarily Jewish nihilism.[24] Levinasian Judaism, the Judaism which sees itself as "the sublime other of modernity" (a phrase which can be equally used to describe the anti-Hegelian portrait of liberal Judaism found in Hermann Cohen's posthumously published *Religion of Reason Out of the Sources of Judaism* as well as the ultra-Orthodox polemics in the early nineteenth century written by such rabbis as Moses Sofer[25]), is a "Buddhist Judaism." If this is Judaism, then Jews deserve the rancor of Nietzsche's critique in *On the Genealogy of Morals*: "to command me to sacrifice myself in sublime passivity for the other, with no political expression for any activity, is to command in *ressentiment*." Moreover, there is nothing which justifies this religion, for it proceeds "without evidence."[26] The Hegelian critique of Levinas is damning, and no scholar of modern Jewish thought or of postmodernism can afford to ignore it. It is not mere and empty polemic; the reader of Rose can reconstruct her critique of Levinas in the following five steps.[27]

1  Levinas separates the violence of ontology in the order of being from the realm beyond being (*epekeina tēs ousias*) which absolutely transcends it.
2  Due to this separation, the absolute beyond being is never knowable, never graspable. It never makes itself present, but only announces indirectly and enigmatically that it has already passed. Consciousness can never meet it face to face.
3  Without knowledge of the absolute, there is no possibility for consciousness to formulate moral imperatives. For knowledge of the absolute, according to Hegel, depends upon recognizing our subjective situation as a determining factor of our acts. Levinas's absolute, being purely transcendent and holy, has no relation to the real world in which we live and breathe.[28]
4  If consciousness does not have the power to formulate moral imperatives, it certainly cannot have the power to act morally. The Levinasian hope for utopia is thus only a fantasy.
5  Additionally, without knowledge of the absolute through either speculative philosophy, natural theology or natural law, it is impossible for Jews to represent the divine will through the development of halakhic jurisprudence. The Levinasian project for a resuscitated Judaism as the completely democratic community fails.

The latter half of *Judaism and Modernity* is a numbing repetition of this argument, applied *pari passu* across the German–Jewish philosophy of the early twentieth century. Rose offers no hope for Judaism from either the American Jewish philosophical tradition, medieval Jewish philosophy, or rabbinic texts.

So it should not be surprising to read of Rose's deathbed conversion. But I would like to suggest that Jews can redeem it by receiving her Hegelian outlook in an erotic embrace. As a philosopher, Rose was unable to recognize her own personal attachment to a certain interpretation of Hegel in the Continental Jewish philosophy to which she was drawn. The account of the sheer transcendence of otherness in her reading of the recent anti-rational strand of Jewish philosophy of religion – echoed in her ravaging critique of post-Holocaust accounts of Jewish religion (e.g. Elie Wiesel, Robert Jan van Pelt) that make catastrophe and destruction the source of transcendent meaning[29] – fails to recognize that identity and otherness always coexist within each and every individual.

> The other is never simply other, but an implicated self-relation. This applies to oneself as other and, equally, to any opposing self-consciousness: my relation to myself is mediated by what I recognise or refuse to recognise in your relation to yourself; while your self-relation depends on what you recognise of my relation to myself. *We are both equally enraged and invested.*[30]

The appearance of otherness, on this reading, would thus already be grounded on an analogical identity between two selves who are engaged in the lifelong process of educating themselves through reconciling the oppositions which the individual understanding constructs within its political and social context. There can be no recognition between this concept of otherness as already a self-relation and the account of otherness in current Continentally infected Jewish thought, in which alterity is transcendence. However, Rose's account of the relationship between identity and otherness is also an account of eros, a "yawning rent of yearning" which "translates the beginning of anxiety, delicate and agitating, into the anxiety of beginning – into politics, erotic and riskful."[31] Eros, for Rose, knows its own dialectic of love and loss in its act of riskful self-positing. The relationship of complete misrecognition between her Hegelian leanings and Jewish philosophy/halakhah led to the ultimate riskful erotic act – the conversion which allegedly brought her to "her true Lover."

Nevertheless, this cannot be the end of the narrative, since the relationship of misrecognition which led to her conversion was asymmetrical. She came to know herself through refusing the self-recognition of Continental post-Holocaust Jewish philosophy. Yet Jewish philosophy has not come to know itself by mediating its own self-relation through her writings. Only when this occurs, only when Jewish philosophers anxiously begin to read her writings, can her death become the expression of Hegelian comedy as a relationship of both misrecognition and recognition. Gillian Rose, in effect, has laid down the gauntlet to Jewish philosophy with the following question. As long as Judaism portrays a relationship with the Absolute in tatters and ruins, and, in gnostic desire, expresses a yearning for holiness that is divorced from politics and the goodness of the created world, then why not convert to Christianity? Certainly on this account, Christianity has more elements of Hegel's philosophical religion than Judaism does. But as long as Jewish philosophers who identify with the philosophies which Rose ravages (Levinas, Derrida, Benjamin) do not recognize the force of this critique, Rose's death is unredeemed, tragic insofar as it occurs only as an undialectical misrecognition.

The task of this essay, then, is twofold. First, it argues that Rose's conversion was unnecessary, by showing that Rose's Hegelian comedy can be recognized in the tradition that has become known as postmodern Jewish philosophy. Here, in accordance with the other essays in this volume, this argument moves from the secular realm. It shows that the Levinasian description of eros – by which I broadly mean the perception of another person's self-expression, i.e. any and all phenomenology of the intersubjective realm – leads to a pathos-filled and anxiety-ridden account of the religious life. In turn, this leads to a risky political existence in the intersection of the finite and the infinite, and not the imperialism of *ressentiment* which Rose finds there. To be blunt, Levinasian philosophy, when properly understood, shares important qualities with the thinking of Hegel, who is uniformly derided by Levinas in his own writings. (I leave analyses of Benjamin, Derrida, Rosenzweig, and Cohen for later occasions.) But only through making this preliminary move can one accomplish the second task. Once both Judaism and Christianity are perceived as possessing the agnostic structure that Rose associates with Hegel, Rose's conversion can be recognized not as a rejection of Judaism, but as a dialectical call to Jewish philosophy to work through its tradition and resuscitate the manner in which its own call to utopia is an embrace of risk, chance and fortune. Christianity and Judaism will thus become actualized as parallel structures of spirit's work. This is a necessary step (and not the only one) toward fulfillment of the expectation that "all of them shall know me from the smallest to the greatest" (Jeremiah 31:33). The recognition of Rose's death which I propose here maintains the comedy of Rose's death, since her choice of a position (Christianity) thereby dissolves itself into a hint of how Christianity and Judaism should serve as representations of philosophical religion. Nevertheless, I await others' dissolution of the position given herein. There will be readers who want more, a proof of Rose's conversion as a lapse in her philosophical gifts, and I empathize with them. On the other hand, Jewish philosophy must not fail to heed her warning that Judaism cannot will itself by fiat into avoiding the risks embedded in the created (and hence good) world through the construction of a philosophy which to some appears otherworldly and dualistic.

Finally, I stress that, although this argument proceeds from within the secular realm, it is also Jewish. The essay is a kaddish (a prayer of mourning) for Rose. Like the Kaddish prayer, it magnifies God by demonstrating the majesty of God's ephemeral manifestation in the intersubjective relationship. It also brings merit to Rose since it is her work which influences the argument below and which should be duly credited as such.

For Rose, the methodological problem with modern and postmodern Jewish philosophy is rooted in, of all people, Rudolf Hermann Lotze. Popular in English-speaking transcendentalist circles in the late nineteenth and early twentieth centuries, Lotze's main contribution to post-Kantian philosophy is a proto-pragmatist move which brackets the classical correspondence notion of truth, and instead claims that truth only refers to linguistic propositions which possess both validity (*Geltung*) and value (*Wert*) through an inscrutable and immediate operation of reason. This style of thinking risks circularity. At the same time that Lotze wants to pass on to his readers a teleological notion of philosophy as aiming at an immediate consciousness of God as the highest value, his analysis of truth necessitates that this transcendent perspective already be implicit in valid propositions. Without this latter element, no individual or community would be able to recognize valid propositions as valid. Therefore, Rose claims that although Lotze's philosophy is rooted in a perceptive critique as to whether Kant's refutation of idealism is belied by other elements of his thinking,[32] the post-Kantian idealistic adventure ends up proclaiming that "validity emanates from a transcendent sphere of value which is both the criterion and object of knowledge."[33] In addition, the role that value plays in Lotze's philosophy renders it otherworldly: value comes from mind and mind alone when reason perceives objects, strips them of the dross of their material existence through its aesthetic employment, and thereby intuits their essential practical worth. The material world is sublated in the most pedestrian sense of Fichtean *Aufhebung*. Especially in Hermann Cohen's brand of neo-Kantianism, the objects of thinking are transformed into "cognemes" (as Rose felicitously translates *Erkenntnisse*).[34]

Husserlian phenomenology, which is usually perceived as a break from neo-Kantian philosophy due to Husserl's suspicion of the applicability of the natural sciences to thinking,[35] is actually for Rose a continuation of the tradition of *Geltungsphilosophie*. This is not a false view of the matter. Insofar as phenomenology views the objects of the world as constituted by human consciousness and its intentional modes of comportment toward them (e.g. desiring, detesting, doubting), the issue of truth-claims about the objective world is indeed bracketed off, and what is left is a "pure and solipsistic consciousness."[36] Insofar as Levinas perceives himself as a phenomenologist,[37] and insofar as his phenomenological analyses are attempts to explain exactly how reason intuits ethical norms and commands *à la* Lotzean project, it makes sense that one might read Levinas's writings as shadowed by an unconscious divine hubris.[38] In addition, reading Levinas within the *Geltungsphilosophie* tradition means reading Levinas as the worst kind of idealist, as his works begin to portray a life of "piety that separates itself from history" that desires only the infinite, and not the other person for his or her own sake.[39]

Nevertheless, to read Levinas in this manner is to *ignore* the grappling within the phenomenological tradition over the issue of the reduction of the world to a series of cognemes, cogs in the quest after the ultimate value and the ultimate source of value. This begins in Husserl himself, and continues through Merleau-Ponty and Levinas. The upshot of this discussion is that phenomenology discloses the relationship between the intentional subject and the world not as one of mere humility (as Rose interprets Levinas's intent) nor one of mere hubris (as Rose suspects to be really the case in Levinas). Rather, phenomenology defends the necessity of the belonging-together of hubris and humility, of appropriation and expropriation, of love and loss, a cluster of themes familiar to Rose's readers. This defense takes place through two arguments: that the mind operates while always ensconced in the world, and that this necessary imbrication in the material realm acts as a check upon the absolutist tendencies of consciousness. Consciousness is thus neither pure nor solipsistic.

During the First World War, Husserl dealt with the problem of how consciousness intentionally constitutes the objects of the world through a phenomenology of the lived body (*Leib*), in the second volume of the *Ideas*.[40] Although they were not officially published until 1952, Merleau-Ponty consulted the manuscripts at the Husserl Archives in Louvain during the Second World War while working on *Phenomenology of Perception*, and there is anecdotal evidence of Merleau-Ponty's enthusiasm for these writings (*ID2* xvi). Both Merleau-Ponty and this set of Husserlian texts convert phenomenology from a straightforward philosophy of cognemes into an empiricist voluntarism. If the advance of *Ideas I* lies in the argument that a properly theoretical attitude reveals that natural objects are constituted through the intentional comportment of consciousness toward them, then the advance of *Ideas II* is the argument that constitution depends upon bodily capabilities. The freedom of consciousness is unthinkable without kinesthetic freedom (*ID2* 61), since "the Body [*Leib*, not *Körper*, the thingly body of nature] is, in the first place, the medium of all perception . . . all that is thingly-real in the surrounding world of the Ego has its relation to the Body." Thinking is dependent not simply on the cognitive impulse, but on the will to engage with the empirical world. There is an ego-faculty more primary than thinking (*ID2* 160): the ability "to freely move this Body and to perceive an external world by means of it."

At first glance, this conclusion resolves the mind–body problem inaugurated in the sixth Cartesian *Meditation* at a far more satisfactory level than seventeenth-century theories of occasionalism had attempted to do. For at a level far more basic than that of how sensations of pleasure and pain are comprehended by the mind, Husserl is able to explain how the spontaneous comportments of the body lead to the ability of consciousness to adequately describe objects. Sensation is not a challenge to the mind, as in Descartes. Rather, tactility (to take one example) is a necessary part of the constitution of the object, since it gives still other aspects or adumbrations (*Abschattungen*) of the object. In a language which hearkens back to Democritean descriptions of sensation in which atoms jump into the hand, ear or eye, Husserl describes the way that properties of objects move into the sensing bodily organ.

> My hand is lying on the table. I experience the table as something solid, cold, and smooth. Moving my hand over the table, I get an experience of it and its thingly determinations. At the same time, I can at any moment pay attention to my hand and find on it touch-sensations, sensations of smoothness and coldness, etc. In the interior of the hand, running parallel to the experienced movement, I find motion-sensations, etc. Lifting a thing, I experience its weight, but at the same time, I have weight-sensations localized in my Body.
>
> (*ID2* 153)

The shift from objective weight to subjective weight-sensations means that even if I were only to be dreaming of lying on the floor (for example), I would still have touch-sensations on my back. I might even go as far as to sense a splinter from a loose floorboard, even though no such splinter or floor exists in objective reality. Without such kinaesthetic sensations, I would be unable to describe the proper predicates of an object (*ID2* 157): "the touch-sensing is not a state of the material thing, hand, but is precisely the *hand itself*, which for us is more than a material thing." Here one can easily state, with Rose, that the physicality of the body is extirpated in the phenomenological exploration of what it means to be embodied. In stating that the body is more than a material thing, it approaches the status of a cogneme, with no explanation of what the criterion for the knowledge attained by this touch-sensing might be.

But Husserl continues this sentence by asserting that "the way in which it is mine entails that I, the 'subject of the Body,' can say that what belongs to the material thing is its, not mine." Here the ambiguity of bodily sensing enters onto the phenomenological scene. For the criterion of the validity of touch-sensing and the supra-material essence of the body is precisely the very materiality of the body which Husserl appears to want to extirpate. The lived body is both of the world and above it, a material thing and a spiritualizing power. It thereby becomes best expressed through the figure of the Janus-face. Both receiving sensations and constituting their meaning, it lies on the borderline between the material and the ideal. On the one hand, the lived body is an "aesthesiological" sensorium, the material organ for perception (*aisthesis*) of surrounding material objects. On the other hand, it is "for the will, the freely moving Body" which has its own reality insofar as kinaesthesis reveals it to be the spiritualizing agency that allows me to constitute anything in the first place and thereby act upon the world, and not merely intuit it. Husserl therefore describes the Body as a "two-sided" or "double" reality (*ID2* 297). The relation between these two poles of embodied existence is difficult to delineate. One cannot say which is prior. Certainly from the point of view of the *ordo essendi*, it is the case that the aesthesiological stratum "is always a presupposition" for the possibility of any free movement. Yet I cannot know this to be a fact outside of my own kinaestheses; in *ordo cognoscendi*, it is movement itself that is the transcendental condition.

Therefore, it is always wrong to claim that Husserlian consciousness is pure in the Kantian sense, even if Husserl himself at times states that this is indeed the case. Nevertheless, one might reply by pressing Husserl and making the critique that even in *Ideas II*, despite the importance of the empirical, there is still a hegemony of the mental which uses matter merely as an instrument for proclaiming its own superiority. It is Merleau-Ponty who responds to such a critique by arguing that Husserl's phenomenology of the body challenges the primacy of thinking, theory and subject in the more dominant strands of Husserl's writing, for example in *Ideas I* and *Cartesian Meditations*. (As I shall show below, Levinas extends this critique to argue that *Ideas II* contains an implicit critique of the hegemony of the ego in both Husserl and Merleau-Ponty, demonstrating that the gain in knowledge of the world which phenomenology gives us is never without a concomitant loss.)

In 1960, Merleau-Ponty published *Signes*, which includes a long summa-tion of his view on Husserl, "The Philosopher and His Shadow."[41] This essay is simultaneously excessively slavish to and excessively critical of Husserl. For Merleau-Ponty, Husserl is always and everywhere correct – in *Ideas II* (and Merleau-Ponty also mentions *Ideas III* and a text on the Copernican revolu-tion). But this also means that Husserl is wrong in describing the ego as a pure entity that has knowledge of being as thought. The body complicates the devaluation of naturalism which one finds in "Phenomenology as Rigor-ous Science" and *Ideas I*. Since mind depends upon world, there is no possi-bility of bracketing it away completely without bracketing away thinking itself.

> From *Ideen II* on it seems clear that reflection does not install us in a closed, transparent milieu, and that it does not take us (at least not immediately) from "objective" to "subjective," but that its function is rather to unveil a third dimension in which this distinction becomes prob-lematic. . . . From *Ideen II* on, Husserl's reflection escapes the tête-à-tête between pure subject and pure things.[42]

The necessary embodiment of reflection, over and above its nature as a men-tal process,[43] displays phenomenology's own interruption of itself.[44] Husserl's description of tactility contests "the unidirectional relationship of the one who perceives to what he perceives."[45] When I rub my hand across a table, it is the smoothness of the table which transfers itself into my hand in the act of sensation. (Merleau-Ponty uses Husserl's example from *Ideas II* §36 of one hand touching another; here "the touched hand becomes the touching hand."[46]) Because of the priority of matter in *ordo essendi*, it becomes dif-ficult to tell what is properly called subject and what is properly called object: the unique intentionality-structure of embodied consciousness blurs the dif-ference between the two. Indeed, Merleau-Ponty goes on to hint that embodiment threatens the very distinction between noesis and noema (between intentive thought and hyletic data) upon which the model of consciousness in *Ideas I* is predicated.[47] The mind thinks bodily, and thinks alongside matter. This does not under any circumstances mean that the mind abnegates itself because of the transcendental priority of the object in *ordo essendi*; it means that consciousness is always subject and object at the same time. For Merleau-Ponty, then, the double status of the body reveals the following circle: matter gives consciousness its ego, but it is consciousness, in its tarrying with the world, that shows this to be the case.

Yet even this may give too much authority to consciousness, as Levinas claims in his contribution to the conversation. To sum Levinas's position on Merleau-Ponty in Rose's language, one might say that Merleau-Ponty does not quite fulfill phenomenology's promise of ambiguity, "to know and yet not to know."[48] In the 1980s, Levinas published two brief articles on Merleau-Ponty's treatment of Husserl which were later reprinted in *Outside the Subject*.[49] While they endorse Merleau-Ponty's strategy of using *Ideas II* to critique the notion of pure consciousness found in *Ideas I*, Levinas still finds that Merleau-Ponty's body-philosophy does not go far enough. Even though the body plays an essential role in the mind's constitution of the world, Levinas still critiques Merleau-Ponty for adhering to a cognitive prejudice in his proto-deconstruction of the subject–object relation: "we know far more about [things] in the natural attitude than the theoretical can tell us – and above all we know it in a different way."[50] The position is the inverse of Kant: Husserl has no problem with the noumenal knowledge of the thing-in-itself in *Ideas I*; this is the *Wesenschau* which the discovery of intentionality affords us. But when faced with the irreducible *belonging-together* of the noumenon with the phenomenon, a barrier complicates the elucidation of gnosis – now the natural attitude is shrouded in "mystery." But for Merleau-Ponty and Husserl, gnosis is not impossible; there is simply a different kind of knowing which is inscrutable. This different knowledge is immediate and self-validating. For Merleau-Ponty (as well as for the Husserl of *Ideas II*), concrete experience of another's body gives an immediate knowledge of that person; the postulation of an analogy between my embodied consciousness and that of the other comes after. In a gloss on *Ideas II* §45, Merleau-Ponty claims that the "transferred co-presence" of the other by which I come to the conclusion that my sensation of another is self-validating – the act of empathy or intropathy (*Einfühlung*) – occurs with "neither comparison nor analogy nor projection."[51] When one hand touches another, there is no doubting the validity of my sensation of that hand *whether or not* it belongs to me or to someone else, and just as there is an immediate transfer of texture from one hand (or a table) to another hand, there is a similar transfer from one person to another. Embodiment thus guarantees that sociality is a real possibility for the relation of consciousness to the world; sensibility guarantees that I can understand another through the transfer of sense that occurs here.

For Levinas to critique this kind of knowledge, as he does in these two essays, is to critique the very *Geltungsphilosophie* that Rose associates with the putative self-validating command of the face in Levinas and the general primacy of practical reason which modern Jewish philosophy shares with Lotze. Levinas sees the sociality deduced from philosophy of the body in Merleau-Ponty as bolstering and completing the authorization of the solipsistic consciousness: "sociality does not break the order of consciousness any more than does knowledge, which, cleaving to the known, immediately coincides with whatever might have been foreign to it."[52] Thus, the possibility of sociality revealed by the body is co-opted into the pure stream of mental processes, and becomes a consolation for the fear of being unable to break out of solipsism.

This critique is familiar; Levinas wants to avoid reducing the social to the status of a cogneme. Yet this is not simply a dogmatic assertion. Levinas grounds his argument that the order of consciousness can be broken – that solipsism is only a possibility for sophists, not for genuine philosophers – in the writings of Husserl himself, which require "an attentive ear throughout, despite the apparent immobility or restating of the main theses."[53] In the latter of the two essays on Merleau-Ponty ("In Memory of Alphonse de Waelhens"), there is a strange paragraph which simultaneously valorizes and dismisses the practical upshot of the ambiguous structure of knowledge in *Ideas II*. It is worth quoting in full.

> Husserl's texts on empathy, which were published in *Ideen II*, present the meaning of this knowledge in a manner that is indeed particularly impressive in its phenomenological preciseness. These analyses, many years earlier than those of the fifth meditation in Husserl's *Cartesian Meditations* seem to me, paradoxically, richer than the latter. Specifically, I have in mind the whole of paragraph 56 of this dense but so very rich volume – and even more specifically the inimitable pages (248–59) on the understanding of "spiritualized" objects (contrasted with our knowledge of all other meaningful objects): cultural and written ones. I have in mind the admirable effort to bring out, through the phenomenological analysis of appresentation, sociality and society in their height and preeminence in relation to the perception of objects simply endowed with "signification." Yet at no point in the course of that very beautiful analysis is the (ultimately or originally) cognitive structure of the lived put into question, in order to conceive of the cognitive accession to the objectivity of the other person on the basis of his or her proximity as neighbor, rather than founding the latter on the former.[54]

On the one hand, Levinas critiques Husserl for finally falling prey to the analogical and fungible view of persons which Levinas everywhere associates with totality and the violation of the other's otherness. On the other hand, Levinas does not find mistakes in Husserl's phenomenological investigations themselves; they are impressively precise. This gives the reader two options for interpretation: either Levinas is breaking with phenomenology *tout court*, since not even the most precise of phenomenological models can ground ethics, or Husserl is ignoring an element in his observations which would ground a more Levinasian ethics.

An interpretation of §56 and especially §56h (the section Levinas emphasizes) decides for the latter option. Here, the relationship between the self and the Other is one of both recognition and confrontation, identity and difference, peace and conflict. It is hardly utopia, although the relationship does allow for the construction of ethics. In §56, Husserl gives the reader the social upshot of the discovery of consciousness as intentional. One can sum up the argument in five steps:

1    Because consciousness is necessarily embodied, sensibility prohibits con-sciousness from separating and reifying "subject," "object," "material" and "mental." (This is the point which Merleau-Ponty stressed.)
2    When I constitute other people, I am therefore prohibited from perceiv-ing them as a mind–body duality. The other person is given to me as "one with [his or her] Body" (*ID2* 245).
3    Because mind and body are co-present in the stream of my conscious processes (as I have already discovered in phenomenological reflection upon touching a stone or a table, for example), I "introjectively posit" a similar unity in the other person (*ID2* 240).[55]
4    This means that the "psychic grounds" of constitution (*ID2* 234) cannot be found in the natural physicalist order. Because the material already appears to me as animated by the Other's mental stream of intentional acts, a different order of causality appears which Husserl terms "motivation" (*ID2* 241).
5    This sets up the possibility of conflict and contestation. The motivation of the Other confronts me bodily and determines my response. It is always possible for my phenomenological empathy to lead to conflict on the empirical level.

> I hear the other speaking, see his facial expressions, attribute to him such and such conscious lived experiences and acts, and let myself be deter-mined by them in this or that way. The facial expressions are . . . immedi-ately bearers of sense indicating the other's consciousness, e.g. his will which, in empathy, is characterized as the actual will of this person and as a will which addresses me in communication. The will characterized in this way . . . then motivates my counter-willing or my submission, etc. . . . The mien of the other determines me (this is already a kind of motiva-tion) to join to it a sense within the other's consciousness. . . . We are altogether outside the attitude required for grasping natural causality.
>
> (*ID2* 247)

This is where the phenomenology of the other person stands at the beginning of §56h. In this section, Husserl extends the phenomenology of constitution from an account of how I can have a relation with a single other person to a general humanism in the socio-ethical realm. The transcending of the natural attitude which Husserl finds in sociality means that the sensation of the Other communicates meaning to me (as opposed to the sensation of physical objects, which only teaches me about the nature of my own embodiment) – an aspect of worldly existence which I have not yet constituted. The appresentation of the other person's body to me, insofar as it cannot be separated from the motivation of the other person's mind, is always an appresentation of the other person's soul (*ID2* 252): "each movement of the body is full of soul, the coming and going, the standing and sitting, the walking and dancing, etc." In this manner, Husserl writes that other persons are like texts, in which the physical book is always animated by the sense–meaning "fused" with the signifying words. Moreover, because the appresentation of the other person's soul is an appresentation *to me*, I have a right to posit a higher realm which would encompass the bridge between myself and the other person: for Husserl, this is *spirit*. Therefore, the observation of the other person's expressive acts – facial gestures, sauntering, come-hither motions, pouts of frustration – authorizes me to constitute a spiritual world of a free poietic culture over and above the natural world of mechanically determined object. Finally, the most important point: the apperception of the other person as "spiritualized" leads to a *new self-apperception*. Here, the soul which I had posited in the other returns to me as spirit. The analogy now works in reverse, affording me a self-apperception as part of this cultural world, an apperception to which I had no access in my self-inspection. Finally (*ID2* 254), I am able "by means of this apprehension, with its complicated structure, [to] fit myself into the family of man, or rather, I create the constitutive possibility for the unity of this 'family.'"

Of course, I constitute my own Body and my own material–mental nature before I constitute the soul of the Other, even if this act of constitution has unforeseen cultural benefits. Yet just as Merleau-Ponty manipulated the distinction between the priority of the mental and the priority of the material to challenge the Husserlian phenomenology of *Ideas I*, so does Levinas manipulate this tension to challenge the dominance of the ego in most of Husserl. Levinas's favorite section of *Ideas II* §56h contains the following brief passage (*ID2* 257):

> It must be noticed, however, that the *unity of expression* [the expression of the other person's soul through his or her bodily acts] is a *presupposition* for the constitution of the founded reality as one which encloses levels, but that it is not already in itself this reality. We could formulate it this way: it is only by means of expression that the person of the other is there at all for the experiencing subject, and the person must necessarily be there first in order for him to be able to enter . . . into a real unity of a higher level and indeed to do so together with that which serves as expression.

Even if the ego is empirically prior, then, there is no guarantee that it is transcendentally prior. Without following up on this paragraph elsewhere in *Ideas II*, Husserl here most boldly retreats from the theory of *Ideas I* that objects are given to me in accordance with my constitution of them, and thereby fully dependent upon consciousness.[56] Here, it is not phenomena that depend upon consciousness, but consciousness that depends upon the phenomenon. The expressivity of the body is given from an I-know-not-where, conditioned by something unnameable. And this unnameable is *necessary* for me to constitute the other person as a participant in the spiritual realm. To be sure, this is always and everywhere *my* constitution of the other person *as* spiritualized; the spirit of the other person does not visit upon me from above and catch me by surprise. Yet in the act of phenomenological reflection, the transcendental priority of the other person (and thus the Other's transcendence over me) reveals itself as I reconstruct the path by which I come to make sense of the other person as a spiritualized being.

I claim that it is this passage in *Ideas II* which serves as the locus of the Levinasian enigma *within* Husserl, and the ground from which Levinas deduces the possibility of being able to speak, within the bounds of phenomenology as rigorous science, of "the other in the same" as he does throughout *Otherwise than Being*. It is in this passage where Husserl's argument should but does not lead him to conclude that the cognitive access to the intersubjective is grounded on the Other's proximity. For if it is true that the Other's unity of expression and expressed (in the bodily gestures I perceive) are the transcendental condition of cognition, then it must also be true that this unity depends upon a nearness sufficient for me to perceive these bodily gestures in the first place.

It is in no way possible to read Levinas as Rose does, as promulgating an argument that good phenomenology contains an imperative that "to become ethical, the self is to be devastated, traumatised, unthroned by the commandment to substitute *the other* for itself."[57] Power and powerlessness go hand in hand for Levinas, as do knowing and not knowing. Certainly, Levinas does note that the phenomenology of the body demonstrates that the self is not the all-powerful king of its environment. Part of what body gives to consciousness is the fact that the body is an epistemological block, and therefore knowledge of the world is always characterized by privation. The gap between consciousness and the objects of its knowledge means that the alterity of the world can never be extirpated by intentionality; the self-expression of the Other's body (and at least all other moving objects, although one might also believe that still objects express themselves in and through their materiality as well) always transcends consciousness. But at the same time, this powerlessness of the self is paired with the self's freedom and power. For without the gap between consciousness and the object (i.e. without the object's transcendental priority), there is nothing that could possibly ground the freedom of the self. For Husserl and the French phenomenological tradition, it is the freedom to take up different bodily positions with respect to the object that constitutes transcendence in the phenomenological sense – the ability for thought to leave behind the borders of its interior space and literally move over into the world which it perceives through bodily kinaestheses. The structure of the objective world is dependent upon me. But this power has an ironic effect: power comes up against its limits because the spatial mobility of the self necessitates that an object can appear to the self in a multitude of ways, based on the self's spatial position at a given moment.

> The philosophy that contributed the idea of eidetic structures, ends up also radically denouncing the idea of structural fixity – its undephasable simultaneity – by introducing movement into the subjectivity of the subject and conditional motivation into its very presence.[58]

Phenomenological existence is best expressed through an odd pairing of opposite terms, a matching through mismatching. Life and power are the representations of the death of the understanding and the powerlessness of the self. This does not make life and power any less real. But life and power are never only life and power. The self's being transcended by the other person's originary self-expression manifests itself in the movement of the self who continually tries to gain new angles of perception in order to cognize the object better. The "animation" of sensed content by intentionality, which gives it spirit and hence life, manifests the death of the material content itself. As soon as consciousness gains meaning, it realizes that there is more meaning to be gained, and that each act of cognition comes with a loss that contests the subjectivity just acquired. Existence in Levinas is *always* agonistic: the subject asserts itself, the meaning of this assertion is contested by another perspective or by the object's transcendental priority, and then the subject asserts itself anew, and differently, in the light of this new assertion.[59] It is obvious that there is never any complete epistemological security in Levinas's elucidation of the nature of phenomenological subjectivity, but neither is subjectivity banished from thought in the mistaken idea that the "I" is always already contaminated by the dregs of fascist violence. The contestation of the subject by virtue of its always arriving late at the scene (the other person is there first, expressing him- or herself), or the radical givenness of the Other, is always constituted by consciousness in its moment of subjectivity: "alterity is only possible starting from me."[60] It is only the I that is unwilling to see itself as contested that is worthy of dismissal.[61]

This oscillation of phenomenological reason, always enthroned and deposed at the same time,[62] is also found in Levinas's depiction of the erotic scene.[63] Eros is always both happy and unhappy, both "joy and agony"[64] for Levinas. The beloved has complete power over the lover, and transcends him absolutely. He (the beloved)[65] has already expressed himself as soon as he makes his motions to disrobe, or at the moment at which he gives me the look that invites me to disrobe him. When I touch him, in the desire to map out this foreign land, the spirit of the expression disappears – all I touch is skin.[66]

The erotic touch gives no properties outside of dermality: the slight paleness that is the scar stretching from the left side of his mouth up to his nose, the pores at the base of his graying chest hair, the curve of the skin at his index finger. This is not what I desired; I wanted something strange to become familiar, the penultimate salvation from my solipsistic loneliness as "my over-charged imagination [is] released inside your body, taken up into mine with attack and abandon."[67] Instead, he has become more strange, collapsing into a mass of profane fleshy parts. Eros does not allow for reification. My power to touch contests my power to know. Nevertheless, this is still my power; the *dynamis* of my desire perseveres insofar as there are hints in the other's self-expression that next time he might be a little less strange to me.[68] Certainly I enjoy this power; the reduction of the unitary erotic Other to a mass of unassemblable parts converts the erotic relationship into one which satisfies only physical needs, what Levinas terms "voluptuosity." This satisfaction cannot be denied. Must one tell this story again? (I would only narrate it badly.) The Levinasian point, however, is that the satisfaction of the voluptu-ous cannot take place without the erotic Other's transcendence of me in his always prior self-expression. If the other person were essentially the "exorbi-tant ultra-materiality" as he appears to me,[69] then there would be no expres-sive gesture that would have attracted me to him in the first place, and I could not exercise my power over the Other and gain satisfaction. If the Other had no material component whatsoever, then my desire could never come to any satisfaction, since my relationship would be one of powerlessness alone. Only in the ensoulment that is not written on the body but exists in "my over-charged imagination" alone is it possible to experience erotic joy, although it is never without the pain of its inability for ontological fulfillment. The loss of love in the erotic act apotropaically guards against the greater loss that inevitably results when love falsely believes itself to be perfectly fulfilled and eternal. So that a perfect union may not reveal itself as a smothering trap, the loss of love ensures "a distance, a boundary for love [allowing lovers to] approach and retire so that love may suspire."[70] Its validity is always unsure, never quite adequately guaranteeing itself, eternally on the precipice. This critique of imperialist eros without letting go of the agency of the self is common to both Rose and Levinas.

The above description of Levinasian eros does not yet prove that the self can be more than a power that flails in its limits and, in its moments of dissatis-faction, is tempted to bite the bars of the cage that imprisons it. Levinas and Rose argue for the equivocality of power. But it is Rose who more explicitly claims that for power to be truly equivocal, it must be able to posit itself in new ways over a period of time. The self's act cannot simply be a Levinasian "passivity beyond passivity"[71] (beyond passivity because the self cannot decide to give up its power, since the Other in his or her transcendental priority has already made this decision). It must also be an "activity beyond activity", an account of "this constant risk of positing and failing *and positing again.*"[72] This third step marks the boundary between tragedy and comedy. Where is this in Levinas? Rose finds it nowhere. For her, Levinas is unwilling to critique the peace he finds in Talmudic jurisprudence with an attentiveness to the mutating nature of social relations: "reconstructing the changing relation between universal, particular and singular . . . this is experience, the struggle to recognize – to know, and still to misknow, and yet to grow."[73]

But on the basis of the argument above that, for both Levinas and Rose, love/eros already involves the exercise of both power and powerlessness simultaneously, it becomes possible to mend Rose's misrecognition of Levinas here. If Rose describes love and the state, the private and the public, the social and the sacred, in these equivocal terms as a critique of Levinas's putative valorization of my powerlessness with respect to the erotic and social Other, then how does this argument change when the discourse of power in Levinasian eros is shown to be more nuanced? If the Levinasian subject possesses an ambiguous power, how does this power exercise itself within the political realm?

For Levinas, eros and its equivocation of power is the basis of a theological politics. This is implicit in one of Levinas's first Talmudic readings, delivered in 1961 and published two years later as the second half of the essay "Messianic Texts" in *Difficile Liberté*. The Talmudic passage under discussion (B. Sanhedrin 99a) and Levinas's commentary on it, read as follows:

> R. Nachman said: If he [the Messiah] is among those living, it might be one like myself, as it is written: "And his chieftain shall be one of his own [lit. from himself], and his ruler [*moshlo*] will come out of his innermost [places]." (Jer. 30:21)

> Jeremiah's text concerns an age in which sovereignty will return to Israel. The Messiah is . . . the absolute interiority of government. Is there a more radical interiority than the one in which the Self commands itself? . . . The Messiah is the King who no longer commands from outside – this idea of Jeremiah's is brought by R. Nachman to its logical conclusion. The Messiah is myself; to be myself is to be the Messiah.[74]

This Talmudic passage is usually understood to signify that the Messiah will come from the same Davidic lineage from which R. Nachman is descended. Yet the verse from Jeremiah is easily associated with the thematics of caress and sensibility found in other writings of Levinas. The verse could easily have used a more traditional example of the Hebrew Bible's royal ideology of messianism than the word *moshel*, "ruler." Why not the obvious *melekh*, "king," or even *nasi'*, "prince"? (Indeed, later in the passage, Rab responds to R. Nachman by hypothesizing that if the Messiah does live, it is Judah ha-Nasi, the codifier of the Mishnah.) But the verse uses *moshel*, and the divine word of Torah is never arbitrary. *Moshel* is a nominalization of the verb *mashal*, "to touch" or "to handle"; the idea being expressed here is that the ruler is a person who can handle and manage everything well.[75] This section of the Talmud thus claims, at the literal level, that the Messiah is the person who touches (dare one say caresses?) his or her community from the depths of interiority. Because the Messiah is literally "from himself," there is no reason why one should take the text as necessarily referring to a distinct messianic figure; "Messiah" becomes the name of a universal human potential.

In the transformation of the erotic scene from the boudoir to the *polis*, sex becomes amplified into redemption, and messianism becomes the way in which passivity beyond passivity becomes represented in the social sphere as something other, as activity beyond activity. I cannot touch the entirety of my community, although a single erotic scene and the hunger it inaugurates prove to me that all others are transcendentally prior to me, and I am thereby under their authority. Yet the erotic scene, in its elucidation of the gap between my mental processes and the Other's skin, also reveals that I have the power to engage with the world. In the social sphere, this means that I have the capability, in my action, to care for and alleviate the individual afflictions of those whom I encounter. (This would not be possible if Levinas were Lotze, if there were no moment in which the priority of the Other questioned the validity of my intentional aims.) But there is no guarantee that my alleviation of suffering will be successful. My act will have effects that engender another form of the suffering and violence which I have attempted to relieve, although hopefully the suffering is quantitatively and qualitatively less. It may lessen violence but will not extirpate it. It may have violent consequences for others, and I may not have expected this situation. If the other person is transcendentally prior, by the time that I perform my act of alleviating suffering, new events have occurred; my act has become merely a stopgap band-aid. What once appeared to be recognition now appears as misrecognition.[76] I must try yet again to minimize the lag between my consciousness and the other's priority, and must therefore reposit myself and act yet again.[77] Redemption is not instantaneous, but a struggle which involves my personal growth in the face of new scenarios, new visions, new sets of information, which I must introject and process if comedy is to persevere.

Levinas describes this political scene as an infinite oscillation between the skepticism of consciousness's mastery and the refutation of that skepticism in the writing of law codes which reflect the belief in mastery at a given moment. This oscillation between validity and its contestation in every historical situation manifests the resistance of the infinite/transcendence/Saying to its thematization in an ontological principle – the shadowy appearance of God within secular history through the realization that what does appear is not God. Skepticism "states the rupture, failure, impotence or impossibility of disclosure,"[78] but this does not make Levinas a latter twentieth-century reincarnation of Sextus Empiricus. Skepticism does not open up a self-contradictory discourse that marks the failure of all attempts at cognition beyond appearance-to-me and the ensuing sadness of necessary solipsism, but rather to a hearing of "the trace of saying," the shadow of transcendence in the other person's priority that lies behind his or her appearance. This transcendence commands me (it has more power than I do) to act anew and broaden the framework of government, to revise the lawbooks and the scientific paradigms which are complicit in violence. Then, later, I will have to act again. Insofar as these continued re-positings of the subject are made in the shadow of the transcendence which always contests the validity of my actions, God enters into community as its incipient substance, always on the verge of being born through the *Bildung* of its members.

Levinas writes that "philosophy is not separable from skepticism, which follows it like a shadow it drives off by refuting it again at once on its footsteps."[79] For Rose, the relationship between recognition and misrecognition is the same. Skepticism is philosophy's sidekick, its comic foil which always exposes the ephemerality of the validity of our acts, and reveals revision as the absolute in human action. Skepticism and misrecognition show that the revelation we experience in the Other's disrobing is instantaneously lost, that transcendence is so majestic as to hide from us and cause us to search for it always and everywhere in the midst of the public sphere. Only in the light of this comedy can one truly glorify and sanctify the name of God, and say Kaddish.

## Notes

1 Gillian Rose, *Mourning Becomes the Law* (Cambridge: Cambridge University Press, 1996), p. 72.
2 Rose, "Ethics and *Halacha*," in *Judaism and Modernity* (Oxford: Blackwell, 1993), pp. 25–32; also see *The Broken Middle* (Oxford: Blackwell, 1992), pp. 272–7.
3 Brief narratives of Rose's deathbed conversion can be found in the following sources. Martin Jay, "The Conversion of the Rose," *Salmagundi* 113 (Winter 1997), pp. 40–52; Arnold Jacob Wolf, "The Tragedy of Gillian Rose," *Judaism* 46 (1997), pp. 481–8; and the Archbishop of Canterbury's sermon for Christmas Day 1996 (http://anglicancommunion.org/acns/acnsarchive/acns1000/acns1064.html).
4 Rose admits something like this in her autobiography, *Love's Work*: "The unemphatic truth is that I have trouble imagining, publicly or privately, that everyone is not made exactly as I am myself." Rose, *Love's Work* (New York: Schocken, 1995), p. 95.
5 Rose, *Hegel Contra Sociology* (London: Athlone, 1981), p. 98.
6 G. W. F. Hegel, *Phenomenology of Spirit*, trans. A. V. Miller (Oxford: Oxford University Press, 1977), par. 763.
7 Rose, *Hegel Contra Sociology*, pp. 112–17. Thus, Christ is always both particular and abstract. John Milbank writes both that "Jesus, therefore, figures in the New Testament primarily as a new Moses, the founder of a new or renewed law and community. It is for this reason that he cannot be given any particular content," and that "the universal repeatability of Jesus is made possible by his specific historic occurrence." John Milbank, "The Name of Jesus," in *The Word Made Strange* (Oxford: Blackwell, 1997), pp. 152, 158.
8 For a summary of these ideologies, see Peter Schäfer, "Diversity and Interaction: Messiahs in Early Judaism," in *Towards the Millennium: Messianic Expectations*

*from the Bible to Waco*, eds. Peter Schäfer and Mark R. Cohen (Leiden: E. J. Brill, 1998), pp. 15–35.

9  Rose, *Mourning Becomes the Law*, pp. 126–9, esp. p. 129: "I cannot live if death be nought, but neither can I die if life be not aught."

10  Ibid., p. 72.

11  Jay, "Conversion of the Rose," p. 47.

12  David Novak, "Edith Stein, Apostate Saint," *First Things* 96 (October 1999), p. 17.

13  Ibid., p. 16.

14  Rose, *Hegel Contra Sociology*, p. 77.

15  Ibid., pp. 76, 208–9.

16  Rose, *Mourning Becomes the Law*, p. 74.

17  Ibid., p. 75.

18  Robert R. Williams, "Theology and Tragedy," in *New Perspectives on Hegel's Philosophy of Religion*, ed. David Kolb (Albany: State University of New York Press, 1992), p. 52. Williams's argument that "reconciliation presupposes negativity" is unclear: is it the case that tragedy and comedy are inseparable from each other at every historical moment, or is the anguish of tragedy only the temporal precondition for love? Rose argues for the former option; the latter is not sufficiently agonistic for her.

19  Rose's reading of Kierkegaard's *Fear and Trembling* as the expression of the dialectical depth of the Hegelian system is key to this argument. See Rose, *Broken Middle*, pp. 147–52; *Mourning Becomes the Law*, p. 121; *Judaism and Modernity*, pp. 155–73, esp. pp. 171–2.

20  Rose, *Love's Work*, pp. 105–6.

21  Rose, *Mourning Becomes the Law*, p. 146.

22  Rose, *Love's Work*, pp. 23–4.

23  For example, see Hegel, *Phenomenology of Spirit*, par. 393.

24  Even the critique of Derrida in *Mourning Becomes the Law* (pp. 65–9) is not a critique of Derrida as a post-Husserlian phenomenologist, but of Derrida the messianic thinker in the tradition of Walter Benjamin. Rose does not grapple with Foucault or Deleuze after *Dialectic of Nihilism*.

25  Hermann Cohen, *Religion of Reason Out of the Sources of Judaism*, trans. Simon Kaplan, 2nd edn (Atlanta: Scholars Press, 1995); Moses Sofer, "A Reply Concerning the Question of Reform," trans. S. Fischer and S. Weinstein, in *The Jew in the Modern World: A Documentary History*, 2nd edn, eds. Paul Mendes-Flohr and Jehuda Reinharz (New York: Oxford University Press, 1995), pp. 169ff.

26  Rose, *Love's Work*, p. 135.

27  My primary source here is *Broken Middle*, pp. 261–4, but the reader should be aware that a reading of *Hegel Contra Sociology*, esp. pp. 92–120 and pp. 204–11, is of great assistance in comprehending the denseness of the latter work.

28  It seems that this argument lies behind John Milbank's assertion that Judaism is not monotheistic, since the negative commandments of the Hebrew Bible and their halakhic applications exhibit "residues of dualism." See Milbank, "'Postmodern Critical Augustinianism': A Short *Summa* in Forty Two Responses to Unasked Questions," *Modern Theology* 7/3 (April 1991), p. 230. (Note the implication at the top of p. 231 that Jews are Christ-killers.)

29  Rose, *Mourning Becomes the Law*, pp. 99–100; *Broken Middle*, pp. 288–94; *Judaism and Modernity*, pp. 33–6, 226–57.

30  Rose, *Mourning Becomes the Law*, pp. 74–5.

31  Rose, *Broken Middle*, pp. 122–3.

32  Rose, *Hegel Contra Sociology*, p. 4: "If the idea that the mind synthesizes the objects of knowledge is accepted, then it can be argued that it makes no sense to retain 'reality' for something beyond our knowledge. The production of objects

may equally well be said to be the production of their reality, not of their appearance."

33 Ibid., p. 9.

34 Ibid., pp. 5–10.

35 See Edmund Husserl, "Philosophy as Rigorous Science," trans. Quentin Lauer, in *Phenomenology and the Crisis of Philosophy* (New York: Harper & Row, 1965), pp. 71–147. In addition to the standard English accounts of German philosophy in the late nineteenth and early twentieth centuries – Klaus Köhnke, *The Rise of Neo-Kantianism: German Academic Philosophy Between Idealism and Positivism*, trans. R. J. Hollingdale (Cambridge: Cambridge University Press, 1991), and Herbert Schnädelbach, *Philosophy in Germany, 1831–1933*, trans. Eric Matthews (Cambridge: Cambridge University Press, 1984) – Steven Galt Crowell has written two excellent brief encyclopedia articles on the continuities and discontinuities between neo-Kantianism and phenomenology: "Neo-Kantianism," in *A Companion to Continental Philosophy*, ed. Simon Critchley and William R. Schroeder (Oxford: Blackwell, 1998), pp. 185–97 and "Twentieth-Century Continental Philosophy: The Early Decades," in *The Columbia History of Western Philosophy*, ed. Richard H. Popkin (New York: Columbia University Press, 1999), pp. 667–75.

36 Rose, *Hegel Contra Sociology*, p. 23. Also see Edmund Husserl, *Ideas Pertaining to a Pure Phenomenology and to a Phenomenological Philosophy. First Book: Introduction to a Pure Phenomenology*, trans. Fred Kersten (Dordrecht: Kluwer Academic Publishers, 1989), §§27–8 and pp. 35–6.

37 Emmanuel Levinas, "Questions and Answers," trans. Bettina Bergo, in *Of God Who Comes to Mind* (Stanford, CA: Stanford University Press, 1998), p. 87; "Que savons-nous de la mort?" in *Dieu, la Mort et le Temps*, ed. Jacques Rolland (Paris: Bernard Grasset, 1993), p. 21; "On Jewish Philosophy," trans. Michael B. Smith, in *In the Time of the Nations* (Bloomington: Indiana University Press, 1994), p. 180.

38 Rose, *Judaism and Modernity*, p. 213.

39 Rose, *Broken Middle*, p. 257.

40 Husserl, *Ideas Pertaining to a Pure Phenomenology and to a Phenomenological Philosophy. Second Book: Studies in the Phenomenology of Constitution*, trans. Richard Rojcewicz and André Schuwer (Dordrecht: Kluwer Academic Publishers, 1989). Hereafter cited in the body of the text as *ID2*.

41 Maurice Merleau-Ponty, *Signs*, trans. Richard McCleary (Evanston, IL: Northwestern University Press, 1964), pp. 159–81.

42 Ibid., pp. 162–3.

43 See Husserl, *Ideas I*, p. 68 (§36).

44 This motif of self-interruption is dominant in Jacques Derrida's most recent critique of Levinasian phenomenology. Jacques Derrida, *Adieu: To Emmanuel Levinas*, trans. Pascale-Anne Brault and Michael Naas (Stanford, CA: Stanford University Press, 1999), p. 51.

45 Merleau-Ponty, *Signs*, p. 166.

46 Ibid.

47 Ibid., p. 167. See Husserl, *Ideas I*, §85 and §88.

48 Rose, *Mourning Becomes the Law*, p. 123.

49 Emmanuel Levinas, "On Intersubjectivity: Notes on Merleau-Ponty" and "In Memory of Alphonse de Waelhens," in *Outside the Subject*, trans. Michael B. Smith (Stanford, CA: Stanford University Press, 1994), pp. 96–115.

50 Merleau-Ponty, *Signs*, p. 163.

51 Ibid., p. 168.

52 Levinas, "On Intersubjectivity," p. 101.

53 Ibid., p. 98.

54 Levinas, "In Memory of Alphonse de Waelhens," pp. 112–13. I have slightly altered the translation to reflect the English edition of *Ideas II*.

55  For Husserl's use of "introjection" and its root in the writings of Richard Avenar-
    ius, see John Scanlon, "Objectivity and Introjection in *Ideas II*," in *Issues in* Ideas
    II, eds. Thomas Nenon and Lester Embree (Dordrecht: Kluwer Academic
    Publishers, 1996), pp. 213–22.
56  See Maurice Natanson, *Edmund Husserl: Philosopher of Infinite Tasks* (Evanston,
    IL: Northwestern University Press, 1973), p. 98; Levinas, *The Theory of Intuition
    in Husserl's Phenomenology*, 2nd edn, trans. André Orianne (Evanston, IL:
    Northwestern University Press, 1995), p. 48, but see also pp. 150–1.
57  Rose, *Mourning Becomes the Law*, p. 37.
58  Levinas, "Intentionality and Sensation," in *Discovering Existence with Husserl*,
    trans. and eds. Richard A. Cohen and Michael B. Smith (Evanston, IL: North-
    western University Press, 1998), p. 148.
59  One might argue here that even if the subject is dephased in the act of perception,
    the Husserlian *Wesenschau* allows for this dephasing to be conquered through the
    assemblage of a number of perspectives of an object over a certain period of time.
    This would be the cognitive equivalent of the cinematic technique used in the
    film *The Matrix* and recent advertising campaigns in which the director is
    able to give the audience a 360-degree view around a still object by placing numer-
    ous cameras around it and using a computer to triangulate the gaps in perspective.
    In both "Intentionality and Sensation" and in *Otherwise than Being*, Levinas uses
    Husserl's lectures on the phenomenology of internal time-consciousness (specifi-
    cally the irrecuperability of the *Urimpression* which runs away from consciousness,
    only appearing through temporal retentions) as arguments against this possibility.
    For example: Husserl argues that the phenomenon of temporal retention (in the
    constitution of a melodic sequence) demonstrates that "the consciousness of the
    now is not itself now." Levinas glosses this idea in claiming that "the *Urimpression*
    already deviates from that needlepoint where it matures absolutely *present, and
    through this deviation* presents itself, *retained*, to a new punctual present. . . . [This]
    divergence of the *Urimpression* is the event, in itself primary, of the divergence of
    dephasing." See Husserl, *On the Phenomenology of the Consciousness of Internal
    Time (1893–1917)*, trans. John Barrett Brough (Dordrecht: Kluwer Academic
    Publishers, 1991), p. 345; Levinas, "Intentionality and Sensation," pp. 142–3;
    *Otherwise than Being, or Beyond Essence*, trans. Alphonso Lingis (Dordrecht:
    Kluwer Academic Publishers, 1991), p. 33.
60  Levinas, *Totality and Infinity: An Essay on Exteriority*, trans. Alphonso Lingis
    (Pittsburgh, PA: Duquesne University Press, 1969), p. 40. For a different account
    of Levinas, see Jean-Luc Marion, "The Other First Philosophy and the Question
    of Givenness," trans. Jeffrey Kosky, *Critical Inquiry* 25/4 (1999), pp. 785–800.
61  Thus, "ethics conserves the I." Levinas, *Totality and Infinity*, p. 305.
62  John Milbank finds a similar structure in the writing of Gregory of Nyssa: "Fre-
    quently we pass from what one might dub a 'neoplatonic' stage when reason
    'mirrors' God to either a sublime drive of the will to a God whom we realize we
    cannot exhaust (but only 'touch') or else a 'wounding' of our tranquil contem-
    plation of beauty by a sublime desire." Milbank, "The Force of Identity," in *The
    Word Made Strange*, p. 203.
63  I do not mention the Levinasian trope of the "face of the Other" here for two
    reasons. First, secondary literature has virtually exhausted the topic. But more
    importantly, the face is a modification of a more phenomenologically primordial
    erotic experience. The face shows itself, in its manifestation, to be a "pheno-
    menon" (in scare-quotes) that cannot sate human needs as the world can. The
    result for the subject who experiences this manifestation is that, as Edith Wyscho-
    grod writes, "the hunger experienced in the presence of the Other feeds upon
    itself" and becomes ever greater. This is already the sublime madness of Plato's
    description of eros in the *Phaedrus*. See Levinas, *Totality and Infinity*, pp. 179–80;

Wyschogrod, *Emmanuel Levinas: The Problem of Ethical Metaphysics*, 2nd edn (The Bronx: Fordham University Press, 2000), p. 89. This parallels the path which Levinas took in his writings: the concept of erotic alterity, established in 1947 in *From Existence to the Existent* and *Time and the Other*, is magnified into the concept of ethical alterity by the 1961 appearance of *Totality and Infinity*. Eros is the scene which discloses a general economy of self–other relations; this insight then gets transferred to non-libidinal interpersonal relations.

64 Rose, *Love's Work*, p. 59.
65 The pronouns used by the reader may vary.
66 "The caress consists in seizing upon nothing." Levinas, *Totality and Infinity*, p. 257.
67 Rose, *Love's Work*, p. 69.
68 In the last chapter of *Mourning Becomes the Law* (pp. 127–8), Rose cites a poem from the Sufi mystic Rumi that contains a wonderful example of this modality of desire perpetuating itself in the agon of its success and failure: "For a sign, the tip of the Beloved's curl became a centre of revelation / As yet the tip of that fair curl was not."
69 Levinas, *Totality and Infinity*, p. 256.
70 Rose, *Love's Work*, pp. 142–3.
71 Levinas, *Otherwise than Being*, pp. 51, 108.
72 Rose, *Mourning Becomes the Law*, p. 13.
73 Rose, *Broken Middle*, p. 264.
74 Levinas, "Messianic Texts," in *Difficult Freedom: Essays on Judaism*, trans. Seán Hand (Baltimore, MD: Johns Hopkins University Press, 1990), pp. 88–9. The Talmudic passage under discussion can be found at B. Sanhedrin 99a.
75 Another nominalization of the verb, *mashal*, an allusive tale or a parable, is thus a technique by which Torah becomes more tangible and thereby more easily comprehensible to the audience.
76 In the political sphere, this is most apparent in the example of Western nations doing battle against their own weapons sold to "developing" nations in the interest of securing friendship.
77 The lag between myself and the objects in my field of perception that Levinas purports to demonstrate in his phenomenology of the body has recently been correlated by a study of the so-called "flash-lag effect" (the gap between the emanation of light and its perception) which supports the hypothesis that consciousness is always playing catch-up with all the information streaming into it. David M. Eagleman and Terrence J. Sejnowski, "Motion Integration and Post-diction in Visual Awareness," *Science* 287, no. 5460 (17 March, 2000), 2036–8 (http://www.sciencemag.org/cgi/content/full/287/5460/2036).
78 Levinas, *Otherwise than Being*, p. 168.
79 Ibid.

# 8 The gift of prayer

*Theresa Sanders*

> He alone feels authentic sorrow who realizes not only *what he is* but *that he is*. Anyone who has not felt this should really weep, for he has never experienced real sorrow.
>
> *The Cloud of Unknowing*[1]

Why should being be a cause for sorrow? Why should we weep to know that we are? Why should we despair over the gift that was given to us in the beginning, in the beginning when, according to the Bible, God breathed life into the nostrils of the creature made from dust and cared for it and clothed it and spoke to it?

After all, the Book of Genesis tells how on the sixth day of creation, after human beings had been placed upon the earth, God looked at all the things that had been made and judged them to be not just good but indeed very good. In light of this goodness, in light of the sheer unexacted and unexpected outpouring of generosity that Genesis says the creator showed in bestowing life upon the earth, the author of *The Cloud of Unknowing* sounds positively ungrateful in urging us to weep over our existence. Why should the gift of being be such a burden and cause for tears?

*The Cloud* seems to recognize that its words may be taken as discourteous, and it hastens to affirm, "[A man] rejoices that he is and from the fullness of a grateful heart he gives thanks to God for the gift and the goodness of his existence." Nonetheless, the text continues: "At the same time, however, he desires unceasingly to be freed from the knowing and feeling of his being."[2]

Thanks, but no thanks.

Given the ambiguity of the gift of our being, what should be our response be? *The Cloud* warns against one option: rejecting the gift outright, or tossing it aside as worthless. The author reflects, "And yet in all this, never does [a man] desire to not-be, for this is the devil's madness and blasphemy against God."[3] It is blasphemy to give the gift back once it has been given. It is madness to throw it away.

But neither can we simply accept the gift gratefully, joyfully reveling in our own beingness. True, the author of *The Cloud* manages to give thanks and to do so with a full heart. However, he then immediately looks for a way to be loosed from the burden that has been bestowed upon him, unable to stand his awareness of its weight. His "thanks" is sincere and yet pervaded by a sadness so profound that any joy is swallowed up by his weeping.

This sorrow seems to be the fate of humankind as we live out the unbearable ambiguities of our being. But what if there were a way to escape from the sorrow? What if the gift could be refused before it was received? In other words, what if there were a way, a way perhaps only barely glimpsed, a way certainly never spoken, but a way to refuse the gift before it becomes a gift so that it becomes neither a burden for which we must be grateful nor a cause for madness and blasphemy? What if both our sorrow at our beingness, on the one hand, and our desire to be freed from being, on the other, could find . . . not articulation, no, but rather enactment, in a single gesture? What, in other words, if we could pray?

It may seem strange to speak of prayer in a world that has witnessed the Death of God. Prayer, having lost its addressee, would seem now to be nothing more than a curiosity. Certainly it is not a topic that has found much attention in postmodern theology; a quick glance at the indexes of deconstructive theological works shows that the word "prayer" seldom even appears. This is true despite a large and growing body of literature concerning the relation between deconstruction and negative or apophatic theology. Since negative theology, at least in the Christian tradition, nearly always occurs in the context of prayer, it is odd that so little attention has been paid to the subject. And yet, deconstructive literature has virtually ignored it.

What this essay hopes to do is to indicate what meaning prayer might have in a postmodern theological context. It will propose a definition of prayer as gift, taking into account the difficulties such a definition entails. The essay's thesis is that prayer is a conscious refusal of the gift of being. Better: it is a refusal of the consciousness of the gift of being, and this refusal in fact constitutes being as a gift.

## I. The gift

In recent years there has been a proliferation of writing concerning the notion of "the gift." At issue is whether or not there really is such a thing as a gift, or if gifts are not rather part of a carefully calculated economy in which nothing is given without expectation of a return. For example, observing patterns of exchange among peoples in the South Seas, anthropologist Marcel Mauss noted that "Gifts circulate . . . in Melanesia and Polynesia, with the certainty that they will be reciprocated."[4] According to Mauss, there is a variety of rules regarding the paying back of a gift: a certain amount of time must elapse, for instance, between the original donation and its return if the return is not to be seen as an insult. But these rules regulate rather than negate the dynamic of give-and-take. Gifts are exchanged in a perpetual flow of credit and debt in which who owes what to whom is conscientiously observed and recorded.

Complex rules regarding gift-giving and reciprocity are not limited to the South Seas, as any advice column or book of etiquette will demonstrate. Given the exchangeist character of gifts, however, a question arises: if a gift is given with the knowledge, or at least with the expectation, that the giver will receive something in return, does it still qualify as a gift? That is, what distinguishes gift-giving from systems of exchange such as barter or contractual obligation? Moreover, if all gifts fall into this same pattern of donation and return, is "gift" even a coherent concept, or should the word rather be abandoned in recognition of the inherently reciprocal character of all human interactions?

On the one hand, one might conclude that the give-and-take of human relations does not diminish but rather enhances the possibility of gift-giving. Consider, for example, a situation in which a giver continually showers a recipient with gifts that are neither solicited nor desired. Suppose that the gifts are given over the protestations of the receiver and that they do not stop even when the receiver insists that they must. In such a situation, we would not praise the giver as being exceptionally kind and generous. On the contrary, we would see the giver at best as annoying and at worst as potentially threatening. Indeed, if the situation were serious enough, we might consider notifying the police of the giver's actions, or suing the giver for harassment.

Now consider the same situation, but imagine that periodically the receiver responds to the giver with some gift in return: a small token, perhaps, or simply a note expressing gratitude. In this case, where the giving is not entirely one-sided, what is originally given by the giver might be truly called a gift. It is offered not simply because the giver wishes to give regardless of the impact of the gift on the receiver; rather, it is given because the receiver indicates a wish to receive the gift and participates in and encourages the giving by responding in kind.

One might conclude then that a gift is only truly a gift if it is reciprocated in some way. This is in fact the position of British theologian John Milbank as expressed in his essay "Can a Gift Be Given?" Milbank contends that it would actually be undesirable to strive for an ethic of utter self-giving. Such an ethic, he says, tends toward a kind of sacrificial suicide: "That is to say, it tends ineradicably to depersonalize or devolve into a will to be a fully usable object."[5] As we have seen, it also tends towards a kind of imposition on those to whom the gifts are given.

Milbank is writing in the context of Christian theology, and thus he takes up the question of giving in light of the Christian imperative towards *agape*. He argues that Christian charity is not about "pure" gift-giving at all, in the sense of giving without return or expectation of thanks. Rather, *agape* is a kind of "purified gift-exchange." Invoking Jewish and Christian notions of covenant, Milbank argues that even divine giving is rightly and necessarily characterized by a logic of exchange. This exchange "commits the very being of the giver to the gift and the expected return of the gift in reciprocal relation . . ."[6] Even the giving of God's divine Son in the Incarnation, notes Milbank, was not done unilaterally; rather, it depended upon the Virgin Mary's prior offer of herself as mother. Only Mary's "Let it be to me according to your word" could clear the way for the entrance of Jesus into the world. In this context, a "pure gift" from God, even if it were possible, would violate the reciprocal nature of the divine–human relationship.

Having considered one side of the debate about the nature of gift-giving, however, we must return to the question of what distinguishes the gift from the contractual obligation. For it must be noted that as soon as a gift is recognized as a gift, it establishes a kind of credit on behalf of the giver at the same time that it indebts the recipient. Gift-givers, even if they act in secret, cannot keep the secret of the gift from themselves, and thus they have the satisfaction of knowing themselves to be generous. Gift-receivers, on the other hand, even if they do not know the source of their gift, are expected at the very least to be grateful. If they do know who their benefactors are, then they are expected to reciprocate with a gift in return, even if that gift is only a word of thanks.

In the thinking of French philosopher Jacques Derrida, this sense of obligation that is entailed in gift-giving means that the only possible gift would be the one that is neither given nor received. A gift that is given is a gift that is repaid, if only with the satisfaction of knowing that it has been given. And a gift that is received is not a gift but a debt that cannot be repaid at once but must nonetheless be repaid at some point in the future. The only possible gift, then, in Derrida's thinking, is an impossible gift.

As an impossibility, "the gift" in Derrida's thought assumes a crucial role. It is a way of expressing disruption: what is outside all possible anticipation and reckoning. It signifies the "outside" of any system of meaning or exchange. It is a trope, in fact, for the end of metaphysics, as the true gift gives "*nothing that presents itself as present, nothing that is.*" The true gift cannot appear as a gift any more than the present (that is, now) can appear as present. Just as the present never fully is (since, at the moment we recognize it as present it is already past), so the gift cannot be. And yet, the very fact that it cannot be weighs upon us, says Derrida. It is, he says, "The secret of that about which one cannot speak, but which one can no longer silence."[7]

It is perhaps no accident that in Derrida's writing, the notion of the gift assumes a quasi-religious character. "Gift" is, after all, a profoundly religious concept. In a theological context, or, more specifically, in a Christian theological context, gift-giving is implicated in issues related to Trinitarian theology, Christology, eucharistic theology, liturgy, ethics, Mariology, and theologies of revelation. The Gospel of John proclaims that "God so loved the world that he gave his only Son, that whoever believes in him should not perish but have eternal life" (3:16). But given all that we have said thus far, we must ask: if God gives, whether God's Son or eternal life, does God really expect something in return? And if so, are God's gifts in fact donations or are they rather obligations? If they are obligations, then they must be repaid. But what sense could it possibly make for human beings to give something (back) to God?

## II. The gift of being

Thus far we have explored two sides of the question of gift-giving. From one perspective, it is good and proper that gifts be reciprocated; if they were not, they would not be gifts but rather impositions. From another, however, we observe that a gift that is reciprocated is not a gift but rather an obligation. It demands that the recipient respond with a gift in return, setting up an endless cycle of credit and debt. Unreciprocated gifts are impositions: reciprocated gifts are obligations. We seem to have arrived at an impasse.

It is, in fact, the same impasse encountered by the author of *The Cloud of Unknowing*. That author, having received the gift of being, can neither throw it away (which would be madness) nor refuse to be grateful (which would be blasphemy). Nor does he have any hope of ever evening the score by giving to God something of equal value. He has nothing to give that God does not already have. In the end, all he can do is weep.

Weep, that is, and pray. For what I will suggest is that we might break through the impasse regarding the gift by using the same method recommended by *The Cloud*: prayer. Prayer is an enactment of Derrida's impossible gift: the gift given by no one to no one which, in the end, is nothing to give at all.

Before we can move to a consideration of prayer, however, we must first come to a clearer conception of what, precisely, the gift is that causes so much anguish to the author of *The Cloud*, and why exactly this gift is such a cause for sorrow.

It is clear that the gift under consideration by the author of *The Cloud* is being: "He alone feels authentic sorrow who realizes that he is." Or again, "Every man has plenty of cause for sorrow but he alone understands the deep universal reason for sorrow who experiences *that he is*."[8] Being is what we are. Being is what we have been given.

And indeed, for John Milbank, being is precisely the gift that is offered to us by God. Milbank, in "Can a Gift Be Given?" finds himself in an extended argument with French philosopher Jean-Luc Marion over the question of what exactly it is that God gives to humans. The details of that debate need not concern us here, but the argument may be summarized in this way: for Marion, God loves before God is. More precisely, God is love (*agape*). When God gives, what God gives is first of all God's self, *agape*. This giving precedes the giving of being. Thus not only beings but even non-beings receive God's goodness.[9] In other words, according to Marion, charity is the primary gift, and then "Charity delivers Being/being."[10]

In Milbank's eyes, however, this amounts to saying that when God gives, what God gives is literally nothing. That is, giving must give some thing, something in the realm of being. Writes Milbank, "The gift without being is not a gift 'of' anything, and so is not a gift."[11] If being is not the primary gift, if being is given only as an afterthought, as it were, then giving itself disappears because there is no thing being given and no being to whom one can give. Giving, in Milbank's eyes, thus becomes an empty and ultimately nihilistic gesture.

But if being is a gift, it is not a gift without price. Milbank does not hesitate to declare that our existence does indeed indebt us to God. We receive from God an ontological deficit which we must repay, endlessly and imperfectly, simply by our very being: "The Creature only is, as manifesting the divine glory, as acknowledging its own nullity and reflected brilliance. To be, it entirely honours God, which means it returns to him an unlimited, never paid-back debt."[12] One could, of course, refuse to repay the debt by refusing to acknowledge or proclaim one's status as indebted. This is the root of sin, the ancient adamic transgression of wishing to be like God. Moreover, this refusal, according to Milbank, is self-contradictory in that one can refuse to acknowledge that one has received being only because one has already in fact received being.

Whether we believe, like Marion, that the divine gift is *agape* which then delivers being, or we believe with Milbank that God's gift is being itself, there are two more observations we must take into consideration. First, the fact remains that our being, no matter how we account for it, is not a fullness of being. It is instead marked by incompletion. From a Scholastic perspective, one might say that we are both presence-to-self and absence-from-self, or both *esse* and *materia*. From a post-Cartesian perspective, we might agree that "I am, I exist, is necessarily true, every time I express it or conceive of it in my mind."[13] Yet we are also aware both that we are not all that there is to be thought, and that not all that we are is accessible to thought. We are both conscious of ourselves as beings and aware of what is not subsumable to our consciousness.[14]

Second, this limitation of our being only appears to us as the frustration of an unrestricted desire for being. That is, we only know objects to be limited because we wish for illimitation. Our reach for being, experienced in a transcendental movement, constantly and necessarily exceeds our grasp. Thus, what we know when we know a thing is not simply the object itself. We know a limited instantiation of being, yes, but also an unlimited desire for being, as well as a difference between the two. That difference appears as what is other than being.

Thus, we cannot hold that "the gift" that we are given, whether primarily (as for Milbank) or derivatively (as for Marion), is simply being. It is also the knowledge, however halting, of what is outside of or otherwise than being, and a desire that nothing be outside of being. We do not receive simply existence but also the limitation of existence, testimony to what cannot be accounted for under the rubric of being. These conditions of our knowing cannot be extracted from the experience of ourselves.

### III. The gift of prayer

It is this knowledge of what is otherwise than being, and the desire for unrestricted being, and not simply the knowledge of his own being *per se*, that afflicts the author of *The Cloud*. That is, it is not being itself that is ultimately so burdensome to him, but rather the experience of this being: as he puts it, the "knowing and feeling of your own being." Again and again, the author wishes to be freed from the "naked knowing and feeling," by which he is "crushed."[15] He is crushed not by his existence in itself but by the knowledge of his existence. That knowledge prevents him from encountering his Beloved, who is inaccessible to thought and understanding and feeling. The author advises his readers, "Long after you have successfully forgotten every creature and its works, you will find that a naked knowing and feeling of your own being still remains between you and your God."[16]

Moreover, the author's sorrow is rooted in a recognition that insofar as anything is, including ourselves, God is not. That is, anything that participates in being is an instantiation of something other than God, who is "wholly other."[17] Thus, in advising his readers about how to pray, the author counsels: "I do not want you to be anywhere; no, not outside, above, behind, or beside yourself." Why not? Because to be somewhere is to be still in the realm of things. All things are to be left behind by consciousness, and devotees are to enter into a realm where they know only nothingness: "Never give up but steadfastly persevere in this nothingness ...". For myself, I prefer to be lost in this nowhere, wrestling with this blind nothingness, than to be like some great lord traveling everywhere and enjoying the world as if he owned it.[18]

This is why "the gift" is such an ambiguous endowment. It is not really that our being is itself a cause for weeping. It is rather the knowledge that being is not all there is, and that what there is other than being is inaccessible to us except in a perpetual withdrawal from what is, that tears at our hearts. That is why we find ourselves divided between gratitude and despair, between the desire to sing praise with joyful hearts and the urge to throw our lives away in what *The Cloud* called a kind of blasphemous insanity.

Gift or burden? What has been given to us?

As we have seen, Milbank has no hesitation in describing our being as a divine gift despite the fact that it places us in a debt that can never be exhausted. He uses the word "gift" even though refusing to acknowledge and be grateful for this gift is a sacrilege and a sin. Gift-giving, he says, relies on an exchange between two parties, and one-sided giving on God's part would violate the reciprocal nature of the divine–human relationship. Thus we must offer God our praise and thanksgiving if the covenantal bond between God and us is to be preserved.

More than that, we must give what we have to others as a way of extending the generosity of God. In a discussion of Jewish and New Testament understandings of gift-giving, Milbank observes, approvingly, "As God gives to us, who are infinitely needful, so we should give to the needful, without stint or 'counting of the cost'. Only gratitude and 'good use' are expected in return."[19]

Surely it is not irrelevant to point out here, however, that monitoring whether or not one's donation has been "put to good use" is precisely a way of counting the cost. The implication is that if gifts are not in fact put to good use, or if the recipients are not sufficiently grateful, the gifts may stop. It is difficult to see how this is reconcilable with the notion of "giving without stint."

Moreover, our giving to others, no matter how generous it might be, does not exhaust our debt to God. That debt is permanent; no jubilee year could ever erase it. And our giving to others actually causes debt to proliferate, sending out new shoots and putting down roots into our interpersonal relationships. Once we have given to others, they are indebted to us as well as to God.

In other words, despite Milbank's description of the divine–human relationship as a reciprocal bond, in truth there is no reciprocity in the relationship. God gives a gift that cannot be repaid, and humans are described as existing in a kind of perpetual servitude such that no matter what they offer, their debt cannot be canceled. If they offer nothing, the debt does not remain the same but becomes even more abysmal. If they offer something to others as a way of paying the debt to God, they not only do not pay off the debt but they manage to increase others' indebtedness. Such a scenario sounds more tragic than donative.

Is there any alternative? It would seem not. Humans are contingent, thrust into being before consent could be a meaningful term. They are not the authors of their own existence. They are limited instantiations of being with a taste for the unlimited and an awareness that being is not all that there is. They are, as *The Cloud* observes, a cause for weeping.

And yet, the author of *The Cloud* does not stop with weeping.

Instead, he offers a prescription for joy and "greatest delight." He advises his readers to enter into contemplative prayer, fixing their attention on no thing whatsoever and leaving behind all experience. Methods for doing this vary. Readers should entertain only "a naked intent toward God." They should choose one simple word and repeat it over and over, using that one word to banish all thought and feeling.[20] If they find themselves unable to leave behind the things of the world, they should pretend not to notice these distractions, looking beyond them or over the distractions' shoulders, as it were.[21]

Determination to abide in this prescribed nowhere-nothing is arduously difficult to maintain, according to *The Cloud*. Accustomed to constant stimulation, our senses and intellectual faculties imperiously demand input and become frustrated and restive when it is not provided. And yet if we persist, our willingness to abide in darkness will be more pleasing to God, says the text, than anything else we might offer.

This kind of prayer, then, is something that we can offer. It is a gift, our gift given to God. And yet at the same time it is God's gift to us, according to *The Cloud*: "Contemplative prayer is God's gift, wholly gratuitous. No one can earn it. It is in the nature of this gift that one who receives it receives also the aptitude for it. No one can have the aptitude without the gift itself."[22]

Prayer is a wholly gratuitous gift from God to us. Since it is gratuitous, nothing is expected in return. It is given with no strings attached and no account books kept. And yet at the same time, and in precisely the same act, contemplative prayer is humans' gift to God, a gift so precious that it "gives God the greatest delight," causes the devils to rage ceaselessly, and makes the angels "hasten to assist you in every way."[23] How can one and the same act be a gift both to and from? And if it is a gift that is exchanged, how can it still be a gift rather than an item of barter? It is given by God to humans to be given back by humans to God. In truth, it sounds less like a gift than like a type of coinage, passed from hand to hand as an abbreviated message of good will. Can contemplative prayer really be thought of as a gift?

In Derrida's consideration of "the gift," we saw that for him the only possible gift is the one that is neither given nor received: the impossible gift. Prayer, I contend, is that impossible gift.

The ability to pray, to offer contemplative prayer, to offer the kind of prayer that *The Cloud* describes, is a gift truly given to no one because there is no one who could receive it. Since it is the condition of being "neither outside nor above nor behind nor beside yourself," of leaving the self behind, the facility for contemplative prayer cannot be received by anyone. This is not an eradication of the being of the self; it is not the madness of suicide or the will, as Milbank put it, to become "a fully usable object." It is the dissolution of the experience of subjectivity. In this dissolution there can be no awareness of having received the gift, or indeed any awareness of a gift at all.

Likewise, there can be no awareness at the moment when the gift is offered in return by the pray-er (that is, the one who prays) of anyone offering it, or of anything being offered. There is in that moment only darkness, only clouds of forgetting and unknowing. There is not even a clear sense of the one to whom the prayer is offered: "A man may know completely and ponder thoroughly every created thing and its works, yes, and God's works, too, but not God himself."[24]

In addition, what is offered is offered without desire for anything in return, since there is no one who could experience such desire or who could receive compensation for the gift of prayer.

But here we must be careful. Is it true that the one who prays expects nothing in return? Is not prayer always prayer for something, if only for the experience of God itself? *The Cloud* would seem to tend in this direction. Throughout the text, readers are advised to focus only on their desire for God: "For I tell you this, one loving blind desire for God alone is more valuable in itself, more pleasing to God and to the saints . . . than anything else you could do."[25] Again, "The path to heaven is measured by desire and not by miles."[26] Desire here seems teleological, as if tending towards some future fulfillment or recompense.

It seems to be simply common sense that prayer is teleological. People pray to someone for something. They ask for things, if only for the presence of the one whom they ask. Expectation seems to be part of the structure of prayer itself. Prayer issues demands: Give! Receive! Help! Come! It waits for answers, for assistance, for certitude and for satisfaction. It waits to know that it has been heard.

And yet surely this is not the only meaning that prayer can have. It is not the meaning that prayer has in *The Cloud*. There, devotees are not assured that whatever they pray for will be delivered. Indeed, they are not instructed to pray "for" anything at all. Some of those who pray, observes the author, receive great spiritual consolations. Others do not. Some feel swelling waves of sweet satisfaction. Others are left desolate. And yet "prayer" is not defined by any of these things, nor does it fail if it does not receive them. Prayer, for *The Cloud*, is simply the persistent offering of love towards the God whom it does not know.

Nor is there a promise, no matter how implicit, that one day it will know God: that all darkness and forgetting will be wiped away. Of the one who persists in prayer, the author of *The Cloud* notes,

> And finally there will come a moment when he experiences such peace and repose in that darkness that he thinks surely it must be God himself.
>
> Yes, he will suppose this nothingness to be one thing and another, yet to the last it will remain a *cloud of unknowing* between him and his God.[27]

Thus prayer can be understood as something received by no one and then offered in return (no, not offered in return: simply offered) by no one to one who is so unknown as to be no one at all. It is a gift, an impossible gift. The impossible gift.

## Notes

1  *The Cloud of Unknowing* ed. William Johnston (New York: Image Books, 1973), p. 103.
2  Ibid., p. 104.
3  Ibid.
4  Marcel Mauss, *The Gift: The Form and Reason for Exchange in Archaic Societies* (London: Routledge, 1990) p. 36. Mauss's book was first published in 1950.
5  "Can a Gift Be Given? Prolegomena to a Future Trinitarian Metaphysic," *Modern Theology* 11/1 (January 1995), p. 132.
6  Ibid., p. 144.
7  Jacques Derrida, *Given Time: I. Counterfeit Money*, trans. Peggy Kamuf (Chicago: University of Chicago Press, 1992), p. 147.
8  *The Cloud of Unknowing*, p. 103.
9  Jean-Luc Marion, *God Without Being*, trans. Thomas A. Carlson (Chicago: University of Chicago Press, 1991), p. 76.

10  Ibid., p. 102.
11  Milbank, "Can a Gift Be Given?", p. 137.
12  Ibid., p. 135.
13  René Descartes, *Discourse on Method and the Meditations*, trans. F. E. Sutcliffe (New York: Penguin, 1968), p. 103.
14  See Charles Winquist, *Desiring Theology* (Chicago: University of Chicago Press, 1995), esp. pp. 8–16.
15  *The Cloud of Unknowing*, p. 104.
16  Ibid., p. 103.
17  Ibid., p. 79.
18  Ibid., p. 136.
19  Milbank, "Can a Gift Be Given?", p. 148.
20  *The Cloud of Unknowing*, p. 56.
21  Ibid., p. 88.
22  Ibid., p. 91.
23  Ibid., p. 48.
24  Ibid., p. 54.
25  Ibid., p. 60.
26  Ibid., p. 127.
27  Ibid., p. 138.

# 9 And maker mates with made

## World and self-creation in Eriugena and Joyce

*Thomas A. Carlson*

The following passage concludes Jorge Luis Borges' two-page text titled "Everything and Nothing":

> History adds that before or after dying he found himself in the presence of God and told Him: "I who have been so many men in vain want to be one and myself." The voice of the Lord answered from a whirlwind: "Neither am I anyone; I have dreamt the world as you dreamt your work, my Shakespeare, and among the forms in my dream are you, who like myself are many and no one."[1]

A God of the whirlwind (chaotic, incomprehensible) realizes himself both as many and as no one in and through the world that he dreams – wherein likewise the modern playwright and poetic genius, an image of the creative (and incomprehensible) God, realizes himself both as many and as no one in and through the work that he dreams (wherein we can imagine that there appears a God . . . ). With astounding economy, Borges articulates here the theme that I want to develop (less economically) in what follows: the polyonymous anonymity of the human reflects perfectly (because abyssally) the polyonymous anonymity of the divine insofar as both the human and the divine would realize themselves in and through a creation that is also self-creation. In both cases the "subject" of such creation assumes any and every identity to the degree that it finally ignores or dissolves any identity – and vice versa. From this perspective, self-creation would imply a mystical foundation of unknowing according to which the self-creative subject is fundamentally absent in the act of its self-creation.[2]

This theme arises in light of recent and ongoing discussion concerning the relation between "negative" (or "apophatic") and "mystical" theologies, on the one hand, and, on the other, the tendencies of late modern or postmodern philosophy (especially post-Heideggerian and post-structuralist). I have argued elsewhere[3] that the current fascination among philosophers and theorists with largely medieval traditions of mystical and negative theology must be understood in relation to a kind of "negative anthropology" that haunts postmodern thought: the negative forms of language surrounding the ineffable God of Dionysian traditions (from Pseudo-Dionysius through Eriugena to Meister Eckhart, Nicholas of Cusa, and so on) resonate significantly with the negative forms of language today surrounding finite, mortal subjectivity and the experience of "unknowing" in all its various figures (above all "Being-toward-death" and "the gift," but also desire, love, justice, decision, etc.). Within this context, the language and experience of unknowing would signal a critique or rejection of the active and self-grounding subject who dominates the modern thinking that begins with Descartes' formulation of truth as certitude and reaches its height in Hegel's absolute knowing; the alternative model of subjectivity that emerges within current discussions of negative and mystical theology insists on the radical passivity and receptivity out of which subjectivity would first be called – and here these discussions are tied intimately to a fairly constant philosophic heritage, from Heidegger through Levinas and Derrida to Marion. Granting the necessity and productivity of this emphasis on passivity and receptivity within current understandings of the subject, however, and granting likewise the powerful connections to be made between such understandings and the deeper traditions of negative and mystical theology, one should not allow the emphasis on passivity to obscure the decisive role of self-creation both within the traditions of mystical and negative theology and within certain lines of postmodern thought. I therefore aim here to open a discussion of self-creation by addressing its role both in a figure pivotal to the history of negative and mystical theology in the West (John Scotus Eriugena, for whom, as Borges indicates, "all our history is merely an extended dream of God's, one which eventually devolves on God"[4]) and in a figure decisive to any understanding of late modern or postmodern thought and culture (James Joyce, whom Borges rightly places alongside Eriugena within a single line of Irish genius that "extends itself," as Umberto Eco puts it, "to the limits of reason, always on the border of provocation and fragmentation"[5]). A comparison of these figures, I believe, will help to demonstrate and elucidate a quasi-mystical dimension in the culture today where we must ceaselessly–and above all technologically–create and recreate ourselves while fully comprehending neither who we are in creating nor who we are as created.

"The first troubling voice of medieval Neo-Platonism" (Eco, *Aesthetics of Chaosmos*, 78), and at the same time strikingly modern in his thinking,[6] John Scotus Eriugena (ca. 810–877) arises here as pivotal because he establishes for the Western mystical traditions the essential interplay of apophatic theology and apophatic anthropology within a mystical conception of the cosmos. In doing so, he synthesizes and develops the important anthropological insight of the fourth-century Cappadocian Gregory of Nyssa (ca. 335–ca. 394), according to whom the human subject created in the image of an incomprehensible God is likewise incomprehensible to itself,[7] and the cosmic vision of the late fifth-century father of mystical theology, Pseudo-Dionysius, according to whom the mystically unknowable God assumes all names and no name insofar as he both reveals and conceals himself through all of creation. By means of this synthesis Eriugena will arrive at a radical and very powerful theological (and anthropological) innovation: the unknowable God who both reveals and conceals himself throughout the creation in which he realizes himself remains at the same time, ultimately, incomprehensible to himself – just as the human subject created in that God's image is both self-creative and incomprehensible to itself. A brief discussion of Eriugena's system will help to fill out the ground and significance of this innovation, to which in turn we will relate Joyce's vision in *Finnegans Wake*.

The core dialectic of Eriugena's masterwork *On the Division of Nature* (or the *Periphyseon*[8]) recapitulates Dionysius' Christian version of the Proclean scheme of procession, return and remaining (*prohodos, epistrophē, monē*). According to that dialectic, the super-essential cause of all things moves through all things as immanent to them and stands beyond all things as transcendent of them. As cause, the divine is all in all – and so addressed, metaphorically, by affirmative or kataphatic theology (P, I, 458B), but as super-essential, the divine is nothing in anything – and so most properly addressed by negative or apophatic theology (P, I, 458A–B). As in later thinkers such as Meister Eckhart (ca. 1260–1327) and Nicholas of Cusa (1401–1464), this dialectic of immanence and transcendence seeks to indicate that God, who is both all in all and nothing in anything, named infinitely and infinitely nameless, illuminating all and beyond all in a brilliant darkness, is finally distinct by his indistinction, different thanks to his indifference – absent in his very presence.

In his innovative treatment of this dialectic, Eriugena argues not only that the divine "is all things as the Cause of all things" but indeed that the divine creates *itself* in and through all that it creates:[9] "God is the maker of all things and is made in all things" (P, III, 682D). For Eriugena, this self-creation of the divine – and it alone – gives the subsistence of creatures: "For when it is said that it creates itself, the true meaning is nothing else but that it is establishing the natures of things [*nisi naturas rerum condere*]. For the creation [*creatio*] of itself, that is, the manifestation [*manifestatio*] of itself in something, is surely that by which all things subsist [*omnium existentium profecto est substitutio*]" (P, I, 455A–B). Creation itself, then, the whole of the intelligible and sensible world, is for Eriugena God's own self-creation and self-manifestation.

Thus, interpreting the cosmic dialectic of divine immanence and transcendence as divine *self*-creation, Eriugena, like Dionysius, can see all of the cosmos as an infinitely varied showing or appearance of God. Just as the Scripture in which God reveals himself opens way to an endless variety of possible readings, where one meaning leads to the next within an endless exegetical *transitus* toward the absolutely simple and inaccessible source of all meaning,[10] so the cosmos offers an endless multiplicity of theophanies that can be read (P, III, 679A) to show the invisible God from as many different angles as there are holy souls to desire God's appearance (see, e.g., P, I, 448C–D). Indeed, as Dermot Moran suggests, Eriugena's theo-cosmic perspectivalism already signals the "infinity of worlds" that will often be associated (as in Joyce) with Cusa and Giordano Bruno and often be taken to mark a break between the late medieval and early modern visions.[11]

Within this theophanic play of the cosmos, where God's self-manifestation is actually self-creation, Eriugena emphasizes, further, the fundamentally *co-creative* interplay between Creator and creature: "we ought not to understand God and the creature as two things distinct from one another," Eriugena insists, "but as one and the same. For both the creature, by subsisting, is in God; and God, by manifesting Himself, in a marvelous and ineffable manner creates Himself in the creature" (P, III, 678C). Much like Hegel, though with an apophatic intention that is deeply absent in Hegel, Eriugena insists that God realizes himself in and through the creature, just as the creature finds its subsistence in God; God achieves self-consciousness in and through the crea-ture's consciousness of God.[12] It is in these dynamic, co-creative terms that "the Creator of all things" is "created in all things"[13] – which means that every creature is at bottom a paradoxical theophany, from the celestial essences down to the very last bodies of the visible world (see P, III, 681A–B). All of creation offers a field of luminous appearance that makes manifest the inaccessible darkness of the super-essential (see, e.g., P, III, 681B).[14]

Operating according to the paradox of God's brilliant darkness, wherein the invisible becomes visible, the theophanic in Eriugena follows the Dionysian logic of "dissimilar similarity," and thus it proves equally theocryptic:

> For everything that is understood and sensed is nothing else but the apparation of what is not apparent, the manifestation of the hidden, the affirmation of the negated, the comprehension of the incomprehensible, the utterance of the unutterable, the access to the inaccessible [. . .] the visibility of the invisible, the place of that which is in no place, the time of the timeless, the definition of the infinite, the circumscription of the uncircumscribed [. . .]
>
> (P, III, 633A–B; see also P, III, 678C).

In sum, the theophanic self-creation of God constitutes a movement from the transcendence of super-essential Nothingness, which is absolutely simple and incomprehensible, into the manifold immanence of all created things, which can be known; that immanence, however, is always an immanence *of* the transcendent, and it can therefore ultimately signal only the impossible appearance of the inapparent – the limited and knowable determinacy of God's absolutely unlimited and unknowable indeterminacy.[15]

Eriugena elucidates the logic of this theophanic self-creation, where the something of creation, which we can know, issues from the self-negation of the divine Nothingness, which we cannot know, through the "example" of our own human nature – and at this point, the indispensable anthropological dimension of Eriugena's theological project becomes clear:

For our own intellect [*intellectus*] too, although in itself it is invisible and incomprehensible [*invisibilis et incomprehensibilis*], yet becomes both manifest and comprehensible [*et manifestatur et comprehenditur*] by certain signs [*signis*] when it is materialized in sounds and letters and also indications as though in sorts of bodies; and while it becomes externally apparent in this way [*et dum sic extrinsecus apparet*] it still remains internally invisible [*semper intrinsicus invisibilis permanet*], *and* while it breaks out into various figures comprehensible to the senses it never abandons the incomprehensible state of its nature; and before it becomes outwardly apparent it moves itself within itself; and thus it is both silent and cries out, and while it is silent it cries out and while it is crying out it is silent; and invisible it is seen and while it is being seen it is invisible; and uncircumscribed it is circumscribed, and while it is being circumscribed it continues to be uncircumscribed [. . .]

(P, III, 633B–C).

The theophanic God, who through self-creation makes manifest his uncreated invisibility, is mirrored in the human intellect, which, in itself indefinite and invisible, defines and shows itself through its self-expression, all the while remaining indefinite and invisible. In both cases, Eriugena signals the incomprehensible ground of creativity itself, a mystical foundation of unknowing out of which creation would spring.

Of course, this human example is not simply an example, since it is grounded in Eriugena's understanding of the human subject as incomprehensible *image* of the incomprehensible God. While every creature in Eriugena constitutes an appearance of God (or a *theophany*), the human creature alone constitutes an image (or *imago*) of God – and it constitutes an image of God not simply to the degree that the human intellect, like the divine, becomes self-conscious in and through its own self-expression but, even more, insofar as the human intellect, again *like the divine*, ultimately proves through that very self-consciousness – or in the deepest ground of that self-consciousness – to be incomprehensible to itself.[16] The human image of the divine is distinctive in that it is *both* self-conscious *and* incomprehensible to itself, or incomprehensible in that self-consciousness. Eriugena's apophatic anthropology, insisting on the incomprehensible image of the divine in the human, comes to play a decisive theological role, therefore, since in knowing the deepest incomprehensibility of the human, we come in fact to know the true incomprehensibility of God. In both cases, such incomprehensibility is at the same time the very ground of self-consciousness, for it is the incomprehensibility of a Nothingness which is the ground of that creation in and through which alone self-consciousness is realized.

Here, Eriugena's apophatic anthropology complements his apophatic theology: neither God nor the human subject created in His image can comprehend *what* they themselves are – even as they achieve, through their own self-creative self-expression, a self-conscious awareness *that* they are:

> For the human mind [*mens*] does know itself [*et seipsam novit*], and again
> does not know itself [*et seipsam non novit*]. For it knows that it is [*quia
> est*], but does not know what it is [*quid est*]. And, as we have taught in
> earlier books, it is this which reveals most clearly the Image of God to be
> in man [*maxime imago Dei esse in homine docetur*]. For just as God is
> comprehensible in the sense that it can be deduced from His creation that
> He is, and incomprehensible because it cannot be comprehended by any
> intellect whether human or angelic nor even by Himself [*nec a seipso*]
> what He is, seeing that He is not a what but superessential [*quia non est
> quid, quippe superessentialis*]: so to the human mind it is given to know
> only one thing, that it is – but as to what it is no sort of notion is
> permitted it.
>
> (P, IV, 771B).[17]

As becomes clear in this passage, Eriugena wants to insist not only that the
human cannot comprehend God, nor even simply that the human created in
the image of the incomprehensible God is itself incomprehensible – but also,
in full consistency with these first two principles, that even God finally cannot
comprehend himself.[18] In light of such thoroughgoing divine ignorance Eriugena can insist that "the human mind is more honored in its ignorance than
in its knowledge" (P, IV, 771C) – for in that ignorance above all the image of
the divine in the human achieves its perfection. And so it is that "the ignorance in it of what it is is more praiseworthy than the knowledge that it is, just
as the negation of God accords better with the praise of His nature than the
affirmation . . . " (P, IV, 771C).

Eriugena's apophatic celebration of ignorance here – both theological and
anthropological – is intended to mark the manner in which both the divine
and the human substance ultimately exceed or transcend all ten of the categories or "predicables" delimited by that "shrewdest of the Greeks," Aristotle (P, I, 463A). One of those categories, however, assumes a particular
importance: that of place, *locus*, or *topos* (and its twin, time). In seeking to
articulate the excess of the divine and its image over the categories, Eriugena
emphasizes above all the impossibility of *locating* either the divine or the
human substance, and he does so because it is above all *locus* that marks the
kind of limitation, circumscription or definition that alone make knowledge
(or discourse) possible: "the Divine Likeness in the human mind is most
clearly discerned," Eriugena insists, when it is "not known what it is" – precisely because "if it were known to be something, then at once it would be
limited by some definition, and thereby would cease to be a complete expression of the Image of its Creator, who is absolutely unlimited and contained
within no definition [*qui omnino incircumscriptus est, et in nullo intelligitur*],
because He is infinite, beyond all that may be said or comprehended, super-
essential [*quia infinitus est, super omne, quod dicitur et intelligitur, superessen-
tialis*]" (P, IV, 771C–D). The super-essential God who remains beyond all
that can be spoken or understood is a God beyond the definition or

circumscription of any *place* (or time); indeed, he is for Eriugena the placeless place of all places, "present to all things by his immeasurable circumambience of them" (P, I, 523B) – and thus in that very presence to things beyond all things to which he is present.[19] Since knowledge for Eriugena implies the definition or location of the object known, the unknowable God and its human image alike stand beyond all location.

At the same time, such definition or location is the very condition of all creation. Thus, insofar as self-creation implies definition or location, even as it issues from – and returns to – a nothingness that cannot be defined or located, we can see in the movement of self-creation an interesting intersection between self-awareness and ignorance of self.[20] That is, the creative intellect (human or divine) must define or locate that which it – only thereby – comes to know, and in that which it comes to know it achieves its own self-consciousness or self-awareness, its subsistence; at the same time, however, the same creative intellect necessarily exceeds or stands beyond that which it creates, and to that degree it remains beyond all location and thus incomprehensible – even to itself. The ground of definition and knowledge is itself indefinable and unknowable.

This interplay between the self-consciousness and self-ignorance of creative intellect, between knowable creation in all its multiplicity and the unknowable simplicity of creation's ground, comes to light most forcefully in Eriugena where the divine and the human are most essentially united – in the Word of God as Reason or Cause of the universe:

> The Word of God is the creative Reason and Cause of the established universe, simple and in itself infinitely multiple; simple, because the universe of all things is in Him an indivisible and inseparable One, or rather the indivisible and inseparable unity of all things is the Word of God since He is all things; and not unreasonably understood to be multiple because He is diffused through all things to infinity, and that diffusion is the subsistence of all things. For He spreads mightily from end to end and sweetly disposes all things. Also in the Psalm: "His speech runneth swiftly." By "speech" [*sermo*] the prophet meant the Word [*verbum*] of the Father which runs swiftly through all things in order that all things may be. For its multiple and infinite course through all things is the subsistence [*subsistentia*] of all things.
>
> (P, III, 642C–D).

As the self-expression of God, the Word creates all things and is created *in* all things (P, III, 646C); it is the creative Wisdom (*sapientia creatrix*) of the Father (P, III, 646A) whose providence "proceeds into all things and comes into being in all things and contains all things, and yet because of its pre-eminent self-identity it is not anything in anything through anything, but transcends all things" (P, III, 644D). The core Eriugenian dialectic of immanence and transcendence here comes to expression through the Word that is the center of God's self-expression: the God who as Word runs through all things and is their subsistence at the same time remains transcendently simple in Himself. As beginning, middle and end of all things, the Word is both creative and salvific ground.[21]

Now, in this understanding of the Word as that which "runs" through all things so as to make them be and bring them back into God, Eriugena is alluding to one of two etymologies that he invokes elsewhere to articulate the meaning of the Greek name for God: if *theos* derives from the verb *theō*, or "I run," he reasons, then it articulates the sense in which God "runs *throughout all things* and [. . .] by His running fills out all things, as it is written: 'His Word runneth swiftly' " (P, I, 452C); if *theos* derives from the verb *theorō*, "I see," then it articulates the sense in which God "sees in Himself all things that are [while] He looks upon nothing that is outside Himself because outside Him there is nothing" (P, I, 452C). The God who "runs" through all things to make them be is also the God who creates and sustains all things by *seeing* all things in himself – and himself in all things. As maker and made, seer and seen (P, III, 677C), the God who expresses himself through his Word is at once most present and most hidden, all things in all and nothing in nothing (P, III, 668C). The ineffable intellectual light present to all but contained by none, He is, in short, the placeless "place of all places" that can be defined neither by itself nor by any other intellect, the placeless place from which all things proceed and to which all things return.[22]

In this light we can situate the end of Eriugena's entire vision: the unification (*adunatio*) of the world with God in and through the human subject implies a deification (or theosis) achieved only insofar as the human creature, in perfect likeness with God, transcends all location through "the ascent beyond places and times" (P, I, 482D), for those "*who participate* in the eternal and infinite beatitude will be encompassed neither by place nor by time" (P, I, 482D).

One should emphasize here that the human subject who would be capable of such transcendence over place and time is not only the subject who proves incomprehensible to itself; it is also – to the very same degree – the subject who *comprehends* all of creation, which it *can* transcend thanks only to that comprehension. In this regard, a significant conjunction emerges in Eriugena's anthropology between the ultimately unknowing subject, on the one hand, and the all-knowing subject, on the other hand – the subject made in the image of the incomprehensible God who himself sees and comprehends all by his presence.

The fact that the human is created in God's image means for Eriugena not only that the human mind is ultimately incomprehensible to itself but also that the same human mind, like the divine, contains within itself all of creation. God "has created in man all creatures visible and invisible [*omnem quidem creaturam visibilem et invisibilem in homine fecit*]" (P, IV, 763D) in the sense that the "notion of nature, created in the human mind and possessed by it" *is* the "substance of the very things of which it is the notion, just as in the Divine Mind the notion of the whole created Universe is the incommunicable substance of the whole" (IV, 769A).[23] It is this comprehension of all creation that signals the distinctive transcendence of the human who is created in the image of God.

God wills to make every creature in man, Eriugena argues, "because He wished to make [man] in His image and likeness, so that, just as the primal Archetype transcends all by the excellence of His Essence, so His image should transcend all created things in dignity and grace" (P, IV, 764A). The incomprehensible transcendence of the divine that contains all things within itself is imaged, then, in the transcendence of the human creature who comprehends all creation even as it remains incomprehensible to itself. This means, in short, that the apophatic or unknowing subject in Eriugena is also an all-comprehending subject – and vice versa.[24] The "mastery" of comprehension, then, would be established in Eriugena on the basis of an incomprehensible ground – just as the incomprehensible ground of Joyce's comprehensive vision will resist all mastery.

If Eriugena offers in the medieval context a strikingly modern vision that understands world- and self-creation in terms of an infinite self-expression (both human and divine) that is at bottom apophatically mystical, then James Joyce in the modern context offers a strikingly medieval vision – most notably in his final masterwork, *Finnegans Wake* (1939), where the self-expression of an absent subject (not quite human, not quite divine, and incomprehensible to itself) can be taken as the creative ground of an apophatic and mystical cosmos in and through which that subject ceaselessly composes, decomposes and recomposes itself.[25] And if Joyce articulates already the logic of our late modern or postmodern worlds, even as he simultaneously recapitulates the mystical logic of Eriugenian tradition, then a reading of Joyce in light of Eriugena should help us to establish and elucidate a mystical dimension within the forms of self-creation (above all the technological) that frame our current situation.[26]

Like Eriugena's theophanic cosmos and scripture, the infinitely variable world of *Finnegans Wake* can seem to show or to say both everything and nothing. Because the work draws on sixty or seventy languages while respecting the rules and boundaries of none, the barely – or perhaps excessively – readable language of the *Wake* offers an incalculable syntactic complexity and semantic density (exemplified above all in the pun[27]) within whose immeasurable network of possible relations – and hence possible meanings – all culture and history, all humanity and divinity, can seem to appear and disappear at once: because it can seem to say everything, the *Wake* can seem also to say nothing – and from this perspective, the *Wake* could be taken to recall for a distinctly late modern or postmodern world the kind of co-implication between polyonymy and anonymity that we saw in Eriugena's medieval cosmos, where the God who is both all in all and nothing in anything is reflected in a human subject through whom divine creation and self-creation unfold.

But if Eriugena's medieval cosmos would find its beginning in the logic or reason of the Word, Joyce's modern "chaosmos" would find its "buginning" in the dissemination of the "woid."[28] An expression of both word and void, the *Wake*'s language-world amounts to a "Soferim Bebel" or a writer's (Hebrew *soferim*[29]) Babel/babble in which "every person, place and thing in the chaosmos of Alle anyway connected with gobblydumped turkery was moving and changing every part of the time" (*FW*, 118). Because the *Wake* remains without stable plot or characters, time or place,[30] and because every event, personage, moment and location that emerges in the work conjures immediately a measureless web of allusions and resonances, every event or personage, every moment or location, is always both more and less than itself – always other than itself within an uncontainable flow of movement and change (both linguistic and conceptual). The writer's Babel/babble of the *Wake* is thus also a kind of Bible in motion, or a whirlwind "tour of bibel" (*FW*, 523): its "proteiform graph" constitutes a "polyhedron of scripture" (*FW*, 107) in which one encounters "the traveling inkhorn (possibly pot), the hare and the turtle pen and paper, the continually more and less intermisunderstanding minds of the anticollaborators, the as time went on as it will variously inflected, differently pronounced, otherwise spelled, changeably meaning vocable scriptsigns" (*FW*, 118). In short, because "every word will be bound over to carry three score and ten toptypical reading throughout the book of Doublends Jined" (*FW*, 20), the endlessly changeable, shifting meanings of the "scriptsigns" in this "seemetery" (*FW*, 17) or "semitary of Somnionia" (*FW*, 594) give us a "world, mind," that "is, was and will be writing its own wrunes forever, man, on all matters that fall under the ban of our infrarational senses" (*FW*, 19–20).

As in Eriugena's simultaneously scriptural and cosmic exegesis, where every sign points the soul onward toward other signs within a *transitus* that never reaches or comprehends the God who simultaneously reveals and conceals himself in all signs (thus rendering each sign both excessively full and empty of sense), so the connectivity of Joyce's *Wake* world generates an endless movement among possible meanings that cannot be fixed or unified by reduction to some stable, comprehensible ground. At this level, the medieval quality of Joyce's language is striking: the endless "interpretive labor" required by the *Wake* "reflects a medieval taste, the idea of aesthetic pleasure, not as the flashing exercise of an intuitive faculty but as a process of intelligence that deciphers and reasons, enraptured by the difficulty of communication" (Eco, *Aesthetics of Chaosmos*, 81). At the same time, however, the linguistic and cultural complexities of the *Wake*'s writing and exegesis are also markedly modern or postmodern – even evoking the logic of late- or post-modernity's elaborate and automated technological systems.

Already in 1962, Umberto Eco understands the *Wake*'s operation according to its "cybernetic" quality: the *Wake* constitutes a radically "open work" because its structure sets in motion "a machinery of suggestion, which, like any complex machine, is capable of operating beyond the original intentions of its builder [. . .]; the force of the text resides in its permanent ambiguity and in the continuous resounding of numerous meanings which seem to permit selection but in fact eliminate nothing" (Eco, *Aesthetics of Chaosmos*, 67). Twenty years later (1982), Jacques Derrida takes a similar approach by likening the *Wake* to a computer (*ordinateur*) with respect to whose "wiring" (*câblage*) he can ask, "How to calculate the speed at which a mark, a marked piece of information is related to some other within the same word or from one end of the book to the other? At what speed, for example, is the Babelian theme or the word Babel, in each of their components (but how to count these?), coordinated with all the phonemes, semes, mythemes, etc., of *Finnegans Wake*?"[31] And in response he concludes that "to count these connections (*branchements*), to calculate the speed of the communications, would be at the least impossible, in fact, inasmuch as we would not have constructed the machine capable of integrating all the variables, all the quantitative and qualitative factors. This is not going to happen tomorrow, and that machine in any case would be but the double or the simulation of the 'Joyce' event, the name of Joyce, the signed work, the Joyce *logiciel* today, the *joyjiciel*"[32] (Derrida, *James Joyce*, 205–6). Both Eco and Derrida recognize that the excess and incalculability of the *Wake*'s language issue from the irreducible complexity and connectivity of that language and its world: every word in the *Wake* is a "crossroads of meaning" within the flow of an ever evolving and unpredictable "communication network"[33] whose multiple linguistic and cultural registers can never be translated into the unity of any one language. This, indeed, would be at the heart of Derrida's decisive and influential engagement with the *Wake*: the paradigm of *Finnegans Wake*, which repeats before the fact the logic of today's computers and networks (and whose strategy would stand in contrast to Husserl's search for a transparent, univocal language),

> repeats and mobilizes and babelizes the (asymptotic) totality of equivocation, it makes this its theme and operation, it attempts to make emerge the greatest synchrony possible, at full speed, the greatest power of the significations hidden away in each syllabic fragment, splitting each atom of writing in order with it to overload the unconscious with the entire memory of man: mythologies, religion, philosophies, sciences, psychoanalysis, literatures. This generalized equivocation of writing does not translate one language into another on the basis of cores of common meaning, it speaks several languages at once, draws on them parasitically.
> (Derrida, *James Joyce*, 207).[34]

Hence, at once deeply scriptural and already cybernetic, the *Wake* would offer a pivotal work in which we are forced to reflect on the intersections or resonances between two logics often dissociated in twentieth-century thought: the exegetical logic of a mystical cosmic vision like Eriugena's and the cybernetic and differential techno-logic that seems to appear in Joyce and frames our virtual worlds today. To the degree, then, that the *Wake* gives a world that "is, was and will be writing its wrunes forever," it speaks at once the ruins of our modern and technological chaosmos and the deepest mysteries (AS *run*, a mystery, secret) of traditional and archaic religion, myth, letters and poetry (*rune*).[35]

Articulating "a theory none too rectiline of the evoluation of human society and a testament of the rocks from all the dead unto some the living" (*FW*, 73), the *Wake* seeks (and seems), in its endless circularity,[36] to encompass all of human and divine history, from the age of fallen Adam to the age of the annihilated atom. Flowing from "the obluvial waters of our noarchic memory" (*FW*, 80), the "immermemorial" (*FW*, 600) *Wake* seeks to articulate both the deepest recesses of our forgetting and the endless power of recollection – and to the degree that it draws its dynamism from the oscillation between forgetting and recollection (or between "feeling aslip and wauking up, so an, so farth," *FW* 597), the *Wake* constitutes a world that remains comprehensive but also open and evolving:

> Forget, remember! [. . .] Our wholemole millwheeling vicociclometer [. . .] autokinatonetically preprovided with a clappercoupling smeltingworks exprogressive process [. . .] receives through the portal vein the dialytically separated elements of precedent decomposition for the verypetpurpose of subsequent recombination so that the heroticisms, catastrophes and eccentricities transmitted by the ancient legacy of the past, type by tope, letter from litter, word at ward, with sendence of sundance [. . .] all, anastomosically assimilated and preteridentified paraidiotically, in fact, the sameold gamebold adomic structure of our Finnius the old One, as highly charged with electrons as hophazards can effective it . . .
>
> (*FW*, 615).

The logic of decomposition and recombination articulated here within a passage that moves from Adam to the atom by means of type/tope and letter/litter and word/ward and sendence/sundance would apply to the *Wake* as a whole, a work that seems indeed to articulate the "exprogressive process" of an ever recurring, cosmic and world-historical decomposition and recombination of an unidentifiable or absent subject's self-expression and recollection. As the *Wake*'s central "Night Lessons" will suggest within a discussion of the polyonymously anonymous "median, hce che ech" (*FW*, 284), the simultaneously self-identical and self-differing nightworld of the *Wake* is infinitely multiple and revisable because it rests on the nullity of a "surd" (which would explain its laughable absurdity): for "whereat samething is rivisible by nightim, may be involted into the zeroic couplet, palls pell inhis heventh glike noughty times ∞, find, if you are not literally cooefficient, how minney combinaisies and permutandies can be played on the international surd" (*FW*, 284). The "samething" (or something) of the *Wake*'s nighttime would be repeatedly visible (or risible) and endlessly revisable because it marks the infinite multiplication of a nullity, which allows for countless many (and minute) combinations and permutations, wherein "the mystery repeats itself" (*FW*, 294). Here and elsewhere, the *Wake* suggests and enacts its own infinite revisability, highlighting the sense in which the work and its world constitute a "contonuation through regeneration of the urutteration of the word in progress" (*FW*, 284) – and from the continuous regeneration of the primal iteration of this word in progress would issue a "whorled without aimed" (*FW*, 272) that is a "whirled without end to end" (*FW*, 582).

Opening such an excessive field of potential combination and permutation, (de)composition and recombination, the *Wake* might be read both in (quasi-) anthropological and in (quasi-) theological directions, both as the "meander-tale" (*FW*, 18) of "morphyl man" (*FW*, 80), who as the "truly catholic assemblage" of "Here Comes Everybody" (*FW*, 32) is also the anonymous "quisquis" of "mister-mysterion" (*FW*, 301) *and* as the story of "Ouhr Former who erred in having" (*FW* 530), or "oura vatars that arred in Himmal" (*FW*, 599), the "Great Sommboddy" (*FW*, 415) and "Pantokreator" (*FW*, 411) "in whose words were the beginnings" (*FW*, 597) and in whose sacrament we would consume "Real Absence" (*FW*, 536).[37] The two stories, of course, imply and repeatedly collapse into one another. As of the "four clay-men" in their "starchamber query" on "Yawn," so we might say of the inter-play between human and divine in the *Wake*'s meandertale (and hence in our own): "he was ever their quarrel, the way they would see themselves, everybug his bodiment atop of anywom her notion, and the meet of their noght was worth two of his morning" (*FW*, 475). If in this "meet" of their "noght" (naught/knot/night) we might see that "we haply return [. . .] to befinding ourselves when old is said and done and maker mates with made" (*FW*, 261), then the *Wake* might tell the tale of the eternally cyclic repetition of the decomposition and recombination of the (not quite) human and (not quite) divine in relation to one another. It would do so, however, in such a way that the human is never fully or clearly identifiable as human nor the divine fully or clearly recognizable as divine: each would just barely appear only in order then to slip away – so that each would reflect the polyvalent nullity or abyss of the other. Just as "Fidaris will find where the Doubt arises like Nieman from Nirgends found the Nihil" (*FW*, 202), so the divine and human here, in the meet of their naught/knot/night, where "maker mates with made," would find in each other the abyssal mirror of their own endlessly imaged obscurities. This, I believe, can be read as a late modern version of Scotus Eriugena's medieval insight that the incomprehensible and anonymous God shows itself infinitely or abyssally in, through, and to the self-creation of a human subject who proves likewise incomprehensible and anonymous. "The one the pictor of the other and the omber the *Skotia* of the one" (*FW*, 164), Joyce might put it,[38] "each was wrought with his other [. . .] no thing making newthing wealthshowever" (*FW*, 252–3).

Now, if in the Eriugenian context the self-creation of an incomprehensible God occurs in and through the self-creation of His incomprehensible human image, these two movements, which would stage the "wealthshow" of a theophanic and theocryptic cosmos where "no thing" really does make "newthing," are essentially bound within the cyclic dynamic of a Neoplatonic procession and return. And if the cyclic structure of *Finnegans Wake* is famously inspired by the historic cycles of Giambatista Vico's *New Science*, which treats the "uncertain, formless and obscure material"[39] of human and divine institutions in their historic interplay, it is structured also according to various movements of descending and ascending (*FW*, 298), catastrophe and anabasis (*FW*, 304), systole and diastole – or "systomy dystomy" (*FW*, 597) – that can be taken to issue from (or to echo) "the babbling pumpt of platinism" (*FW*, 164).[40] Such movement, of course, is fundamental in the Christian traditions both to Augustine (the story of his "every man" in the *Confessions* follows the structure of descent and ascent) and to Aquinas (the *Summa*, while famously informed by Aristotle, is also structured according to the Neoplatonic movement of procession and return), but the language and movement of the *Wake* seem ultimately less like that of Augustine or Aquinas (who are not profoundly apophatic) and more like that of the radically apophatic traditions that emerge from Dionysius and Eriugena,[41] who both appear in the opening pages of the *Wake*, and who constitute an indispensable foundation for later figures like Cusa and Bruno, who themselves recur throughout the *Wake* and inspire its central vision of coincident opposition and the infinity of worlds.

In the *Wake*'s opening pages both the Dionysian and Eriugenian visions appear explicitly in order to announce the sense in which the endlessly shifting, multiple and all-encompassing world of the *Wake*, "the miraculous meddle of this expending umniverse" (*FW*, 410), originates (almost) from (next to) nothing. Like the polyonymous HCE (here, "Haroun Childeric Eggeberth"), "Bygmester Finnegan"

> would caligulate by multiplicables the alltitude and malltitude until he seesaw by neatlight of the liquor wheretwin 'twas born, his roundhead staple of other days to rise in undress . . . a waalworth of a skyerscape of most eyeful hoyth entowerly, erigenating from next to nothing and celescalating the himals and all, hierarchitectitiptitoploftical, with a burning bush abob off its baubletop and with larrons o'tollers clittering up and tombles a'buckets clottering down.
>
> (*FW*, 4–5)

A distorted, drunken or dream-like image of the Dionysian and Eriugenian cosmoi, the world of the *Wake* will "eriginate" "from next to nothing" (suggesting the Eriugenian understanding of creation ex nihilo), and its movement, "clittering up" and "clottering down," will recapitulate and thoroughly unsettle the well-ordered hierarchies of the medieval Dionysian cosmos ("celescalating the himals and all, hierarchitectitiptitoploftical . . . ") by dispersing their members throughout a complex network that lacks the linear or sequential coherence of traditional hierarchy.[42] "Panangelical" (*FW*, 407), the *Wake* is suffused by angelic messengers whose displaced, distorted light and language render them "holy messonger angels" (*FW*, 405): as the function of an ever evolving network, every message can and must be read here in several directions at once – and hence every message always harbors the potential of the *mensonge*.[43] The messonger angels and their dispersed hierarchies appear, then, throughout the work – from its initial "erigination," where the angels celescalate the himals and all, through Book IV, where the celestial and ecclesiastical hierarchies punctuate St. Kevin's rafting trip, and perhaps most notably in the central Night Lessons, where the name and movement of HCE himself are signaled by "The Ascending. The Descending." (*FW*, 298) of the angels (from Jacob's dream in Genesis 28:12[44]) along the "Ecclesiastical and Celestial Hierarchies" (*FW*, 298).

Within that movement, as the lesson elaborates, "the logos of somewome to that base anything, when most characteristically mantissa minus, comes to nullum in the endth" (*FW*, 298). Erigenating from (next to) nothing, and moving ultimately back into the abyssal (and endlessly regenerative) waters of "salvocean" (*FW*, 623), the logos or word of the *Wake* belongs to an anonymous "somwome" (neither fully divine nor fully human) whose relation to "that base anything" comes in the end, and endlessly, to "nullum." The movement of procession from and return to this nullum ("my safe return to ignorance," *FW*, 446) can be read equally (and undecidably) from the angle of the "human" or of the "dayety"[45] – and in both directions a tie might be established between the creative power of language and the nothingness that grounds it. Such a tie recurs everywhere in the "nat language" of the *Wake*'s "Nichtian glossery" (*FW*, 83), and it is indispensable to the understanding of creation that takes shape there.

If, as Joyce scholar John Bishop convincingly argues, the world of the *Wake* is created (and re-created) in the "image, memory and language" (*FW*, xix) of an "absent subject" who is "unconscious of and to himself" (*FW*, xix) and whose "elusive presence is felt everywhere throughout the book but who is nowhere within it definitively characterized or even given a stable name" (*FW*, xvii)[46] – or if, as the *Wake* itself suggests, its "disunited kingdom" has been reared "on the vacuum" of a "most intensely doubtful soul" (*FW*, 188), then we might indeed see here a repetition or image or shadow of Eriugena's mystical approach to creation *ex nihilo* – where both God, as the placeless place of places, an indefinable no-thing, and the human subject, as incomprehensible image of that placeless nothing, would alike signal the ground out of which creation issues (and to which it returns) through the multiplicity and simplicity of the Word.

Word, indeed, proves creative throughout the *Wake*, as throughout

Eriugena, by virtue of its proximity to the void, and the *Wake*'s overall "systomy dystomy, which everabody you ever anywhere at all doze" (*FW*, 597) could be taken to signal the multiple goings and comings of Here Comes Everybody out of and into the obscurity and unknowing of that void (sleep, death, ignorance, ocean, etc.), for "In the buginning is the woid, in the muddle is the sounddance, and thereinofter you're in the unbewised again" (*FW*, 378). Emerging out of the void/word as "everabody . . . anywhere" in the "muddle" of the "sounddance," HCE incessantly slips back into that void as a "nomad . . . nomon" (*FW*, 374) who, "touring the no placelike no time-like absolent" (*FW*, 609), appears nowhere. "Who was he to whom? [. . .] Whose are his placewheres? [. . .] [T]he unfacts, did we possess them, are too imprecisely few to warrant our certitude" (*FW*, 56–7). The indeterminate "subject" in whose mind (or body) the *Wake* world appears finds reflected there an image of its own chaotic nullity, for "an you could peep inside the cerebralised saucepan of this eer illwinded goodfornobody, you would see in his house of thoughtsam [. . .] what a jetsam litterage of convolvuli of times lost or strayed, of lands derelict and of tongues laggin too" (*FW*, 292). Just as the divine and/or human subject in Eriugena constitutes the placeless place of places in whose absent presence everything and nothing would appear, so the "goodfornobody" at the heart of the *Wake* marks a void out of which and into which the multivalent thoughtsam and jetsam of the *Wake*-world would flow.

Joyce himself makes this connection between creative expression and mystical void already in a 1912 text that relates the art of William Blake to the theology of Pseudo-Dionysius. Attempting "to paint his works on the void of the divine bosom,"[47] Blake would give expression to the infinitely unnameable within a creative process that recalls the apophatic ascent into God as imagined by the traditions of Dionysian mysticism:

> Dionysius the pseudo-Areopagite, in his book *De Divinis Nominibus*, arrives at the throne of God by denying and overcoming every moral and metaphysical attribute, and falling into ecstasy and prostrating himself before the divine obscurity, before that unutterable immensity which precedes and encompasses the supreme knowledge in the eternal order. The mental process by which Blake arrives at the threshold of the infinite is a similar process. Flying from the infinitely small to the infinitely large, from a drop of blood to the universe of the stars, his soul is consumed by the rapidity of flight, and finds itself renewed and winged and immortal on the edge of the dark ocean of God.
>
> (*Critical Writings*, 222).

Artistic creation, on this reading, would be endlessly open and on the move ("renewed and winged and immortal") to the degree that it – like the whole of the *Wake*, or like a "rough breathing on the void of to be" (*FW*, 100), or like "a flash from a future of maybe" (*FW*, 597) – rests "on the edge of the dark ocean of God." As in Dionysius and Eriugena, where bottomless denial and unknowing go hand in hand with endless affirmation and imagination, so with Blake and Joyce ceaseless creation renews itself on the edge of a void whose darkness and depth escape both the infinitely small and the infinitely large – which thereby come to intersect or coincide, both equally approximating and falling short of the void. Just as the infinitely small and the infinitely great can intersect or coincide within the Romantic vision, and just as the human can contain the universe in Eriugena, so in every word of the *Wake*, part and whole intersect or coincide, for "it will remember itself from every sides [. . .] in each our word" (*FW*, 614).

Such an intersection, fundamental to the *Wake*'s "imaginable itinerary through the particular universal" (*FW*, 260), can be traced both to a Romantic vision such as Blake's and to influential heirs of Dionysius and Eriugena such as Nicholas of Cusa (1401–1464) and Giordano Bruno (1548–1600), for whom "in each thing is realized everything and everything is in each thing. Each thing finally appears as a perspective on the universe and a microcosmic model of it" (Eco, *Aesthetics of Chaosmos*, 73). Thus, if the *Wake*'s infinitely variable world is not inspired directly by Eriugena, it clearly is inspired by Eriugenian tradition. In this direction, Joyce takes inspiration from the coincidence of absolute maximum and minimum as expressed in Cusa, according to whom "because the absolutely maximum is absolutely and actually all that can be, and it is without opposition to such an extent that the minimum coincides with the maximum, it is above all affirmation and negation. It both is and is not all that is conceived to be, and it both is and is not all that is conceived not to be. But it is a 'this' in such a way that it is all things, and it is all things in such a way that it is none of them."[48] Just as the *Wake*-world can seem to express all things and no thing in the chaotic language of a late modern vision, so the Cusan maximum expresses in late medieval and early modern terms the coincidence or indiscretion of everything and nothing. Reading this Cusan doctrine in light of Bruno's insistence that "it is necessary that of the inaccessible face of God there be an infinite simulacrum (*simulacro*) in which, as infinite members, are found innumerable worlds,"[49] the *Wake* is able itself to suggest that "the dialectic of the finite and infinite is accomplished only in the ceaseless process of cosmic metamorphosis" (Eco, *Aesthetics of Chaosmos*, 73) – and in this sense the *Wake* will follow the "tendency of Frivulteeny Sexuagesima to expense herself as sphere as possible, paradismic perimutter, in all directions on the bend of the unbridalled, the infinississimals of her facets becoming manier and manier as the calicolum of her umdescribables . . . shrinks" (*FW*, 298).

Inspired by Cusa and Bruno, the infinity of worlds opened by the *Wake*, wherein finite and infinite, part and whole, would ceaselessly cross and recross, is a function of the linguistic explosion upon which the work is based. As with the fission of the atom, where the infinitely minute proves immeasurably powerful, so in the *Wake*, the smallest linguistic units, reflecting the whole of the *Wake*'s reality within themselves, split, explode and scatter in a process of creation from annihilation: "The abnihilisation of the etym [. . .] expolodotonates through Parsuralia with an ivanmorinthorrumble fragoromboassity amidwhiches general uttermosts confussion are preceivable moletons skaping with mulicules" (*FW*, 353). Thus, combining the language (almost) of late medieval and early modern mysticism (Cusa, Bruno) with that of modern calculus (evoked by Frivulteeny Sexuagesima above) and science (the annihilation of the atom here), the *Wake* heaves "alljawbreakical expressions out of old Sare Isaac's universal of specious aristmystic unsaid" (*FW*, 293) – and according to that "aristmystic" the nothing out of which creation issues provokes an endless naming or linguistic dissemination precisely to the degree that it can be approached asymptotically but never reached.

This word/void through which creation issues, both in Joyce and in the mystical traditions, is, among other things, the self-expression of the God who in Exodus 3:14 announces himself as "I am that (or as) I am," which, as Meister Eckhart indicates, is the most appropriate name for God because it says everything and nothing at once. The "I am that I am" takes numerous forms in the *Wake* ("I yam as I yam," "I am yam," "I am, I am big alltoog-ooder," "what I (the person whomin I now am)," "thou-who-thou-art," "we there are where are," etc.[50]) and if read in this apophatic sense it would constitute one of the most powerful figures for the co-implication or co-incidence of (not quite) divine and (not quite) human anonymity within the cosmic process of self-creation. "A being again in becomings again" (*FW*, 491), the "I am that I am" of the *Wake* constitutes a "howtosayto itiswhatis hemustwhomust worden schall" (*FW*, 223) whose "darktongues, kunning" (*FW*, 223) give expression both to a multivalent and not quite human figure and to a multivalent and not quite divine figure who, in their indiscretion, and by means of "ineffable tries at speech unasyllabled" (*FW*, 183), create, undo and recreate themselves endlessly within "the untireties of livesliving being the one substance of a streamsbecoming" (*FW*, 597).

Seeming to include while dissolving the history of all theological and anthropological imagination, this being in becoming, this "constant of flux-ion" (*FW*, 297) that defines the *Wake*'s countless goings and comings, would ground (and unsettle) the chaosmos of All within which the human and divine I or "Egoname" (*FW*, 485) would seem to be embodied, put to death and resurrected eternally. The polyonymous anonymity of this I, which travels "the void world over," would signal, then, in both modern and mystical language, the immanence of a self-less "Allself" who echoes the mystical "I am":

> for Earl Hoovedsoon's choosing and Huber and Harman orhowwhen theeuponthus (chchch!) eysolt of binnoculises memostinmust egotum sabcunsciously senses upers the deprofundity of multimathematical immaterialities wherebejubers in the pancosmic urge the allimmanence of that which Itself is Itself Alone (hear, O hear, Caller Erin!) exteriorises

on this ourherenow plane in disunited solod, likeward and gushious bodies with (science, say!) . . . intuitions of reunited selfdom (murky whey,
abstrew adim!) in the higherdimissional selfless Allself.

(FW, 394–5)

If "that which Itself is Itself Alone" expresses itself today, "on this ourherenow plane," it does so in the polyonymous anonymity of just such a selfless
Allself, which is named (and unnamed) throughout the *Wake* not only by the
countless names of world historical gods, angelic hierarchies, or sefirothic
emanations, but also, equally, by the innumerable "illassumed names [. . .] of
a tellafun book" (*FW*, 86) – the all too human and undifferentiated names of
a modern mass culture. The anonymity that comes to expression in the *Wake*,
indeed, draws not only on the deepest memory of archaic and traditional
religion, myth and ritual, but also on our most modern mass culture – the
culture of electronic networks wherein tele-vocal and tele-visual media
give voice and visibility to the nameless and faceless Allself of everabody
anywhere, who as such is a nomad nomon nowhere.

"As modern as tomorrow afternoon and in appearance up to the minute"
(*FW*, 309), the *Wake* is a world in which "wires hummed" (*FW*, 98) and
"aerials buzzed" (*FW*, 99), and the oscillations of a modern "dielectrick"
throughout that world render word tele-vocal by means of a "tolvtubular
high fidelity daildialler [. . .] equipped with supershielded umbrella antennas
for distance, getting and connected by the magnetic links of a Bellini-Tosti
coupling system, with a vialtone speaker, capable of capturing skybuddies,
harbour craft emittences, key clickings, vaticum cleaners, due to woman
formed mobile or man made static and bawling the whowle hamshack and
wobble down in an eliminium sounds pound so as to serve him up a melego-
turny marygoaraumd, electrically filtered for allirish earths and ohmes" (*FW*,
309–10). As tele-vocal, modern word or speech here is "electrically filtered"
for all humanity (every hearth and home) by means of network linkages and
coupling systems through which emissions and transmissions cover unseen
distances – like angelic "messongers."[51] Indeed, this is the world in which "we
are now diffusing [. . .] the dewfolded song of the naughtingels"[52] (*FW*, 359),
and in such a world, where technology can turn nightingales into naught
angels, the comings and goings of electrified "messongers," like the epic comings and goings of the *Wake* as a whole (from Adam to the atom, through the
obluvial waters of noarchic memory), would be contained in a "harmonic
condenser enginium" equipped with a "a gain control of circumcentric
megacycles, ranging from the anttidulibnium onto the serostaatarean" (*FW*,
310). Thus charged with modernity's dielectrick pulse, the *Wake*'s all-
encompassing machinery of suggestion becomes, "in cycloannalism, from
space to space, time after time, in various phases of scripture as in various
poses of sepulture" (*FW*, 254) a "radiooscillating epiepistle to which [. . .] we
must ceaselessly return" (*FW*, 108).

Now, if it is true that the electrified scripture of the *Wake* becomes a radiooscillating epiepistle giving voice to a networked telephony, it is also true that "television kills telephony in brother's broil" (*FW*, 52) – and hence that the word and voice of the *Wake* become also (like the Eriugenian God who "runs" through all things) image and sight. While the *Wake* is famously and rightly known as a "lingerous longerous book of the dark" (*FW*, 251), a "funnaminal world" that "darkles" wherein "we are circumveiloped by obscuritads" (*FW*, 244), it is also illuminated throughout by the resplendence of photographic, filmic and televisual image – the electronic light-writing of our late modern mass culture: "In the heliotropical noughttime" of the *Wake*, indeed, "the bairdboard bombardment screen [. . .] tends to teleframe and step up to the charge of a light barricade. Down the photoslope in syncopanc pulses [. . .]. Spraygun rakes and splits them from a double focus: grenadite, damnymite, alextronite, nichilite: and the scanning firespot of the sgunners traverses the rutilanced illustrated sunksundered lines" (*FW*, 349). Just as the "nighttime instrument" or "faroscope" (*FW*, 150) of television shoots a stream of electrons upon a screen where images constantly appear, shift about, transform and disappear, *ad infinitum*, so the *Wake* shoots upon the reader's mind a stream of words and letters that become (like the words and letters in the illuminated *Book of Kells*) light and image – appearing, shifting about, transforming and disappearing within the endless spirals and inter-lacings of color and shape, sound and smell, place and time, plant and animal, humanity and divinity. And just as the reader might indeed see traces of theological vision throughout the *Wake*, so does the *Wake* see in its own television that "A gaspel truce leaks out over the caseine coatings. Amid a fluorescence of spectracular mephiticism there coaculates through the iconocsope stealdily a still, the figure of a fellow-chap in the wholy ghast" (*FW*, 349). Thus, in the "chiaroscuro" (*FW*, 107) of the *Wake*'s "philophosy" (*FW*, 119), "revealled by Oscur Camerad" (*FW*, 602), we would become, along countless twisting paths of an endless "photophoric pilgrimage" (*FW*, 472), "searchers for tabernacles and the celluloid art" (*FW*, 534) – and so the darkness of mystical interiors would merge with superficial screens of photoplay where "flash becomes word" (*FW*, 267).

In the electrification of voice and the illumination of word, then, the "day-noight" (*FW*, 412) of the *Wake* promises "new worlds for all" – worlds that would be "scotographically arranged" according to the measureless ano-nymity of a "scripchewer in whofoundland" (*FW*, 412). Perhaps indistinguish-able from the creative divinity who is all in all and nothing in anything, the humanity that creates and inhabits these worlds might be a "new 'electronic' humanity [. . .] whose depth is indistinguishable from its surface or mask [. . .]. Its actual name would be everyone and no one at once, an everyone who can only be no one."[53] If read as a late modern rendering of the interplay between polyonymy and anonymity within the process of self-creation, the *Wake* would offer to this humanity, as did Eriugena's cosmic God to every soul, its abyssal image – where we would stare into "that multimirror meg-aron of returningties, whirled without end to end" (*FW*, 582). In order to inhabit that world – which means in order endlessly to create and recreate both that world and, through it, ourselves, we would need to become "the readers of tomorrow [. . .] the readers of a possible society in which exercise in the multiplication of signs will not appear as a game for the elite but as the natural, constructive exercise of an agile and renewed perception" (Eco, *Aesthetics of Chaosmos*, 85). And if the *Wake* can teach us to become such readers and thus to renew our perception, it would do so by forcing us to recognize ourselves "in the ignorance that implies impression that knits knowledge that finds the nameform that whets the wits that convey contacts and sweeten sensation that drives desire that adheres to attachment that dogs death that bitches birth that entails the ensuance of existentiality" (*FW*, 18).

## Notes

1 Jorge Luis Borges, *Everything and Nothing*, trans. Donald A. Yates *et al.* (New York: New Directions, 1999), pp. 77–8.

2 While I cannot develop the connections here, the function I assign to this mystical foundation would have significant ties to the function of mystical foundation in Jacques Derrida's widely noted analyses. See especially Derrida's "Force of Law: The Mystical Foundation of Authority," in Drucilla Cornell (ed.), *Deconstruction and the Possibility of Justice* (New York: Routledge, 1992), and the discussion of mystical foundation in relation to religion and technology in "Faith and Knowledge: The Two Sources of Religion at the Limits of Reason Alone," in Derrida and G. Vattimo (eds), *Religion* (Stanford: Stanford University Press, 1998).

3 *Indiscretion: Finitude and the Naming of God* (Chicago: University of Chicago Press, 1999).

4 Jorge Luis Borges, *Atlas*, trans. Anthony Kerrigan (New York: Dutton, 1985).

5 Umberto Eco, *The Aesthetics of Chaosmos: The Middle Ages of James Joyce*, trans. Ellen Esrock (Cambridge, MA: Harvard University Press, 1989; originally published in 1962 as part of Eco's *Opera Aperta*).

6 On the modern (especially idealistic and Hegelian) dimensions of Eriugena, see especially Dermot Moran's fine study *The Philosophy of John Scotus Eriugena: A Study of Idealism in the Middle Ages* (Cambridge: Cambridge University Press, 1989); and, for a brief treatment, Werner Beierwaltes, "The Revaluation of John Scottus Eriugena in German Idealism," in *The Mind of Eriugena*, ed. John J. O'Meara and Ludwig Bieler (Dublin: Irish University Press, 1973), pp. 190–9.

7 See above all chapter 11 of Gregory's treatise "On the Creation of Man" (*peri kataskeuēs anthrōpou/De hominis opificio*): "since one of the properties of the divine essence is its incomprehensible character [*to akatalēpton tēs ousias*], in that also the image must resemble its model [*anangkē pasa kai en toutō tēn eikona pros to archētupon echein tēn mimēsin*]," in J. P. Migne (ed.), *Patrologiae Cursus Completus Series Graeca*, vol. 44. In my translation I have relied on the original Greek and on the French translation, *La création de l'homme*, trans. Jean Laplace (Paris: Editions du Cerf, 1944).

8 *Periphyseon (The Division of Nature)*, trans. I. P. Sheldon Williams, revised by John J. O'Meara (Montreal: Editions Bellarmin, 1987). All citations will be given parenthetically, according the Migne pagination, as follows: P, Book #, Migne column # and letter. Citations of the Latin original are taken, for Books I and II, from I. P. Sheldon Williams (ed.), *Periphyseon (De Divisione Naturae)* (Dublin: The Dublin Institute for Advanced Studies, 1968, 1972), and, for all other books,

from J. P. Migne (ed.), *Patrologiae Cursus Completus Series Latina*, vol. 122 (Paris: Migne, 1853).

9  Eriugena explicitly attributes the teaching that God both makes and is made in creation to Pseudo-Dionysius: "Therefore God *is* everything that truly is because He Himself makes all things and is made in all things, as St. Dionysius the Areopagite says" (P, III, 633A).

10 As Bernard McGinn points out, "John stressed that creation and scripture were two parallel manifestations of the hidden God" (*The Growth of Mysticism*, vol. 2 of *The Presence of God* (New York: Crossroad, 1994), p. 93), and he "often used the term *transitus* ('dynamic passage from one state to another' would be a possible translation) to describe the process of how the exegete moves through the infinity of textual meanings to the hidden divine unitary source" (*Growth of Mysticism*, p. 94). Werner Beierwaltes will emphasize that this movement of human *transitus*, wherein the believer passes through the infinity of God's scriptural and cosmic showings to return into God himself, answers to the divine *transitus* that is the very nature of both divine and created being: "transition expresses an essential feature of divine being: the movement in which it develops itself and creates the world," from "Language and its Object," in *Jean-Scot Ecrivain*, ed. G.-H. Allard (Montreal: Editions Bellarmin, 1986), p. 224.

11 On the infinity of universes in Eriugena, see Moran, *Philosophy of John Scotus Eriugena*, p. 260. On the infinity of universes in Cusa and Bruno, see the first two chapters of Alexandre Koyré's study *From the Closed World to the Infinite Universe* (New York: Harper Torchbooks, 1958), and the passages quoted below. As we will see then, this notion of infinite worlds will be fundamental to Joyce, who most likely takes the idea from Bruno.

12 For a clear instance of this in Hegel, see, for example, *Lectures on the Philosophy of Religion*: "Finite consciousness knows God only to the extent that God knows himself in it" (1831, in the 1827 One-Volume edition, p. 392, n.3). On the "apophatic erasure" that Hegel effects in his reading of the speculative mystics, see Cyril O'Regan's *The Heterodox Hegel* (Albany: State University of New York Press, 1994).

13 Divine self-manifestation, then, signals not simply the Incarnation but indeed more broadly "the ineffable descent of the Supreme Goodness, which is Unity and Trinity, into the things that are so as to make them be, indeed so as itself to be, in all things from the highest to the lowest, ever eternal, ever made, by itself in itself eternal, by itself in itself made" (P, III, 678D).

14 Several commentators have made this point with some force. See, for example, Don Duclow: "Conceived as theophany, the entire created order becomes a field of translucent symbols which yield knowledge of the divine nature, even though this position knowledge [*sic*] remains metaphorical and partial throughout," from "Divine Nothingness and Self-Creation in John Scotus Eriugena," *Journal of Religion* 57/2 (April 1977), p. 118.

15 As Duclow puts it, "the divine *nihil* constitutes the ground for theophanic self-creation, which in turn cannot be thought apart from the transcendence which it manifests in the otherness of created essence and being." Duclow, "Divine Nothingness and Self-Creation," p. 119.

16 McGinn puts all of this quite well: "If all things are God manifested, then humanity is God manifested in the most special way. It is the true and only *imago Dei*, because, like its divine source, it does not know *what* it is (it is not a *what* at all), but it does know *that* it is – namely, it possesses self-consciousness. Thus, the primacy of negative theology in Eriugena is complemented by his negative anthropology: Humanity does not know God, but God does not know God either (in the sense of knowing or defining a *what*); and humanity does not know itself, nor does God know humanity insofar as it is one with the divine mind that is the cause of itself.

This brilliant anthropological turn, hinted at in Gregory's *The Image*, was brought to full and daring systematic expression in the Irishman's writings. It is the ground for a remarkable elevation of humanity (at least the idea of humanity) to a divine and co-creative status," in *Growth of Mysticism*, p. 105.

17 To elucidate more fully this interplay between the human creature's self-consciousness and its ultimate incomprehensibility to itself, one would have to note that Eriugena distinguishes two aspects of the human substance: as created among the intelligible Causes in God, that substance is utterly simple and thus incomprehensible; as generated among the effects of those Causes, however, the human substance takes on the kind of determination that renders it comprehensible, as indicated by P, IV, 771A: "No, I should not say that there are two substances, but one which may be conceived under two aspects. Under one aspect the human substance is perceived as created among the intelligible Causes, under the other as generated among their effects; under the former free from all mutability, under the latter subject to change; under the former simple, involved in no accidents, it eludes all reason and intelligence; under the latter it receives a kind of composition of quantities and qualities and whatever else can be understood in relation to it, whereby it becomes apprehensible to the mind." Having made this distinction, however, Eriugena finally insists, apophatically, on the ultimate incomprehensibility of the human substance – at the level *both* of generated effect *and* of created cause: "So it is that what is one and the same [substance] can be thought of as twofold because there are two ways of looking at it, yet everywhere it preserves its incomprehensibility [*ubique tamen suam incomprehensibilitem custodit*], in the effects as in the causes [*in causis dico et in effectibus*], and whether it is endowed with accidents or abides in its naked simplicity: under neither set of circumstances is it subject to created sense or intellect nor even the knowledge of itself as to what it is [*nec a seipsa intelligitur quid sit*]" (P, IV, 771A).

18 For a concise and rigorous analysis of these three theses – with an insistence on their essential interconnection, see McGinn, "The Negative Element in the Anthropology of John the Scot," in *Jean Scot Erigène et l' histoire de la philosophie*, ed. René Roques (Laon: 1975), pp. 315–25.

19 On the place-lessness of God's causal presence, see also, for example, P, I, 468D–469A: "For everything that is in the world must move in time and be defined in place; even place itself is defined and time itself moves. But God neither moves nor is defined. For (He is) the Place of places by which all places are defined, and since He is not fixed in place but gives place to all things within Him, He is not place but More-than-place. For he is defined by nothing, but defines all things: therefore He is the Cause of all things." The inextricable tie between definition and location runs throughout Eriugena's thinking, for "place is definition and definition is place" (P, I, 485B).

20 As Marta Cristiani puts it, one can see throughout Eriugena "the clearest affirmation that *place* is identified with the activity of the human, angelic or divine intellect that localizes and circumscribes beings, that knows reality thanks to that very act, thanks to that power of definition, which is considered at the same time as the power of *creation*," in *The Mind of Eriugena*, p. 47.

21 As Don Duclow summarizes: "The Father cries out through the Word, and this cry first establishes all created natures [. . .]. The Word's second cry occurs through the flesh and constitutes the Incarnation, which sets in motion the return of all things to God," Duclow, "Divine Nothingness and Self-Creation," p. 122. On this double cry, see also McGinn, *Growth of Mysticism*, p. 108.

22 See especially those passages such as P, II, 592C–D: "The Divine Nature is without any place, although it provides place within itself for all things which are from it, and for that reason is called the Place of all things; but it is unable to provide place for itself because it is infinite and uncircumscribed and does not allow itself to be

located, that is, defined and circumscribed, by any intellect nor by itself. For from it, being infinite and more than infinite, all finites and infinites proceed, and to it, being infinite and more than infinite, they return"; or P, III, 643C: "For who, taking thought for the truth, would believe or think that God had prepared for Himself places through which he might diffuse Himself, He who is contained in no place since He is the common place of all things and therefore, as Place of places, is held by no place . . . ?"

23 See also P, IV, 764A: "no part of [the sensible world] is found, either corporeal or incorporeal, which does not subsist created in man, which does not perceive through him, which does not live through him, which is not incorporated in him."

24 Indeed, the concept of man "stands above all definition" to the very extent that "it has been given him to possess the concept of all things which were either created his equals or which he was instructed to govern" (P, IV, 768D), for man possesses the concept of all things only insofar as he constitutes the perfect image of the incomprehensible God who knows all.

25 On the medieval and mystical dimensions in Joyce, see especially Eco, *Aesthetics of Chaosmos*. Colleen Jaurretche's recent study, *The Sensual Philosophy: Joyce and the Aesthetics of Mysticism* (Madison: University of Wisconsin Press, 1997), is also insightful and informative, especially on the importance of John of the Cross's theology for Joyce's artistic vision.

26 It bears noting that I am not attempting here to demonstrate any direct "influence" of Eriugena in Joyce – though he did recognize and admire in Eriugena the innovator and "mystical pantheist, who translated from the Greek the books of mystical theology of Dionysius, the pseudo-Areopagite [. . .]. This translation presented to Europe for the first time the transcendental philosophy of the Orient, which had as much influence on the course of European religious thought as later the translations of Plato, made in the time of Pico della Mirandola, had on the development of the profane Italian civilization," in "Ireland, Island of Saints and Sages," in *The Critical Writings of James Joyce*, ed. Ellsworth Mason and Richard Ellman (Ithaca: Cornell University Press, 1989), p. 160.

27 On the poetics of the pun in Joyce, see especially Eco, *Aesthetics of Chaosmos*, pp. 65–70.

28 James Joyce, *Finnegans Wake* (New York: Penguin, 1999). Hereafter cited parenthetically as "*FW*."

29 Here and elsewhere throughout my reading, I rely on Roland McHugh's invaluable *Annotations to Finnegans Wake* (Baltimore: Johns Hopkins University Press, 1991). Also immeasurably helpful to an exploration of the *Wake* is Clive Hart's *A Concordance to Finnegans Wake* (Mamaroneck, NY: Paul P. Appel, 1974), which I have likewise consulted extensively.

30 Something *like* plot and characters can, however, be traced (if sketchily) in the *Wake*. For a brief and helpful summary, see John Bishop's "Introduction" to the 1999 Penguin edition of the *Wake*.

31 Jacques Derrida, "Deux mots pour Joyce," in *James Joyce* (Paris: Editions de l' Herne, 1985), p. 205. Translations are my own.

32 *Logiciel* is the French term for "software," and Derrida's play on the term here seems, appropriately, untranslatable.

33 Marshall McLuhan was using this language of technological "network" and "flow" with respect to Joyce already in 1953. See "James Joyce: Trivial and Quadrivial," in *Thought* 27 (Spring, 1953).

34 This Derridean reading, with which I am in agreement here, is central to Mark C. Taylor's critique of Thomas J. J. Altizer's "total presence." See Taylor, "p.s. fin again," in *Tears* (Albany: State University of New York Press, 1990). For Altizer's very powerful reading of Joyce, see especially "Joyce and the End of History," in *History as Apocalypse* (Albany: State University of New York Press, 1985). While

I cannot do justice to Altizer's reading of Joyce here, its influence can and should be noted (even if I am finally more in line with Derrida and Taylor on the question of presence).

35   "Rune" can refer generally to poetry, verse or song; more specifically to ancient Scandinavian poetry; and most specifically to the ancient alphabet of Scandinavians and other Germanic peoples. The central character of the *Wake*, of course, is of Scandinavian descent.

36   The work begins in the middle of a sentence whose beginning comes at the work's end.

37   A powerful sacramental reading of the *Wake* is to be found in Altizer, which in this direction draws deeply on David Leahy. See "Joyce and the End of History," pp. 244ff.

38   Perhaps even evoking the darkness (*skotos*) of the Scot's thought.

39   Giambattista Vico, *New Science*, trans. David Marsh (New York: Penguin Books, 1999), p. 28. "By studying the common nature of nations in the light of divine providence," Vico's *New Science* "discovers the origins of divine and human institutions in the pagan nations" and on that basis delimits three ages within the course of world history: the age of the god, the age of the heroes, and the age of men (p. 22).

40   As well, of course, as the pagan mystery rites surrounding the solar cycles, the cycles of the Catholic liturgical year, etc. On these, see e.g. McCluhan, "James Joyce: Trivial and Quadrivial," p. 85.

41   Also decisive in this direction would be the traditions of Kabbalah, which appear in the *Wake* (e.g. *FW*, 261) and whose thinking Gershom Scholem has likened to that of Dionysius and Eriugena: "This *Nothing* from which everything has sprung [. . .] is infinitely more real than all other reality. Only when the soul has stripped itself of all limitation and, in mystical language, has descended into the depths of Nothing does it encounter the Divine. For this *Nothing* comprises a wealth of mystical reality although it cannot be defined," in *Major Trends in Jewish Mysticism* (New York: Schocken Books, 1995), p. 25. For the comparison to Dionysius and Eriugena, see p. 354, n.24 – and for speculation concerning Eriugena's direct influence in the Hasidic context, see p. 109, which notes the Eriugenian derivation of the Hasidic phrasing "For Thou shalt be everything in everything, when there shall be nothing but Thee alone."

42   The shift from hierarchy to network in the *Wake* becomes very interesting in light of complexity theory. In a provocative study (though one unnecessarily hostile to post-structuralist theory), Thomas Rice Jackson rightly indicates that "the measure of complexity in a system is directly proportional to the precedence of the network (the parallel system) over the hierarchy (the serial system) in its structure [. . .]. [T]he networked, 'proteiform graph' of *Finnegans Wake* (*FW* 107.8) virtually eliminates hierarchies for the sake of a 'geodetic' structure (*FW* 114.15) that generates progressively higher degrees of complexity, complexity that apparently defeats mastery," in *Joyce, Chaos and Complexity* (Urbana: University of Illinois Press, 1997), p. 132. To situate this within a deeper historical perspective, one might note with Eco "the early moderns" like Bruno, Pico and Ficino who "knew by imagination, before mathematical formulation, that the universe was no longer a rigid hierarchy of immutable and definitive modules of order but something moving and changing. In such a universe, contradictions and oppositions do not constitute an evil to be reduced by abstract formulas, but they form the very core of reality" (Eco, *Aesthetics of Chaosmos*, p. 83).

43   One should relate this possibility of the *mensonge* to Derrida's remarks on the role of *forgery* in the *Wake* (forged words, phrases; invented histories, cultures, etc.): "In the simulacrum of this *forgery* [in English in the original], in the ruse of the invented word the greatest possible memory is struck and founded. *Finnegans*

*Wake* is a little, a little what? a little, a very little grandson [*petit-fils*] of occidental culture in its circular, encyclopedic, Ulyssean and more-than-Ulyssean totality. And then it is at the same time much greater than that odyssey itself." (Derrida, *James Joyce*, pp. 206–7).

44  "And [Jacob] dreamed that there was a ladder set up on the earth, and the top of it reached to heaven; and behold, the angels of God were ascending and descending on it."

45  On the human and the deity/dayety within the cyclic dynamic of procession and return: "Now, to be on anew and basking again in the panaroma of all flores of speech, if a human being duly fatigued by his dayety in the sooty [. . .] were at this auctual futule preteriting unstant [. . .] accorded, throughout the eye of a noodle, with an earsighted view of old hopeinhaven with all the ingredient and egregiunt whights and ways to which in the curse of his persistence the course of his tory will had been having recourses, the reverberration of knotcracking awes [. . .] could such a none [. . .] byhold at ones what is main and why tis twain, how one once meet melts in tother, wants poignings, the sap rising, the foles falling, the nimb now nihilant" (*FW*, 143).

46  For the full-scale development of this perspective, see John Bishop's superb study *Joyce's Book of the Dark: Finnegans Wake* (Madison: University of Wisconsin Press, 1985), which reads the *Wake* in terms of the sleep that traverses the body and mind of an absent subject.

47  Joyce, "William Blake," in *Critical Writings*, p. 222.

48  *On Learned Ignorance*, Book I, Ch. 2, § 12, in *Nicholas of Cusa: Selected Spiritual Writings*, trans. H. Lawrence Bond (New York: Paulist Press, 1997).

49  Bruno, *De l'infinito, universo e mondi*, in Giovanni Aquilecchia (ed.), *Giordano Bruno, Oeuvres Complètes, iv: De l'infini, de l'univers et des mondes* (Paris: Belles Lettres, 1995), p. 77; on Bruno's debt here to Cusa, see the helpful introduction by Miguel Angel Granada, p. lvi: "as the necessary effect of the divine power in which that power realizes itself fully, the infinite universe is *image, mirror, trace* and *simulacrum* of the divinity. Bruno can thus read literally the famous verse from the Psalms according to which *coeli enarrant gloriam Dei* (18:2): the infinite universe is certainly the self-expression of God or – as Bruno says, using the Cusan terminology: cf. *De docta ignorantia* II, 3 and 4 – the *explicatio* or *contractio* of that which in absolute simplicity and in the divine unity is *implicated*." As I note above, the notion of an infinity of worlds as perspectives on God actually emerges already in Eriugena.

50  Respectively, *FW*, 604, 481, 358, 484, 418, 260.

51  The connection here in Joyce between the angelic and the modern/technological resonates very powerfully with Michel Serres' fascinating and far-reaching meditation *Angels: A Modern Myth* (Paris: Flammarion, 1995). As Serres indicates, "these ancient mediators [. . .] provide a perfect image for our telegraph operators, postmen, translators, representatives, commentators . . . the armies of our new labor processes. [. . .] But also fiber optics, and the intelligent machines that we have built to connect networks between them."

52  As McHugh notes, in 1924 the BBC gave a live broadcast of Surrey nightingales.

53  Thomas J. J. Altizer, *The Contemporary Jesus* (Albany: State University of New York Press, 1997), p. 187. The most important recent analyses of this electronic humanity and its religious significance are those of Mark C. Taylor, whose influence in the present essay, if not explicit, should be noted. See especially *Hiding* (Chicago: University of Chicago Press, 1997).

# 10 Kenotic existence and the aesthetics of grace

*Luca D'Isanto*

> One cannot speak about the Great – the fulfillment of utopia – but only bear witness to it.
>
> Walter Benjamin[1]

In *The Philosophy of Symbolic Forms*, Ernst Cassirer associates the aesthetic vocation of mankind with the vision of the human being as a creator of forms.[2] Cassirer is the heir of a classical tradition that seeks in the beautiful image, in the symbolization of human space, the announcement of humanity's ontological destiny. However, the question of aesthetics does not lie merely in the beautiful; rather, it has to do with certain dynamics – the mobilization of force, of intensity, of lines of flight, of the solidity of "planes." In this chapter, I discuss the question of force in aesthetics – most cogently articulated by Deleuze in *Francis Bacon. La logique de la sensation* – in relation to the mystic tradition on the one hand, and early romanticism on the other hand. My choice of these fields of comparison is shaped by the fact that one finds addressed in both the relation between aesthetic vision or image, and the figural presentation of the divine. Both mystical and early romantic traditions share the idea, common to Greek philosophers and poets, that beauty, or "*more than*" beauty, is divine, and that the poetry of spirit is divine as well. But it is precisely the tantalizing residual of the "more than," of the ungraspable excess, which Kant and others somehow subsumed under the heading of the true sublime, that underscores the limitations of an aesthetics grounded in beautiful forms *per se*. Hence, my interest in Deleuze's dynamic approach to aesthetics, to the effects of figuration – lines of flight, planes, forces and so on – for the viewer's sensory apparatus, which is productive of an incapacity to translate the experience into a pattern of meaning. This, in turn, is at the center of the theological concept of *kenōsis* (abasement, self-emptying, depletion), in which all attempts to give meaning to an experience of presence to the divine are abandoned, along with the illusory notion that such experience can be intelligibly communicated to others. In sum, this chapter is about the hermeneutic and aesthetic strategies deployed by those who wanted to explore the liminal experience of vision and its language.

I argue that while much of aesthetics focuses on how it raises one to the intuition of the infinite, there is another movement which is much more important, namely, the logic of the fall. This consists in the trajectory of descent of the subject into the roots of existing, which is productive of an equally fundamental recovery of the world. Mystic and early romantic "flights of the imagination" toward the apex of divinity – in poetry, art, painting and ascetic practice, are driven by an active force that draws the subject to face up to the *abyss* of existence, and hence to the risk of insanity. But it is this very risky process that enables the subject to participate in the world of historical choices.

The connecting link between mystic and early romantic literature is in the shift from the figurable (the teleological idea of the beautiful) to the unfigurable (the presentation of the "almost unpresentable," that is, the sublime). The shift in emphasis (though they remain complementary) from one to the other concept consists in the transition from the figurative presentation of the divine – understood as teleological purposiveness and meaning – to the liberation of the divine Figures where meaning is understood as force, intensity and direction. The force surging through Figures opens up the abyss of existence, and lowers the subject down to earth, where a sense of existence (but not its absolute meaning) can spring forth.[3] Indeed, the German word for art (*Kunst*) has its etymological root in the verb *können*, which means to be possible or to make possible.[4] This etymology too brings into view the proximity of aesthetics to the question concerning the maturation of existence. What is at stake in historical debates concerning divine beauty and sublimity is the possibility of grasping a direction of sense, and a possibility of decision in the exigency of the instant.[5]

## I. Aesthetics and the logic of the fall

Aesthetics must transcend the realm of the figurative (illustration, representation, narrative, sequential history), drawing closer to the realm of the figural. In other words, figures must escape all figuration.[6] In a text concerning El Greco's *Burial of Count Orgaz*, Deleuze noted that the lower part of the painting told the story of a burial. Even though El Greco's signature style of stretching lengthwise the human form was already at work, narrative figuration still predominates. However, in order to reach the upper part of the painting, where Christ sits in glory in heaven, the count's soul is distorted, as are the other figures in this space. Thus Deleuze concludes: "One cannot say that religious feeling sustained figuration in ancient painting: on the contrary, it made a liberation of the figures possible, a surging of Figures outside of all figuration."[7] El Greco liberated the figure from its slavery to realism, to imitation and to the idea of representation in order to unleash sublime forces in painting. Figures are removed from narrative sequence, temporal chain, and exploded into a world of light. What matters in the figural world is not the perspective, the story, the structure, but the liberation of the form, the excess that enables the figure to emerge from obscurity. The force that exerts pressure on it matters more than the actual thought. Hence, Deleuze's emphasis on the act of creation as the *genesis* of thought. Art traces the *becoming* of lines of flight, the difference of becoming, the intersections, the play of capture. However, the sensation produced by the surge of El Greco's Figures above the world, and history, is accompanied by the intensity of the fall. It is the descending movement of intensity that supplies in sensation the effects of its ascent above the limits of the historical world. The crystallization of the effects of ascent constitutes the original moment of the creativity of art, and of the possibility of living in the historical world.

Moving from the figurative to the world of the figural requires that one thematize the synthetic role of sensation. A sensation is that which is transmitted directly without having to tell a story.[8] The point is not to return to the immediacy of experience in order to apprehend things in themselves, but to recover the *insignia* supplied in aesthetics, or *aisthēsis*, that is, in a sensible intuitive immediacy. *Insignia* have the character of a point, which cannot be reached by continuous progression, but rather by a leap. "This leap is an event that transforms existence. It transforms the structure and meaning of existing."[9] What is given in the surge of the figural is not an immediate awareness of being, but rather the possibility of making a leap into the incarnate world. The aesthetic might then be the locus of transformability of the subject in *communion* with others.

Sensation is closely related to a field of invisible forces, in such a way that a force exerts itself on a body in order to produce sensation. Then one may become aware of the intensities crossing the body surfaces, the traces left on the differential structure of experience. Deleuze appeals to the Kantian "principle of intensity," that is, to the idea of a maximum magnitude apprehended in the instant through sensation. "Sensation is not in itself an objective representation, and since neither the intuition of space nor that of time is to be met with in it, its magnitude is not extensive but *intensive*."[10] Sensation cannot be synthesized in the continuity of space, but rather only in the instant of the moment, because intensity is its modality. "Apprehension by means of sensation occupies only an instant, if, that is, I do not take into account the succession of different sensations."[11] What is generated in the apprehension is an intensive magnitude, a pressure on the senses. According to Deleuze, this maximum degree of intensity can be felt in the experience of the "fall" (*la chute*). The fall is an *active* movement of descent into the circulation of sensation, it is the difference of the "planes" within sensation. Indeed, the fall constitutes the difference of plane as such.[12] It is not a deadening, but rather the most "living" movement in the experience of a sensation. Hence, the task of reflection is to grasp *becoming* in the intensity of lines of flight exploding at the center, where the figural world springs forth.

The descending logic of the fall, I argue, appears especially in mystic *kenōsis*, both in the idea of the descent of the divine in the human form – to the abasement of the cross – and in the practice of detachment from the world of the senses, and of the figurative, on the part of the mystic subject. In this perspective, the fall presents the modality in which invisible forces, intensities and trajectories mark the coming into existence of subjectivity and meaning, that is, the way in which the subject can fully own up to its own history. As Nietzsche reminds us, the beautiful can only be grasped by a thought that has abandoned itself to the grace and generosity of being, that is, that has assumed upon itself the full meaning of the world, of incarnation. In this sense, the principle of the fall, understood as an active force that lowers the subject into the roots of existing crosses the mystic tradition, from its inception to the dawn of modernity, as well as early romanticism's reflection on aesthetics.[13] My argument then moves between the demand of kenosis that the subject detach itself in order to allow the appearance of divine Figures, and the subject's necessity to own up to the historicity of existence. Hence, the questions I pursue here are as follows: what does it mean to "sense" the other in the movement of kenosis, in descending into the roots of existing? How to figure the unfigurable in sublime abandonment, that is, in the poverty and suffering of existence? What is the relation between Figure and ineffable silence? In what follows, I begin by tracing the arts of the fall in mystic literature.

## II. Mystic *kenōsis* and the nonvision of God

Early patristic thought contrasted the logic of knowledge to the logic of perception (*aisthēsis*) in order to draw the limits of theological knowledge. It is the very contrast to which Baumgarten, the founder of the modern science of aesthetics, appealed in order to defend the rational foundation of the new science. Whereas knowledge is the special object of logic, says Baumgarten, perception is the object of aesthetics, thus separating aesthetics from logic.[14] A paradigm of the patristic debate concerning the perception of the divine can be found in John Chrysostom's *On the Incomprehensibility of God*.

Chrysostom opposes any claim that God might be fully visible and transparent, or that divine essence might be knowable in its totality, because of the fundamental gap between knowledge and God's being. It is not so much a question of affirming the unknowability of the divine, as of formulating the conditions in which the unknowable becomes accessible to finite experience, by accommodating itself, but also partially by withdrawing from visibility. These conditions of knowing are discussed in aesthetic and phenomenological terms as the im-possibility of grasping a pure *aisthēsis* of the divine in the midst of the human world.

The analysis of the conditions in which the perception of God is possible must pass through the recognition of the radical finitude of perception. This finitude implies the abyss between the figuration of beauty and its direct apprehension. The latter, for Chrysostom, is impossible. Immediate vision of divine beauty is so unbearable for the sensible eyes that even the angels, these beautiful figures of mediation, are forced to turn their eyes away from God.[15]

The splendor of divine beauty clashes with the misery of the fallen angels, those intermediate creations that are somehow responsible for the appearance of evil in the created universe. Here, though, it is a fall that does not reconstitute the continuity of existence, but rather annihilates it.

Hence, the recognition of the ineffability of God's essence: "Let us call upon him then, as the ineffable God who is beyond our intelligence, invisible, incomprehensible, who transcends the power of mortal words. Let us call upon him as the God who is inscrutable to the angels, unseen by the Seraphim, inconceivable to the Cherubim, invisible to the principalities, to the powers and to the virtues, in fact to all creatures without qualification, because he is known only by the son and by the spirit."[16] In tracing the limit of human knowledge about God, Chrysostom draws a zone of darkness which provides the condition for God's revelation. Even the biblical visions of God suggest that it is impossible to see God and remain alive. What then is the meaning of God's apparitions? Chrysostom writes that "God condescends whenever he is not seen as he is, but in the way one incapable of beholding him is able to look upon him. In this way God reveals himself by accommodating what he reveals to the weakness of a vision of those who behold him."[17] The emphasis is removed from the contemplation of the figurative object (the essence of God) to the only imperfect and partial human capacity of sensing the divine Figure and of being known by the divine. Hence, the idea that it is God's infinite capacity to adapt himself according to the individual, and so to appear as a different "figure" to each. Chrysostom tells us that "God is simple being; he is not composed of parts; he is without form or figure. But all the prophets saw different forms and figures."[18] The plurality of the divine Figures does not present the divine figuratively once and for all, but rather liberates the divine from the constraints of a particular form.

The liberation of the divine can be understood as a "force" that reduces the subject to silence, and that protects the secret of its invisibility. This, however, is not the positive force about which Deleuze and the modern mystics will speak. Rather, the latter has to be understood in terms of charity, that is, as the possibility of relation, of exposition to a community. What then is the relationship between vision and silent witnessing? To see a vision in which nothing is beholden by the eyes is to bear witness to the one who steals away the word.[19] The witness renounces the attempt at grasping the Figure, preferring instead an attitude of silent adoration. Yet, such a silence is filled with expectation insofar as Chrysostom "writes" it, that is, points to it as a residual of ineffable splendor, thereby cutting out a "place of silence." This is the place where, according to Lacan, the message of the subject is inscribed.[20] In this sense, the witness, unconsciously or not, is always already implicated in the logic of writing, of "transcribing" or giving speech to the demand of the other.[21] As we shall see, this is the demand that brings the witness to the risk of exposition, of communication.

In the mystical tradition of modernity, *kenōsis* is understood as a practice of detachment from the world of figuration for the sake of relation with the other, and with all others. As Michel de Certeau demonstrated in *The Mystic Fable*, modern mystics are travelers in search of the lost object of love. They are not comfortable with the silence of the absolute. They are rather wounded by it. Hence, their mysticism consists in revisiting the prophetic figures of the past that no longer speak in the present, in order to make them tell the truth of the subject. Their mysticism is thus a *pragmatic* of communication, that is, an effort to make silence speak. The fundamental attribute of mystics is the desire for exposition, for communication with a community that might understand the nature of their desire. They are wounded by the absence of the beloved, and of a community of souls, and so they remain isolated. They are pilgrims in a foreign land. Their mystic corpus springs forth from the radical movement of kenosis.

In *The Ascent of Mount Carmel*, John of the Cross suggests that to encounter the divine (vision) the soul must learn the path of renunciation. This practice must remove all the obstacles posed by understanding, imagination, feeling, and sense. The resulting entrance into the sphere of unknowing can lead to a true encounter of the divine.[22] It is neither a question of finding the right method, exercise or intention, nor of cultivating the right understanding. People who enter into the state of unknowing, says John, no longer have any modes or methods, still less are they – nor can they be – attached to them."[23] Rather, they depart from any prior understanding, imagination and sensory experiences in order "to be empty and free."[24] Thus, "no created thing is God, and because every created thing has form, all forms must be surmounted and abandoned if the vision of God is to be possible."[25] Renunciation is at the same time necessary and impossible. It is necessary because sense cannot "comprehend" God. The Kantian tradition will agree that the idea of God "exceeds" the realm of the senses, and cannot be grasped by the intellect. Kant makes use of the figure of *hypotyposis* to speak of the beautiful as the *symbol* of the morally good. *Hypotyposis* is the rhetorical operation of putting in view something that corresponds to an invisible object.[26] Etymologically, it is a stand-in that is known to be inadequate.

However, such renunciation (of the figure) remains an impossible gesture, because it is in danger of destroying the very possibility of sensing the divine. In order to think at all, the intellect must be presented with some content "by means of the senses, and so it needs the figures and forms of objects, which are present either in themselves or in their likenesses."[27] In detachment from the senses, the soul becomes aware of its nakedness and perceives the nakedness of the divine. "Placed before the naked reality of the Absolute, which presents itself to her in the mode of privation and dispossession, the soul endures an 'infinite death,' in her languishing and suffering, a living image of that infinite privation."[28] In the end, the destitute soul is confronted by the power of a vision that consists in a nonvision, that is, in a visible apparition of the divine in the mode of deferral. The consciousness of divine apparition is always already a deferral in relation to experience. The modality of deferral is not phenomenologically empty but rather fully experienced as a trace that has always already escaped the grasp of consciousness. The impossibility of grasping the divine apparition makes aesthetic experience collapse. Indeed, the kenotic process of stripping the soul of any attachment to the senses, and in particular to the forms of the visible, corresponds to the demand that existence disown itself for the sake of relation, with the other, and with all others. This collapse raises the question of love as that which resists identification, and remains open to the relation with the absolute. "For though love may throw herself into an encounter with the unknown, she knows that she has been taken hold of and carried further; rather than emptying herself, she is emptied."[29] The trajectory toward ecstasy, the state of being outside of oneself, is well under way.

Here the Christian thinker echoes the philosophical thematic assigned to Diotima in Plato's *Symposium*, and the Neo-Platonic speculation of Plotinus on the dialectic of Eros and Beauty. Thus Socrates, recollecting a dialogue with Diotima, spells out the idea that love is relational insofar as it is directed to an object. It is characteristic of love to "stand in relation to something."[30] This relation, however, stands under the mark of privation, for the lover does not own what she loves. Socrates speaks of the offspring of privation and indigence, but also of abundance. He speaks of love being the child of both lack (indigence, and privation) and inventiveness in the service of desire. The lover wants to possess the beloved for all eternity, for all immortality, but that goal is always deferred.[31] It is then the characteristic of love to give away that which it does not possess, a maybe, a surprise, a promise.

Following Plato, Plotinus builds his reflection on the dialectic of Eros as the desire of what the soul is always lacking, as a privation that needs to be filled up in eternal plenitude of the Good. Plotinus argues that in order to attain to beauty the soul must ascend through the steps of knowledge, reaching the place where nothing can be conceived any more. "When therefore we name beauty, all such shape must be dismissed; nothing visible is to be conceived, or at once we descend from beauty to what but bears the name in virtue of some faint participation. This formless form is beautiful as form, beautiful in proportion as we strip away all shape."[32]

What does the mind grasp when presented with the force of invisibility? It is not presented with an identifiable object that it can grasp or name. It may be called the One, says Plotinus, but not in the sense of a mathematical unity or of a single substance. One is then presented with an excess, the pure and endless power of all, the *apeiron*, the unlimited sphere of ungraspable plenitude.[33] Here, however, the idea of the active fall, of true kenosis, seems to be absent. The force of the invisible Figures does not draw the subject down to the roots of existence, but rather upward toward the sun of hyper-beauty. The subject is transformed into the movement of pure light, and becomes "the only eye capable of seeing supreme beauty."[34] To behold a vision is then, for Plotinus, to *conform* oneself to the archetype. Such a movement lifts the soul to the archetype, but does not seem to throw existence back into the incarnate world.

Gregory of Nyssa already stated that "everything that participates of something transforms in itself that which it participates with."[35] To behold the invisible is to receive the sublime offer of a communion, which may bring the soul back to the originary freedom of creation. This is the basic meaning of the doctrine of the restoration (*apokatastasis*) of sinful being within the providential scheme of the history of salvation. It is also the basic content of the messianic promise of the fulfillment (*plērōma*) of existence, articulated by the apostle Paul. The doctrine has to do with the possibility that faith might bring back the past into the future of creation. This interlacing of the mystical and the messianic shows the prevailing aspect of the incarnate world, and of the possibility of its redemption. If existence can be taken up as a whole, it can establish a continuity of its inner history. "If you know that, you have grasped what lay in the origin, the creation in the image and resemblance of God."[36] The mystic tradition – from Augustine's vision of the *City of God* to Eckhart – stresses in the aesthetic the possibility not merely of conforming oneself to the *Urbild*, but also of receiving the sublime offer of a transformation of the self in the incarnate world.

However, there are certain conditions for receiving this sublime offer of communion and transformation of existence, which have to do with the proper understanding of the practice of renunciation. True renunciation can occur only if the subject assumes fully the ontological priority of the divine origin, that is, if the world is not taken as the antecedent, the origin of being and meaning. In particular, Augustine condemns the role of habits in carrying along the past in ways that impede kenosis. "In habit's attachment to the wrong before of the world, it would make something imperishable out of itself, a life that surrenders itself to this world and its imperishable as if it were its antecedent. In habit, life always belongs only to what it has once taken up; it has bound itself over to its own past, which is precisely its sin."[37] Hence, true renunciation demands that one relinquish all bonds with the crushing weight of the sinful past, and place oneself outside of oneself before God (*coram Deo*). How to relinquish that which is most one's own, how to disown oneself and place oneself outside in the presence of God? For Augustine, it is a question of referring back, of returning to the forgotten origin and meaning of existence. But the origin cannot be reached once for all by archaeological or teleological thought. The process of referring back to the origin is a perpetual movement of return that is made possible by the always already ad-venient (grace of) God.

For Augustine, existence cannot accomplish on its own the ultimate renunciation of itself, it cannot give itself up completely. As long as human beings hold on to the will, they do not disown themselves, and consequently cannot love God's creation. This means that the human being cannot fulfill the central demand of love, that is, true relation with others. Human beings are restricted to the enjoyment of what they produce on their own. "Though the command to return to Being as our source is within conscience, the granting of the power to do so, which is divine grace, comes from outside ourselves."[38] Augustine believes that it is not a matter of persuading oneself that redemption has taken place, or of waiting for divine action. "Man cannot call himself into existence and cannot make anything out of nothing; in other words, he lacks true creative power."[39] The power of correcting the trajectory of existence lies in something that definitely interrupts the will to will, even the will not to will, for redemption consists in the transformation of will into love. "There is no greater assertion of something or somebody than to love it, that is, to say: I will that you be – *Amo: Volo ut sis.*"[40] The transformation is brought about by an encounter, by an experience of transformation that is made possible by an act of grace. Grace, then, is the most sublime metamorphosis of love.

Modern mystics – John of the Cross, Theresa of Avila, Meister Eckhart, and so on – understand the search for the divine origin as an act of departure, as a voyage that transforms the subject. The creation of the mystical corpus itself supplies the power of making one depart. "Sixteenth-century linguistics," says Michel de Certeau, "as has often been emphasized, often takes the direction of a 'mystics of the beginning' and a 'mystics of unity.' But it must be understood that the origin sought after is not a dead past. It had to be a 'voice' that returned under new guises, still breathing its 'force,' into present-day words."[41] To refer to the Augustinian desire of the forgotten origin is to learn to hear in the language of the Scripture and in the language of the body the Voice of the beloved. Thus language becomes a site of testing the limits of existence, and a machine for travelling adrift following the echoes of the divine Voice. Words become the very operators of detachment. They are "machines for setting adrift – machines for voyages and ecstasy outside of received meanings."[42]

Mystical discourse produces a space of fiction operating at the level of practice, involving the whole existence of the subject. The shift to practice is achieved by the abuse of translative processes, that is, by playing *kenotic* games with language. Names are borrowed from the corporeal world and from the biblical corpus, to supply the terms of dissimilarity. "The dissimilar, a discrepancy in relation to the analogy conceived by the understanding, becomes a body, transformed and altered, the movements of which form the illegible vocabulary of an unnameable speaker."[43] These passions – together with the conflicts they unleash – are "displaced, closed in a language, hidden again, and submitted to the constraints of another system of expression."[44] Language becomes the site of mystic passions, overflowing the border between individual existence and social relation. Thus they bring to the extreme the question concerning the potentiality of existence, which is understood as a blank text where the self writes its own story of departure. It is then a question of passing beyond, to the other border, to the *rivage* of the other. And in the process, listening to the Voice through the decoding of the very name of God in the language of the other, according to the codes of the Other Scene.

For de Certeau, the passion enveloping the mystic body borders on a primal form of sado-masochism, because this experience results precisely from descending into the roots of existing.[45] It bears witness to a "non-idealist vision of humanity," says de Certeau.[46] This vision is translated pictorially into the dispersion of fragments of rays resulting from the unleashing of passion, the altered and altering force of sense painted on the canvas. "In the paintings, the passions depicted portray mainly a passion of the forms and colors subjected to the delicious tortures of an art."[47] These techniques of figuration are renderings of a scene handed over from the past. Divine beauty is related to the love of abjection, of the humiliated body.

Thus the divine excess overflows the abyss of existence, trespassing into bare existence. To invoke God is to turn the eye to the mystery of the humiliated body, and to the passions experienced in privation. God ultimately is uncovered as perceivable body, voice and smell.

> God is no longer the subject who sustains the surface of things, and which a hermeneutic might decipher through it; he is brought to a surface of which he occupies only one of the places; he is given"there," immediate and un-covered. The clothes which once concealed him have now become the bare, indecent skin (*chair*), because there is nothing else for which they are the vestment.

To attain peace of heart, says Jean-Joseph Surin, "there is nothing like the love of abjection and of its miseries such as they might be. Love of one's own abjection draws profit from everything, even from its falls."[48] Thus, the mystical notion of the fall sees this as the site of divine beauty, though it appears in the experience of privation, of poverty and of suffering in which the senses persecute the mystic body. Angela da Foligno had already spelled out the meaning of the divine's descent into the depth of the world, as a choice for a life of abjection. She writes:

> Then he said to me, "I have shown you something of my power . . . behold now and see my humility." There was I given so deep an insight into the humility of God toward man and all other things that when my soul remembered His unspeakable power and comprehended his humility, it marveled greatly and did esteem itself nothing at all, for in itself it beheld nothing but pride.[49]

These practices cut out a new sacred territory, where the machinery of sense becomes a figure of pure passage, and waiting for the other. They are *artifacts* of silence, ways of making silence speak, through the perceivable – despised, humiliated – body. What is at stake in the mystical utterance is therefore the possibility of the birth of the subject – the birth of sense – out of the fragments of dispersion swirling like sand and storm in the desert of modernity. The mystic poetry of the spirit is the promise of "the creation of the subject who assumes a new order of symbolic relations to the world."[50] This *terra sacra* was to become the dream of aesthetic idealism, and of early romanticism. In romanticism, the dream of a new mythology translates into the desire of a new language, of new forms of communion.

## III.  Romanticism and the kenosis of beauty

The early romantic circle of Schelling, Hegel, the Schlegel brothers, Novalis, and Tieck was directly influenced by the resurgence of the mystic gesture through the recovery of speculative mysticism (Eckhart and Böhme). In these mystic authors, the experience of kenosis is related to the creation of a new language, of a new poetry of the spirit. Eckhart produced some of the more interesting mystical concepts by translating them from Latin into German. Böhme translated the insights of the mystical heritage – by reconciling them with the symbols of Jewish kabbalah and alchemy – into a theology of nature. However, the experience of kenosis – understood as the force of descending into the roots of existing – is somewhat obscured by the interlacing of kabbalistic and alchemical motives. In what follows, I look at the way in which early romantic authors like Schelling and Schiller freely appropriate the kenotic gesture of the mystic tradition, and testify to an art of descent as the possibility of the transformation of existence.

In the lectures given at Erlangen in 1810, Schelling debates critically the dialectical gesture of mysticism. The beginning of philosophy, says Schelling, lies in abandonment, in detachment from knowledge, will and desire. The person who wants to philosophize must be ready to feel the poverty and nakedness of existence, that is, he must abandon everything in order to gain everything.[51] He is, however, critical of the mystic appeal to the ineffability and incomprehensibility of God, because the logic of negation seems to bind the divine to structures of finitude. Mystical reserve does not do justice to the absolute, because it finds no place in which to grasp it. The premise of the objection lies in the status of the aesthetic. It is necessary for the absolute to make itself graspable in a form or figure, in order to participate in being.

In the dialogue *Bruno, or on the Natural and the Divine Principle of Things*, Schelling recognizes the limit of finite knowledge enunciated by the mystic tradition. "Nevertheless, it is difficult to express the inner essence of the eternal in mortal words, since language is derived from images and is created by the understanding."[52] However, Schelling does not abandon the quest for the form in which the absolute can be graspable. He seeks this form in art and nature: "we experience this indivisible identity of God and nature as destiny, but to behold it in direct, supersensible intuition is to be initiated into the supreme bliss, which is to be found only in the contemplation of the most perfect."[53] But given the limit of finite perception, what are the conditions in which such a beholding is possible? How to ascend to the divine forms or figures? The *Bruno* appeals to the spiritual ascent of the soul toward the splendor of beauty

> and we will follow this path upward until we see the point where absolute identity appears divided into two relative identities; in the one, we will recognize the point of origin for the real or natural world, in the other, that of the ideal or divine world. Within the first world, we celebrate the eternal incarnation of God; in the second, the inevitable divinization of mankind. And as we move up and down the spiritual ladder, freely and without constraint, now descending and beholding the identity of the divine and natural principle dissolved, now ascending and resolving everything again into the one, we shall see nature within God and God within nature. Now when we have scaled this peak and beheld the harmonious light of this wondrous cognition, we shall realize that this cognition is at the same time that which is real in the divine essence; then we shall be granted the favor of seeing beauty in its brightest splendor and not be blinded by the sight, and we shall live in the blessed company of all the gods.[54]

The mystic thematic of the spiritual ascent of the mind is lived through the consummation of the divine principle. Like the mystics, Schelling sees in the Figures the medium of presentation of the divine. Art is an autonomous locus of the reflection of the absolute.[55] It is "the absolute revelation of God, the artist is the prophet, artistic intuition is harmony with God; that is, true religion."[56] In the *Philosophy of Art*, the reflection as in a mirror of the divine in nature and art reveals the form in which the mind can grasp the unfigurable. The role of art forms (figures) lies in *hypotyposis*, that is, in the visible exhibition of the invisible. Schelling speaks of the *tautegorical symbol* as the actual manifestation of the absolute. While rejecting the hypothesis of the allegorical reading of mythology, and of art as a whole, he appeals to the force of the *tautegorical* symbol that contains the absolute content within itself. Thus "each figure in it is to be taken as that which it is, for precisely in this way is each also taken as that which it means or signifies. Meaning here is simultaneously being itself, passed over into the object itself, and one with it."[57]

The absolute can only be apprehended through a medium. "Complete revelation of God only occurs where in the reflected world itself the individual forms resolve into absolute identity, and this occurs only within reason. Reason is thus within itself the All itself the full reflected image of God."[58] Hence, the work of art is the full revelation of the absolute only to the extent that it reflects the unity of the absolute principle of identity. From this perspective, every event can be divine, though no event can be identified with the divine itself. If one were to do so, the consequence would be a loss of differentiation, of the absoluteness of God, and the subject would sink perhaps even into madness. Conversely, the universe is grasped as an absolute work of art itself.

The Platonic unity of Beauty and the divine is preserved. Thus, says Schelling, "the *basic law of all portrayals of the gods is the law of beauty*, for beauty is the absolute intuited in reality. Now since the gods are the absolute itself intuited actually (or synthesized with limitation) within the particular, their basic law of portrayal is that of beauty."[59] But what kind of beauty can be adequate to the figuration of the divine? The mystic tradition stressed the need of exploding the figures and forms of the beautiful in order to reach the ineffable presence of the true God. Schelling argues that the beautiful "reveals itself eminently as the canon of all concepts of the gods" by alleviating "all that is frightful and terrible by means of the beautiful."[60] Kant had defined beauty as "the form of purposiveness in an object so far as this form is perceived in it without the concept of a purpose."[61] However, he had to introduce the notion of the sublime as an appendix to the analytic of the beautiful to open up the totality of the figure to something that exceeds all possible figuration.

For Schelling, the beautiful consists in the in-forming (*Ineinbildung*) of the finite into the infinite. The beautiful maintains the harmonious relationship between the finite and the infinite. Thus, the infinite is contained from the beginning within the finite, it is not "added" to it. Whereas "the intuition of the sublime enters when the sensual, concrete intuition is found to be inadequate for the greatness of the concrete object, and then the truly infinite appears for which the merely concretely infinite is the symbol."[62] The sublime has an element of coercion as well – the coercion of the infinite that subdues the finite.

Schelling appeals to the principle of incomprehensibility – following Schiller's argument on the sublime – to define the aesthetic condition for grasping the divine under the conditions of finitude. The idea of the incomprehensible can enable the mind to have an intuition of what transcends the realm of the understanding.[63] Thus, the incomprehensible "can serve to give an idea of the supersensuous infinity."[64] Without the principle, the imagination would be unable to give a positive content to the apparition of something of the highest magnitude, for which no measure can be found. Since the sublime has no other measure than itself, the imagination is presented with something that cannot be schematized, although it can catch a glimpse of it.

The presentation of the sublime occurs like an actual combat, involving a fight between two equal opponents whose language is different. "There are cases," says Schiller – on whom Schelling's argument is based – "where fate 'overpowers' all ramparts, and where the only resistance is, like a pure spirit, to throw freely off all the interest of sense, and strip yourself of the body."[65] This overpowering force presents a challenge to the human spirit to transcend itself, to extend itself and to maintain a dignified control before the apparition of force. It is a matter of resistance, which testifies to the freedom and autonomy of the human being. At the same time, the trial involves suffering, and its tragic re-presentation. "Man can defend himself with the help of common sense and his muscular strength against the 'object' that makes him suffer."[66] Hence, the appropriate setting of the sublime is the theatre, the tragic, which demands that suffering and resistance to it be staged as the source for manifesting the infinite meaning of moral freedom. This process leads to the recognition of strength. "The noble man finds true harmony between reason and sense, inclination and duty. Grace is the expression of harmony in this sensuous world."[67] The staging of the sublime becomes the locus for reconstituting sense, and for resolving conflicts that might otherwise overpower the subject. The function of the aesthetic is to render visible the spiritual forces that appear on the scene for the trial of the subject.[68]

The dissemination of force manifests a world dominated by lawlessness. The understanding must find a symbol of reason within this very lawlessness.[69] The condition of independence of every phenomenon exposes the understanding to chaos as the general law of experience. In this sense, chaos "is the fundamental intuition of the sublime, for our vision perceives as chaos even the great mass that transcends our sensuous vision, as well as the sum of all the blind forces too powerful for our mere physical strength."[70] The feeling of the sublime then discloses a force which is capable of lacerating and overstepping the world of the senses. "It is not little by little (for between absolute dependence and absolute liberty there is no possible transition), it is suddenly and by a shock that the sublime wrenches our spiritual and independent nature away from the net which feeling has spun around us and which enchains the soul all the more tightly because of its subtle texture."[71] This force has a gravitational pull that can lift up the mind toward the heights of the spiritual world. For "the very thing that lowers one to the earth is precisely that which raises the other to the infinite."[72] As in Deleuze's formulation of the liberation of the Figures, the aesthetics of the sublime testifies to an excess of figuration. The excess occurs through the fall of the subject in the abyss of and through the liberation of sensuous vision from the constraints of the figurative.

How then to translate the idea of the fall into the possibility of the leap of the subject into the incarnate world? Like mystic kenosis, true elevation (which is capable of lowering down the subject) is made possible only by absolute detachment from the weight of the world. But this world is also the object whose contemplation produces the experience of the sublime. Appropriate detachment determines the relation of the self to the world. Nietzsche argues that "elevation" means finding the right distance between the self and the sublime object, so that the latter might be truly grasped. If we take a bird's eye view of our existence – but not the teleological view represented by God's eternity, which would be a denial of our finitude of perspective – we realize that the obstacles we thought so overpowering have been overcome. The ideal of an elevated humanity lies in learning to look from above at our existence, taking a "rest from ourselves, and turning our sight from down there on us, laughing and crying over ourselves from an artist's distance." There is grace in this elevated gaze, for the graceful expression can manifest itself in learning "to see – to accustom the eye to composure, to patience, to letting things come to it; to put off judgement . . . to be able to put off a decision."[73] Learning to keep a distance from the self involves evaluating the hierarchy of values on which existence is based. The order of the sublime, then, must be inverted. "If he grew weary of his sublimity, this sublime man, only then would his beauty rise up – only then will I taste him and find him tasty."[74] True elevation, says Nietzsche, consists in a true descent into visible beauty, that is, a descent into the historical world of human relations. "To stand with relaxed muscles and unharnessed wills: that is the most difficult thing for all of you, you sublime men. When power grows gracious and descends into the visible: call such descending beauty."[75] In the language of the mystics, descending beauty involves the transformation of the violent will into charity, because beauty demands the renunciation of all violence. "Beauty is unattainable by violent wills."[76] Violent wills, for Nietzsche, are the metaphysicians who want to get the truth by an act of force, that is, by an act that cannot be negotiated. Conversely, true beauty has to do with the question of love, of the recovery of communion with others. The vertical hierarchy of values must be transformed horizontally.

Elevation is essential to the self-realization of the self, for existence in order to fulfill itself must reach beyond itself.[77] An elevated existence is the condition for reconstituting an inner continuity of the self. But it is possible to overextend oneself, and to forfeit the possibility of an authentic transformation, remaining trapped in the temporal flow of decision. The existentialist psychiatrist Ludwig Binswanger – who is influenced by Heidegger and Nietzsche – has shown that the experience of being carried above is constitutive of the dream, and of the aesthetic as a whole. The imaginary flight is necessary for the mind, which can lead either to the fulfillment or to the paralysis of existence. What determines the ontological effectiveness of the imaginary flight, is the Nietzschean test. In other words, if there is a proportion between the vertical and the horizontal vectors of meaning, then existence has a chance to fulfill itself, and reach the process of self-realization. True elevation is the condition for getting a view from which to grasp the totality and continuity of one's own existence. In other words, it is the occasion for reviewing one's hierarchy of values. "It does not mean the adventurer's circumnavigation of the world in the sense of worldly experience; it means, rather, the strenuous and painful scaling of the rungs on the ladder of the problem of evaluation, i.e. of establishing an order of preference."[78] Hence, to rise beyond oneself means to choose oneself, and thus to realize oneself."[79] It means understanding existence in terms of potentiality, that is, regaining the point of view of the one who says, "I can." In mystic terms, true elevation functions only if the subject is thrown back into the incarnate world.

However, if the self gets stuck somewhere in the course of its imaginary flight, whether in a dream, vision, or idea, the flight has no positive ontological significance.[80] It is then captive to the imaginary, that is, it remains disproportionately in the vertical vector of meaning to the detriment of the horizontal one. This in turn undermines the reconciliation between the self and others. The harmony between heights and breadth, far and near, withers, so that communion and communication are impossible. Hence, the demand for a practice of renunciation, for putting off judgement, decision, and reaching beyond immediate stimuli. This is an expression of sobriety. To live accordingly means to enter the world of history, of arduous choices, and realization. It is the condition for recovering the experience of a radical encounter, the intimate communion with others as a form of luminous grace.

## IV. Conclusion

Kenosis then is a true descent of the subject into the roots of existing, and an exploration of the full meaning of mortal language. Is it possible to paint the silence of the absolute? Christian mystics testify to the silence of the beloved, the divine, by offering their own body as a living sacrifice. In other words, the absolute is no longer sought outside as something that stands in opposition to the inwardness of the soul. To withdraw into the self is to go in search of the absolute, opening oneself to the possibility of a surprise. It is also to expose oneself to the inevitability of its absence, for the beloved has always already left the trace of its passage across the humiliated body.

Modern mystics are profoundly aware that the divine can be experienced only in the abjection of the body, and thus offer an actual phenomenology of the senses. What the mystic body manifests is the flesh, the smell, the cry of the heart as the site marked by the absence of the absolute. Nothing remains outside of the perceivable body, except the intensity of the cry for the absence of the other. Lacan has shown that the silent cry can be re-presented only as laceration. "The body appears as the place where the desire of the other is expressed through the figure of a lack: image for language, language for image."[81] The body is an image that renders something visible and an image that speaks in eloquent silence.

The space opened up by mystic and romantic discourse is a pure passage, a pure waiting. "Pure waiting divides naturally into two simultaneous currents, the first representing what is awaited, something essentially tardy, always late and always postponed, the second representing something that is expected and on which depends the speeding up of the awaited object."[82] Thus the mystic voyage is an infinite kenosis, that is, a descent into the roots of the self in search of the Voice of the Divine. It is also the demand of communion with a community of souls that might understand the pain left on the humiliated body. It is an eminently ethical space where communion can be established, for the self opens itself to the surprising ad-vent of the other.

Similarly, Schlegel reminds us that romantic "knowledge proceeds exclusively toward the inside; it is in itself and for itself incommunicable, that is the way in which in common parlance the one who meditates gets lost inside himself. . . . It is only through exposition that he reaches . . . communion. . . . It is possible to assume that an inner knowledge existed before exposition or outside of it; but it is incomprehensible as long as it is deprived of exposition."[83] In both cases, the possibility of figuring the invisible lies in communicating something inexhaustible, which is open to the infinite movement of interpretation. It is, perhaps, because existence is incommunicable, unless it is exposed, or ex-scripted.

## Notes

1   Walter Benjamin, "Paul Scheerbart: Lesabéndio," in *Briefe* (Frankfurt am Main; Suhrkamp, 1966), p. 130. (My translation.)
2   Ernst Cassirer, *The Philosophy of Symbolic Forms*, vol. I (New Haven: Yale University Press, 1953).
3   Lyotard too argues that "the analysis of the beautiful allows one to hope for the advent of the subject as unity of the faculties, and for a legitimation of the agreement of real objects with the authentic destination of this subject, in the idea of nature." But the introduction of the analytic of the sublime "seems to put an end to these hopes. Yet what is of interest in sublime feeling is precisely what detonates this disappointment." Jean François Lyotard, *Lessons on the Analytic of the Sublime*, trans. Elizabeth Rottenberg (Stanford: Stanford University Press, 1994), pp. 159–60.
4   Henry Maldiney, "Ludwig Binswanger et le problème de la réalisation de soi dans l'art," in Ludwig Binswanger, *Henrik Ibsen et le problème de l' autoréalisation dans l'art* (Brussels: DeBoeck Université, 1996), p. 114.
5   Kant speaks of the feeling of respect for the sublime in nature as of respect for our ontological destiny (*Bestimmung*), for our common destination. Immanuel Kant, *Critique of Judgement*, trans. J. H. Bernard (New York and London: Hafner, 1951), p. 257.
6   Gilles Deleuze, *Francis Bacon: Logique de la sensation* (Paris: Éditions de la différence, 1984), p. 13.
7   Ibid., p. 14 (my translation).
8   Ibid., p. 28.
9   Henry Maldiney, "Ludwig Binswanger et le problème de la réalisation de soi dans l' art," p. 113 (my translation).
10   Gilles Deleuze, *Francis Bacon: Logique de la sensation*, p. 54 (my translation).
11   Immanuel Kant, *Critique of Pure Reason*, trans. Norman Kemp Smith (New York: St. Martin's Press, 1965), p. 202.
12   Gilles Deleuze, *Francis Bacon: Logique de la sensation*, p. 54.
13   Von Balthasar has made the category of kenosis central to an interpretation of the history of theological aesthetics by expressing the necessity of the trajectory of descent and ascent of the divine logos in the incarnation, the depletion of God into the servant figure of Christ. "The whole world is a free descent by the divine spirit into the hells of createdness and materiality, and it is this very descent, this humility and poverty of God, that radiates forth in glory from all things." However, I depart from Von Balthasar insofar as I want to express more radically the experience of the human subject in the Levinasian terms of kenotic existence, that is, an existence in depletion, poverty, and abandonment for the sake of others. The question of sense, of sensing the divine, is addressed here from the perspective of kenosis, as the transmission of something that is given only in the modality of the trace. Trace, however, does not merely imply that there cannot be an experience of fullness, of fulfillment, of plenitude in aesthetic and religious experience. Rather, it points to an experience which so fills the human subject that it impels an ascent above experience, making possible the intervention of the subject into the world of

history. Thus the trajectory of ascent and descent indicated by mystic and philo-sophical texts from the heights of the sublime into the world of the senses is a movement that leads back to the roots of historicity, to worldliness, to the secular. See Hans Urs Von Balthasar, *The Glory of the Lord: A Theological Aesthetics* (Edinburgh: T & T Clark, 1986 (1969)), p. 258.

14  Alexander Gottlieb Baumgarten, *Meditationes philosophicae de nonnullis ad poema pertinentibus*; *Reflections on Poetry*, trans. K. Aschenbrenner and W. B. Holtner (Berkeley and Los Angeles: University of California Press, 1954), p. 78.

15  Adorno contends that the "image of beauty as that of a single and differentiated something originates with the emancipation from the fear of the overpowering wholeness and undifferentiatedness of nature. The shudder in the face of this is rescued by beauty itself by making itself impervious to the immediately existent; beauty establishes a sphere of untouchability." What is articulated in the "blinding glare of beauty" has to do with the coerciveness emanating from the form, the distance from any materiality. The kenosis of beauty consists in the limitation of coercion, in charitative relation. Theodore Adorno, *Aesthetic Theory* (Minneapolis: University of Minnesota Press, 1997), p. 51.

16  Jean Chrysostom, *On the Incomprehensibility of God* (Washington: The Catholic University of America Press, 1982), p. 97.

17  Ibid., "Mystic Fable," p. 141.

18  Ibid.

19  Giorgio Agamben, *Quel che resta di Auschwitz. L'archivio e il testimone* (Turin: Bollati Boringhieri, 1998), p. 99.

20  Françoise Fonteneau, *L'ethique du silence. Wittgenstein et Lacan* (Paris: Éditions du Seuil, 1999), p. 187.

21  Avital Ronell, *Dictations: On Haunted Writing* (Bloomington: Indiana University Press, 1986), p. xiv.

22  John of the Cross, *The Ascent of Mount Carmel*, trans. E. A. Peers (New York: Image Books, 1958), p. 86.

23  Ibid., p. 87.

24  Ibid.

25  Von Balthasar, *The Glory of the Lord*, p. 127.

26  Kant, *The Critique of Judgement*, pp. 221–5.

27  Von Balthasar, *The Glory of the Lord*, p. 127.

28  Ibid., p. 110.

29  Ibid., p. 145.

30  Plato, *Symposium* (Oxford: Oxford University Press, 1994), 199-d.

31  A. H. Armstrong, *The Divine Enhancement of Earthly Beauties: The Hellenic and Platonic Tradition*, in *Eranos* lectures, 6, "On Beauty" (Dallas, 1987), pp. 41–73.

32  Plotinus, *Enneads* 6.7.32–3; also quoted by Sixten Ringbom, "Transcending the Visible: The Generation of the Abstract Pioneers," in *The Spiritual in Art: Abstract Painting 1890–1985*, ed. Edward Weisberger (Los Angeles: Los Angeles County Museum of Art, 1986), p. 132.

33  Von Balthasar, *The Glory of the Lord*, p. 303.

34  Jean-Luc Nancy, *The Muses*, trans. P. Kamuf (Stanford: Stanford University Press), p. 89.

35  Gregory of Nyssa, *De Virginitate*, XL VI, 364 B–C.

36  Jean Daniélou, *Platonisme et théologie mystique: essai sur la doctrine spirituelle de Saint Grégoire de Nysse* (Paris: Aubier, éditions montagne, 1944), p. 137.

37  Hannah Arendt, *Love and Saint Augustine* (Chicago: University of Chicago Press, 1996), p. 83.

38  Ibid., p. 88.

39  Ibid., p. 82.

40 Hannah Arendt, *The Life of the Mind* (New York: Harcourt Brace Jovanovich, 1978), p. 201.
41 Michel de Certeau, *The Mystic Fable*, vol. 1: *The Sixteenth and Seventeenth Century*, trans. Michael B. Smith (Chicago: University of Chicago Press, 1992), p. 123.
42 Ibid., p. 148.
43 Ibid.
44 Michel de Certeau, *La possession de Loudon* (Paris: Julliard, 1970), p. 45.
45 For a discussion of the relation between masochism and mysticism, see Luca D'Isanto, "Dépouillement du sujet et surgissement de l'être dans l'expérience mystique," *Rue Descartes* (1999).
46 Michel de Certeau, "Historicité mystique," *Recherches de science religieuse* (Paris) (1985), fn. 7, p. 331.
47 Ibid., p. 141.
48 Jean Joseph Surin, *Triomphe de l'amour divin sur les puissances de l'enfer et science expérimentale des choses de l'autre vie* (Grenoble: Jerome Millon, 1990), p. 417 (my translation).
49 Angela da Foligno, *Il libro dell'esperienza*, ed. Giovanni Pozzi (Milan: Adelphi, 1992), p. 130; *The Book of Divine Consolation of the Blessed Angela da Foligno*, trans. Mary G. Steegmann (New York: Cooper Square Publishers, 1966), p. 172.
50 Cited in Fonteneau, *Ethique du silence*, p. 176.
51 Freidrich Wilhem Joseph von Schelling, *Sämtliche Werke*, IX (Munich: Beck, 1927–59), p. 218.
52 Friedrich Willhelm Joseph von Schelling, *Bruno, or on the Natural and the Divine Principle of Things*, trans. M. Vater (Albany: State University of New York Press, 1984), p. 199.
53 Ibid., p. 203.
54 Ibid., p. 222.
55 Paul Tillich, *Mysticism and Guilt-Consciousness in Schelling's Philosophical Development*, trans. Victor Nuovo (Cranbury, NJ: Associated University Presses, Inc., 1974), p. 57.
56 Friedrich Willhelm Joseph von Schelling, *System of Transcendental Idealism* (1800), trans. Peter Heath (Charlottesville: University of Virginia Press, 1978), p. 231.
57 Friedrich Wilhelm Joseph von Schelling, *The Philosophy of Art*, trans. Douglas W. Scott (Minneapolis: University of Minnesota Press, 1989 (1859)), p. 49.
58 Ibid., p. 27.
59 Ibid., p. 40 (italics in the original).
60 Ibid.
61 Immanuel Kant, *The Analytic of the Beautiful* (New York: Bobbs-Merill, 1963), p. 45.
62 Schelling, *The Philosophy of Art*, p. 86.
63 Ibid., p. 88.
64 Friedrich Schiller, *Essays Aesthetic and Philosophical* (London: George Bell & and Sons, 1875), p. 138.
65 Ibid., p. 141.
66 Ibid., p. 149.
67 Ibid., p. 203.
68 This exposing of the imagination to an overwhelming force introduces a violent incommensurability into the system. In his discussion of the Kantian sublime, Derrida has demonstrated that the presentation of such an overwhelming force involves the violence made by the imagination to the senses. It is the imagination itself, for Derrida, that turns violence against the self, thus mutilating and sacrificing itself. However, this apparent sacrifice consists in organizing its own expropriation with a view to gaining an overwhelming victory. "But through this

violent renunciation the imagination wins in 'extension' and power." Jacques Derrida, *La vérité en peinture* (Paris: Flammarion, 1978), p. 150.

69  Ibid.
70  Ibid.
71  Ibid., p. 136.
72  Ibid., p. 134.
73  Friedrich Nietzsche, "What the Germans Are Missing," in *The Twilight of the Idols*, trans. R. Port (Indianapolis/Cambridge: Hackett, 1997), p. 48.
74  Friedrich Nietzsche, *Thus Spoke Zarathustra*, trans R. J. Hollingdale (London: Penguin Books, 1969), pp. 139–41.
75  Ibid.
76  Ibid., p. 140.
77  Henry Maldiney, "Ludwig Binswanger et le problème de la réalisation de soi dans l'art," in Ludwig Binswanger, *Henrik Ibsen et le problème de l'autoréalisation dans l'art* (Brussels: DeBoeck Université, 1996), p. 127.
78  Ludwig Binswanger, "Extravagance," in *Being-in-the-World: Selected Papers of Ludwig Binswanger*, trans. Jacob Needleman (New York: Basic Books, 1963), p. 345.
79  Ibid.
80  Ibid., p. 346.
81  Fonteneau, *Ethique du silence*, p. 189.
82  Gilles Deleuze, "Coldness and Cruelty," Introduction to Leopold von Sacher Masoch, "Venus in Furs", in Gilles Deleuze, *Masochism* (New York: Zone Books, 1991), p. 71.
83  Cited in Walter Benjamin, *Der Begriff der Kunstkritik in der deutschen Romantik*, in *Gesammelte Schriften*, I (Frankfurt: Suhrkampf Verlag, 1974), p. 41 (ff22).

# 11 Theography

## Signs of God in a postmodern age

*Victor E. Taylor*

My purpose is to tell of bodies which have been transformed into shapes of a different kind.

Ovid, *Metamorphoses*

*This* was Naso's path. Banned from Rome, from the realm of necessity and reason, the poet had finished telling his *Metamorphoses* beside the Black Sea, transforming this barren craggy coast, where he froze and ached with home-sickness, into *his* coast, transforming these barbarians, who harassed and drove him to the forsaken world of Trachila, into *his* characters. And telling *every* story to its conclusion, Naso had freed his world of human beings, of their rules and regulations. And then no doubt he had himself entered the landscape devoid of humans – an indestructible pebble rolling down the slopes, a cormorant sweeping above the foam-crested breakers, a swatch of triumphant purple moss perched atop the last crumbling wall of a town.

Christoph Ransmayr, *The Last World: A Novel with an Ovidian Repertory*

In the thirteenth century James I of Aragon (1213–76) opened an assembly of religious leaders with a provocative line of "Scripture": "Nor is it less a talent to protect what you have than to find it."[1] The line, of course, is not from "Scripture," but from Ovid's *Ars Amatoria*. It is interesting to note that while the line is not scriptural, it could have been or, at least, was perceived by those in attendance to be theological in character. This, one could argue, is the challenge of all poetry, to aspire to sacrality, to sound theological. Given that passages from Ovid's epics and elegies often have been misidentified over the centuries[2] as originating from sacred texts, it is accurate to say that he met this poetic challenge with tremendous success. One could go so far as to claim that Ovidian verse is, in a manner of speaking, essentially theological, especially with opening lines that chronicle the beginning of the Cosmos: "Before there was any earth or sea, before the canopy of heaven stretched over-head ... [n]othing," Ovid writes in the *Metamorphoses*, "had any lasting shape, but everything got in the way of everything else; for, within that one body, cold warred with hot, moist with dry, soft with hard, and light with heavy."[3] This "strife," as Ovid describes it, is brought to an end by "a god"; "a natural force of a higher kind, who separated the earth from heaven, and the waters from the earth, and set clear air apart from cloudy atmosphere."[4]

At the immanent level, Ovid's epic poem recounts the transformation of shapelessness into a "harmonious union."[5] This "unbroken thread of verse, from the earliest beginnings of the world, down to [his] own times," does much more than chronicle the forming of Order from Chaos, it purportedly creates it through the force of poetic language. Ovid's "unbroken thread of verse" provides the universe with *provenance*, revealing the mytho-narrative structures of his times. The "unbrokenness" of the *Metamorphoses* also suggests a theory of poetry, with verse representing the eternal dialectical inversion of order and chaos, a mimetic after-effect of a more encompassing process of creation. Ovid's epic, with its discontinuities of style, content and voice, aligns words and things, revealing a precarious harmony that is simultaneously linguistic, cosmological and theological.

The *Metamorphoses*, as it attempts to give structure to the 250 interconnecting myths, legends and stories within stories, is fundamentally an extension of creation, a bringing forth, as both creative process and product, of the categorization of a "shapeless uncoordinated mass" that pre-existed the earth, sea and heaven. Shaping shapelessness as a theo*logical* endeavor that forms an analytics of order in the form of poetry, for Ovid, is underwritten by a subtle dialectical inversion of separated similarities. When released from the constraints of kinship in "that one body," these become theo*graphical* in character, allowing for the emergence of a radical difference that is prior to a primal equivalency as a condition of meaning. This primal equivalency of logos and cosmos, however, undergoes an initial transformation in the *Metamorphoses* as Ovid manipulates the ambiguity of words across shifting contexts. A second, more radical, transformation at the interpretive level occurs within the postmodern moment as words transform into signs escaping ambiguity, with logos and cosmos giving way to signification. Before examining this concept of radical linguistic heterogeneity and ambiguity giving way to signification, however, it is necessary to delineate the poetic imagination's traditional function as a uniting force bringing, as Ovid states, shape to shapelessness.

### Limit, depth, surface

The nineteenth-century literary critic and essayist Walter Pater (1839–94) noted in his seminal study of Dionysus that religion is an indispensable element of all literature, classical and modern. He wistfully reflects on the classical mind and on "the dainty *Metamorphoses* of Ovid [as] a fossilised form of one morsel here and there, from a whole world of transformation, with which their nimble fancy was perpetually playing."[6] Pater's impulse toward a comparative science of religion is with us today in the form of dialectical literary criticism attempting to bring these "morsels" from here and there together again. The result of this interpretive endeavor is a remarkable re-positioning of language–story–theology uniting all three within the spatiality of God. It is through an analysis of this traditional triangulation that a postmodern secular theology will emerge.

The language–story–theology interplay within religion and literature studies attempts to bridge the great divide between the finite and the infinite. John Dominic Crossan in *The Dark Interval: Towards a Theology of the Story* begins his analysis of theology and narrative form with an extended passage from Rilke's *The Duino Elegies*:

> But because being here is much, and because
>    All this
> That's here, so fleeting, seems to require us
>    And strangely
> Concerns us. Us the most fleeting of all.
>    Just once,
> Everything, only for once. Once and no more.
>    And we, too,
> once. And never Again. But this
> having been once, though only once,
> having been once on earth – can it ever be cancelled?[7]

Crossan's explication emphasizes the elegy's theme of finality (finitude) expressed through the repetition of "once," leaving the reader to ponder the unsettling thoughts of a fleeting "life-towards-death." While death is indeed a limit, it is not the "fundamental limit" that Crossan sees as most significant in Rilke's elegy. "[D]eath," Crossan writes, "may be only a sign and a reminder of this more fundamental limit." A fundamental limit "which is language itself."[8] Quoting Wittgenstein's aphorism that "man has the urge to thrust against the limits of language … but the tendency, the thrust, points to something,"[9] Crossan offers a theory of language that is fundamentally allegorical; that is, Crossan *à la* Wittgenstein sees language pointing toward something beyond itself, referring to a primal identity that is "deeply" theological. Rilke's elegy, then, while turning on the theme of human finitude, also becomes a crypto-poetic exercise in which language initially fails then succeeds in revealing a depth to human experience. Poetic language as a language toward depth rests on a notion of direct referentiality that requires a recoverable transcendent "synapse" linking words and things. Crossan is by no means alone in this assertion. Early writings of Wittgenstein offer a "picture theory of language" in which words are reconciled to mental images. The later work of Wittgenstein, however, rejects this "picture theory" in favor of the "game theory" of language in which meaning is determined by the use of a word in context. For literary critics of the early 1980s, this accepted disciplinary departure by philosophers from Wittgenstein's earlier rigidity meant a re-appraisal of ordinary language philosophy that provided a ready, albeit ineffective, defense against deconstructive criticism.[10] Crossan subtly adopts this "philosophico-literary" approach, with the idea of "language-games" providing a necessary metaphysical element within his literary aesthetic. Taken at its least radical instantiation, then, "language games" debunk a naïve correspondence theory of language, words to things, in favor of a neo-correspondence theory of words to actions. "Ordinary language philosophy," Carl A. Raschke writes, "has served well to direct our attention to speech in its lived concrete setting, but it has proven remiss in showing us what, like the pearl of great price, lies buried in our field of inquiry."[11] As much as Wittgensteinian language theory moves the debate over meaning away from mysticism, words, nevertheless, find new meaning in relation to a "re-mystified" exterior space, concrete or mental. Whether words point back toward a thing in the world, a mental picture, or a use in context, the results are the same, a linguistic allegory in which language functions referentially, revealing a depth to the world (ontology), humankind (anthropology), society (sociology) or God (theology).

The "thrust" that points toward something, a depth, as Crossan suggests, leads to a false "language-limit" to the extent that language is forced to operate under an extra-linguistic demand which may be characterized as theological insofar as the "other" of language is determined to be God. The structure of narratives or stories within this conceptual model, argued by Crossan, necessarily directs language toward a foundation (God) of meaning that is, as he states, "found only at the edge of language and the limit of the story and that the only way to find that excitement is to test those edges and those limits."[12] The interesting issue here is not the deferred invocation of God one finds throughout Crossan's text, but the use of spatial metaphors to express (repress) a supposed inevitable transcendent readerly experience. "Edge" quietly invokes an inestimable "center" upon which the narrative or story must rest. One easily can substitute "surface" for "edge" and "depth" for "center" to arrive at a more precise binary opposition that informs Crossan's theo-literary critical approach to God as an extra-linguistic presence in/outside narrative.

A story or narrative's meaning, Crossan argues, generates from a tension between "edge" and "center" or "surface" and "depth." Within this traditional approach, language is poised against its "other" (God); an "other" that is accessible only through reflective experience: the greater the depth, the greater the meaning, the greater the experience. Theo-literary approaches to narratives, as we have seen, require that the "concept" of depth be articulated as a temporal (Rilke) or spatial exigency, rectifying the *mysterium* of poetic language. A postmodern theology, as a secular theology, forms at the conceptual limit of this crypto-poetics with a notion of "depth," as Charles E. Winquist observes in *Desiring Theology*, configured as "a complex inscription on the recording surface of experience."[13] Winquist's argument for a postmodern secular theology begins with an analysis of a cultural despondency over the lack of meaning and value in everyday life that does not force discourse toward an inestimable center or unfathomable depth. This lack of "depth," as Winquist sees it, incites a desire for theology as a longing for connectedness that "begin[s] [as] an interrogation of life."[14] This imperative to interrogate life allows Winquist to turn to the existential (secular) theology of Paul Tillich in such a way as to open an inquiry into the nature of theology itself; a move Crossan resists. Contrary to the crypto-poetic aesthetic honoring spatial "depth" that is advanced within a traditional theo-literary perspective, Winquist comes to revalue "surface" as an occasion for thinking theologically and poetically.

The crisis identified by Crossan in Rilke's elegy, as his explication would suggest, may be construed as a recasting of an age-old bi-partition of world in which language (phenomena) must continually yield to God (noumena), reinscribing meaningfulness as a product of transcendence. Theology and literature, within this perspective, are symbiotic, revealing depth through (extra-linguistic) symbols. The exigency of theology and literature, for Winquist, however, necessitates a thinking *in extremis* that reformulates spatial relations into linguistic relations:

> Conceiving of theology as a minor literature is a tactical implementation of the multiple strategies of acoluthetic reason, erring, deconstructive and hermeneutical tropologies, bricolage, radical criticism, parabolic and paradoxical narratives in the context of a dominant discourse of commodification. A minor literature is made of texts that are unsafe and are a contagion that makes all texts unsafe. Minor literatures teach us to stammer in our own language.[15]

Crypto-poetics asks, how does one come to know depth through literature? Postmodern theology sees the problem of "knowing depth" as a linguistic problem, not a metaphysical one reuniting words and ideas. That is, language doesn't fail to (re)present "reality," it deconstructs that reality through a differential sign system that is inextricably woven in to the fabric of lived experience. Depth, then, is a linguistic surface, not a spatial limit.

## Ending words

Winquist's postmodern theology depends upon a thinking *in extremis* that is linguistic, not epistemological, nor metaphysical. *Desiring Theology* or a desire for theology begins with a concept of "unconditionality" that one finds articulated in Paul Tillich's sermon entitled "The Depth of Existence" in which two epigraphs designate the aim of theological thinking:

> But God hath revealed them unto us by his Spirit:
> For the Spirit searcheth all things, yea, the deep things of God.
>
> 1 Corinthians 2:10

and

Out of the depth have I cried unto thee, O Lord.

Psalm 130:1

For Winquist, depth, as a concept, retains "a secular mandate for theology even in the context of transitoriness, contingency, and dissimulation of post-modern thinking."[16] In this regard, spatiality undergoes a deconstruction in Tillich's sermon, with the words "deep" and "depth," Tillich notes, being "used in our daily life, in poetry and philosophy, in the Bible, and in many other religious documents, to indicate a spiritual attitude, although the words themselves are taken from spatial experience. Depth is a dimension of space; yet at the same time it is a symbol for a spiritual quality."[17] How should one define this "spiritual quality" to which Tillich refers? First, we must consider the meaning of depth and its apparent opposite, surface. Tillich views the tension between "surface" and "depth," like Crossan, as a spatial representation of humankind's quest for meaning and value, which is much in the same way Ovid offers verse as a reconciliation of chaos to order. This spatial limit is breached, however, by the introduction of spiritual "quality" in which the "surface" of experience is argued to be mutable, inauthentic; it is, Tillich writes, "that side of things which first appears to us."[18] And it is this first appearance that is, finally, disappointing. Depth, on the other hand, is pre-sumed to be that side of things that only appears to us through theological reflection beyond the limit of language. The "quality" of depth, for Tillich, is more than the supposed inauthenticity of appearance; it is an apprehension of a profound, sublime, "spiritual quality," a truth which does not "disap-point."[19] How could one come to a theology that does not disappoint without returning to Crossan's transcendent poetics? Find a truth that, in the end, is not deep, but nevertheless meaningful? Find a way of thinking about God as a surface.

## Theology in ruin

Postmodern theology begins with a turn away from words towards signs, abandoning, as Carl A. Raschke observes in *The End of Theology*,[20] the "west-ern epoch of metaphysics."[21] While theology in the postmodern moment is characterized by an abandonment of metaphysical discourse, questions con-cerning meaning and value in lived experience endure. Along with these ques-tions comes the significance of the sign of God, not as a metaphysical entity but as a linguistic construct offering a logic of heterogeneity and a "dis-junctive diversity"[22] resulting in text production, the "unconditionality" of artistic creation. The sign of God is not the "name of God," the inadequate linguistic expression of an all-powerful being, but a condition of the possibi-lity of signification. The sign of God is an economy of concepts that takes "shape" as grammatological arrangements. God, freed from a spatial limit, no longer is language's "other"; nor is God philosophy's first principle – God is a sign-network. And, in this regard, it is important to remember that a theology that can only "simulate" its first principles, Winquist writes, "need not be a cause of despair."[23] The loss of modes of transcendence, opportunities for realities more real than language allows, permits a re-valuation of the limit; a limit that is not an "edge," but an illimitable surface for recording signs, a network. Theology's "unconditionality," then, is found in Tillich's reformulation of depth as a "quality," signaling, as Winquist writes, a forthcoming problem in which "[t]he experience of originality without origins and serious thinking without foundations keeps us bound to surfaces that are the space and theater of meaning."[24] In the absence of originality with origins, thinking with foundations, we are forced to return to the theater of meaning as space for staging the Ovidian impulse to give shape to shapelessness through poetic expression, to mark surfaces. However, this is no simple return to creative activity; it is a reversal of that initial creative act articulated by Ovid: "My purpose is to tell of bodies which have been transformed into shapes of a different kind." Postmodern theology, as an artistic endeavor, transforms shape into shapelessness, with shape refigured as a "disbecoming."

Clearly, the brief history of postmodern theology takes "shape" around the concept of "shapelessness" and "disbecoming." As we have seen, Charles E. Winquist advances a desiring theology precipitated by a longing to "interrogate life" as an extended surface of experimental constructions, epistemological as well as ethical. Other postmodern theologians, Carl A. Raschke and Mark C. Taylor, have argued for a theology emancipated from metaphysical discourse. For instance, Raschke writes, "[m]etaphysical thinking has always been based on difference, which is at the same time a dissemblance, a sheer taking off and putting on of comparative disguises."[25] Metaphysical thinking's "disguise" is its "depth," a concealing of signification with spatiality. This metaphysical (de)masking returns us to Winquist's "theater of meaning" in which theology becomes theography, the (un)writing of God, an anti-*Metamorphoses*.

## Signs and stones

> Now sailors spread their canvas to the winds, though they had as yet but little knowledge of these, and trees which had once clothed the high mountains were fashioned into ships, and tossed upon the ocean waves, far removed from their own element.[26]

> A hurricane – a swarm of birds high in the night, a white swarm rushing ever closer, cresting suddenly into a monstrous wave that lunged for the ship. A hurricane – screaming and weeping in the dark below deck and a sour stench of vomit, a dog gone mad in the pitching seas and ripping at a sailor's tendons, spume closing over the torn flesh. A hurricane – the journey to Tomi.[27]

Theography is the disjunctive arrangement of distinctive conceptual fields, theology and anything else. The "disjunctive" quality prohibits one conceptual field from eclipsing another, as we saw in the crypto-poetic approach advanced by Crossan. Theography, then, marks the removal of spatial depth from theology, replacing it with a non-spatial surface for signification. In this respect, all conceptual fields (disciplines) operate on the same discursive plateau, one beside the other. Theological–philosophical–literary–historical thinking does not move spatially, towards a depth, but differentially across a sign-network. For Mark C. Taylor, this emphasis on the surface amounts to an "axiological" change in the way spatiality is construed: "When depth is reinscribed in a superficial play of figures formed and deformed along fractal faults, fissures, gaps, and seams, this ancient hierarchy, which has long grounded being and knowledge, collapses. Order seems to give way to chaos in an endless flux of appearance."[28] Order giving way to chaos reverses Ovid's poetic enterprise and the direction of the criticism that generated around it, leaving in its wake a "fractal" theology, a theography, an immeasurable linguistic coastline, as it were. This new economy of the concept as an immeasurable linguistic coastline allows for a (mis)alignment of signifying movements that a return to literature may clarify.

As Ovid's *Metamorphoses* attempts to remedy shaplessness with shape, Christoph Ransmayr's[29] *The Last World: A Novel with an Ovidian Repertory* (*Die letzte Welt*) deconstructs Ovid's poetic achievement insofar as he presents the "harmonious union" of word and world transforming into signification. The novel's protagonist, Cotta, sets sail on the *Trivia* in search of the exiled poet Naso (Ovid). The novel brings the Roman Empire into the present through an anachronistic presentation of Ovid's life and final work. The characters that populate the island of Tomi, to which Cotta ventures, are recreations from the *Metamorphoses*, with each one "disbecoming" into his or her corresponding mythological character at the end of the novel. Cotta's journey becomes an anti-journey in which language, reality and representation ultimately fail, leaving him bereft of meaning beyond the infinite distribution of signs into the world. Ransmayr's tragic hero is man seeking "depth," hoping to find the great Naso who will reveal to him the transcendent meaning of his works.

His investigation leads nowhere, with insane figures supplying him with bits and pieces of useless information until he comes upon fifteen inscribed stone columns on the outskirts of town:

> Cotta unriddled and whispered the words like someone learning to read, tearing a blanket of slugs away with his bare hands wherever he suspected new words. He patched together what was revealed, checked it for sense and syntax, discarded it once, twice, began anew elsewhere, until at last it seemed to him that he had exhausted all the possibilities for combining and connecting fragments into a single message:[30]

I HAVE COMPLETED A WORK
THAT WILL WITHSTAND FIRE
AND IRON
EVEN THE WRATH OF GOD AND
ALL-CONSUMING TIME

WHENEVER IT WILL LET DEATH NOW COME
HAVING ONLY MY BODY
WITHIN ITS POWER
AND END MY LIFE

BUT THROUGH THIS WORK
I WILL LIVE ON AND
LIFT MYSELF HIGH ABOVE THE STARS
AND MY NAME
WILL BE INDESTRUCTIBLE[31]

Cotta solves the riddle and is energized by his findings and even though he knows only one man who could have created the column he calls into "the darkness" to Naso's insane servant, Pythagoras, "Who wrote this?" The quest for Naso and the secrets he may reveal lead Cotta through his own metamorphosis. He sees the people of the island transform into birds and beasts, causing him to look more intensely for the great poet and his book. In his exhaustion, Cotta comes to realize that "reality, once discovered, no longer needed recording."[32] Naso, the book, the promise of transcendence are gone, leaving one final inscription to discover: "He would find it on a banner buried in the silvery luster of the Trachila or on the boulder-strewn flanks of the new mountain. He was sure it would be a small banner – after all, it carried only two syllables. When he stopped to catch his breath, standing there so tiny under the overhanging rocks, Cotta sometimes flung those syllables against the stone, and answered, *Here!* as the echo of his shout came back to him. For what reverberated from the walls – broken and familiar – was his own name."[33]

Ransmayr's *Last World* is more than a protracted allusion to Ovid; it is richly diverse text that disallows symbolic correspondences between surface and depth, edge and center, with the *Metamorphoses* refraining from playing the part of the Ur-narrative. In fact, Ransmayr's novel returns us to Winquist's "theater of meaning" as the repertory elements suggested by the novel's subtitle interrupt the possibility of *a* story. In this sense, *The Last World* enacts a theographical logic by resisting the metaphysical reflex, allowing the "broken and familiar" nature of signs to reverberate back to Cotta, to us. While Ransmayr leaves Cotta distributed across the sign-universe, answering his own call, "*Here!*," he re-affirms Naso's (Ovid's) immortality by making him responsible for the transformation of the island and its people into "*his* characters." Ironically, by the novel's end, Naso achieves the opposite of what literary history has given him credit for, creating order. Ransmayr's

"Great Poet" transforms shape into shapelessness that is beyond the laws of Rome and the gods.

Theography, or signs of God, begins with an identification of a theo-literary tradition that synthesizes diverse conceptual elements into a unity, a spatial depth. Ovid, the poet of ages, stands within this tradition as the exemplar of this poetic activity of bringing "shape" to "shapelessness." Through a deconstructive analysis of the spatial metaphors and presuppositions regarding the primacy of identity in language, Derridean metaphysics of presence, we arrived at a re-valuation of "surface," not as the spatial opposite of "depth" but as a separate category of thinking. That is, surface denotes a turning away from words towards signs, leaving aside a referential schema grounding meaning in theology and literature. In this sense of theography, "meaning" is distributive across singular economies of signs precariously arranged within narrative forms. These conceptual singular economies are overdetermined[34] and may be viewed as narratives within narratives, referring to Ransmayr's Ovidian repertory. Secular theology, then, is theography, a non-allegorical linguistic "journey" designating "meaning" through differential signifying chains located within irreducible economies of meaning. Cotta's journey, in this regard, becomes an anti-journey, a journey without closure, without an endpoint. In the postmodern situation and at the end of spatiality, all texts and all journeys, like those of Ovid and Cotta, may be confused with "Scripture" insofar as all texts simulate their first principles, rehearsing Cotta's own moment of inescapable self-referentiality, *Here!*

## Notes

1 Sara Mack, *Ovid* (New Haven: Yale University Press, 1988), p. 164.
2 Ibid., p. 163.
3 *The Metamorphoses of Ovid*, trans. Mary M. Innes (New York: Penguin Books, 1971), p. 29.
4 Ibid.
5 Ibid.
6 Walter Pater, *Greek Studies: A Series of Essays* (New York: The MacMillan Company, 1901), p. 3.
7 Rainer Maria Rilke, *Selected Works*: II, trans. J. B. Leishman (New York: New Directions, 1967), p. 244.
8 John Dominic Crossan, *The Dark Interval: Towards a Theology of Story* (Sonoma: Polebridge Press, 1988), p. 2.
9 Ibid.
10 M. H. Abrams, *Doing Things with Texts: Essays in Criticism and Critical Theory* (New York: Norton, 1989).
11 Carl A. Raschke, *The End of Theology* (Boulder: Davies Group, 2000), p. 12.
12 Crossan (*Dark Interval*, pp. 29–30) posits that God is either "inside" narratives (imaginative idol) or "outside" narratives (transcendent unknowable), rejecting both in favor of a default quasi-transcendental experience on the "edge of language." It is worth noting that even though God is removed from narrative Crossan proceeds to offer "parable" as a means for "experiencing" God.
13 Charles E. Winquist, *Desiring Theology* (Chicago: University of Chicago Press, 1995), p. 138.

14  Ibid., p. 7.
15  Ibid., p. 129.
16  Ibid.
17  Paul Tillich, *The Shaking of the Foundations* (New York: Scribner's Sons, 1948) p. 52.
18  Ibid., p. 53.
19  Ibid.
20  Raschke, *The End of Theology*.
21  Ibid., p. 101.
22  Winquist, *Desiring Theology*, p. 138.
23  Ibid., p. 139.
24  Ibid., p. 138.
25  Carl A. Raschke, *Fire and Roses: Postmodernity and the Thought of the Body* (New York: State University of New York Press, 1996), p. 36.
26  *Metamorphoses*, p. 32.
27  Christoph Ransmayr, *The Last World: A Novel with an Ovidian Repertory* (New York: Grove Press, 1990), p. 3.
28  Mark C. Taylor, *The Picture in Question: Mark Tansey and the Ends of Representation* (Chicago: University of Chicago Press, 1999), p. 107.
29  The aesthetic, historical, philosophical and political crises of a postmodern age are exquisitely rendered and further exacerbated in Christoph Ransmayr's novels. His works are deeply postmodern, with his early days as a student of philosophy at the University of Vienna, where he studied the social and aesthetic theories of the Frankfurt School, serving as the rich intellectual *mise en scène* of his literary style.
30  The *Metamorphoses* ends with Ovid's declaration of his own immortality:

> My work is complete: a work which neither Jove's anger, nor fire nor sword shall destroy, nor yet the gnawing tooth of time. That day which has power over nothing but my body may, when it pleases, put an end to my uncertain span of years. Yet with my better part I shall soar, undying, far above the stars, and my name will be imperishable. Wherever Roman power extends over the lands Rome has subdued, people will read my verse. If there be any such poets' prophecies, I shall live to all eternity, immortalized by fame.
>
> (*Metamorphoses*, p. 357)

31  Ransmayr, *Last World*, p. 38.
32  Ibid., p. 219.
33  Ibid.
34  In this context, "overdetermination" is not in reference to (post-)Althusserian ideology critique in which economic laws "determine" the meaning of events; instead, I am using the term to suggest an epistemological inability to decide a "last instance" along a signifying chain.

# 12 Contact epistemology for the sites of theology

## Clayton Crockett

According to Jacques Lacan, Freud described the reception of psycho-analysis in the United States by claiming that "they don't realize we're bring-ing them the plague." This statement refers to the simple-minded embrace of Freudian psychoanalysis by many of its American adherents (which Lacan attacked), although Freud knew full well that many opponents of psycho-analysis did treat it like the plague.[1] This description of the reception of psychoanalysis could also refer to the American reception of postmodern-ism. On the one hand, many scholars dismiss contemporary Continental phi-losophy as irrational, nihilistic or irresponsible, that is, as a plague, while on the other hand, many proponents of postmodernism embrace it uncritically and pronounce its slogans without fully grasping their theoretical signifi-cance. In order to provide complexity and specificity for a theological encounter with "postmodernism," this essay develops an epistemology of contact, drawing on the work of the historian of religion Charles H. Long. An understanding of such intellectual influence as contact allows an exploration of the interaction between American pragmatism and radical empiricism, as well as Anglo-American process thought, and Continental philosophy, poststructuralism and/or postmodernism, and suggests impor-tant implications for theological thinking. I will briefly survey four sites of contact, in order to provide resources for thinking such connections. Finally, I will conclude by suggesting that psychoanalytic theory serves as a medium or catalyst for allowing such contact to take place in a fruitful manner.

In his book *Significations*, Long grapples with methodological and her-meneutical issues surrounding the interpretation of religious ideas and people in terms of symbols. He writes, "For my purposes, religion will mean orientation – orientation in the ultimate sense, that is, how one comes to terms with the ultimate significance of one's place in the world."[2] Long defines religion broadly as orientation, and he discusses the problematic nature of signification, that is, the signification of human beings who practice religion, by scholars of religion. In situations of Western imperialism and global conquest, the categories and meanings are imposed upon oppressed groups and peoples, who are precluded from signifying their own practice. Long holds on to the complex power dynamics at work in situations of cultural contact such as the "discovery" and inhabitation of the New World by Europeans, as well as New Guinea cargo cults, and he develops a discourse which allows so-called vanquished peoples not only to signify their own cultural and religious situation, but also to deform or deconstruct the discourse used to render them invisible.

> This opacity of vision forces the vanquished to come to terms in a concrete manner with what has happened to them. They had to take account first of the conquerors and their initial wrong perceptions of them and their intentions. They had to make sense of the trauma and the decentering and destruction of their cultures. They had to come to terms with the fact that their cultures would never be the same.[3]

This necessary opacity of vision issues in a "theologies opaque" which takes into account race and color as well as socioeconomic location in any theoretical discourse about the interpretation of religion.

Long develops an epistemology of contact to take into account the contextual situation of cultural contact and conquest. This epistemology is not only an acknowledgement of the ability of marginalized, vanquished or oppressed people and groups to speak, signify and interpret themselves religiously and culturally, but it also understands that there is no neutral discourse to describe the contact situation itself. In addition, what is created out of the encounter is a third discourse, pressured by both of the other two discourses, and determined in different ways by the power dynamics at work in the situation. This epistemology of contact can be applied to all kinds of cultural and religious situations, not only cross-cultural and post-colonial, but also theoretical, interdisciplinary, historical and theological discourses. I am applying Long's work to the situation of a contact or encounter between American and Continental philosophical and theological discourses, in order to assist in the construction of a radical theological discourse or theoretical discourse about religion.

# I

I will describe four sites of contact. Contacts are not static, and must also be understood in terms of currents. A current may be thought metaphorically in terms of ocean currents, and/or as an electronic current or flow.[4] The use of the term current to supplement Long's notion of contact is intended to supply a directionality to the contact surveyed. One site is the contact/current from Kant to William James, where the unknown status of things in themselves leads to a pragmatism regarding our concepts which does not thereby become an instrumentalism.

In the *Critique of Pure Reason*, Kant secures objective understanding of phenomena only by denying knowledge of things as they are in themselves. This is not a theory of idealism, because there is no doubt whatsoever that things in themselves exist, but, paradoxically, the condition for knowledge of things as they appear to human perception and understanding is that things as they are in themselves remain unknown to us. Kant is not a simple Platonist either, because there are not two different things or realms which must then be related; rather there is only one thing, but we must make a distinction between how that thing appears to us under the guise of human representation and how that same thing is in itself apart from any categories of human understanding. This is Kant's "Copernican revolution," that our knowledge of things conforms to the conditions of human representability rather than vice versa. He writes, "we suppose that our representation of things, as they are given to us, does not conform to these things as they are in themselves, but that these objects, as appearances, conform to our mode of representation."[5]

Subsequent German idealism, including Fichte, Schelling and Hegel, attempts to rejoin what Kant has put asunder, that is, to find some means of bridging the gap between things as they appear and things as they are in themselves. For William James, however, this irreducible gap leads to a philosophy of pragmatism, because truth applies to the realm of conceptual understanding rather than the things themselves, which are inaccessible. In his book *Pragmatism*, James casts his theory as a resolution of the dilemma between idealism and empiricism, and he adopts Charles Peirce's statement about the meaning of ideas that "conduct is for us its sole significance."[6] According to James, Kant undermines the possibility of a correspondence theory of truth whereby our concepts and ideas mirror things as they are in themselves. James's solution is to focus on the definite difference an idea makes to human beings in concrete life. The pragmatic method is a form of radical empiricism, and it understands theories as instruments, rather than as solutions. "Pragmatism unstiffens all our theories, limbers them up and sets each one to work."[7]

Now, the language James uses makes it sound like pragmatism is a robust American instrumentalism, a typical philosophy for a practical people concerned less with empty speculation than with getting things done. This instrumentalism can then be criticized as simply a means to an end, whereby any means is valid provided it gets us from one point to another, and we possess no criteria to evaluate ends. This superficial understanding of James's pragmatism as instrumentalism fails to follow the implications of such thinking very far. James follows Kant in focusing on human concepts and understanding, rather than the reality of things themselves. This is not a naïve (or more consistent) Kantianism that simply lets go of things as they are in themselves, since "purely objective truth . . . is nowhere to be found."[8] We cannot simply talk about a reality independent of human thinking, because our concepts are so intimately implicated in our understanding of such a reality. In fact, our concepts and understandings make or constitute that reality for us. What James accomplishes, however, is the folding of the notion of things as they are in themselves back into the idea of things as they appear to us. He writes, "The truth of an idea is not a stagnant property inherent in it. Truth *happens* to an idea. It *becomes* true, is *made* true by events. Its verity *is* in fact an event, a process."[9] The only standards of verification, however, are ultimately aesthetic, because "the connexions and transitions come to us from point to point as being progressive, harmonious, satisfactory. This function of agreeable leading is what we mean by an idea's verification."[10] This operation destroys any instrumentalism, because we lack an objective standard of measurement to evaluate whether and how an instrument works. Pragmatism is far more radical and far more Kantian than many of its adherents admit, because we constitute the measure for what a concept accomplishes at the same time as we evaluate the concept itself in its ability to accomplish something. This passage from Kant to James produces a radical undecidability of the status of our concepts, at the same time that it acknowledges the necessity of such concepts for human meaning and production. In some ways, James's extension of Kant's critical idealism into pragmatism rebounds back towards the *Critique of Judgment*, where the aesthetic judgment of beauty lacks objective content but expresses a finality without end, or a purposiveness without purpose.[11] The end does not remain, static and invisible, to be presupposed and invoked by any pragmatic operation of truth. No, the end becomes folded back into the process of conceptual working itself, dislocating the certainty of any adequacy of the means.

## II

The second site or situation is a movement from Charles Sanders Peirce to French semiotics and structuralism, which is a preoccupation with signs that enables many of the poststructuralist insights and critiques to occur. Despite the fact that Ferdinand de Saussure in his *Course in General Linguistics* considers both synchronic and diachronic aspects of linguistic signs, both Saussure and many thinkers influenced by him have emphasized the static and synchronic over the dynamic and diachronic elements of signification. Derrida appeals to Peirce's semiotics in order to move beyond some of the constrictive conclusions of French structuralism.[12]

Saussure divides the sign into signifier and signified, where the signifier indicates the vocal sound pattern (or graphic image) a word takes, whereas the signified refers to the conceptual content. These two aspects of a sign can be distinguished but never separated, even though the specific connection of sound and concept is arbitrary, and language as a system of signs constitutes the structure of differences which organizes meaningful significations by classification.[13] On the other hand, in his essay "Logic as Semiotic: The Theory of Signs," Peirce divides the sign into three parts, what he calls a "triadic relation." What he calls "First" is the internal logical relation of a sign in itself, which relates to logic and intrinsic possibility. "Second" is the relation to an external object, or what we commonly think of as a referent. Peirce also uses the word Representamen. Finally, "Third" is the Interpretant, or the relation to reason, general law and/or the thinker who uses the sign, although

Peirce also calls it a symbol. Each of these triadic relations is "genuine," and cannot be ignored or left out of consideration.[14]

Peirce's language is complex, because he creates neologisms to express his thought, but "First," "Second" and "Third" expresses the basic structure of his semiotics. This triad is then tripled into three trichotomies, or three ways of distinguishing these three fundamental relations, as a first, second and third of each "First," "Second" and "Third."

> Signs are divisible by three trichotomies; first, according as the sign in itself is a mere quality, is an actual existent, or is a general law; secondly, according as the relation of the sign to its object consists in the sign's having some character in itself, or in some existential relation to that object, or in its relation to an interpretant; thirdly, according as its Interpretant represents it as a sign of possibility or as a sign of fact or a sign of reason.[15]

We could also return to Long's epistemology of contact here, and think "First" as the subject or interpreter, while "Second" would be the object or people interpreted or studied. Finally, "Third" would be the result of such an encounter, or contact, which must take into account *both* the reflexive methodological categories and self-understandings of the interpreter *and* the transformation upon the entire hermeneutical situation by the agency, actions and self-understandings of the so-called object of study. Keep in mind that for Long the traditional Kantian subject–object representational paradigm of knowledge (retained to a certain extent by Peirce) is replaced by a subject–other relational paradigm of knowing and encounter.

In *Of Grammatology*, Jacques Derrida makes use of Peirce's dynamic theory of signs as part of his critique of Saussure and structuralism. Although Saussure provides resources to think signs and signification temporally and diachronically, the focus of French structuralism was mainly on language as a static system of signifiers and signifieds. Derrida puts Saussure's linguistics in motion, appealing to Peirce's notion of the symbol, which Peirce associates with "Third" in "Logic as Semiotic." The process or flow of signification means that the dynamism of the chain of signifiers is not undergirded by a transcendental signified which restricts the relation of a given signifier to a given signified once and for all. Despite Saussure's recognition of the arbitrariness of the signifier, he fails to go far enough, according to Derrida. Peirce draws attention to the "becoming unmotivated of the sign," by means of his awareness of the dynamic nature of the symbol, or "Thirdness" and its resonating effect upon the entire structure of the sign in itself and its relation to an object. Derrida claims that Peirce recognizes, on the one hand, that "the symbolic . . . is rooted in the non-symbolic, in an anterior and related order of signification: 'Symbols grow.'" On the other hand, "no ground of nonsignification . . . stretches out to give it foundation under the play and the coming into being of signs. Semiotic no longer depends on logic. Logic, according to Peirce, is semiotic."[16] Peirce enfolds the referent of a sign into the process of semiotics itself, and thus "Peirce goes very far in the direction that I have called the de-construction of the transcendental signified. . . . What broaches the movement of signification is what makes its interruption impossible. The thing itself is a sign."[17] Derrida appeals to Peirce to argue that signification or semiotics in a broad sense cannot be delimited by a naïve appeal to a non-symbolic real. At the same time, however, the nonsymbolic is always already at work within the process of signification itself. Finally, in this relation of Peirce to Derrida it is not simply a question of the struggle for originality, whether Peirce anticipated Derrida's insights or whether Derrida distorted or transformed Peirce, but of the contact, the encounter, or the "Third" which emerges from the trajectory of Peirce to Derrida.

## III

The third site is more complex, consisting of a movement from Kant to Whitehead on the one hand, and from Whitehead to Deleuze on the other. Kant's transcendental imagination has structural similarities with White-head's notion of the subject–superject, and Whitehead's systematic ontology takes a swerve in relation to Deleuze, who appropriates a Whiteheadian epistemology for his notion of an event of thinking, in which Deleuze shares Whitehead's fundamental valuation of novelty.

In the *Critique of Pure Reason*, the section on the "Transcendental Deduction," along with the dense chapter on the "Schematism of the Pure Concepts of Understanding," is Kant's account of how knowledge works by combining sensible intuitions with conceptual categories. Central to this process, although Kant neglects to provide as secure a status for it as for most of his important notions, is the role of transcendental imagination. Phenomenal knowledge, according to Kant, is the synthesis of a manifold of sensible intuitions under a determinate concept or category. The "transcendental synthesis of imagination" makes knowledge possible by reproducing the sensory appearance in a way that enables it to be grasped conceptually by the understanding. At the core of Kantian epistemology, the transcendental imagination mediates sensible intuitions and conceptual categories, and thus "we must assume a pure transcendental synthesis of imagination as conditioning the very possibility of experience."[18] In *Kant and the Problem of Metaphysics*, Heidegger focuses on transcendental imagination as the central active force in human knowing, and suggests that imagination forms the "root" of the two stems, intuition and understanding. To a certain extent, however, "Kant shrank back from this unknown root" because an emphasis upon imagination seriously compromises the objectivity of the determinate result of understanding.[19]

The mathematician and philosopher Alfred North Whitehead is often seen as a philosopher of science and nature, and his masterwork, *Process and Reality*, appears as a complex achievement of speculative ontology.

Whitehead's final chapter, "God and the World," along with his acknowledged enduring interest in religion, has been appropriated for an elaborate process theology by Charles Hartshorne, John Cobb and others. On the other hand, and despite Whitehead's profound criticism of Kant's over-reliance on Newtonian physics, one can trace a Whiteheadian epistemology that possesses important affinities with Kant's epistemology. In his book on *Symbolism*, Whitehead shows how symbolic reference mediates between causal efficacy and presentational immediacy in a way similar to how transcendental imagination mediates between sensible intuition and conceptual understanding for Kant. The working of symbolic reference is implicit and presupposed in *Process and Reality*, but explicit in *Symbolism*. Causal efficacy refers to the actual processes at work in the world, many of which are microscopic and molecular, and thus beyond the range of ordinary human perception. Presentational immediacy means the vivid sensory impressions, which should not be mistaken for reality itself. Whitehead attacks Hume and the tradition of British empiricism for its over-reliance on sense perception, which he calls "The Fallacy of Misplaced Concreteness." The incongruity of presentational immediacy and causal efficacy is problematic in human experience. "The contrast between the comparative emptiness of Presentational Immediacy and the deep significance disclosed by Causal Efficacy is at the root of the pathos that haunts the world," writes Whitehead.[20] This is the problem of appearance and reality, and causal efficacy for Whitehead is not simply the Kantian understanding, but also includes reason and its consideration of things in themselves. The actual causal efficacy of things is not available to human perception, and in line with the findings of modern physics, this is inherent to the things themselves (which are processes), rather than a situation which can be resolved by refining our instrumentation as an extension of our sensory apparatuses. What is ultimately at stake in symbolism is a "symbolic transfer of emotion" in an explicitly aesthetic sense as well as a broadened metaphorical sense.[21] Symbolic reference suggests that feeling is an irreducible component in working through the passage from causal efficacy to presentational immediacy. Here is a line traced from a Kantian to a Whiteheadian epistemology, and this encounter suggests that Whitehead's systematic effort in *Process and Reality* is not a naïve scientism or ontology.[22]

Deleuze's philosophy appropriates Anglo-American empiricism as a counter to the dialectics and phenomenology pervading French thought; his dissertation, *Empiricism and Subjectivity*, deals with Hume. Deleuze's late work on Leibniz and the construction of a neo-baroque also involves a turn towards Whitehead. *The Fold* develops a metaphysics of folding and unfolding, of pleats of matter and folds of the soul, which avoids the negativity so problematic in Hegelian and existentialist thought. *The Fold* is an intervention between the pure thought of Spinoza and the irresolvable antinomies of Kant, which elaborates an aesthetics of chiaroscuro, or a harmonious interplay of light and shadow. The complexity of the neo-baroque fold possesses affinities with Whitehead's *Process and Reality*, centered around the question "What is an event?"[23] For Deleuze, an event is an event of thinking, or a "logic of sense" but not in exclusion or separation from of the actuality of ontological events. In terms of *What Is Philosophy?*, an event expresses the reality of philosophy's creation of concepts. Deleuze claims in *The Fold* that based on his thinking about the event, Whitehead "stands provisionally as the last great Anglo-American philosopher before Wittgenstein's disciples spread their misty confusion, sufficiency and terror."[24]

*Process and Reality* can be read as an elaborate scheme illustrating the nature of an event, which is the process of concrescence for an actual entity which prehends an eternal object in accordance with its subjective aim. The goal is enjoyment, or satisfaction, and Whitehead describes both conscious and unconscious, organic and inorganic processes. I am assimilating White-head's understanding of an event to an event of thinking, specifically in reference to his notion of subject–superject. In Kantian terms, there is a distinction between the subject as subject, that is, the transcendental I or unity of apperception which performs the synthesis of transcendental imagination, and the subject as object, that is, the empirical self represented to and for the "I think." Whitehead criticizes Kant by means of expressing a similar conception. "For Kant, the world emerges from the subject," he writes; "for the philosophy of organism, the subject emerges from the world – a 'superject' rather than a subject."[25] Of course, Whitehead holds on to the necessary interconnection of a subject who sub-jects the world to her own existence in thinking and living, and the subject who is super-jected by the world in its process of actualization. There is never a subject without a superject and vice versa.

Deleuze appropriates his notion of the subject as a fold specifically from Heidegger, where the fold is what distinguishes and relates being and beings.[26] At the same time, however, Deleuze in *The Fold* and *Foucault* elaborates his thinking of subject as fold in relation to both Leibniz and Whitehead. For Deleuze, "folds are in the soul and authentically exist only in the soul," despite the appearance of a cosmological language, as in Whitehead.[27] "The fold is Power," and "force itself is an act, an act of the fold."[28] The Fold in itself always occurs between two determinate folds, and an object becomes what Deleuze calls "objectile." "The object here is manneristic, not essentia-lizing: it becomes an event," while the subject becomes a point of view, which is a perspectivism related to the Whiteheadian superject. The object is trans-formed by the activity of the human subject as subject; it becomes an event. The subject is also transformed by its contact with the becoming of the object: it is super-jected. Deleuze explains:

> That is why the transformation of the object refers to a correlative trans-formation of the subject: the subject is not a sub-ject but, as Whitehead says, a "superject." Just as the object becomes objectile, the subject becomes a superject.[29]

The complex encounter between Kant and Whitehead on the one hand, and Whitehead and Deleuze on the other, allows a thinking of event (of thinking as profound contact, which refers back to Long's notion of contact at a micro-epistemological level) in which processes of imagination and symbolic reference effect a transfer of feeling that affects both object and subject. The trajectory from subject to object is what Whitehead calls subject and Deleuze calls objectile; the trajectory from object/event to subject is what Deleuze calls point of view and Whitehead calls superject.

## IV

Finally, the fourth site is the encounter of American Death of God theology with contemporary Continental philosophy, and it is this site which needs to be fleshed out for the purposes of contemporary theological thinking. In many respects, the delineation of the other three sites provides theoretical resources to understand the nature and stakes of this encounter, which is the primary topic of this essay and in some respects the book overall. Although identified publicly with Thomas J. J. Altizer and sometimes dismissed as a fad, Death of God theology's roots are located in a radical Tillicheanism, and its effects have shaped the reception of Continental philosophy in an essential way in the creation of a postmodern theology.

In some ways, Tillich can be seen as the first theologian who accomplishes the Death of God, and this is neither the traditional notion of God dying kenotically on the cross, nor the expiration of deity in the modern world. Tillich claims that any talk of God is inherently symbolic, while the only non-symbolic statement about God is that God is "being-itself." The insistence on the nature of symbolic language frees theology from enslavement to an implicitly cosmological discourse, where divinity expresses some spatial reference "out there" in the universe, whether understood in traditional terms or revised in reference to modern physics.[30] Rather, God is a sign among other signs, and the Death of God refers to the deconstruction of theology. Derridean deconstruction disallows the operation of a transcendental signified, or a master-sign which would halt or determine the flow of signification. This is extremely threatening to traditional theology, despite the fact that Derrida has written about religion in passionate and positive ways. If the word God is a sign, then it possesses no special status in relation to every other sign. Although Tillich's exception, that the sentence "God is being-itself" is a non-symbolic statement, appears to preserve an exemplary reference for the word God, his statement should be understood in relation to Lacan's triad of imaginary, symbolic and real. In this case the phrase, "God is being-itself" refers not to the symbolic, but to the real, not in a naïve literal way, but in a specifically Lacanian way, where this phrase should also be supplemented with Lacan's claim that "God is unconscious." Being in itself, the real, is unconscious, that is, inaccessible to human conceptual thinking as such, although it does disturb and disrupt conscious thinking.

The Death of God is a radical displacement of theological discourse from a secure and certain object, and theology is then thrown back on itself into the mode of a concern with the form of theological language. Paradoxically, this loss frees theology from rigid dogmatic and conceptual constraints, and allows it to undertake powerful and intensive investigations into the significance of human thinking, signifying and cultural identity form(ul)ations.[31] If God is a sign/event, then the concept "God is Dead" represents a metonymical displacement of traditional theological discourse, as well as a pressure point to interrogate that discourse and a tool to create a radical theological discourse.

American radical theologians influenced by Tillich and informed by Death of God theology did not simply import French philosophy into an empty shell, or appropriate wholesale the theories of Derrida, Deleuze, Lacan and Kristeva (not to mention Heidegger). The creation of a postmodern theological discourse in the 1980s around figures such as Mark C. Taylor, Robert P. Scharlemann, Charles E. Winquist and Carl A. Raschke involved a complex encounter in which the legacy of American radical theology influenced by American radical empiricism, pragmatism and process thought came into creative contact with contemporary Continental philosophy in order to generate new ways of thinking theologically. This tradition of radical American theology has been overshadowed somewhat by the emergence of Radical Orthodoxy in the United Kingdom and Jean-Luc Marion in France. These latter thinkers have overtaken the name and public identity of postmodern theology, and have deployed theology in more traditional and conservative ways, despite their sophisticated readings of Continental philosophers. A contextual awareness of the tradition of American radical theology, along with its resources for contact with contemporary postmodernism, creates an opening for a continued transformation of theological thinking. Such thinking allows for the formation of a sophisticated theoretical discourse about religion that is not hostile to the general project of the academic study of religion.

Psychoanalytic theory provides a medium through which to think these sites of theoretical contact. Lacan's quote of Freud sets up the situation of an American theological appropriation of postmodern Continental philosophy. I appeal to Long's contact epistemology to provide a theoretical resource to make sense of this appropriation or encounter, which is neither a naïve appropriation of Continental philosophy or theology as it is in itself, nor a simple-minded assimilation of Continental thought to American channels, but the creation of a new theoretical discourse. A psychoanalytic understanding suggests that a too-quick embrace and celebration of postmodernism is unhealthy, which is Lacan's spin on Freud's statement, that Americans do not realize the nature of the beast they are welcoming with open arms, the announcement of a "plague." This raises the question of nihilism, and opens up three possibilities: whether (1) the Continental theorists in question are active promoters of nihilism, which is seriously in question for any scholar who has carefully studied their work; (2) they are announcing and warning a situation or condition of nihilism and attempting to respond to it, which is the basic standpoint of Nietzsche, the diagnostician of Western European nihilism; or finally, (3) there is nothing nihilistic about their work at all, rather the impact it has had on other traditions, thinkers, etc., is taken to be nihilistic by defenders of those traditions and other readers. On the other hand, a superstitious disavowal of postmodernism as dangerous and destructive risks a return of the repressed which is even more dangerous than the theory itself (the "cure" may be more deadly than the disease).

## Conclusion

In some ways, what it (postmodernism) *is* is less significant that what it *does*, which is both a Deleuzian and a pragmatic approach. The construction of a radical postmodern theological discourse is the attempt to put European postmodernism to work, to experiment with what becomings it can effect, rather than a sterile discussion about its limits and determinations. In conclusion, I want to return to a consideration of currents to discuss what Lacan says about a door. In Seminar Two, during a discussion of psychoanalysis and cybernetics, Lacan claims that the door expresses "relation as such, of access and closure. Once the door is open, it closes. When it is closed, it opens."[32] Lacan is referring to the operation of a door rather than a physical entity. In the case of an electrical circuit, closing a door closes a circuit and allows the current to flow within a certain area. To open a door is to break the circuit, or short-circuit the current. Lacan refers to the use of digital numbers 1 and 0 to represent a closed (0) or open (1) door. Feedback is what allows the successive states of open and closed to affect each other in increasing layers of complexity, so that doors open and close in a sequence or meaningful operation.

Lacan argues that human beings are very similar to digital machines here, but he is actually using Freudian psychoanalysis to overcome a narrow mechanistic structuralism, because the insistence of unconscious speech opens up a beyond of the pleasure principle, which as death drive represents the institution of the symbolic order. At the end of the Seminar, Lacan concludes: "The symbolic order is simultaneously non-being and insisting to be, that is what Freud has in mind when he talks about the death instinct as being what is most fundamental – a symbolic order in travail, in the process of coming, insisting on being realized."[33] Speech is the articulation of a subject beyond the control of the conscious ego. In the case of the door, the door "is a real symbol, the symbol par excellence, that symbol in which man's passing, through the cross it sketches, intersecting access and closure, can always be recognized."[34]

Closing a door closes the circuit, allowing the current to flow. Opening a door is a short-circuit, which redirects the current but does not allow a circuit to form and a current to flow unless there exists a closed door further out to establish a new circuit. If we consider America, or philosophy and theology within the United States, as a circuit, then we may want to keep the door closed in order to preserve the circuit which has been set up. On the other hand, to open a door is at once to allow currents to flow beyond the circuit, and to short-circuit American philosophy and theology. At the same time, we must close another door which will allow American and Continental philosophy and theology to form a new circuit. One of the questions that arises is what doors to open and close, which is akin to the distinction made by William James between live and dead options, live and dead circuits. Circuits used to be carried by wires, but now with wireless networks and communications we no longer need to be able to see the cables, or the strings which pull the connections and conceptions being established.

Theological thought may need to experiment with opening and closing doors, and at the same time pay attention to the hinge on which the door turns, the passage granting access and closure, and the conditions allowing circuits, currents and contacts to be created. Some contacts are grounded, and others may contain live wires or charges that may be explosive. To open one door is necessarily (or at least inevitably) to close off another. Are there doors which cannot and should not be opened? Are there doors which cannot be kept closed, despite our efforts to prop and jam? Is God a giant doorkeeper, guarding entrance and exit, or can a radical theological interrogation roll a gigantic stone from the entrance to what cannot be other than a tomb, an invisible door to an empty tomb? And is this "good news"?

## Notes

1  See the discussion in Elizabeth Roudinesco, *Jacques Lacan*, trans. Barbara Bray (New York: Columbia University Press, 1997), p. 265.
2  Charles H. Long, *Significations: Signs, Symbols, and Images in the Interpretation of Religion* (Philadelphia: Fortress Press, 1986), p. 7.
3  Ibid., p. 108.
4  For an example of the use of a metaphor of an ocean current, or more specifically ships in motion across continents, see Paul Gilroy, *The Black Atlantic: Modernity and Double Consciousness* (Cambridge, MA: Harvard University Press, 1993).
5  Immanuel Kant, *Critique of Pure Reason*, trans. Norman Kemp Smith (New York: St. Martin's Press, 1965), p. 24 [Bxx].
6  William James, *Pragmatism* (New York: Dover Publications, 1995), p. 20.
7  Ibid., p. 21.
8  Ibid., p. 25.
9  Ibid., pp. 77–8.
10  Ibid., p. 78.
11  Immanuel Kant, *Critique of Judgment*, trans. Werner Pluhar (Indianapolis: Hackett, 1987), p. 84: "Beauty is an object's form of purposiveness insofar as it is perceived in the object without the presentation of a purpose."
12  Derrida is not the only French thinker influenced by Peirce, even though I focus on Derrida in this essay. In *Negotiations 1972–1990*, trans. Martin Joughin (New York: Columbia University Press, 1995), Gilles Deleuze admits the crucial

significance of Peirce for his thinking of signs. He writes: "The significance of a logician like Peirce is to have worked out an extremely rich classification of signs, relatively independent of the linguistic model" (p. 47). And relative to his work on cinema, Deleuze claims: "It's signs that realize Ideas. Images, in cinema, are signs. . . . If I've used Peirce, it's because in Peirce there's a profound mirroring of images and signs. If, on the other hand, a semiotics based on linguistics worries me, it's because it does away with both the image and the notion of sign" (p. 65).

13  Ferdinand de Saussure, *Course in General Linguistics*, trans. Roy Harris (LaSalle, IL: Open Court, 1986), p. 67.

14  Charles Sanders Peirce, "Logic as Semiotic: The Theory of Signs," in *Philosophical Writings of Peirce* (New York: Dover Publications, 1955), p. 100.

15  Ibid., p. 101.

16  Jacques Derrida, *Of Grammatology*, trans. Gayatri Chakravorty Spivak (Baltimore: Johns Hopkins University Press, 1976), p. 48. See also Charles S. Peirce, "What Is a Sign?" in *The Essential Peirce: Selected Philosophical Writings* (1893–1913), vol. 2, ed. the Peirce Edition Project (Bloomington: Indiana University Press, 1998), pp. 4–10.

17  Ibid., p. 49.

18  Kant, *Critique of Pure Reason*, p. 133 [A101].

19  Martin Heidegger, *Kant and the Problem of Metaphysics*, trans. Richard Taft (Bloomington: Indiana University Press, 1990), pp. 95, 110.

20  Alfred North Whitehead, *Symbolism: Its Meaning and Effect* (New York: Fordham University Press, 1985), p. 47.

21  Ibid., p. 85.

22  Despite their extremely different languages, significant connections could be made between *Process and Reality* (1929) and Heidegger's *Being and Time* (1927), both of which reconceptualize thinking, being and temporality.

23  Gilles Deleuze, *The Fold: Leibniz and the Baroque*, trans. Tom Conley (Minneapolis: University of Minnesota Press, 1993), p. 76.

24  Ibid.

25  Alfred North Whitehead, *Process and Reality* (New York: Free Press, 1978), p. 88.

26  See Gilles Deleuze, *Difference and Repetition*, trans. Paul Patton (New York: Columbia University Press, 1994), "Note on Heidegger's Philosophy of Difference," pp. 64–6: "The difference is not 'between' in the ordinary sense of the word. It is the Fold, *Zwiefalt*. It is constitutive of Being and the manner in which Being constitutes being, in the double movement of 'clearing' and 'veiling'" (p. 65).

27  Deleuze, *The Fold*, p. 23.

28  Ibid., p. 18.

29  Ibid., pp. 19–20.

30  Levinas makes a similar point in his essay "God and Philosophy," where he claims that "rational theology, fundamentally ontological, endeavors to accommodate transcendence within the domain of being by expressing adverbs of height with the verb 'to be.'" Emmanuel Levinas, *Of God Who Comes to Mind*, trans. Bettina Bergo (Stanford: Stanford University Press: 1998), p. 56.

31  See Deleuze's quote in the appendix to the *Logic of Sense*, trans. Mark Lester (New York: Columbia University Press, 1990), p. 281: "it is our epoch which has discovered theology. One no longer needs to believe in God. We seek rather the 'structure,' that is, the form which may be filled with beliefs, but the structure has no need to be filled to be called 'theological.' Theology is now the science of nonexisting entities, the manner in which these entities – divine or anti-divine, Christ or Antichrist – animate language and make for it this glorious body which is divided into disjunctions."

32  Jacques Lacan, *The Seminar of Jacques Lacan Book II: The Ego in Freud's Theory and in the Technique of Psychoanalysis*, ed. Jacques-Alain Miller, trans. Sylvana Tomaselli (New York: Norton, 1988), p. 302.
33  Ibid., p. 326.
34  Ibid., p. 302.

# 13 Malformed essence, misplaced concreteness and the law of the indifferent middle

*Noëlle Vahanian*

What is evil? Evil is not a Platonic form. And evil is not an extraordinary form of formlessness, a monstrous body with its attendant monstrous soul.[1] Evil is the force of mass, of massive indifference, but not especially an indifference to a real fact occurring next door or overseas. This indifference is a modality of being, an *a priori* principle of human nature – a natural principle of individual protection against the hopeless burden of not being whole and good.

Is this modality of being, after all, quite human – should I borrow Nietzsche's formulation *all-too-human* (and I fear its boggling meaning would be lost to the cliché of a word that has traveled too much and spread too thinly) – is this modality of being, indifference, the evil instinct that is – dormant or not – in all of us? Or some predisposition?

## The condition of individual consciousness

I would argue, first, that indifference is the condition for the possibility of individual consciousness, for the daunting experience of one's reflexivity bounced back from the mirror of an experiential world. How ugly we become in our own eyes when we look around and discover the horrors of evil. And how distant we become from that horrifying world: selfish. Our lofty morals and ideals suddenly turn into a call of duty, but what can we really possibly do? Nothing, really. Or pray! Or fall apart.

The expression "condition for the possibility of individual consciousness" deserves an explanation. Yes, I am co-opting the Kantian argument of the Transcendental Aesthetic, where the debate is overtly epistemological, not yet ethical, and where the reasoning that brings about *a priori* conditions for the possibility of knowledge finds justification for its radical innovation of philosophical intuition in the long-standing logic of truth (a logic of truth landmark of philosophy since Plato and Aristotle[2]) as cause or principle, necessary, universal and thus certain. But, more important, this reasoning finds its inspiration in Hume's own challenging of the same logic of truth.[3] So truth is a habit of belief, and habit itself, good or bad, is, after Kant, the transcendental form of the understanding independent of experience, the intuition of space and time. Habit, good or bad, objective or subjective, is, in itself, universal and necessary, and thus certain. The logic of truth justifies its refutation, so that the truth of logic refutes the logic of truth. I mention this revolution of epistemology from ontological truth to subjective truth because I argue that the Kantian use of *a priori* categories of knowledge implies that this revolution has occurred. The point here is that intuition (of space or time) now complicates the notion of a condition for the possibility of experience, in the sense that the possible is not limited by the actual (so that the *a priori* is no more the condition of an actual experience than it is of speculative experiences that have never seen the light of day) in so far as the intuition of space and time is the virtue of experience, whereas you could say that wisdom is the virtue of intuition. For we know that the correct intuition of space and time, so to speak, is, for Kant, in the end, only controllable if it is a wise intuition – or, specifically, willed in accordance with the imperative of an intuitive sublime – a sublime intuition.[4] In any case, the intuition of space and time, as a condition for the possibility of experience, is not wise and it is not satisfying either – and is this not the virtue of experiences that they are always new, particular and different, and in need of an interpretation or a paradigm to serve as or substitute for an object of curiosity or desire?

Hence, when I refer to indifference as the condition for the possibility of individual consciousness I am only intensifying how the problem of knowledge had already become, with Kant, the problem of the logic of truth, that it is a secondary process of thinking, and that experience, not knowledge, is a symptom of a primary process of thinking, a manifestation of the unthought in consciousness, brought on by virtue of intuition (that intuition is of space and time is almost irrelevant, since intuition is of itself the habituation, the formation, of the habit of blurred impressions which, through repetitive exposure to the blur of impressions, selects only in terms of duration and expansion to sensitivity and/or to numbness what it otherwise presents to consciousness. This selection is causality for us because space and time censor what, perhaps, would be too numbing: an infinite blur of impressions; or too demanding: to feel and *sense* more than the *common*). *Indifference is a thoughtless defense-mechanism.*

Indifference is the condition for the possibility of individual consciousness after intuition as intuition has caused a deep manifestation of the resonating waters of consciousness. Indifference is not a metaphysical instinct or predisposition for evil. And it is not what makes individual consciousness actual, since it is a general condition that develops subsequently to the blow of reality to which the cruelty of intuition as intuition condemns us. It's a human condition: the condition for the possibility of individual consciousness. *Indifference – the condition for the possibility of individual consciousness is our condemnation to indifference towards our freedom.*

The truth is that our will, our courage to fight for our ideals and beliefs, comes from the heart, and reason will never master the heart that pumps the spirit of life into the will, unless reason can actually convince you that life is worth living: for that, reason would have to prove it to you. It would amount to reasoning with a fool in love: to nothing or to anger and, last, to despair. Reason is like our hands, it comes in handy, and, with dexterity, it can also excite, sooth, and play-dough. But reason alone cannot give you a reason to stick to your ideals. Reason alone is the worm in the heart of man, as Camus would put it.[5] Though you will not find a worm in a bad apple.

I don't want to speculate on the nature of evil and offer a map of a territory that I have not conquered. I don't want to compare and contrast other maps either. I don't want a puzzle (complete or not). I want to confront evil, rebel against indifference, my own and that which I see around me. Which means that I don't want to settle for the comfort that speculative analysis provides (that it provides for a while at least, until the real grabs your handiwork and crushes it with its strong hold). I want to confront evil by evoking evil without explaining it, like a work of art that depicts reality without comprehending it, because evil is pointless, and its territory can not be mastered. But my paintbrushes are words, and my canvas is consciousness, so my strokes, in as much as they are artistic, are descriptive, but my art, in as much as it is the art of speaking, is a point of view and my strokes are also interpretations.

### Indifference, not evil, is a Platonic form

It is a Platonic form in the sense that the sun is the source of all the seen: without it, there is darkness; with it, there is blindness. In between, there is the seen, the best we've got, neither all, nor nothing.

> "Weren't we saying before that if something should come to light as what *is* and as what *is not* at the same time, it lies between that which purely and simply *is* and that which in every way *is not*, and that neither knowledge nor ignorance will depend on it, but that which in its turn comes to light between ignorance and knowledge?"
> "Right."
> "And now it is just that which we call opinion that has come to light between them."
> "Yes, that is what has come to light."
> "Hence, as it seems, it would remain for us to find what participates in both – in *to be* and *not to be* – and could not correctly be addressed as either purely and simply, so that, if it comes to light, we can justly address the opinable, thus assigning the extremes to the extremes and that which is in between to that which is in between. Isn't that so?"[6]

The seen, what has come to light, is consciousness: a scenario, neither psychotic nor psychic, but erotic, sensual and reasonable. Leave the seen, distance your self from your consciousness, and the seen is a *fait accompli*, a shadow, a cliché – indifferent to the unseen. And then: "those who look at many fair things but don't see the fair itself and aren't even able to follow another who leads them to it, and many just things but not justice itself, and so on with all the rest, we'll assert that they opine all these things but know nothing of what they opine."[7] Return to the seen, invest yourself in your consciousness, and the seen is an event, an epiphany, a singularity – indifferent to the unseen. And lovers of opinion, we "love and look at fair sounds and colors and such things but can't even endure the fact that the fair itself is something."[8] Whichever way we turn, we encounter our own indifference: sometimes we are indifferent to it – because *we are dreaming*, we opine; other times we are indifferent to the dream – *we are awake* because we see that the fair itself is something about which we really know nothing at all. *The truth is that indifference is the blueprint of Platonic Recollection: Indifference is the virtue of representation that in its most correct and dialectical process it mis-represents.* Truth is the principle of contradiction whereby the indifferent middle sees both what *is* and what *is not*. Truth is literally a metaphor instituted by a regime of power.

Foucault speaks of truth as a regime. Truth is not a realm of forms, it is not a riddle, and it is not arbitrary and subjective. "Truth is a thing of this world: it is produced only by virtue of multiple forms of constraint. And it induces regular effects of power."[9] We hear Nietzsche in the background who chuckles, because his description of truth as "a mobile army of metaphors, metonyms and anthropomorphisms" is Foucault's regime "of multiple forms of constraint." Compare the two passages that follow. First, Foucault:

> In societies like ours, the political economy of truth is characterized by five important traits. [1] "Truth" is centered on the form of scientific discourse and the institutions which produce it; [2] it is subject to constant economic and political incitement (the demand for truth, as much for economic production as for political power); [3] it is the object, under diverse forms, of immense diffusion and consumption (circulating through apparatuses of education and information whose extent is relatively broad in the social body, notwithstanding certain strict limitations); [4] it is produced and transmitted under the control, dominant if not exclusive, of a few great political and economic apparatuses (university, army, writing, media); lastly, it is [5] the issue of a whole political debate and social confrontation ("ideological" struggles).[10]

Then Nietzsche:

> What then is truth? [1] A mobile army of metaphors, metonyms, and anthropomorphisms – in short, [2] a sum of human relations, which have been enhanced, transposed, and embellished poetically and rhetorically, and [3] which after long use seem firm, canonical, and obligatory to people: truths are illusions about which one has forgotten that this is what they are; metaphors which are worn out and without sensuous

power; coins which have lost their pictures and now matter only as metal, no longer as coins.

[4] We still do not know where the urge for truth comes from; for as yet we have heard only of the obligation imposed by society that it should exist: to be truthful means using the customary metaphors – [5] in moral terms: the obligation to lie according to fixed convention, to lie herd-like in a style obligatory for all . . .[11]

The army of metaphors, metonyms and anthropomorphisms is, I would argue, more evocative than the blatant, politically charged notion of truth as a regime of power. Perhaps this is why it is easy to dismiss Nietzsche's passage as an interesting allegory that is, however, without any direct practical relevance to our contemporary situation. We might feel that it is too philosophical to be taken at face value even though it is still something to think about. So it is more evocative because it is charged with epistemological complexity, which makes it more problematic and evaluative than descriptive or heuristic. But I am not interested, here, in merely pointing what after all is not such a surprising similarity between two thinkers whose genealogical approaches are genealogically linked. Rather, I am timidly attempting to continue the investigation of an intricate web of epistemological, ethical, political and human relations.

The *regime* is an economy of power in tandem with a political structure. The economy of power is metaphorical and metonymical. For instance, the Constitution stands, at least in the eyes of the law-abiding citizens, for the truth, and justice is when the truth prevails, or when constitutional rights are repaid. The metaphor is the equation of truth with the law – as a general, universal and biblical concept. The metonym is the equation of the truth with human, constitutional, individual rights, or the equation of the truth with what is fair, with the law of the heart. So the president is most powerful by right of his office, and Bill Gates is most powerful by right of his property, while the street prostitute is powerless by right of her officiousness, and the welfare recipient is powerless by right of his poverty. The political structure is anthropomorphic, that is, democratic and hierarchical, guided by universal human indifference and individual human interests. If we were to ask if there is an intrinsic reason why the president did not become a prostitute instead, I do not believe that merit or integrity would necessarily come to mind. What, then, does come to mind? Ambition, instruction, and a strange need to imitate God, because power transcends the world within individual, accidental, arbitrary consciousness. You might call this power of transcendence, optimism, and its lack, pessimism, and what is real is neither the optimistic illusion that the world without is one with the world within nor the pessimistic disillusion that the world without senselessly fetters the world within; what is real is what is indifferent to your mood, which is life.

## Moody consciousness

Indifference is a Platonic form and life is indifferent to our moods. So how is indifference related to our moods? Are moods forms of indifference toward the indifference of life? For life goes on, while moods fluctuate. Life does not ask for your opinion. It does not stop to let you catch your breath. If we were indifferent to this life that goes on with or without us one way or another, would we have a mood? It seems that our moods reflect rather our inability to live indifferently to the indifferent course of life. We assess what cannot be assessed. We value what is invaluable.

Freud seems to have linked the value we place on existence to the pleasure principle (the title of one of his works, intended to demonstrate that "what decides the purpose of life is simply the programme of the pleasure principle," is none other than *Civilization and Its Discontents*[12]). It is clear that we are not indifferent to pleasure or pain. You could, therefore, say that our moods reflect, less than a state of mind, a conscious physical state. The problem, however, seems to be the lack of correlation between the infliction of physical pain and felt sadness, sorrow, despair or hurt. Though discontent feels bad, physical comfort or affection usually does not seem to be enough to make one feel better. The point, here, is that meanings, interpretations, descriptions or explanations are integral parts of our moods. So much so that it is basically ludicrous to establish a certain distinction between meaning and sensing. Indeed, prolonged physical pain always becomes emotional pain and the converse is no less true. Just as we are not immune to physical violence, so too we are not immune to verbal violence. Otto Fenichel points out that "every disease is 'psychosomatic'; for no 'somatic' disease is entirely free from 'psychic' influence – an accident may have occurred for psychogenic reasons, and not only the resistance against infections but all vital functions are continually influenced by the emotional state of the organism – and even the most 'psychic' conversion may be based on a purely 'somatic' compliance."[13] What cannot be assessed is not whether we feel pain in our joints because we are getting older or fear old age because we feel the pain in our joints. What cannot be assessed is the what in itself that exists independent of our pain or pleasure, or interpretations – that is, what this in itself indifferent to us might be, want or mean: life as a whole, contingent cause of pain and pleasure, meaninglessness and meaningfulness.

Our moods are like a price tag on green paper. The paper is life as a whole, indifferent to, independent of us. Do you earn your life and deserve the life that you have earned? Are you a slave to life by nature? Is the price of life not an issue for you? Are only the just rich? How does the economy of moods function? In *Madness and Civilization*, Foucault has already shown how the birth of the asylum and the medical secularization of madness resulted from the simultaneous secularization and civil instauration of religious morals in the Classical age. In Medieval times and until the Renaissance, the slothful suffered his plague because he had lost faith and the mystic spoke, not his own words, but the voice of God. Once, however, work becomes an ethic and gradually gains political recognition, the idle beggar who wanders like a madman and thinks that he is God needs to stand corrected.[14] Madness becomes a disease; it ceases to be a legitimate form of expression, and instead, becomes the symptom of the absence of sense, senselessness. To treat the disease means to discipline the patient so that he comes to view his fears as irrational and inappropriate responses, learns to properly repress (or objectify and silence) his demons, and relinquishes his individual power to become a cog in the machinery for the benefit of productivity.[15] While the psychoanalyst encourages the patient to silence the voices of unreason by labeling them as such and in this way can be said to treat a patient, the psychoanalyst also stands for life itself, life as a whole, indifferent to his patient's moods. But, unlike life itself, he hears the patient's plaints. And he still does nothing to change life itself. And in this way he can be said to challenge the voices of unreason.

Is bliss ignorance? What does happiness have to do with morals? These questions cannot be answered rationally. They cannot be answered hyperbolically either.

In the first case, the answer would be dialectical and painstakingly irritating, like Socrates in Book I of Plato's *Republic*, who argues that a just man can do no evil and is happy, while an unjust individual is harmful and unhappy.[16] The logic of Socrates' argument rests on a dualism between a rational soul and an irrational body which is as reductive as the dualism implied by the term "psychosomatic." It is no wonder, then, that unless "the philosophers rule as kings or those now called kings and chiefs genuinely and adequately philosophize . . . there is no rest from the ills of the cities . . . nor I think for human kind."[17] It is no wonder, "For it is hard to see that in no other city would there be private or public happiness."[18] As regards the economy of our moods as contrasted with life itself, the just who are rich have joined the company of a few good men who enjoy the sweetest rewards of all, the stillness of wisdom in the after-life.

In the second case, we are spared the argument. The shock of the absurd is what is meant to convince us that "the last will be the first, and the first last" (Matthew 20:16). But there is no Platonic justice here. Your rewards are not based on your earthly worthiness. What makes one a just person is not one's usefulness or efficiency. "For the kingdom of heaven is like a householder who went out early in the morning to hire laborers for his vineyard. After agreeing with the laborers for a denarius a day, he sent them into his vineyard." All day long the householder went about recruiting all those who were idle and unemployed. "And when evening came, the owner of the vineyard said to his steward, 'Call the laborers and pay them their wages, beginning with the last, up to the first'" (Matthew 20:1–17). But those who worked all day received as much as those who did not. Only God knows God's Justice. All we have of this is God's Word which we speak and either gratefully keep or begrudgingly break.

## Misplaced truth in malformed knowledge

Representation, in Plato's ontology, is the verbal re-presentation (the copy) of a visual mis-(re)presentation (a shadow) that participates in the intelligible universal image or form (the real thing) of an invisible Idea (the being of the real thing, its eternal actuality). The representational copy justifies that the shadow that appears to the senses is a good, correct rendering of an archetypal idea. By the same token, however, representation loses what makes it credible to begin with, which is its capacity to recall an experience by means of resemblance or, otherwise put, to recognize this.

Hannah Arendt writes that *"Every mental act rests on the mind's faculty of having present to itself what is absent from the senses."*[19] It is in this sense that Magritte's painting of a pipe is not a pipe: it looks like a pipe, but it is an image. The ability to recognize a pipe when you see one is the ability to paint a mental image of what you see, to keep the impressions together, to make them last and remember them. Common sense is what takes us home, so to speak. Without it we become strangers in a strange land. Common sense does not take us back to the Same (in the sense that no one can ever really go back home or back in time), it takes us home, it makes us feel at home, where we have nothing to fear, because we "know" the people at home, as if we were habituated to them. They "are" us; we take who they are for granted, as we take Magritte's pipe for a pipe. This common sense, then, *is* epistemological indifference as a condition for meaningful experiences. The senses do not lead us to the abyssal ground of reason, and initially they do not serve the strictly utilitarian purpose of preservation. "It," explains Arendt, "rather looks as though, on the contrary, the inner, non-appearing organs exist only in order to bring forth and maintain the appearances."[20]

Whether something is beautiful because it appears to be in the likeness of the Beautiful that stands opposite to the Ugly or simply because it appears to be the Beautiful itself of which, however, it is only in the likeness – whether thinking is knowledge or opinion – is a secondary concern. Epistemology comes as an afterthought: the superficial event, the shadows and the images, are the *raison d'être* of the intellect. Or, what is clear and distinct, the hallmark of Cartesian certainty, is what is evident – *even to the senses*.

Foucault credits Descartes for the historical reversal of the ground of certainty. Knowledge becomes empirical and certainty becomes whatever is evident to the senses apart from the ambivalent epistemological status of appearances once Plato's dialectic becomes the dialogical Cartesian method. In an oral interview conducted by Paul Rabinow and Hubert Dreyfus, Foucault schematically describes this historical reversal of the status of subjectivity characteristic of the shift to Modernity:

> In Western Culture up to the sixteenth century, asceticism and access to truth are always more or less obscurely linked.
>
> Descartes, I think, broke with this when he said, "To accede to truth, it

suffices that I be *any* subject which can see what is evident." Evidence is substituted for ascesis at the point where the relationship to the self intersects the relationship to others and the world. The relationship to the self no longer needs to be ascetic to get into relation to the truth. It suffices that the relationship to the self reveals to me the obvious truth of what I see for me to apprehend that truth definitively. Thus I can be immoral and know the truth. . . . After Descartes, we have a non-ascetic subject of knowledge. This change makes possible the institutionalization of modern science.[21]

The Same Idea is the true, just and correct representation of the original Idea itself. But the subject cannot authenticate the original Idea unless the representation is false, unjust and incorrect. Since he cannot authenticate the thing in itself or the original Idea, the Cartesian subject declares, first, that nothing is certain that is not clearly and distinctly so. The imperative forces him to verify his assumption, rather than to authenticate it. This leads to his second declaration, that nothing is clear and distinct that is not also evident. To verify means nothing other than to localize the original Idea and the copy in one self-same subject: I am certain that I exist, because I think; likewise, I know that forms are beings, because I can only copy them or represent them. Hence, if the return to the Same is impossible because we need appearances to recognize similarities to begin with, going home is possible: we cannot be in different places at the same time, but we can be in the same place at different times. Otherwise put, experience is what we know best, because it is what we recognize first. Even though experience is only real by virtue of being an appearance of an uncertain origin instead of a form, this reality of representations is how we measure certainty and come to doubt whatever we assent to. The logic of assent is not tautological or representational, it is *valuative – it values what is invaluable*. As Foucault points out, with Descartes, we can be certain of our knowledge when what we know is what is evident, but then, certainty or correctness is not truth in a moral sense (it is not God's Will). Rather, it is true in an aesthetic sense (it is the copy of a form because it has the evidence of an appearance: it appears, but it is not a sense-perception, it is not the image of a thing, it's the image of a thought, the subject or self which has no material basis = certain knowledge).

In some desperate introductory textbooks to philosophy, it is not uncommon to read a blurb on Plato's theory of forms that, in spite of the sterile, impartial and standardized discourse of the textbook, sounds naïve and preposterous – especially to the students. In such books, we read that Plato *believed* in a realm of forms (I have in mind a pictorial equation with on one side logs of wood as matter plus the blueprint of a table as form, and on the other a wooden table as a wooden table. The legend reads: "Form and matter as conceived by Plato. Plato believed that the form of a table existed in a world of perfect forms"), *believed* that what we call learning is in fact a remembering of what we already knew before we were born (the only disclaimer states that forms mean a great deal more than just ideas in the mind – as if their perennial existence answered the student's genuine and legitimate concerns: "how did we know then what we remember now if we never really learned it once?" Or "if we were a soul before and now we're a soul and a body, then how did the soul become a soul and body if it is still the same soul but we've changed?").[22] The problem, here, is that for the sake of sound-bite pedagogy, subtlety is struck. Imagine having never read Plato or any philosophy. Why would you want to start after that introduction? "I've never had to try to understand what I was reading before," is the comment that sound-bite pedagogy cannot solicit. "Philosophers believed that their theories were true, but we all have different beliefs and what is true to someone may not be true to someone else. I believe Plato was right about the immortality of the soul because that is what I was taught to believe"; such are the comments that sound-bite pedagogy is more likely to promote. What, then, about Plato's theory of forms could have prompted so much interest that we still bother with him? Why did it take so long to reverse his theory which seems so immediately naïve and wrong to today's sound-bite culture?

Even more puzzling is why, as Whitehead suggested in *Process and Reality*, all Western philosophy is a footnote to Plato. Clearly, there was more to Plato's idealism than his *belief in a world of perfect forms*. Perhaps one could simply start by looking at what about his world might have prompted his *belief* in some other perfectly abstract world. What was he running from? And why are we not? Or if we are, why is it naïve and preposterous to posit that the really real is a realm of forms of which we are only the mere appearances?

Arendt reminds us that Greek myths divinize nature because of the quest for immortality.[23] The Gods are human-like, they fight, they kill, they procreate and prosper – but they never die. So they will fight again, and kill, and cry, and love. Who is man in this god-like world? A slave, of course. A slave to nature. Freedom from the wrath of unpredictable gods, is freedom from their lure – the alluring beauty of nature. Freedom comes with a price, though: meaning is the price. The truth is good and it means nothing and it does not blackmail or require sacrifices. Over against a temperamental, cruel nature, it is happiness in the absence of pain and pleasure. Meaningless: it can only disappoint.

"Both the world and men stand in need of praise lest their beauty go unrecognized."[24]

## The place of meaning in the formation of analogy

We value what is invaluable because there is an analogical rapport between opinable common sense and the sublime sense of reason. This rapport establishes that the relation between sensible objects of common sense and objects in themselves is equivalent to the relation between intellectual objects of the sublime sense of reason and sensible objects of common sense (i.e., A:B_C:D). Analogy is a step forward, even though it is a step that is so ordinary, so natural that we forget about it, much like in actual walking, we forget the difficulty of taking our very own first steps. And, since one never crosses the same river twice, analogy is like taking a step in the mud: the ground is not solid, even if it is a common ground to both sides of the equation. For Aristotle, this mud, this common ground, is *being qua being*, or, to deter our penchant for metaphysical fallacies, it is something, which by virtue of being whatever it is, whenever it is what it is, possibly anything or everything, is not nothing. It is not *non-being* even if it is not what we say it is – it cannot be said (or predicated) of a subject, nor is it present in a subject as one of its properties,[25] but it subjects every object to the test of dialectical illusion and makes the dream of metaphysics to return to the Same not only impossible, but especially detestable and nihilistic. *Ineffable, invisible* and absolutely *impassible. Being qua being is the indifferent middle.*

The Aristotelian Werner Marx refers to the study of *being qua being* as *Ousiology* to mark the distinction with ontology and the trend, amongst Aristotelian scholars who acknowledge that First Philosophy is Theology, to confound Theology, the science of divine substances, with Plato's realm of forms.[26] By contrast with Plato's ontology, Aristotle's *Ousiology* is not logocentric, where meanings belong to the being of ideas, but not to their signifiers. Rather, Aristotle's *Ousiology* associates the *logos* with the *topos* by analogy, that is, in theory or by virtue of the imagination which marks the absence in thought of a material presence in perception and which marks the limits of perception with a presence in thought of an absence in perception. The meaning marks the being of thought, its activity, and the being of common-sense appearances by analogy, where the relation sound–hearing–understanding is equivalent with the relation seen–seeing–comprehending so that words can be heard without being spoken out loud – they can be thoughts – or they can be read without being written down – they can be appearances.

Meanings, here, signify both the being of ideas according to which, as Berkeley would put it, their being is to be perceived (by the mind), and the being of appearances, according to which their being is to be perceived (by the senses), even though the passage from common sense to thought necessitates a withdrawal and a disengagement from the world of common sense – so as to "stop – and think."[27]

The speculative move that allows us to contemplate, understand and comprehend through the concentration of and the attention paid to several particular thoughts – some being memories and abstractions, some appearances, some abstract anticipations of appearances, or again abstract fantasies – this line of thought is, indeed, what Whitehead called the "flight of an aeroplane," an adventure in the etymological sense of the word, or, if you like, the pursuit of experience (before the age of computers) in virtual reality.

This speculative move is a suspension of knowledge, because (1) the virtue of the move is its aesthetic: "like knows like." The desire to know gets in the way of knowledge, because it seeks what is beyond the field of evidence: beyond the now, the instant, to create an eternal field of evidence where the old is never lost and the new is ever present, where what happens again and again never feels the same or never gets old and where what will never happen does.

Hence, this speculative move is also a suspension of knowledge because (2) epistemology is not its final end, it is only its efficient end. This simply means that to desire to know is how one loves wisdom, but it is not how one knows. The interpretation, the generalization, presupposes an epistemological gap. Aristotle is clear on that point when in his *Metaphysics* he tries to define the subject of philosophy, being *qua* being, as either a this that we can induce (like nature which is the this that physics induces in order to deduce its what), or it is not. If we can induce the this of being *qua* being, then it is nature as nature is to physics, and we can know it completely as such a substance. But, what if it is not something that we can induce, what if it is eternal and separable, and immovable, and so forth? Are we to deduce what it is without even knowing that it is? Is there a what without a this? How could there be? It must be then that there is a this, a being *qua* being, that we cannot induce nor know.[28]

This Aristotelian definition of method is a pre-Anselmian ontological argument for the existence of God, but it is also a pre-Kantian critique of pure reason: it is a speculative move that refers outside of the sensible realm, and not just away from the sensible realm into (fanciful) abstractions derived from the sensible world, because it refers to what cannot be derived from the sensible world, it cannot be abstracted, it cannot even be thought in terms of abstractions (as in made-up). But also, just because we cannot know it through experience, since all our knowledge begins with experience, does not mean that it does not exist. Aristotle's *Ousiology* considers this latter possibility, but, say, unlike Plato who only considers this possibility – and this is why we speak of ontology – Aristotle shifts the purpose of philosophy "to know thyself," for "all that one knows is that one knows nothing," to know thyself, for the love of life.

Epistemology is a knowing of speaking – it is already an afterthought. As such, it is not wisdom, rather, it is *in need of wisdom*, and as such, it is not being as being, rather it is a contemplation of being as being by calling to mind the absence of a material sense-perception (its purpose is only that of making one stop – before one speaks, so that one considers all possibilities). It is a propaedeutic for speaking, for pointing to that which is other than logic or common sense, and which, without this forced moment of interpretation, appears as what it is – as what cannot appear or be evident – absurd and meaningless. Epistemology is, for Aristotle, the way to speak being, not the way to know being. Analogy, which, in a first moment, serves to enlighten the world of thinking, then provokes a return to the world of common sense. And from one flight to the next, for we are forced to land, even though we always want to take off again, we pursue the plane of evidence. Hence, meanings do not belong to the being of ideas, nor do they belong to the beings of their signifiers. Meanings are not said of a subject either. The being of the logos is the end of the logos: to value what is invaluable. And meanings do not refer to invisible ideas, nor do they refer to visible things. Meanings are metaphors of wisdom or being as being: Aristotle's Ousiology is *logoeccentric*: it reaches out while turning within towards the otherness of being: its ineffability that is also its impassibility, or what being is not which makes it something rather than nothing.

But if we can so readily criticize Plato for turning the philosopher's way of living into a denigration of life on earth, perhaps we can also question the success of Aristotle to turn the philosopher's way of life into an affirmation of life. In *The Life of the Mind*, Hannah Arendt is critical of Aristotle in a way that reminds me of Nietzsche's criticism of Socrates for two reasons. I see in her criticism of Aristotle's *nous* her disappointment with the philosopher's inability to state unambiguously the purpose of philosophy: that it is a quest for meaning and a desperate gesture of longing for immortality.[29] "Socrates' decadence," writes Nietzsche, "is signaled not only by the confessed depravity and anarchy of his instincts, but also by the overdevelopment of the logical and *arthritic nastiness* that characterizes him. . . . I am trying to grasp from what idiosyncracy the Socratic equation – reason = virtue = happiness – stems, the most bizarre equation that there is, and one which in particular has all the instincts of the older Hellenes against it."[30]

It appears, then, that Aristotle was caught in a double-bind: on the one hand, the overcoming of wonder and, the other, the vindication of his "Hellenic instincts." In the *Metaphysics*, wonder at life is first taken to mean puzzlement, or, as is stated, "the desire to know." And, it is true that a student who reads Aristotle and philosophy for the first time is perplexed with the rationale behind the progression from experience and technique (which address the desire to know as a common sense) to speculation (which suspends the engagement with common sense to recreate a similar engagement in thought) and, notwithstanding, suggests that the removal of wonder is still the end of first philosophy, while it becomes more and more obvious to the reader that this end is an abyss. Analogy presupposes a common original ground as nature to both common-sense appearances and thoughts. But thinking which is like a seeing cannot know something unless it thinks about it, just as seeing cannot know something unless it sees it. Hence, the common ground of sense and thought can neither be seen, nor thought, or else the substance of life would look like a this and it would be thought of like an idea, neither of which are in itself or original since they are products of perception and thinking, which presuppose an object to be perceived or thought (the object in itself as the unknowable ground for both the object as it appears and the object as it is thought). So, if being as being is the being of thinking and the being of nature which we sense, what we desire to know cannot be known: we contemplate an abyss that really exists . . . And the removal of wonder, here, is ironic; we will never know, and that is far from wonderful.

But, as Arendt also shows, Aristotle interprets wonder as a traditional longing for immortality, so that to think about thinking perpetuates the circle of life and death – as if that activity which is eternal (in the sense that movement is not rest) immortalizes the one who engages in it (the thinker) as opposed to his thoughts. This is especially true, she says, in the *Nicomachean Ethics*.[31]

I hear her saying: "Is it so hard to be straight about the end of philosophy that it is the affirmation of life over against what we know of it – that it ends, that it is cruel, that it is absurd."

## The surfacing of singularities

We know that we know nothing. We know that we will never know why there is something rather than nothing. We know that we do not know if life has an ulterior motive besides herself, and if she does, we do not know what it is, and if she does not, we do not know why she even bothers to sustain her stupid self.

It is clear enough that we do not know. So why should we cease to be amazed by the pleroma? Why should we cease to be puzzled, dumbfounded, awed, by the ground on which we walk every day? By the pavement and the street-lights? By lions and termites and bears and fish and water and snow and toes and nails and eyelashes and tongues and smells? Why should we hate and kill those who remind us to be puzzled? Why kill the child in man only to create a monster, so that the Nazi is only a beast in his eyes for laying them on the Jewess, and the Southern Christian fundamentalist campus is only compromising its duty to obey the Lord for lifting its ban on interracial dating? Why should we, how can we be indifferent to what is a perennial puzzle? Is indifference a form of life that seeks an end to life in the *whatever* of what Giorgio Agamben calls bare life?

And indifference is then the *logos* and the *telos* of barbaric bare life: the *modus operandi* of life that sustains itself – a cruel and absurd self-sustaining life for its own sake, namely life without the possible goodness of its religious overcoming.

*Telos* and *logos* of barbaric bare life, indifference is the *a priori* Platonic form because it unites nature and human order, *physis* and *nomos*, without a rite of passage, without exemption, without the other. God is not the term of this agreement. He is *nous*, but *nous* is the reason why *physis* sustains itself in flux. *Nous* is the soul of *nomos*, the eternal in the human, but *nous* is also the soul of soul-less *physis*, the immortal in nature. Agamben supports this concept of "indifference as an *a priori* Platonic form" when he cogently notes that Plato dismantles the opposition between *physis* and *nomos* by

> affirming the originarity of the soul and of "all that belongs to what is soul" (intellect, *technē*, and *nomos*) with respect to bodies and the elements "that we erroneously say are in accordance with nature" (892b). When Plato ... says that "law must rule over men, and not men over

law," he therefore means to affirm not law's sovereignty over nature but, on the contrary, its "natural," which is to say nonviolent, character.[32]

So *The Republic*, this theoretical model city-state, impossible in actuality, is a state of nature. Or, it is nature which is dissolved and transformed into human law: the anthropological regime. Whichever way we prefer to see this symbiosis (whether man is the parasite or nature), it foments a sort of atheism – that than which nothing more nihilist, solipsist and unredeemable can be conceived. Yet, it is not only conceivable, it is the fascist state, or Marx in the hands of Lenin. What is corrupt? Is it thinking? Or faith? Man or nature? God Himself? How is it that he who seeks a solution to despair, to cruelty, and to the indifference of life to our moods, conceives the death of God?

## Indifference drowns

Feuerbach's anthropology in his *Principles of the Philosophy of the Future* is the epistemological equivalent of the Platonic naturalization of human order. It is as if Feuerbach echoed Plato, as if he were saying that the atheism of human experience ought to rule over the theism of human idealism in order to affirm, not the faith that transcends the human being, but the natural independence of man from the Other, from any other. Feuerbach's solution to the problem of idealism or speculation – that it alienates man from his world in the contemplation of a ghostly divine essence or in his negation of subjectivity towards absolute spirit – is to empty the *logos* of the power that constitutes it to begin with, of *nomos*.

With arrant analytic genius, Feuerbach uncovers the fact that scandalous liaisons systematically preempt the task of three generations of thinkers to transform and dissolve theology into anthropology.

Reformation theology fails because its atheism is incomplete. God cannot be known, God is dead in our world. He is absent and absurd. But his absurd absence is felt. And the theism of theology moves to religious anthropology while theology is transformed into humanism.[33]

Modern philosophy does not fare any better; on the contrary, it shifts the atheism of Reformation theology to nature and the theism of religious anthropology to philosophy. Whereas, in the philosophies of Descartes and Leibniz, God is the object of thought and man is the subject of thought without an object, here God is the principle of the thinking subject. Modern philosophy is true theism, "for God, in the theological sense, is God only as long as he is conceived as a being distinguished from and independent of the being of man and nature."[34] Modern philosophy is an imaginary pantheism because God's attributes are intelligible, not physical, and they are those of man minus his limitations.[35]

As for speculative philosophy, it alienates man as a thinking being from his own essence. It transforms the atheism of nature into the theism of absolute spirit and the theism of modern philosophy into the atheism of subjective idealism. "Absolute philosophy has indeed transformed for us the other world of theology into this world, but in turn it has transformed for us this side of the real world into the other world."[36] The moments of the Hegelian dialectic affirm the sublation of feeling under subjective abstractions only to affirm the sublation of the subject under absolute abstractness. The double denial of the problem of idealism for the unhappy consciousness is positively alienating all along. Absolute philosophy negates God and negates the negation. It is "at the same time atheism and theism. . . . [And any theism that is also atheism] is pantheism."[37]

The scandalous liaisons are all the result of a covert affair between the atheism of human experience and the theism of human idealism. Feuerbach blames man's inability to accept his finite experience of the infinite on psychological disturbances. Theism is the ghost that haunts the thinker who desires to be a philosopher.

According to Feuerbach, a name is a sign. It ought to be nothing else. It ought to be the sign of an object. It ought not to be the symbol of an empty concept. Hence, speculation is the human activity that subverts the unambiguous sign which a name is of an object by eliminating the reality of the object for us, by eliminating the determination of feeling, of the senses and of the thinker from the concept of an object. What is real is all at once what we can sense, feel and think. We cannot sense, feel and think all at once an idea, and much less can we sense, feel and think all at once the absolute being of an idea, its essence removed from the subjective determination of it as an object of the understanding.

What is real is all at once what we feel, sense and think – it is not what we think, but have never felt or tasted, and it is not how we feel when we do not want to work a room at a cocktail party but would rather stop and think in solitude, for it is not a backward glance at what is forever past or a gaze into the future. Man makes a distinction between his essence and his existence, unlike most animals for whom the true being is their being really there and now, and so, man is neither where his soul is – somewhere else, nor where his body is – somewhere here. Man is truly and really only where his heart is.[38]

But Feuerbach cannot leave it at that. Now man's heart is the union of I and Thou, and whenever man is alienated, and finds himself in between his head and his body, he is not where his heart is – he is heartbroken, perhaps. Feuerbach's new philosophy dissolves theology and speculative philosophy into anthropology to disavow the experience of the broken heart, to prevent and proscribe the broken heart: it is almost as if, or perhaps it is as if, Feuerbach sought a return to an original natural naïveté and spontaneity. Head on his shoulders, feet on the ground: man is neither somewhere else, above, nor somewhere here and now, man is where his heart is.

This heart, union of the I and Thou, is always already full or never empty. It is the heart of the true anthropological form: the atheistic heart of the atheistic man whose desire is neither excess nor lack. Indeed, his lips are sealed, because there is nothing that the heart has not poured out already: it is dry. In the union of the I and Thou, there really and truly is nothing left to say. No desire to speak what has not yet been said even if it all has already been said. No desire to give a name to what is not yet an object of the understanding.

## Robbery

The human power to give a name to something that is not yet an object is sacrificed in order to dismantle the opposition between the order of things and the natural order. Nothing remains outside the naturalized human law – completely nothing. That with which *they, male and female*, sought to overcome *Anankē* and *Thanatos*, is, with Feuerbach, dead and can never return, not even as a ghost. That is, when they trespassed their selfless complementarity, their undifferentiated immediacy, and chose to speak freely, establishing an order proper to themselves out of spite for the sacrificial nature of necessity, and named the novel (the possibility, today, of that which, yesterday, was impossible); when they buried their dead and marked the course of their existence against futility, mummified their bodies to preserve their power over the engulfing hunger of the life-cycle, in order to change their fate from a means to the end of necessary life into the end in itself of a sacred life, that struggle is lost. The anthropological form is thus exempt from the obligation to reciprocate the gift of creation. Unlike *they, male and female*, male, he is not man, and female, she is not woman. Anthropological forms, either male or female, are not made of dust in the image of God. Their flesh is produced to be consumed. They overcome nothing. Nothing overcomes them.

## Generosity

*Telos* and *logos* of barbaric bare life, indifference cannot however exclude that which it does not include. Our world is not *The Republic*. And if our rulers were philosophers, still they would not rule *The Republic*. Our lives spill over the flow of male or female forms of life. And if we can kill our God, still we cannot sacrifice that which remains outside the law of the indifferent middle. The economy of life is not free, but we are free to pay more than we owe.

   Do you remember how the old man, Cephalus, explains to Socrates that wealth has allowed him to be a just man? Socrates is quick to reduce the meaning of Cephalus' words to that of a popular saying according to which a man is just if he speaks the truth and pays his debts.[39] But Cephalus is not strictly talking about repaying no more and no less than what he owes as if he were returning what he had borrowed. Rather, he welcomes his wealth because it allows him to respond to his obligations to reciprocate what has been given to him and that for which he did not ask – his life. His departure does not mean that he is taking his life with him, that his life is just wasted on him in his death. His wealth is his contribution which he owes to the world that has given him life. He is not returning what he borrowed, he is doting on what he was given and gives all, not back, but again. Marcel Mauss, in *The Gift*, had unveiled this uncanny binary between wealth and religiosity in Polynesian cultures. He writes on the exchange of gifts and the obligation to give and receive, that "everything – food, women, children, property, talismans, land, labour, services, priestly functions, and ranks – is there for passing on, and for balancing accounts. Everything passes to and fro as if there were a constant exchange of spiritual matter, including things and men, between clans and individuals, distributed between social ranks, the sexes, and the generations."[40]

Theism is a hot potato. It circulates in the music of language from movement to movement, from one generation to the next. But when the music stops, he who still holds on to the hot potato loses God. For language breaks down when the music stops. It stops making sense when man's heart, either in his stomach or on his shoulders, is not free from necessity; when broken, man prefers not to speak.

## The spiritual cog of society

Indifference, as this Platonic form, marshals the reversal of the Aristotelian hierarchy of ways of living: labor, work, political activism, philosophic contemplation. In the utilitarian society, productivity justifies a way of living and consumption justifies productivity. Otherwise put, the life-cycle is the good which the legislator has in mind when he organizes the life of the *polis* – not freedom. This is perplexing, since Arendt writes that

> What all Greek philosophers, no matter how opposed to *polis* life, took for granted is that freedom is exclusively located in the political realm, that necessity is primarily a prepolitical phenomenon . . . and that force and violence are justified in this sphere . . . violence is the prepolitical act of liberating oneself from the necessity of life for the freedom of world. This freedom is the essential condition of what the Greeks called felicity, *eudaimonia*, which was an objective status depending first of all upon wealth and health.[41]

In the utilitarian or consumer society, what is meaningful is what is useful. "It is 'for the sake of' usefulness in general that *Homo faber* judges and does everything in terms of 'in order to.' "[42] *Homo faber* is not a political or prepolitical animal. His wealth and health are not his private business. He is not the Roman head of a household whose power is over the life of his sons. Nor is he a sovereign whose power it is to let his subjects live because he could just as well have them killed. Rather, *Homo faber* is often likened to a cog in a machine. He serves whomever is directly his superior, and he is served by whomever is directly his inferior. His psychological battles have replaced the prepolitical order, and his personal spirituality, his philosophy of life, is intimated, not voiced. He is not free to aspire to felicity; he is guilty for having unresolved issues.

When the public field is dissolved and transformed into the social sphere, when we are all free to speak (but not during work hours and most certainly not after hours), we choose to value what is useful to our social–economic status. After all, we may be free to speak, to campaign for public support, to withdraw into the life of the mind, observe the spectacle on the world-stage and praise the performance, but without household slaves and a plantation, our freedom may be short-lived. To speak "for the sake of" felicity is not an effort – it is not necessary "in order to" have a wealthy and healthy life.

Until all social animals are wealthy, healthy and idle, there will be no public square in which to philosophize and no spare time to immortalize. Such is life in the utilitarian, consumer society – such is life, eternal flow – not yet immortal.

What is and has always been superfluous is the agora, the public square for spare time.

But this is the religious space. It is not included. It is not excluded. It is free. The religious space is the place where a citizen is a political living being capable of speech, a *zōon politikon* and a *zōon logon ekhon*. This is where she is free to speak, where he wills his power, where she acts, expresses, expends her matter, her soul, where he leaps into otherness. Meaning precedes knowledge. Meaning precedes necessity. Meaning is intending – it is willing and it is trying.

Indifference drowns. Singularities surface.

Robbery. Generosity.

Cog. Spirits.

## Notes

1 Nietzsche writes of Socrates that he is ugly, because he intends to be a caricature of the logical mind that he is, but his motives are ulterior and pressured by his own recognition of the pathetic import in the disposition and temperament of the soul. Hence, Socrates is ugly more than in the physiognomic sense of the times whereby one's complexion or expressions held serious indications about the virtues of one's soul. Socrates is ugly, because he, himself, is the intended victim of his deceitful, ironic pedagogy. He knew that he was, and he, therefore, thought himself the master of his unsatisfied passions. Because he knew that his cure for dissatisfaction was not a cure in the true sense – it was only a "semblance of a cure" – his soul would put on an act for his body, so to speak, as if it were the body that needed convincing, and not the soul – as if one could reason with folly, when reason is the fool who confuses unreasonableness with irrationality. (Friedrich Nietzsche, *Twilight of the Idols: Or, How to Philosophize with the Hammer*, in *Classics of Western Philosophy*, 5th edn, ed. Steven M. Cahn (Indianapolis: Hackett, 1999), §1–10, pp. 990–2).

2 See Plato, *The Republic*, translated with Notes, Interpretive Essay, and Introduction by Allan Bloom, 2nd edn (San Francisco: HarperCollins, 1991), bk. VI, 508e–511c, and Aristotle, *Metaphysics*, in *The Basic Works of Aristotle*, ed. Richard

McKeon, trans. W. D. Ross (New York: Random House, 1941), bk. II, ch. 1, pp. 20–30.

3  See David Hume, *A Treatise of Human Nature*, ed. L. A. Selby-Bigge, rev. P. H. Nidditch, 2nd edn (Oxford: Oxford University Press, 1978), bk. I, part IV, sec. VII, pp. 267–8.

4  Indeed, in *The Critique of Judgment*, Kant postulates that the intuition of the sublime is the condition of possibility of pure reason as pure reason (empty and awesome). But practical reason is supposed to effect a sort of sublime intuition of the formal intuitions of space and time which problematically condition the understanding to subjectivity. The categorical imperative of reason, as a moral imperative, usually appears to play the role of the voice of conscience after the understanding has already cast its subjective judgment. I think, however, that, for Kant, the secondariness is not a transcendental secondariness – since it is what *transcends* the transcendental schematism of the imagination. He writes: "For the beautiful in nature we must seek a ground external to ourselves, but for the sublime one merely in ourselves and the attitude of mind that introduces sublimity into the representation of any particular form in nature, but involves no more than the development of a final employment by the imagination of its own representation" (Immanuel Kant, *The Critique of Judgment*, trans. James Creed Meredith (Oxford: Oxford University Press, (1928) 1952), pt. I, bk. II, §23, 246–7, p. 93).

5  "Beginning to think is beginning to be undermined. Society has but little connection with such beginnings. The worm is in man's heart. That is where it must be sought. One must follow and understand this fatal game that leads from lucidity in the face of existence to flight from light" (Albert Camus, *The Myth of Sisyphus*, trans. Justin O'Brien (New York: Vintage Books, 1983), pp. 4–5).

6  Plato, *The Republic*, bk. V, 478d–e.

7  Ibid., bk. V, 479e.

8  Ibid., bk. V, 480a.

9  *The Foucault Reader*, ed. Paul Rabinow (New York: Pantheon Books, 1984), pp. 72–3: "Truth and Power," from *Power/Knowledge: Selected Interviews and Other Writings, 1972–1977*, ed. Colin Gordon.

10 Ibid., pp. 72–3.

11 *The Portable Nietzsche*, ed. and trans. with a Commentary by Walter Kaufmann (USA: Viking Penguin, 1982), pp. 46–7: *On Truth and Lie in an Extra-Moral Sense*.

12 Sigmund Freud, *Civilization and Its Discontents*, ed. and trans. James Strachey, with an Introduction by Peter Gay, standard paperback edition (New York: Norton, 1961), p. 25.

13 Otto Fenichel, *The Psychoanalytic Theory of Neurosis* (New York: Norton, 1972), ch. 13, p. 237. Fenichel is attacking the modern term "psychosomatic" precisely on the grounds that it suggests a dualism between symptoms and diseases. He prefers the term "organ neurotic," as it dissolves the psychosomatic dualism (between the "realm of organic disorders" and the "field of conversion" that translates "specific fantasies into a 'body language'") to reveal that in the meddled middle "there stretches a large field of functional and even anatomical alterations."

14 *The Foucault Reader*, "The Great Confinement," from Michel Foucault, *Madness and Civilization*.

15 *The Foucault Reader*, "The Birth of the Asylum," from Michel Foucault, *Madness and Civilization*.

16 See Plato, *The Republic*, bk. I: "Then if someone asserts that it's just to give what is owed to each man – and he understands by this that harm is owed to enemies by the just man and help to friends – the man who said it was not wise. For he wasn't telling the truth. For it has become apparent to us that it is never just to harm anyone" (335e).

17  Plato, *The Republic*, bk. V, 473c–e.
18  Ibid.
19  Hannah Arendt, *The Life of the Mind*, one-volume edn (USA: Harcourt Brace, 1977), vol. 1, pt. II, ch. 9, pp. 75–6.
20  Ibid., vol. 1, pt. I, ch. 3, p. 27.
21  *The Foucault Reader*, "On the Genealogy of Ethics: An Overview of Work in Progress," from *Michel Foucault: Beyond Structuralism and Hermeneutics*, pp. 371–2.
22  I do not mean to discredit the valiant efforts of the author to make philosophy accessible to a majority of students, and the text that I am referring to is subtle if one has already a profound understanding of Plato. Unfortunately, I fear that simplicity encourages passive learning and the expectation that teaching is not supposed to challenge the student's intellect. See Helen Buss Mitchell, *The Roots of Wisdom*, 2nd edn (USA: Wadsworth, 1999).
23  Hannah Arendt, *The Human Condition*, 2nd edn (Chicago: University of Chicago Press, 1998), ch. 1.
24  Arendt, *The Life of the Mind*, vol. 1, pt. III, ch. 14, p. 132.
25  This is Aristotle's definition of substance in the *Categories*, ch. 5.
26  See Werner Marx, *The Meaning of Aristotle's "Ontology"* (The Hague: Martinus Nijhoff, 1954) and *Introduction to Aristotle's Theory of Being as Being*, trans. Robert S. Shine (The Hague: Martinus Nijhoff, 1977).
27  See Arendt, *The Life of the Mind*, vol. 1, pt. II, ch. 9.
28  Aristotle, *Metaphysics*, bk. E (VI).
29  Arendt, *The Life of the Mind*, vol. 1, pt. III, ch. 14.
30  Nietzsche, *Twilight of the Idols*, §4, p. 991.
31  See Arendt, *The Life of the Mind*, vol. 1, pt. III, ch. 14.
32  Giorgio Agamben, *Homo Sacer: Sovereign Power and Bare Life*, trans. Daniel Heller-Roazen (Stanford: Stanford University Press, 1998), pt. I, §2.2, pp. 34–5.
33  "The task of the modern era was the realization and humanization of God. . . . The religious or practical form of this humanization was Protestantism. The God who is man, the human God, namely, Christ – only this is the God of Protestantism. Protestantism is no longer concerned, as Catholicism is, about what God is in himself, but about what he is for man; it has, therefore, no longer a speculative or contemplative tendency, as is the case in Catholicism. It is no longer theology; it is essentially Christology, that is, religious anthropology" (Ludwig Feuerbach, *Principles of the Philosophy of the Future*, trans. Manfred Vogel (Indianapolis: Hackett, 1986), §1–2).
34  Feuerbach, *Principles of the Philosophy of the Future*, §14.
35  See ibid., §10.
36  Ibid., §24.
37  Ibid.
38  Ibid., §27.
39  Plato, *The Republic*, pp. 331–2.
40  Marcel Mauss, *The Gift*, trans. W. D. Halls (New York: Norton, 1990), p. 14.
41  Arendt, *The Human Condition*, p. 31.
42  Ibid., p. 154.

# 14   God is of (possibility)

*Peter Canning*

The most compelling definition of God, *scilicet*, the power to exist, is immediately frustrating to the theological desire to know God. Is this power concentrated in One Being, or is it dispersed, distributed nomadically in all beings? Can it be described by physical law? What relation can it have with the human desire for a "moral universe"?

It seems impossible to relate our finitude of power and knowledge to an infinite and absolute power to exist. We cannot know the cause or reason of existence, of creation, nor whether the world was "created" at all; nor is an absolute power to be "cause of itself" fathomable or reasonable. But if we cannot know or experience the absolute except negatively or metaphorically – there is nonetheless a power of existence that is shared by all beings and all material elements. How is it, then, that "I," that we-all – we including all beings, all particles of being on earth and in the universe – can *do* anything at all? How is it that we can exist if not by *our* power to exist? Is that power not related to the divine power? Isn't it the same power or a part of it?

The shift from the divine One (All-One) to the distributed, dispersed but relational all, from Unity to Multiplicity, is an event in the history of Western consciousness. Perhaps it began with Spinoza's consideration of the modes as elements or particles of divine substance, each with its portion or degree of that power. The problem Spinoza could not solve was how the finite power of the modes could be related to the infinite power of the substance, because one cannot add together finite quantities to reach infinity, infinity can only be posited all at once. There is a logical gap there, but Spinoza's suggestion, to consider God as the infinite source (*natura naturans*) of all finite power to exist, act and think, has the advantage of making God thinkable, conceivable, knowable as nature. Theology and science then merge into one. Nature is the manifestation or expression of power, and by studying nature we can begin to know God.

The second problem with Spinoza's idea was that his science of nature was resolutely deterministic, such that all events were necessary and individual freedom was denied. Leibniz opened up an entire new area of thinking with his notion of God as Possibility, a definition that was accepted and critiqued by Kant. Kant argued that the ensemble of possibility could be presupposed as a transcendental category or regulative Idea, but could not be hypostatized as a possible object of experience. Once again, a negative epistemology was asserted and applied to the infinite. Nevertheless, the suggestion that the God of Possibility was a God of multiplicity, of many possible worlds from which He chose the Best for realization, was powerful enough to sustain, if not the developments in Judaeo-Christian theology, then certain considerations of "possible worlds" in (1) the contingent history of a Darwinian process of sorting out among competitors for reproductive presence, (2) the quantum "many-worlds" hypothesis in its various forms, including "possibilities for histories," and (3) the Borgesian Garden of Forking Paths – in which each divergent alternative is realized in its own way, as opposed to God's choosing only one world for realization.

This last development, the multiplicity of diverse worlds realized in "the same chaotic and parti-colored world" (Deleuze) is, paradoxically, the most "solid" basis for the future becomings of theology. For the Deleuzian chaos or chaosmos is not so much chaotic in the sense of "confusing" as it is a reflection of actuality as a process of competing "worldviews" vying for realization as "the" world, and each maintaining its own priority and precedence over the other, but always risking "capture" and "marginalization," or being rendered divergent and inconsequential, "unrepresented" by other "monads" asserting the reality of their vision of the world. In fact, this is exactly what we see all around us, group, community and individual monads struggling to assert their presence and to build their world to the exclusion of others; and Deleuze's version of Leibniz's world-pyramid – a multiplicity of possible, self-realizing monads competing for actuality but without any One-God or Judge to decide which world is the "true" or Best one – is an inspired description of the event. It is also the most compatible with the developing Darwinian doxa, while yet (because it is in implicit dialogue with it) offering certain alternatives . . .

First, it is necessary to hold on to the idea of power as criterion. Power, the Spinozist–Darwinian power-to-exist, -act and -think, prevails over the Leibnizian moral Judge of the "best of all possible worlds." Here the Enlightenment critique has done its work (Voltaire). However, this does not condemn us to resignation and the cynic's "pragmatism" or else the protests and fruitless or hypocritical rebellion of the "beautiful soul." Nor does it justify the Gnostic or Sadean identification of God with "evil" and world-corruption.

For this reason, in the second place, God who is Power remains also Possibility. And just as power, for better or worse, manifests itself and shows its true nature in the competitions among species and individuals for predominance, so possibility shows what it can do in the human world of creativity and ethics. It is still true that not one but many worlds are coexisting in uneasy alliance, reluctant mutual recognition or else open hostility and non-recognition. And within each subject many conflicting possibilities, asserting themselves as realities, may be vying through verbal and imaginary representation for "recognition" and realization. One need only look at the contemporary religious and political scene to verify this quasi-chaos, this "incoherency" which has invaded the human subject under the rubric of "diversity," "cultural relativism" and "postmodernism" – which may be domesticated and marketed by the shopping-mall ideology that "we can all get along," but which we know in our hearts is threatening to realize the Apocalypse that many are waiting for and not a few are working for. It is true that the human subject is "pried open" and made self-divergent, forking away from oneself, by these conflicts and discords within "the" self. But here, I believe, is where a reconsideration of the relations between science and theology can begin to clear a new path.

The "God" of science is simply the power of what is to become and be what it is. It is the actual universe plus whatever science believes is necessary to supplement that actuality – be it a "scalar field" of potentiality, a "quantum chaos," etc., in any case a "force" or set of forces and a set of rules describing the behavior of the force(s). Science studies the design of "this" universe, but also asks, in its honest moments, "what is it that breathes fire into the equations and makes a universe for them to describe?" (Hawking).

However, the God of science, who thus consists in both the power and the knowledge of the universe to exist and to evolve, has become, in the last century, something of an *unconscious* god, in the precise sense that no one, not even God, can know the future as science is coming to understand its production and becoming in relation to the present actuality. The event that has destroyed the very notion of a determined and thus known or knowable future is three-fold. It is, first, the hegemony of Darwinian contingency; second, that of "quantum indeterminacy"; and third, the advent of "chaos theory" and "complexity," which relates indirectly to Darwinian unpredictability and more problematically to quantum uncertainty. Boiled down, the idea unifying all three of these ruptures of the classical Newtonian paradigm is the disruption of determinism by one form or another of radical contingency, and the consequent *intrinsic* unknowability of the future, even by a divine "observer" – just because the future, and its becoming, are simply *not determined in advance of its happening*. Or to put it another way, if there is a god who knows all there is to know, then that god knows precisely all *except* what is inherently unknowable by the nature of things. Here we are back into Leibniz's world-possibility, minus the God who "determines" – understands, knows – all worlds in advance and chooses one – the Best – for realization. That is, the "shape" or the "form" of the god who would be in accord with these scientific developments would not be a god who could know all in advance, since the future is not yet determined, but would be precisely an "unconscious" god in that sense, a god of all power but of only limited knowledge. There are certain "allegories" – most significantly the story of the Garden of Eden and the divine proscription against knowledge – which obscurely, cryptically, and as in a distorting mirror, do indicate that we humans have been thinking about this problem since the beginning of our self-consciousness.

In particular, it has always seemed impossible to reconcile God's omniscience with the reality of freedom. Now freedom is power, the power to choose or to create the future, and it is knowledge, up to the limit of one's own (not God's) science. Traditionally, and most expertly with Leibniz, this incompatibility between divine absolute knowledge and human creative freedom has resulted in a "compromise formation" (to use Freud's term) consisting in a God who knows all, and therein knows all that will necessarily happen, but nonetheless has given humans the freedom to choose and to create a future that they do not know in advance as He does. Of course, the sleight of hand is evident and no thinking person can confuse an unconcious automaton, believing itself free but really programmed to choose the path that has already been mapped out for it by God, with a free being.

Today, however, now that God is *power without (total) knowledge*, a "deconstruction" of power is required, similar to that of knowledge. First, power is decentralized, distributed among all "particles" and combinations, assemblages, compositions of particles. The power to exist, to remain in existence or to survive, and the power to reproduce and thus amplify one's "representation," to "increase in power," as Nietzsche said, involves some kind of knowledge short of the ability to predict the future. It involves a kind of know-how, a know-how to exist, to think and act, which does not necessarily mean having complete knowledge of all the "parameters" determining the outcome. Nor to have control, but to "go with the flow" of things without knowing where it will take us; yet also to "steer" the vehicle one is operating – really, one's own body, and brain – in certain directions depending on the interpretation of certain cues and signs from the environment and from "others" exhibiting indications of their "worlds," their intentions, the possible futures they are trying to realize.

We live today in a world of overwhelming complexity and inconceivable possibility — including, as Kierkegaard said, the possibility of being (or becoming) nothing at all. And it is here that impossibility begins. But also the Blanchotian impossibility of dying begins here. Why? Because "I" can no longer claim mastery of "my" death; I can no longer even claim that it is "I" who dies when it is time to die. It is not possible to experience death as I. As He, or She, or It, perhaps, as "one" or "they." This impossibility of dying as myself leads to the impossibility of living as myself, as it also derives from that impossibility – which is linked to the death of God, when "nothing" became possible. As Lacan said, "If God is dead, nothing is possible."

Yet again, what do we mean by possibility today? Is the possible not that which is to be created?

Deleuze distinguished between the possible that is realized and the virtual that is actualized in a true becoming. But then becoming clearly must create something that did not exist before, that did not pre-exist its own becoming, otherwise it would be indistiguishable conceptually from the realization of the given possibility, or the selection – by chance or by power – of the real from among the set of possibilities. The virtual is not the pre-existent, it is the becoming of reality, the creation of something new – in fact, every true creation makes a new set of possibilities. The creation of possibility is art. Theogony, for example, or the creation of a god, is an art of poetry or architecture or sculpture or painting or music or dance. To create something that did not pre-exist, as opposed to choosing among possibilities, is necessarily to create a god, in the sense that God is possibility and power.

But does power not always exist? How can power be created?

The prime definition of power is: the power to *create itself*. If God is not the power to create itself, then what is God? Eternity? But, as Spinoza realized, "eternity is power or the essence of God" (see *Ethics*, book V). Eternity is the timeless aspect of power; but in time, eternity manifests as the power to create, which implies, as a temporal interpretation of eternity, the power to create itself, *causa sui*. Today this power manifests in a quasi-finite way as a "fractal," including the "eternally self-reproducing fractal inflationary universe" of contemporary cosmology (Andrei Linde), which is highly speculative; but also the fractal nature of innumerable physical processes. I would say that the fractal, as process, can be defined as the "incarnation or realization of infinity in conditions of finitude" (see Mandelbrot, Feigenbaum: "when things work on themselves over and over"). In short, we live no longer in a finite world but in a world that appears to "cross" finitude with infinity, time with eternity, space with infinity; the cross between finite and infinite in realization is a "transversal" – a process that works and plays on itself over and over again. Repetition, variation, self-differentiation.

So this new conception of highly decentralized and distributed power really implies that no One being can have over-all knowledge of everything, because each and every being, every power, is mutually dependent, partially dependent, on other powers, on "others" for its power to complete and realize itself. And some of these other powers are not living in the same universe, are not creating and realizing the same universe as "I" am, even if I am trying to realize something *with* them in cooperation. All together we compose the "god of power" – but none of us knows how it will all turn out; and none can claim to have their script directly from God, although many do make this outrageous and potentially lethal exclusive claim. In fact, even if we did know what God intended for us, would this necessarily mean we should enact His script, realize His program, dance His choreography, play in synchrony the notes of His symphony? What if He were, as Sade and some Gnostics thought, evil or insane? Should we not then listen to our own reason or reasons? And if we are truly free, then are we not free to create the world as we "see" and imagine it – the possible world that is not yet created and waits to be imagined?

God is, and always has been, a name of our unconsciousness. Our obscure drives and ambitions; our vague fear of the unknown; our anxiety in the face of the nothingness of our dead ego, the Impossible; the chanciness of the future; the incomprehensible, existence; the real, the virtual, the possible, what is to come if we make it happen, or if somebody or something else does;

the obscure disaster of our errancy; the unnameable, the unthinkable; the other, the others, all the other worlds I can't imagine – but someone can. And a few other things besides . . .

However, we cannot imagine God just as we please – at least not without "psychosis." Our idea must reflect things as they are even in bending them towards the goal of our desire. So it is necessary to re-examine notions of guilt and innocence, good and evil. The God–Father of Western theology is a power that is sometimes accused of enjoying human suffering, being a "sadist." Thus our story and discourse of God, our theo-logos, has to answer to our concerns. The story of our fall from grace – the Garden of Eden – is the paradigm of a narrative designed to account for human misery in terms of justice, of good and evil, implying a just God and Judge of humanity. In fact most of the Bible has this concern: to justify God to man, and sometimes man to God. This opens up the problematic of *jouissance* – the Lacanian idea of an enjoyment that must be justified, or else accused, its supposed agent charged with wickedness. That pleasure should be a reward for good behaviour, righteousness; that pain is punishment for criminal behavior, transgression – this is the moral logic of *jouissance*. The "*jouissance* of the Other" is a (generally illegitimate or problematized) enjoyment attributed or imputed to an other, or to "the" Other, to God as we cannot help imagining "Him."

The Lacanian thesis is that this Other is modeled after the primary other of our libidinal life, the Mother, our mother; or, since history is written by men: women, the Other is "Woman." Without entering into the labyrinth of this imaginary world of "sexual relation," it is clear that the Freudian–Lacanian idea is to understand the Other as feminine – but then how is it that God is male, is "the Father"? The Father is the agent of prohibition coming between the human "child" and the Other, separating them, and preventing each from "enjoying" the Other without restriction. Thus God is not the Other but the Lawgiver who protects us from the "desire of the Other" – or rather, from the Other's unrestrained *jouissance* or "abuse" of our body and mind. Thus the law forbidding knowledge of the Other is actually a law that protects our finitude from being crushed by infinite *jouissance* which we are not equipped to experience (and go on living). The human imagination cannot invent God or the Law arbitrarily or "as we like it" but must try to address questions of "ultimate concern." It is no longer a question of: are good and evil real or fictional, but: what is evil, why do humans have to invent the notion of crime (and punishment)? And Who invents? Why do we need God to invent this Thing, this Value of Good or Evil?

The second Lacanian theory of relevance is that it is not "we" – human subjects – or any subject that invents the Thing (God, Justice). It is really language itself, its "discursive structure," that insists on presenting us with these notions and producing both accusations and defenses; both utopias and distopias; both good and evil. And society mimics its linguistic structure by producing scapegoats to account for good and evil. The first scapegoat is God, the Father Himself. The reason we are mired in ambivalence toward the

Father is that He is in the position of the Father–Enjoyer who is using and absuing us for His, at best inscrutable, at worst plainly sinister, purposes. It is He who prevents or prohibits us from enjoying the Mother–Other fully; from uninhibited sexual relations; from unrepressed, unconstrained non-stop *jouissance*. Instead we have "desire" – i.e. lack of *jouissance*, lack of satisfaction. It is the Father who, in our fantasy, stands in the way of our full satisfaction.

But that is the Father as Lawgiver, as agent of interdiction. The Other Father is actually the unrestrained Other himself or herself, the imaginary Mother of unrestricted access to our bodies and minds – really the Mother from which the first figure, the Father–Lawgiver, is supposed to protect us. The real Father–Enjoyer, then, is that "ferocious and obscene" figure of the Other who cannot be restrained by any law – as if the father who made the law were also the one whom no one could force to obey it. He gives the law to us human subjects, but He Himself violates it maliciously and at will.

The point is that the image and discourse of God is designed not only through language but even by language and its usage. As though it were language itself that were the God "enjoying" and using us as we enjoy (and use or abuse) it in turn. Of course we use and are used by discourse in relation to "others," to other humans in their bodies and minds. Language occupies our brains and nervous system – an actual language with which we have our own "power relations"; a virtual language which we too create and imagine in our turn. And language is our agency of power, of the exercise of power over others and their domination and (ab)use of us for their purposes. It is this power-language, language "of" power, that is concerned in the discourse of *jouissance* and of its ultimate source in the "shape" or structure of God, of the Other. God is the power "behind" and "within" language – its power to make us dream – literally to force us to dream and "see pictures" when we experience its real-imaginary power, as, for example, when reading or hearing the words "elephants tramping and honking," a subject might be compelled to see and hear something automatically, flickering images, imaginary sound, synthesized and reconstructed; to suggest actions or command them; to "program" its subjects to be actors in a play in which we are free – or forced – to improvise our own script, but are also compelled to respond to others who are constantly re-writing our parts from day to day or moment to moment, and forcing us to take their expressed and supposed intentions into consideration as we plan and reshape our roles from scene to scene, event to event.

This power to create the reality of imagination, the reality of possible worlds, is the awesome power of language – and of other arts, aesthetic processes of composition. The creation of possibility means creation of what is truly possible, not just what might be if the world were designed another way or if our wishes could somehow come true without consideration of "others," if we were ourselves the Other, the divine Power. The fantasy of the Other as oppressor is a neurotic fantasy. It is not that others aren't oppressive; the very structure of discourse, of language, lends itself to abuse, to the triumph of lies and liars, of opportunists and manipulators without regard for truth or fairness, of false accusers who satisfy the people's lust for blood of a scapegoat to make them imagine they are getting even with their abusers, and so on. And the fantasy that one is oneself the Other or its instrumental agent is a perverse, narcissistic fantasy of omnipotence – narcissism, as the amplification of the ego to infinity, being the core of perversion. The delusion that the Other really exists and is acting in relation to oneself or has invaded oneself or that one really is (possessed by) the Other, is a psychotic condition. Language is consistently the medium of the *jouissance* of the Other.

So to imagine possibility, other possibilities, is not to invent arbitrary worlds, but to invent this world in its "otherness." It is what we are all doing already – some more than others, but in dispersal and "dissemination," in nomadic disjunction and without unity or consistency, like the chorus of mice in Kafka's story.

Yet God remains the community of that dispersed multiplicity, the power of each with or against others. God, said Kant, is the Idea that unifies the concept of community. Then today, without God as One, we still have the mutuality of interaction between elements in the "same" world (other worlds begin where "we" no longer interact). "Our" God is the power of Dionysian community, immanent multiplicity, general discordance and cacophony, with occasional harmony. From this condition a *sensus communis* emerges, a possible harmony (and discord), possible unity (and dispersal).

The most obvious possibility is that the old Father–God – the Lawgiver-prohibiter of "knowledge," the enjoyment of the Other; the possible abuser of us all, which is a "hysterical" thesis, the Father–abuser, violater, etc. – is simply no longer possible today. We are living through the event of His impossibilization.

Leibniz saw that the logic of the event implied a bifurcation of time itself, taken as the set of all possible events or alternative worlds. The linear time of narrative history thus determines an exclusive disjunction: if I go one way, I cannot go the other way at the same time. If the naval battle takes place tomorrow, it cannot not take place. Yet, Leibniz claimed, it can take place in another, "incompossible" world, one of the total set of worlds in which all the alternatives to our actual world-event are acted out. Today the logic of incompossibility has moved into our actual world-event, because there is no longer a Leibnizian god to select one world over all others as the best one to realize. Today there are as many worlds vying for realization on the same earth as there are peoples and communities, even individuals, under the command – remote control – of gods telling them how to act and what to do in history: where to go, what land is theirs, who is their friend or foe. Without unity of ego, released into psychic anarchy, it is the very soul of the individual that is the battleground of contrary world-events clamoring for recognition within a "single" self, thus multiplied incompossibly. The clang of arms and clash of bodies in war (history) over realization of competing alternatives in the same earthly location is just the passage into action of that psychic incompossibility.

Perhaps only by affirming the inclusion of others' desire within my own can I be woken from this nightmare into the act of a new nature, a new humanity whose language is free of prepossession by the demons spontaneously generated by unconscious fantasy.

Today the problem of alternative realities, of "many worlds," has become a challenge to the subject: can you stand (tolerate) the unknown desire of the Other? Do you prefer to form a unified unanimous community to authorize and legislate the Truth, to restore the One? The reality of democracy at least *shows* that this is impossible without eliminating disagreement – that is, those who disagree and "cause discord."

Incompatible possibilites are being projected and realized all over the earth. The speaking being invents fictions and delusions of closure it enacts in history. Every hypostatized Other is a structure of language imagined in a story told of injustice, *jouissance*, knowledge, love, desire . . . But the freedom to create fictions (and fantasies), even in ignorance of their physical possibility, is the power of the virtual itself to create possibility. Possibility is that margin of reality created at the edge of time, in the interval-now between past and future. It consists or inconsists in a wish or project, an interpretation, which competes with divergent, incompatible fictions (possibilities) for realization in the same physical world. There are many regions of the world, and each culture tries to finds itself a place to enact its beliefs as rituals and incarnate its fictions in institutions. Conflict begins when they try to establish their presence *in the same place at the same time* by building their world-reality to the exclusion of others claiming that place. There are additional uncertain monads hesitating between alternatives; while still others are self-divided among alternatives within themselves and maintain incompossible versions of reality as "compromise formations."

In the absence of One-God or Judge to decide which world is the universal or "true" or best to realize, the postmodern polytheos of Incompossibles realizes all that have the power to assert themselves, becoming the condition of their passage or communication from one individual to another, the transition from one world to another, and the suspension of reality at the margin of the possible between self and others and between past and future where reality becomes the fiction of its creation, where the outside chance loops back into time to relink with the chain of events, and where the complexity of the person engages a relation with unknown others whose place is within oneself as unconscious Other, which is the spacetime of dialogue. It is at this suspended pass or passage that "others" operate within oneself, expressing other possible worlds, desiring, creating and enjoying worlds to which "my" world, like a door, must be either closed or open, at least a crack. In any case, it is long past closing time.

Only at this instant do I begin to open myself truly to the God of Possibility, that is, the reality of the Other whose image is the plurality of worlds realized as cultures, groups or individuals, or as "works," each (in)consisting in a multiplicity of variations. That is also an image of the creative edge of time, of which all modes of life are the evolving medium, while human language is the unconscious creation of possibility itself.

But God, no longer viable as Father–Enjoyer – of course He was "always already" dead, murdered by His abused children (Freud) – and failing as Father–Lawgiver, is still Possible, the possibility yet to be created. But as we see, the possible is not the arbitrary, and it is not just the "imaginary." Imagination is the power or essence of God, the self-synthesis or mutual synthesis of multiplicity as community, but what-is (the object of science) must still be the basis of what is possible. Otherwise, it is not only the scorn of scientists and technocrats that condemns theology, it is reality "in principle."

Language is not God, but the power of language and art is the power to create the possible. Technology realizes the set of possibilities programmed into nature by its creator, whether One or Multiple, Other or Self; art freely creates possibilities by imagining them; and philosophy reflects them by creating their concepts, even in advance of art or theology. The space of possibility in language is an empty Word, not nothing but the space of the imaginable. This creative void is a future built into language, wherein its fictions can emerge, its possible realities to come. But these depend partially on the series of past realizations for their basis. This partial dependency, this contingency upon the past as presented, forms the ground of a Markovian process, a retroactive selection of the past–present by the future as it emerges. This process of reflecting the past series in a future concept to be created initiates a "generic procedure" (Badiou) by which the emerging present, futuring, selects its own conditions and predecessors. It is a "concept of reflection" (Deleuze–Kant), a concept of the way nature itself emerges, becomes. The becoming of nature, its naturing, is the process-structure of God (Whitehead), the shape of God as shaping of reality.

Art, by creating imaginary worlds, produces possible futures which may be selected for realization – and these are already aesthetically realized as, for example, theater, music, ritual . . . In this sense, art or aesthetic process is immanent in all human activity of any consequence or significance; as philosophy is immanent reflection and diagramming; and science, immanent analysis of the way things are. Should theology not also focus its reflection on creativity and becoming, the manifestation of the power of God, but while also trying to arrange a "symposium of gods" – that is, of religions, of ways of imagining God's possibility on the basis of science; and, especially, while creating the new Image of God, the Idea of God adequate to illuminate this chaotic and terrifying, breathtaking world-process of all cultures and individuals colliding, colluding, conflicting, destroying or allying with each other in the *harmonia discors* of "godless" world-multiplicity? If there is no One God over all gods (which is the Nietzschean evangile), then does theology not "necessarily" become the discourse of that Dionysian multiplicity of god-passions, god-drives, god-images and possiblities? Does it not see the opportunity of selecting among "gods" (images, ideas, discourses of theology) that composite god-assemblage that tells us what we can be, what we are becoming in imagination, not of necessity but freely because we are creating our future, the future of earth?

The discourse of theology, then, is a discourse of desire (Winquist); not what we wish God were but what we ourselves desire to become with each other – since, all together, we (universal particles) are the power of God minus full knowledge of what we are, what our essence is, and what is to become of us, but also plus the conditioned freedom to create our reality despite our lack of knowledge. Or rather, our freedom requires that knowledge of the future be incomplete, even God's knowledge. This "lack," then, as condition of possibility, is what is meant by our desire – which is also the "desire of the other," since it requires that we leave open the possibility that the other we encounter holds a key to our own future. But most of all we encounter the other of our imagination. Here again, Freudian and Lacanian analysis reveals the great danger of "reflecting" or mimicking the other in ourselves and "projecting" our own imaginings into the other as intention or desire or *jouissance*. The "Law of the Father" was designed in (or as) language to mediate this imaginary register and prevent the doubling and psychosis or perversion of desire it fosters. But now that the Father–Law is "dead," or has lost its imaginary foundation, what is to be done?

Something of the Law of the Father remains in force and must be retained as part of any "desiring theology." It is the prohibition, perhaps no longer against divine images or imagining God, but against imposing that image – or idea, or discourse – on others and compelling them to worship our own vision of reality. Thus the world religious crisis we find ourselves in, the rise of fundamentalist hysteria and psychosis, and perverse interpretation and vicious enforcement of the "Law of God," demands intervention on the part of theologians not afraid to measure the full dimensions of the theocratic quagmire nor to invoke and reactualize – really, to recreate – the Kantian–Mosaic law which, by prohibiting an enforced Image of God, holds open the space of God's future possibility. That is the true meaning of the "sublime" law – not that we must "draw a blank" when trying to "figure out" divinity, but that our blank represent and really incarnate the open space of possibility for a desire to come – not a lack but the void of a plenitude of opening. An opening to the other who is trying to create a world.

It is true that the dire law of Nietzsche and Darwin advises against optimism: the law that affirms that it is the "strongest" – the most ruthlessly self-serving, who are not ashamed to lie, to cheat, to slander and produce scapegoats in order to consolidate their hegemony – who will always prevail against the "weak," who open themselves to exploitation or destruction by others in their naïve desire to hold themselves open to the desire of the other. Nevertheless, the new Law must allow for a positive multiplicity of imaginings, without the censorhip implied and enacted in the negativity of the Law prohibiting images of God. It must be negative only in prohibiting the hegemony of one Image and Law of God over all, the subjection of all to one Law, one Signifier.

To this end, there are four requisites for conceptualizing theology in the context of this Law:

1   It is a positive law of desire, to include the desire of the other as an openness, an empty "signifier" fillable by the creation of possibility in the space of interaction between oneself and the other.
2   Theology should stop resisting and denying the validity of science, the reality science describes. It must listen carefully to scientific discourse, not slavishly or in humiliation, but in seeing its opening there where science too, at its most honest, remains open. It does not contest, or vainly try to alter, the "laws" of nature, but it reads science precisely in order to find out, affirm and create its own space of freedom. For example, theology does not deny Darwinism, it questions certain notions and applications of chance, probability and randomness, and the Possibility, the Power implicitly presupposed by them given the fact of our existence. It affirms what science is not (yet) capable of affirming: creativity. It creates what science cannot recognize: the transbiological ethics of freedom, as opposed to the ethology that explains animal behavior. Theology and philosophy do not let science dictate what is "necessary" or predetermined (e.g. genetically) once they have discovered their margin of freedom, precisely in the interstices and at the emerging edge of science (chaos, complexity).
3   Theology (and art) begins where science ends, in the real present. Theology is the art of creating the future image of God, while poetry and art become sources and resources for theology, to find out what is possible, including ideas and images of evil. Art begins creating possible events and future worlds where science leaves off, content to describe and understand things as they are and to suggest possibilities for technology. A theological aesthetics addresses social realities, "rituals" willed by human beings in the name of their images of Power and enacted by them, involving their minds and bodies in a strange, compulsory mode of freedom.
4   Finally, theology today should become a "law of hospitality" that is, I think, twofold: it is a belief in the earth and the possibilities of life (not "afterlife"); by affirming the earth, it affirms "other lives" and life forms – not that it denies the harsh Darwinian law of "differential reproduction" and speciation and extinction; but since humans unavoidably find ourselves in the position of "managing" the earth and earthlings, of "administrating" the processing of natural resources, we are in a position to create a kind of paradise on earth, to become hospitable to nature and other lives, beyond the hegemony of capital and energy-guzzling technology and religions competing by increasing their flocks, all conspiring to deepen the misery. It is true that hysteria, perversion and paranoia are the ordinary human responses to this grotesque hegemony, and that fundamentalism is the obvious reactionary formation. But the theology of

earth and of cosmology demands ethical creativity today as never before. For example, the moral law of capital – always pay your debts on time – and its rule by the signifier of money ordering human behavior can be superseded.

The new law of hospitality orders a new kind of "receptivity" of the other and the other's real or expressible desire. It is a law of mutuality: I receive the other, *a priori*, who receives me; we interact – just as all particles in the universe interact – to create (and destroy) each other's worlds, each "held open" by affirmation of the reality of the other, as opposed to the closed, mutually excluding monads of a post-modern – cynical–nihilist – psychosis. It is an aesthetic *a priori* of creation: what will become of us depends on our "attitude" and what we are already doing, how we are already acting "toward" the other in advance of our meeting. We anticipate a possible agreement, an *a priori* sympathy and the possible "song and dance" we will make together in free obedience to the ethical law – not to "give the law to our nature" as in Kant, but to synthesize the possible. To synthesize the possible community that is already (*a priori*) a kind of ethical reality, a future (virtual) reality: to "catalyze" each other's existence and to improvise the dissonant harmonies, the uncertain rhythms of possible futures is discretely to subvert the laws of capital and to compose a hospitable community whose realizable Idea is the reality of God. For life, in the poet's word, is a "finely tuned tornado" whose eye is of God.

# Index